# SILK
# DRAGON

## MIKE HARRIS

This book is dedicated to my wife Evelyn who stuck by me
through the good times and the bad.

CONTENTS

SILK DRAGON

6

# PROLOGUE

I'm a member of The Explorers Club in New York City and a Fellow of the Royal Geographical Society in London. I get a big kick out of leading expeditions to various places around the world. I also enjoy producing feature-length documentary films on the different expeditions I lead.

So, I wasn't too surprised one day in 1981 when Bradley Hahn Cdr., USN Ret.), a fellow Explorers Club member, asked me a simple question. "Why don't you make a movie on the greatest explorer of all time?"

I thought that sounded like a pretty good idea, but didn't have the slightest idea who he was talking about. When he told me the man's name was "Zheng He" I still had never heard of him! Over the next few weeks, however, Brad began feeding me information on this "unknown" explorer and before long I was hooked!

First, I found out that Zheng He was Chinese, and second, that he was a eunuch servant who conducted six major trade expeditions for Zhu Di, the Third Ming Emperor of China. All this incredible exploration activity took place during the Chinese Ming period in the early 1400's, years before Christopher Columbus, or any of the other European explorers.

What's even more incredible, Zheng He's Ming fleet consisted of hundreds of ships, many of them nine-masted treasure ships, which were over four hundred feet in length. He also carried with him as many as twenty-seven thousand men on one expedition.

Compared to Columbus, who explored the New World with only three small ships and ninety men, this was quite an amazing marine accomplishment!

When I started asking questions that Brad couldn't answer, he introduced me to his close friend, Dr. Daniel Lee, from Annapolis, Maryland. Dr. Lee taught Chinese History at the U.S. Naval Academy and was used frequently by both the U.S. and Chinese governments as a special interpreter and advisor on cultural exchanges between the two countries.

When I first met Dr. Lee, or 'Danny' as all his friends called him, I knew he would be just the person I needed to help me get information on Zheng He. He let me know, that if I wanted to do film work in China, I'd have to get permission from a company in Beijing called China Film Co-Production Corporation. I quickly fired off a letter to them, asking about their great hero, Zheng He, and waited for their speedy reply.

No such luck!

After waiting for over a month and not hearing a peep from anyone, I called Danny at the Naval Academy and asked, "what's taking them so long?" His answer to me was very prophetic.

"When dealing with the Chinese, Michael, you must learn to have patience." He wasn't kidding!

Finally, after about three more months, China Film wrote back and formally requested information about my Tampa company and me. Much to my chagrin, they hardly mentioned a thing about my request to gather information and produce a film on their famous explorer.

I sent a letter back to China Film with the information they requested and resigned myself to the fact that I was dealing with a foreign country and, as Danny had suggested, nothing was going to happen particularly fast. I asked Danny if he would use a little of his influence to help speed things along, which he did, but it still took almost a year and a half before I finally received a formal invitation to visit Beijing.

My wife, Evelyn, and I, along with Dr. Lee and his wife, Lilly, Bradley Hahn and his wife, Ann, all left New York during the summer of '82 and flew to Narita Airport, just outside of Tokyo, Japan. Early the next morning we caught a CAAC (China Airways) flight from Narita to Beijing where several representatives of China Film Co-Production Corporation met us at the airport.

For the next three weeks we enjoyed the sights and sounds and food of a wonderful, friendly people and got to know a little bit about their interesting Ming explorer, Zheng He.

On the international level of cultural exchange, I quickly learned that business meetings and even social functions are conducted in a formal, almost ritualistic sort of a way. Let me give you an example. Whenever we were meeting someone new, as leader of our research delegation, I was always introduced first, then Dr. Lee and Bradley Hahn in that specific order. I was, in turn, introduced first to the head of the Chinese delegation, then to the next most important representative, depending upon his, or her, ranking within the organization and right on down the line.

I also found out that it's customary for the Chinese host to invite his guests to a formal banquet and then we, as guests, were expected to return the favor. These banquet exchanges are also quite formal with each person being seated, again, according to his, or her, rank or social position.

We always received a welcoming toast from our Chinese hosts, and then we, as guests, were expected to offer a toast to them. All of this was quite formal and seemingly a little restrictive, but, of course, it was also just plain good manners.

Because I'm a 'teetotaler', the obligatory toasting with Mai Tai, the very strong alcoholic drink that's present at all Chinese official functions, had me worried for a bit. I'm happy to report, however, that the Chinese hosts were very tolerant of my taking a small sip, instead of gulping down the glass of white liquid, as many foreign guests are wont to do. I don't believe that by not partaking their interesting alcoholic beverage, I lost too many diplomatic points!

China Film Co-Production Corporation officials arranged for me to meet with several distinguished Chinese historians, who were considered specialists in the Ming period. They provided me with quite a bit of valuable information on their explorer, Zheng He. These meetings, almost daily, were also formal and began with the almost obligatory serving of green tea to each member present. After this little formality was completed, the daily work session would begin.

I would usually start by asking our interpreter a specific question about Zheng He. The Chinese interpreter would repeat my question, in Chinese, to one of the government historians. The historian would then begin speaking slowly and deliberately for about ten minutes in Chinese, trying to answer my question as best he could.

While the historian was speaking, the Chinese interpreter would write furiously on a note pad, trying to get everything down that was being said. Since I didn't understand a word of Chinese, I had to sit quietly with my own pad and wait until the historian was finished. When the historian had completed his history lesson, I received the translation in halting English from the interpreter, which was a signal for me to begin writing furiously on my own pad, trying to get it all down correctly.

If the English or Chinese translation didn't come out exactly right, or was somehow unclear, Dr. Lee would immediately interrupt and make sure that any miss-communication in English or Chinese was corrected. Although Danny was fluent in both languages and could have saved us a lot of time by speaking directly to the historians himself, the formality of the meeting always prevailed.

After several hours of this back and forth translation, of English into Chinese and Chinese into English, the morning session would end and we'd all take off for lunch.

The afternoon session would be more of the same, or China Film would arrange a visit to one of their great cultural attractions, such as the Forbidden City, Great Wall, Summer Palace or Ming Tombs.

The visit I think our wives enjoyed more than any other, however, were to a nondescript seven-story building, located in the center of Beijing called the Friendship Store. This building was filled with a magnificent assortment of Chinese goods at excellent prices. It was off limits to the average Chinese citizen during the 1980's, but wide open for foreign tourists!

I was most interested in all of the wonderful historical sites we were allowed to visit, but our wives, I'm certain, enjoyed their world class shopping experience the most!

My first trip to China was, to me, the most memorable, probably because it was the first. Dr. Lee and I eventually made several more trips to Beijing, between '83 and '84, each time getting more and more pieces of the Zheng He puzzle into place. After three years and five trips to China, Danny and I decided we had enough information collected, so I could finally begin writing a book on Zheng He. By now I had to agree that the Chinese admiral, as Bradley Hahn had suggested, was one of the greatest maritime explorers of all time!

Not many westerners today know about the inventions, the military might, the ship building, the exploration, the religious freedom, or the unprecedented international exchange of ideas the Chinese people enjoyed in the early 1400's, all of which, fit together into a pattern of civilization that was unmatched by any other country at that time.

My ultimate goal is to produce a feature film about the Ming period and the incredible eunuch admiral, Zheng He, who helped make this era of Chinese history so special.

Chapter One

---

THE BATTLE

Soldiers from Zheng He's Ming army wade through knee-high murky water at the bottom of a deep ravine. It's night, it's hot, and if the men don't return to the beach soon more than three hundred of their ships could be lost.

Zheng He, Admiral of the Ming Fleet, relentlessly pushes forward beside his exhausted men. There's no thought of slowing down. He holds tightly to the hand of Xi Chen, his beloved lady servant and pulls her along behind.

"Everything is going to be all right", he whispers softly. "Just keep moving."

Unfortunately, his whispered reassurance does little to suppress Xi Chen's growing fear. The last time he told her not to worry, they were captured by Mongols and separated for almost ten years. Nervously, she glances in Zheng He's direction and prays that this time things will be different.

Suddenly, an arrow hisses through the sultry darkness and strikes a soldier close by. Before the man can cry out, thousands of spears and deadly fire arrows begin raining down upon them from above.

Hundreds of soldiers, servants, dignitaries and Ming officials all begin screaming as they vainly search for cover that doesn't exist. There's no thought of returning fire, only of ducking and hiding and trying to escape the terrible onslaught of death from above.

Small fires spring up wherever an arrow strikes, illuminating the murky darkness. Ironically, these intermittent flickering bursts of light, while revealing a route of escape to Zheng He and his men, also endangers them by exposing them to view.

The admiral presses Xi Chen against the canyon wall in a desperate attempt to provide her with some protection. But this move is futile as it subjects both of them to a barrage of spears and fire arrows launched from the opposite rim.

An Arab king and queen traveling with the admiral are caught up in the treacherous attack against the Chinese. Without thinking, Muslim servants throw themselves on top of the royal couple in a desperate attempt to save their lives. Seeing what the Arab servants are doing, Zheng He pushes Xi Chen to the ground and covers her with his own body as well.

Frantically searching for a way to escape, he notices his friend, Friar Odoric, in the middle of the melee of screaming and dying people, on his knees praying. Zheng He screams at the Italian cleric to take cover by the wall.

Though small in stature, Odoric is a sturdy and vigorous man, whose faith remains unshaken by the overwhelming onslaught. He slowly rises to his feet and joins Zheng He as instructed.

"We must escape this hellish betrayal," he yells at the admiral, trying to be heard over the growing din.

Zheng He yells back, "We're trapped, friar! There's no escape."

"Only because we can't see it," Odoric responds firmly, displaying no fear whatsoever.

Appreciating the foreigner's wisdom, Zheng He gently guides Xi Chen into the arms of his Italian friend.

"You must protect her with your life," he tells Odoric, trying his best to express no fear while ducking the flaming arrows and heavy spears. "As my loyal friend, I want you to promise me you will protect her with your life."

Odoric covers Xi Chen protectively with his arms    "I will, Admiral, you have my word.  No harm will befall her.  To my God, I swear.  To your Allah…"


Before the diminutive friar can finish, a barrage of flaming arrows hits a small tree next to them and it explodes in flame!  Odoric instinctively shields Xi Chen from the eruption of heat and flying embers.

The young woman trembles against Odoric, terrified.

Zheng He picks up the sword of a fallen Chinese warrior and turns to face the converging hoards of Ceylonese soldiers, who are now moving towards them, like phantom spirits through the smoke and flames.

Two soldiers suddenly burst into view, charging the Ming admiral. With lightning power, he swings his blade and cuts them down as if he were slicing bamboo. Their severed limbs fall at his feet. Their spinning torsos collapse an instant later.

To his left, down the ravine toward the stream, Zheng He can see a line of armed men, masked by the smoke, moving steadily towards him.  He turns to face them, his sword ready.

But then, to his rear, a Ceylonese warrior bursts from the cloud of ashes and attacks the admiral with a long spear.  Odoric sees the attacker and calls out.

"Zheng He, watch out!"  But his voice is lost in the harsh cacophony of battle.  In an instant, without thinking, the Italian pushes Xi Chen aside and leaps towards his friend to protect him, throwing his own body into harm's way.  The razor-sharp spear strikes Odoric's upper chest.

Horrified, Zheng He decapitates the warrior with one mighty swipe and yanks Xi Chen back to the false safety of the wall. Immediately, he shouts to two soldiers cowering nearby.

"Get Odoric! Get him NOW!"

Reacting to Zheng He's command, the two men rush forward, pick up the badly wounded man by both arms, and look to the Ming admiral for another command.

"Take him to the flagship! As soon as I can, we will follow!"
Though bleeding badly and barely able to speak, the wounded cleric tries to protest.

"Zheng He, please," he gasps, gritting his teeth against the pain and clutching his bloody robe at the chest. "I'll be all right. Just let me rest a few moments..."

13

Xi Chen sees a growing stream of blood staining the Italian's robe and knows he needs help fast.

"Zheng He is right, friar. You must get to the flagship, and quickly. The soldiers will carry you."

Still Odoric tries to protest.

"What about you?" he pleads, clutching at his bloody chest in pain.

"Don't worry about us," Zheng He responds firmly, "we'll be right behind you."

The Ming leader pointed to the two frightened soldiers holding Odoric.

"Get him out of here! NOW!"

Jarred by the admiral's sharp command, the two men begin carrying and dragging their wounded charge through the gauntlet of falling spears and arrows.

Even though Ceylonese warriors and Chinese soldiers are fighting all around, all three are miraculously able to make it out of the ravine safely. But just as they are beginning to climb the dirt trail beyond, a huge tree crashes to the ground behind them. The thunderous, unexpected sound catches the men by surprise. Instinctively, the soldiers stop and turn to see the massive barrier of wood and leaves lying across the muddy trail, blocking it completely.

For an instant they look with concern at Zheng He and his troops trapped on the other side, but then, fearing for their own safety, once again begin half-carrying and half-dragging the bloody Odoric towards the fleet in the bay, as instructed.

Back in the gorge, Zheng He and his men have been able to drive back the warriors who attacked them so treacherously. But this allows only a small respite and he knows he must do something quickly. If he doesn't move his men out of the gorge soon, the Ceylonese will regroup, return with an even larger force, and kill them. He yells at his men to head for the beach.

Many don't move, too frightened of what may lie beyond the raging fires, which now burn all around them. Soon, the intensifying conflagration is so heavy with dark smoke that it's difficult to see more than a spear-length ahead. Ironically, it affords the men a small measure of brief protection.

Gasping for breath, Zheng He knows if they stay where they are, they will all surely die. In desperation, with Xi Chen in one hand and his sword in the other, he starts pushing his men in the direction of the beach. But then, just as he gets them moving, they come upon the huge tree, which, minutes before, had come close to crushing the two soldiers carrying Odoric.

When Zheng He sees the huge obstruction blocking their path, he has no choice but to order his men to turn around, and start heading back in the opposite direction.

"Back! Back!" he screams. "We'll go the other way!"

During all this confusion and activity, the Ming admiral has held tightly to the hand of Xi Chen. She's the love of his life, and if anything should ever happen to her, he knows his own life wouldn't be worth living.

Slowly the formation of Ming soldiers, servants and foreign dignitaries turns and they all begin moving reluctantly back in the opposite direction.

It's almost impossible to breathe. Most cough and choke on the thick smoke. But despite the difficulty, all do as their leader has ordered, with none questioning his decision.

Just as Zheng He, Xi Chen and his men are about to escape from the gorge, a second sprawling tree crashes to the ground, this time blocking their escape to the rear. They're trapped!

While Zheng He and his men struggle to survive in the narrow gorge, the two soldiers bearing Odoric manage to carry him down to the harbor, barely alive. Extremely weak from the loss of blood, he begins fingering the wooden cross that has always hung about his neck and quickly realizes something is wrong. A chip of wood is missing from the right side of the crucifix. It's not a big piece, but substantial enough to let him know its smooth surface doesn't feel right. Then it comes to him. The cross that he has touched and prayed with for nearly his entire life had saved him from certain death. The blade that penetrated his chest would have killed him instantly, if it were not for the blessed ornament around his neck.

Odoric quickly thanks God for his loving benevolence and then begins praying that the two Ming soldiers will be able to get him back to Zheng He's flagship while he is still alive.

When they reach the rocky beach, what Odoric sees is almost more than he can bear. Of the three hundred ships in Zheng He's huge Ming fleet, more than half have been destroyed. Many more are still burning.

Odoric gasps. "How could this have happened?"

The two soldiers find an abandoned outrigger canoe on the beach and commandeer it for their own use. As quickly, and as gingerly as they can, they place the wounded cleric into the crude vessel and begin rowing him out to Zheng He's flagship.

As Odoric looks back towards the shore, he's further horrified to see a steady stream of fire arrows, arching skyward from the surrounding hillsides and onto the ships in the bay. "If the admiral's Baochuan is on fire," he worries to the rowing soldiers, "there may be no hope."

15

As the little outrigger approaches the mass of ships riding at anchor, the unmistakable shape of a huge, nine-masted treasure ship, begins to loom above them from out of the darkness. Large eyes painted near the bow seem to stare down menacingly onto the frail craft as it approaches.

"I pray that's Zheng He's flagship," Odoric again whispers to the soldiers. "That ship is not yet on burning."

As the two soldiers bring them closer to the vessel, fires from other burning ships reflect eerily off the flagship's massive wooden structure and cloth sails. When they reach a position close to midship, the two soldiers begin shouting for help.

Almost immediately, a handful of Ming sailors peer over the side and spot the small outrigger floating twenty feet below. They quickly toss a rope sling over the side and start hauling the wounded cleric up onto the main deck. Without saying a word, four sailors grab his arms and legs and begin carrying him to his cabin at the stern.

Once inside, Ming servants take over and place the bleeding friar, as carefully as they can, onto his own wooden-framed bed. When Odoric complains that he doesn't want to be laid flat, one of the men scurries around and is able to find a few extra pillows from an adjoining cabin. Once they're placed behind his back, Odoric is able to breathe easier. The pain in his chest subsides somewhat, providing some relief now that he's in an upright position.

"That's good," he gasps, while gripping his upper chest and clutching his bloody robe in a tangle of fingers. Silently, he reaches for his broken wooden cross and starts praying to the Almighty.

While one servant takes a rag and tries to clean the blood from around the wound, Odoric begs the other to bring him a pen and a few sheets of paper.

The servant can't believe it. Both then give him an inquisitive look, believing the wounded foreigner is delirious. But Odoric is adamant!

"Bring me some paper and a pen, please!" he gasps, again having to hold his chest against a sudden rush of pain.

Since the servants don't expect Odoric to live beyond the rising of the sun, they silently accede to his wish. It could, after all, be his last request.

While the first servant continues cleaning Odoric's seeping wound, the second silently crosses the cabin in his bare feet and pokes around a small desk until he locates a piece of parchment and a writing instrument. He holds them out to Odoric, sympathetically offering a respectful bow of deference.

"Thank you!" Odoric wheezes, his teeth still clinched against the pain. "Now, if you don't mind, I'd like you to leave so I can be alone."

The two servants look at each other, hesitating, unsure how they should respond.

Odoric waves a sheet of paper at them and protests weakly.

"Just let me rest. I'll be fine."

After making a final adjustment to the friar's bandage, the two servants reluctantly do as they're told. But first they make certain that he has a cup of hot tea beside his bed and the cabin lantern is turned up to afford him a little more light. After bowing in unison, they depart from the cabin, closing the door softly behind them as they leave.

Finally, Odoric is alone. The small cabin is eerily quiet, except for the faint sound of cannon fire and orders shouted from somewhere on an upper deck. The muffled background noise provides him with some comfort, as it probably means the Ming soldiers and sailors are now fighting back.

But he can't dwell on the turmoil outside. That is now Zheng He's difficult burden to bear. Rather, he must summon the strength to recall and record the incredible things that he has experienced over the past thirty years and write them down before he dies... so nothing will be lost.

He closes his eyes, the tumultuous images of his life cascading through his mind. "Why did I travel to China?" he wonders to himself. "To spread the word of God? To bring spirituality to that distant land?"

His eyes suddenly open as a realization washes over him. "Marco Polo."

The name hangs in the air, whispered from his lips. The pen in his hand hovers over the parchment, words ready to flow from its point.

"Yes. I came to China, because of Marco Polo."

Odoric adjusts his bandages, wincing against the throbbing pain. Slowly, and with careful precision and trembling fingers, he begins to write...


"Marco Polo traveled to China in 1275 and upon his return he authored a book which was very popular. The name of it was quite simple. The Book of Marco Polo. I read the volume about a hundred years after the great explorer returned from China. Immediately I became curious about this distant country and its fascinating people."


Odoric again stops a moment to rest and looks, not at his bandage, but for the cup of tea, which the servants had left beside his bed. After

SILK DRAGON

taking a sip of the still hot liquid, he unsteadily returns the cup to the table and continues trying to recall those earlier times...

"It was the year 1385. I was a young friar in Venezia, Italy, and quite anxious to spread my wings. When Bishop Augustine asked for a volunteer to start a mission in China, without thinking, I raised my hand.

An impetuous act, I must admit, and before long, not more than six months, if I remember correctly, I found myself on the back of a long-haired horse, high in the mountains of Tibet.

It was a miracle I didn't freeze to death. But it was also miraculous that I was wise enough to hire a mountain guide. If I hadn't, I never would have survived the journey.

As soon as we got to the highest mountain pass, we were struck by a terrible blizzard. With all the blowing snow, I couldn't see a thing, front or back. All I could do was hang on to the mane of the shaggy horse I was riding and pray to God it wouldn't stray from the trail.

The year was 1381. I was thirty years of age at the time. In that raging blizzard, I was quite sure I wouldn't live to be thirty-one.

We were following the Old Silk Road, which had been a well-worn thoroughfare for merchants and people on the move for more than a thousand years. But up there, on the top of that high mountain, it was hard for me to believe that others had passed this way and lived to tell of it. The road was very narrow in places; nothing more than a narrow and dangerous rocky trail.

When I thought about Marco Polo and his family, traveling on the same road one hundred and six years previously, the enormity of what they accomplished was much more appreciated and magnified.

But it wasn't just the steep rocky path. It was the bitter cold. No matter how many times I tugged on my thick woolen scarf, or hunched down in that uncomfortable wooden saddle, I couldn't get away from it.

And with the blowing wind and snow, it made surviving that much more difficult. The only way I could see at all was to squint into the freezing maelstrom with one eye open and keep the other closed.

I also prayed continually that my horse would stay in line with the others. Since it was impossible for me to see anything to my front or rear, there was nothing I could do to keep the animal headed in the right direction.

From time-to-time, when the wind slackened slightly, I was able to catch a brief glimpse of a frosty blur ahead, but then, just as quickly, the wind harshly returned and the vision disappeared into a blur of white on white.

But it was during the second day of the storm, when conditions grew worse, that I almost lost my life. It started just like the first day, bitterly cold with howling wind and snow, then, sometime before noon, almost without my realizing it, the howl became an inescapable roar. At first, I couldn't tell if what I was hearing was the normal sound of the storm itself, or a more ominous and evil presence trying to frighten me into turning back.

As the sound grew louder and louder, I twisted in my saddle and tried to see where it was coming from. Just at that moment the storm clouds parted and, to my utter horror, I saw what looked like the whole side of the mountain crashing down upon me.

In an instant I knew what was happening. Avalanche! The huge mass of ice and snow was rushing toward me at an incredible speed and there wasn't anything I could do. I closed my eyes and braced for the calamity I was certain would descend upon me. But then, at the very last moment, the frozen river of ice and snow took a slight turn away and miraculously swept past.

The roar was deafening. Bits of frozen debris pummeled my body, but I was left on the trail, shaken, still on the back of my horse. Two pack animals in line just behind me weren't so fortunate. Both were swept from the trail and into the valley below.

Instinctively, I crossed myself and fervently thanked God for miraculously sparing my life. I also prayed, as earnestly as I could, for the mountain guides to rescue me from this insidious folly. I had experienced enough riding for one day and wanted to move someplace, anyplace, that was warm and off this damnable freezing mountain trail.

Realizing I had cursed, I crossed myself again and asked God for His benevolent forgiveness. Then, I prayed even harder that my trusty mountain guides would rescue me from this frozen hell... and soon.

My friends in Italy had told me, many times, that even though I had a short stature and was somewhat heavy-set, I was blessed with a friendly disposition. I must admit their description and assessment of me was true. But on that particular afternoon, when I was almost killed by that thunderous avalanche, my friendly disposition was nowhere to be found.

To take my mind off the harsh cold, I forced myself to think about warmer times and what had caused me to be on that horrible mountain trail in the first place.

Marco Polo. His indomitable spirit had tempted me to leave the welcome climes of sunny Italy in search of unexpected adventures in a strange, unfamiliar land.

What had captured my interest was reading about Marco Polo's family taking friars with them when they traveled east. This one piece of information, probably more than any other, caused me to become fascinated by China and to start thinking about going there myself one day.

But what did the friar's do when they arrived in China? Did they try to teach the Chinese about Jesus? Surely they must have. That would have been their first priority. But if they did attempt such teaching, how did they communicate? Surely no Chinese spoke Italian. And I'm quite certain that none of my Italian brethren spoke Chinese.

An exceptionally strong gust of wind stung my face, quickly jolting me back to reality. I stopped thinking about Marco Polo and the friars. I squinted hard, trying to see the way ahead. The only thing visible was the interminable blowing snow.

But I was still astride my shuffling horse. That was good. And I still hadn't frozen to death. That was also good. Thus far, my prayers had been answered. So, I did the only thing I could; slide deeper into my saddle and allow my mind to continue its curious wandering.

Random questions marched steadily through my thoughts. Did the friar's stay in China attempting to gain converts? Or did they return with Marco Polo and his family to Italy? What happened to the message they were trying to deliver? Did any of the Buddhists become Christians? And were the friars even allowed to talk to the Chinese about other religions?

Another blast of wind-driven snow slapped my face again. The cold was like a physical force, trying to slice through my clothes and body. I tugged harder on my woolen scarf and tried to hunker down even further into my uncomfortable wooden saddle. But no matter which way I turned or twisted, I couldn't escape the unbearable wind and cold. My only escape was to close my eyes and, as before, force myself to indulge in question after question.

"What happened to them? Those friars?" My voice filled the snowy void. I thought if I spoke aloud, perhaps it would wake my spirit and cause me to feel better. But it had little effect, other than to unduly startle my horse. And so, I kept all further questions safely inside my head.

What did the friars accomplish while they were in China? And what of the Chinese people, living their lives, invisible to the rest of the civilized world? How did they manage to develop such an incredible culture? Marco Polo said theirs was more advanced than any civilization in the world? How could that be? To me, a proud and confident Italian, that sounded unbelievable. I had always been taught that we Italians were the most advanced culture in existence. No one in my experience ever thought about the Chinese.

Marco Polo had reported that the Chinese practiced any religion they chose. But weren't they all Buddhists? Marco wrote that some in southern China were Muslim and followed the prophet Mohammed. Muslims in China? It didn't seem possible.

Suddenly, my horse stumbled!

A startled shout of panic burst from me. My heart almost stopped at the same time. I quickly forgot about daydreaming and strained again to make out the horse in front of me. Thankfully, the swaying haunches of the animal drifted faintly into view, plowing clumsily through the ever-deepening snow.

When I realized I was still on the trail and hadn't fallen into a chasm, I offered another prayer of thanks and then, unable to resist the distraction, gradually lost myself in thought once again.

When Bishop Augustine asked for volunteers, why did I raise my hand? Had I completely lost my mind? Now, here I was, six months later, on the back of a horrible animal in the middle of, God knows where, clearly in danger of freezing to death. Lying on my bed in Italy, dreaming of traveling to China, it never occurred to me that I might actually risk killing myself trying to get there.

My thoughts were growing too oppressive. I shook my head, hoping to rid myself of such negative contemplation. I wiggled my fingers and toes, trying to determine if I could feel anything. When I finally realized that I could, I offered another grateful prayer to my Maker and thanked Him, once again, for his generous benevolence.

Shifting in my saddle for the thousandth time, I again squinted into the blowing snow, this time hoping I could locate my trusty mountain guides somewhere ahead.

"Where are you, Chu-ji", I muttered silently to myself. "If we don't stop soon, I'm going to freeze to death."

I had no idea if my intrepid guides had even survived the avalanche. My horse still walked the trail, undisturbed, as if nothing had happened. Surely, if the guides were killed, the horses would have stopped? Wouldn't they?

"Where are you, my friend?" I ventured aloud, becoming more and more desperate. "I don't think I can hold out much longer."

As the sharp, wind-whipped ice crystals again lashed my face, I calmly became resigned to my tragic fate. I was obviously going to freeze to death. Acceptance was the final step toward inescapable bliss and eternal grace.

Just as I began sliding down into a position of least discomfort, I felt a slight tug on my woolen coat and looked up to see, miraculously, what looked like the smiling face of God himself. It wasn't really God, but at that moment, the face of Chu-ji, was the next best thing.

"We better stop now, Father," he yelled, trying to make himself heard over the howling wind. "The snow is getting too deep!"

I eagerly nodded my approval and ducked deeper into my thick woolen scarf.

Chu-ji urged his own horse forward, past mine, and was soon swallowed up in another swirl of white. In just a few minutes, however, I could sense the wind slacking. For the first time in quite a while, the vision of other horses and guides, strung out in front of me and to my rear, began to appear like apparitions.

The guides pulled their animals off the trail and led them towards an area that was located behind a cliff face of solid rock, which, mercifully, blocked the wind. Within minutes the horses were huddled together, packs unloaded and the guides busied themselves setting up camp.

Chu-ji came to me and offered to help me off my horse. I accepted his aid, otherwise I probably would have still been perched there, frozen stiff. I was so cold I could hardly move. Once Chu-ji saw I was on my feet, he moved over to help the guides set up a large round tent, which they called a yurt. I recall that I made a lame effort to help, but was really only interested in staying out of their way. Before long, the round tent, made of slender wooden poles covered with the hides of goat and yak, was in place. Snow was brushed away from the inside. Several guides then spread two thick layers of carpet over the wet dirt floor and invited me to enter. Not needing a second invitation, I dropped to my hands and knees and quickly crawled inside, followed closely by the other guides and Chu-ji, who backed in last and pulled a heavy flap shut. This effectively kept the storm outside.

Immediately, two of the younger guides began building a small fire using dried horse dung as fuel, while a third filled a small copper pot with snow. I knew from previous stops, that within a few minutes they would present me with a welcome cup of hot tea, which, as far as I was concerned, could not come too soon.

I never cared much for the tea they served. To me, it had an unpleasant, bitter taste. But on that day, frozen to the bone, I had no intention of making a complaint.

Chu-ji brushed the snow off my coat then handed me a cup of the strong, black tea. Giving him my friendliest smile, which was difficult, considering I could hardly move my face, I accepted the cup, closed my eyes for a few seconds so I could relish the heat from the metal cup, then took a very long and satisfying sip.

Completely oblivious to the howling storm outside, Chu-ji settled down next to me and started slurping big mouthfuls of the bitter liquid from his own cup. As was his custom, when the scalding tea was gone, he turned to me and with a broad toothless grin. I knew what that meant. It was time once again to practice his Italian.

He wiped his mouth with the back of his hand and began a stilted inquiry. "Why you try make so difficult journey, friar?" he asked, mixing some of his words, but not so many that I couldn't understand. "We no see men like you in these mountains."

Just then, one of the younger guides handed me a bowl of hot soup, which I gratefully accepted before answering. As usual, just to be safe, I surreptitiously sniffed the bowl's oddly aromatic contents. Deciding it was probably not made from some slithery or unsavory animal parts, and not wanting to insult the generosity of my leathery-skinned companions, I took a cautious, but fairly good-sized bite.

Turning to Chu-ji, I swallowed the food in my mouth before responding, offered him another forced smile, then explained to him that I was traveling to China on a mission for my church.

I don't know whether or not he understood what I was talking about. He probably didn't really comprehend it. But, before he could ask another question, one of the other guides offered Chu-ji a bowl of the same, foul-smelling soup, which he accepted without saying a word.

Holding the bowl tightly in both hands, he began slurping big mouthfuls with obvious gusto. When he finished, he held out his bowl for a refill. When his bowl was replenished, as before, he turned the bowl up on end, slurped it down in one long gulp, then finished his meal with even bigger gulps of the bitter black tea. He burped loudly, gave me another toothless smile and then continued our conversation.

"I hear stories, friar, about Mongol leader Kubla Khan. They say Great Khan, he like Marco Polo much. I hear, you travel to China... you say name Polo... Chinese, they treat you like friend."

Another guide refilled Chu-ji's cup, then offered me the same. Since it was hot, I gladly accepted the nourishment, despite its bitterness.

"I hope you're right," I told him. "I have a lot of faith in the heavenly Father guiding me to my destination, but if I can receive a little help from Marco Polo along the way, I certainly won't refuse."

Chu-ji smiled at me again, pretending he agreed. But I had a feeling he didn't truly understand what I had said. We sat together for several hours, drinking tea and struggling to talk about Marco Polo and the Chinese. I thought it was remarkable he could speak any Italian at all. He told me, as best he could, that he had been able to pick up a little of the language from other Italian countrymen he had led across the mountains.

And so it was, that I learned much about the Chinese; their customs, their beliefs and their unique view of the world. And it all came to me in the disjointed, halting and broken Italian muttering of a toothless man sipping bitter soup. Such was the irony of my life.

At the same time that I was quaking and freezing in the mountains of Tibet, a small village on the plains of the Yunnan Province, one of the southern-most Provinces of China, was holding its annual harvest celebration.

Villagers cheered as long strings of brightly bursting firecrackers popped and snaked across the hard dirt. Others drew back in fear and excitement, as multi-colored rockets suddenly whooshed into the clear night sky. When the rockets exploded high overhead in a brilliant flash of color and noise, the rundown village was transformed, at least for a few moments, into a magical land.

Ma He, a Muslim lad of eighteen, was distracted for a moment by the noisy fireworks display, but his eyes quickly returned to the delicate beauty of Xi Chen, the sixteen-year-old girl who stood beside him. Leaning against a rugged stone wall, Xi Chen stared admiringly into his eyes, her attention never drawn away for a moment by the jarring explosions of light.

A short distance away, Ma He's mother sat with Xi Chen's aunt, trying to keep an eye on the two amorous teenagers.

"Look at them," the Ma He's mother purred, "they've been like that since they were babies."

"They're going to be married soon," the young girl's aunt chirped happily. "It's Allah's will."

Ma He and Xi Chen were full Chinese, both having been born in Yunnan Province. But their heritage was definitely mid-eastern. Two generations earlier, the boy's family had been farmers in Persia.

When the great Mongol leader, Kubla Khan, led his army westward, it was not unusual for him to come upon an enemy force much larger than his. When this happened, he would quickly solicit help from as many local villages in the area as he could. The Great Khan was more than happy to offer the villagers free land in China, if they would agree to fight for him and help him defeat his much larger foes.

And so it was, sixty years earlier, when Ma He's grandfather and all the men of his village joined Khan's army and helped the Mongol ruler achieve his victory. True to his word, Khan offered the villagers free land in southern China. Consequently, many of them packed up and made the journey from Persia to China, settling in the southern part of the country in Yunnan Province.

Ma He and Xi Chen were both born in Yunnan Province and were considered full-blooded Chinese yet retained many features of their

Persian forefathers. Not surprisingly, their village, along with other villages in the area, retained many of the Persian customs, including that of honoring Mohammed as their most revered and only prophet.

Xi Chen stared intently into Ma He's eyes. The young lad held her hand nervously and waited for just the right moment to sneak a kiss. She felt his warm breath on her neck.

Xi Chen drew back with a warning gaze. "Be careful," she whispered with caution. "The elders might be watching."

"They are watching," Ma He whispered back. "That's why I'm not kissing you. Yet."

Both youngsters knew it was strictly against village custom to violate a young girl's honor, even in so trivial a romantic display as a kiss on the cheek. They both had to be extremely cautious that no one saw any demonstration of physical affection.

Ma He continued to watch the elders out of the corner of one eye, waiting for just the right time when they'd be distracted by the fireworks and look away.

"The next time one of those big rockets goes off," he whispered again, "be ready to run."

"Run?" Xi Chen asked, surprised at Ma He's words. "Run where?"

"Just be ready," he added, while stealing another look in the elder's direction. "I'll show you."

When six large rockets suddenly whooshed into the sky, spinning wildly in different directions, the two elders instinctively turned to look at the incredible display of flashing light. When they did, Ma He was ready.

"Come on," he shouted and pulled his sweetheart from the wall with a hard jerk.

The two lovers ran together, joyously, hand-in-hand, through the village garden and to the back of the village, where they could safely hide in the shadows of an old stone Mosque. Once there, sheltered in the blackness of the stone edifice, Ma He took Xi Chen in his arms excitedly. "Now I've got you alone and no one is watching."

Trembling with anticipation, the eighteen-year-old lad took Xi Chen's face in his hands to give her a passionate, loving kiss. But as he leaned close, his heart afire, she suddenly turned her face away.

"What's the matter with you?" he begged, obviously shocked and hurt.

"Not until we're married," she responded coyly.

"But I love you!" Ma He wailed, obviously hurt by her unexpected rebuff.

Xi Chen turned to face her frustrated suitor.

"And I love you, my dearest, sweetest, Ma He," she purred with the amorous intensity of youth.

"Well, then?"

Xi Chen looked into Ma He's dark brown eyes and gave him a teasing grin.

"I don't think Allah… or Mohammed, would approve."

With that, she turned and ran off into the night, leaving the lad standing alone in the shadows, disappointed and terribly confused.


But at this time, I was unaware of the drama that played out far away in the Yunnan Province. As we safely emerged from the frigid high country, Chu-ji and his mountain guides moved their horses at a much faster pace. Freezing to death just two weeks earlier, I now had to contend with dust and heat. We walked our weary horses slowly but steadily across a slightly undulating plain that stretched to the horizon.

Since it was no longer cold, I found it necessary to discard my heavy clothing in favor of a dark brown, loose-fitting robe, which I was much more accustomed to wearing. I also found to be the most comfortable of garments.

As I turned in my saddle and looked back towards the mountains far behind us, I was immediately mesmerized by the look of their unbelievable grandeur and beauty. With sweat now dripping from my face, it was hard to imagine that just two weeks previously, I was in swirling snow praying mightily for God's help and quite certain I was going to freeze to death. Now, on the flat plain, almost eight thousand feet lower, I began to feel that I might soon perish from the unbearable heat.

Several days later a large dust cloud hung eerily on the far horizon. Not surprisingly, my mountain guide, Chu-ji, was the first to see it. He moved his mount next to mine and tried to point out the strange looking phenomena to me.

"Friar! Look!" he exclaimed, excitedly, "Over there!"

When I squinted in the direction he was pointing, I thought I saw something moving vaguely in the distance, but still wasn't quite sure of its origin.

"What is it?" I asked uneasily, suddenly feeling terribly inexperienced.

"A caravan," he responded, becoming more excited by the minute. "Perhaps Chinese merchants."

I looked again, now apprehensive. It appeared to be nothing more than a vast dust cloud.

"How can you tell?"

"I cannot… for certain," he shrugged, grinning from ear-to-ear. "But inside, I hear the voice. It tells me… a caravan."

"If so," I responded, "I hope they're friendly."

"Maybe," Chu-ji said, giving me his best toothless expression of delight. "If you lucky, they take you with them."

It wasn't long before the dust cloud did, indeed, reveal a caravan, just as Chu-ji expected. But, they weren't Chinese merchants as he had predicted. It was the caravan of a forty-year-old Chinese king, named Zhu Di. He was traveling north to his home in Beijing after having just completed a leisurely three-month retreat in neighboring Siam.

As the monarch peered out from behind the curtained window of his exquisitely decorated carriage, he was surprised to see us in the distance. I'm certain we appeared to be an oddly rag-tag group. Curious as to who we might be, he immediately called for his senior military officer, Commander Tan.

"Commander!" he shouted, leaning out the window to make sure he was heard, "I'd like to see you for a minute!"

Tan looked around when he heard Zhu Di calling, laid a whip to the flank of his horse and galloped back to where the king's carriage was waiting.

"Yes, Sire?" the Commander asked, offering a respectful dip of his head as he addressed the monarch.

"Take several of your men," Zhu Di said, eyeing us with curious suspicion. "Find out why those people have stopped."

Without saying a word, Commander Tan saluted, backed his horse away and shouted orders to his men. Ten soldiers formed two short columns behind Commander Tan, following him at a slow trot as he moved directly toward us.

As soon as I saw the soldiers coming, I began to worry. Here were ten Chinese soldiers, each wearing bright red coats, armed to the teeth, led by a large, not-so-friendly-looking military commander, heading straight in my direction. Even more sweat began to pour from my face, running into the crevices of my robe, making me shiver despite the heat. Nervously, I began fingered the small wooden cross that always hung about my neck.

"Why are they carrying swords and shields?" I thought anxiously to myself. "Do they think we want to fight?"

The Commander Tan stopped his horse a short distance from us. He did nothing for a few seconds, sitting motionless, studying us carefully. Then, after motioning for the rest of his soldiers to remain where they were, he slowly walked his horse toward us. He paused, squinting a hard gaze, clearly trying to assert his authority.

"I am Commander Tan," his deep voice boomed. "I am military representative of Emperor Hung-wu, protector of His Royal Highness, Zhu Di, the Duke of Yan, king of the northern province. Identify yourselves and state the nature of your travel."

Since I didn't speak Chinese, I had no idea what he was saying. I pulled on Chu-ji's coat, quietly begging for a translation. The mountain guide motioned sharply for me to remain silent. He looked directly at Commander Tan, searching his instincts for the right response, knowing that precisely how he answered could spell our fate.

"We are poor guides," Chu-ji began, trying his best to appear humble. "We travel from the high mountains behind us." He turned in his saddle and motioned towards the snow- covered peaks on the far horizon.

"We take this man, Friar Odoric, across the mountains to China. He is from a country far away. It is called Italy. Friar Odoric is a good man. He would like an honorable man to take him to your country."

I still wasn't sure what Chu-ji had said, but while he was speaking I thought of something I wanted to make sure he communicated to the commander. I tugged on his coat and whispered to him in Italian.

"Tell him I come as a man of peace."

When Chu-ji started to relate this to the commander, I tugged his coat again.

"Tell him I come in the name of Marco Polo."

Chu-ji flashed his toothless grin at me and happily translated what I had said.

The Chinese commander's eyes shifted skeptically to mine, studying me for a long, tense moment with dark suspicion. Then, as I begin to consider my options for a hasty escape on horseback, his face relaxed and he displayed an unexpectedly warm smile.

"You know Marco Polo?" he asked, with a soothing voice that had abruptly lost all its harshness.

When Chu-ji told me what the Chinese officer had asked, I breathed a long sigh of relief and immediately replied, "Si! Si! Senor Polo was from my country… Italy."

And in this moment, the tension all but vanished. Chu-ji continued to translate our conversation, a giddy sense of relief in his newly found enthusiasm.

"My king is quite interested in people from foreign lands," the commander told us. "Perhaps he will desire to meet you. He may even allow you to travel with us to Beijing."

When Commander Tan finished, he abruptly turned his horse around and rode back to where King Zhu Di was waiting in his carriage. The armed soldiers, however, didn't move. They maintained their position nearby, hands close to their swords, unaware of the conversation that we'd had.

"Where's he going?" I asked Chu-ji.

He didn't respond to my question. Instead, he turned away and, in their native tongue, began telling the other guides what was happening. All of them immediately started smiling and talking happily among themselves. I took this as a good sign, feeling more at ease.

After a few minutes, Commander Tan returned and took up his original position in front of his troops.

"My king has agreed to take in this stranger," he stated simply. "He may travel with us to our home in Beijing."

Chu-ji whispered a quick translation to me, then bowed graciously to Commander Tan. He turned to me and gave me a mischievous toothless grin.

"You travel in good hands now, friar." he gushed, obviously delighted that he had cleverly negotiated such a fine arrangement. "It is long a Chinese custom to be friendly with those of other nations."

"You're sure?" I stammered, gazing off at the caravan, still amazed at my seeming stroke of good fortune.

"You will be alive and well fed," Chu-ji joked, slapping me on my back for good measure. "What more could you want? After all, my friend, you travel with the king!"

Since it appeared the arrangement had been made, I immediately began fishing around in my pocket for a small leather pouch. I pulled out several gold coins and held them out to Chu-ji.

"I owe you my life, Chu-ji," I said. "It isn't much, but I'd like you to take this as a sign of my gratitude. You have taken good care of me."

Chu-ji held up his hand in a sign of polite refusal.

"No need!" he told me happily, still smiling broadly. "You pay me enough already."

I persisted, holding out several more coins. He grinned peacefully, gazing off toward the horizon, not giving it another thought. Obviously, it was not a subject for further discussion.

The next thing I knew, I was handed the reins to three horses, all loaded down with my possessions and, I suspect, some additional supplies that I hadn't brought with me.

I was instructed to follow Commander Tan and his red-coated soldiers. I waved a final goodbye to Chu-ji and the other guides, took a deep breath, crossed myself, and headed off on what I knew would be a once-in-a-lifetime adventure.

A great distance away, in the village, Ma He and Xi Chen tried to spend as much time as they could together out of the sight of others.

But it wasn't easy. The village elders continued to watch every move they made. Everyone knew they were in love and they planned to be married soon, so it was doubly hard for them to slip away unnoticed.

One thing that Ma He did enjoy doing was to gallop his horse across the open meadow as fast as he could, showing off for Xi Chen. And he didn't care who was watching. The feeling of the wind blowing through his hair, was a thrill he never grew tired of repeating. Xi Chen, however, worried constantly that he would hurt himself, especially when she saw him jumping on and off his horse, while riding as fast as the horse would go. Or when he rode his horse seated backwards, waving his arms in the air like a crazy man.

But Ma He was an expert rider and knew exactly what he was doing. He loved to give the appearance of great danger and tease Xi Chen into thinking he was about to fall or go sprawling into the hard rocks beneath him.

One stunt he enjoyed, probably more than any other, was to ride towards her as fast as he could, then pull to a stop at the very last second, and jump off, right at her feet. The stunt would scare her, just as he intended, but it also made her angry.

"Why do you take so many chances?" she would complain, pouting. "It's stupid! Don't you know that?"

"I'm just having fun," he would always say, his youthful grin of exuberance stretching from ear to ear.

"Fun! You call that?" she fumed, pretending to be madder than she really was. "Someday you're going to break your neck, Ma He! That's what's going to happen! Then where will I be? I'll tell you. I'll be stuck at home for the rest of my life, taking care of a broken man, his bones twisted and crushed!"

Ma He always tried to calm her down with a gentle, flirtatious kiss.

"There isn't anything to worry about," he would boast. "The horse and I are as one. Someday, you'll see. You'll be proud of me. I'll become a great soldier, ride off into battle..."

Xi Chen hated it when he started bragging.

"And that's another thing, Ma He!" she snapped, shaking her finger and still pretending to be mad. "All you ever talk about is wanting to be a soldier. I don't want you to be a soldier. You'd have to go off and fight battles. I want you to be home with me. To be my husband, and a father to our children."

Once more, Ma He again tried to give Xi Chen a kiss, but she turned away sharply with an exaggerated pout.

"I don't want a husband I will never see," she said, giving him a quick glance just to make sure to be certain he was still listening. "I want…"

He gently pulled her back around to face him, covering her face with tender little kisses. This time, Xi Chen was unable to resist. She melted into his arms and responded with kisses of her own.

Then, suddenly, realizing what she was doing and where it would lead, she suddenly pulled away.

"No, Ma He," she whispered, fighting to catch her, her lips lingering close to his. "I will not kiss you until we're married!"

She firmly removed his arms and pushed him back.

"Any way, someone may be watching."

"I don't care who's watching," he countered eagerly, wanting desperately to continue kissing her. She was the only girl he'd ever loved and the one he intended to marry. Not being able to simply kiss her seemed like a most unfair torture.

"I love you, Xi Chen," he whispered, excitedly, his words and tone becoming more and more passionate. "I love you with all my heart."

He took her face in his hands, speaking to her from the depths of his being.

"I want to promise you, Xi Chen, right here and now, before Benevolent Allah, that I will always love you and I'll never leave you. Not ever! For as long as we both shall live!"

Xi Chen let his words of desire wash over her, weakening her resolve. Slowly, she let her arms slip softly around Ma He's neck. She brushed her lips across his handsome face.

"And I love you, my dearest, sweetest, Ma He. I, too, promise, here and now, before Benevolent Allah, that I'll always love you, I'll never leave you. And I will never allow another man to touch me. Not ever! For as long as we both shall live!"

The two lovers were well aware they shouldn't be kissing, especially in the middle of the open meadow. But their strong youthful desires and proclamations of everlasting love quickly overcame their common sense. They didn't care if anyone's watching or not.

Neither made an effort to stop the passionate kiss. In their hearts, they had sealed their sacred vow of love forever.

From afar, Hadji Ma, Ma He's father, watched the two young lovers kissing in the field. He was stirred by a troubled anger within, not liking what he witnessed. He yelled at them from the front door of his house.

"Ma He! I want both of you to come inside. Now! It's time for you to eat!"

The young lovers were slow to heed his request, continuing their very open display of affection. Hadji Ma shouted at them again… this time much louder and with greater vehemence.

"Don't be slow about it! You hear me? I want both of you in here... NOW!"

Ma He grabbed the mane of his horse and with an easy agility, swung himself upon the animal's back. He reached down, taking Xi Chen's hand, pulling her up behind him.

They trotted unhurriedly across the meadow towards the house. Ma He's father watched them impatiently, shaking his head at the impetuous nature of youth.

Over a simple meal of rice and vegetables, the family talked about the unexpected rush of activity that had been stirring around the village for the past week. Soldiers from Emperor Hung-wu's army had passed through the village every few days, warning everyone to be on the lookout for Mongol horsemen. This had caused much speculation among the local villagers that a great battle could be brewing nearby. Some suggested it might even happen on the flat plain beside the Stone Forest.

The elders recounted stories of the emperor's senior military officer, General Ho. Ma He listened intently to every word. He was barely able to contain himself. He had so many questions.

Xi Chen watched him closely, knowing that if Ma He didn't get his chance to speak soon, he would surely break in and rudely interrupt.

She gave him a kick under the table and a stern look, trying to warn him it might be best if he kept his mouth closed and maintained a respect for his elders. But Ma He was stubborn and determined to speak. He gave his love a brash grin and tugged on his father's sleeve.

"Father..." Ma He interrupted. Hadji Ma turned to him with a scowl on his face. Ma He continued regardless, still confident in his words. "I do not wish to be impolite, but..."

Immediately, everyone at the table stopped talking and turned to look at the precocious boy. They knew well from previous experience that once Ma He started talking about soldiers and battles, he was impossible to stop. And yet, the boy was in no way intimidated by his elders.

"When do you think the battle will come? Soon? And where? Where will they fight...?"

But before his father could even begin a response, Ma He jumped in with another inquiry that flowed from him in a breathless rush of words.

"Are you sure General Ho will lead the emperor's troops? I know he's the senior imperial officer, but surely our emperor wouldn't send him so far from Nanking, just to fight a small band of Mongols? What do you suppose is the real reason General Ho has been sent into our province to fight? There must be another reason, don't you think?"

Hadji Ma heaved a long sigh. He didn't want to get into another discussion of military tactics and political theory with his inquisitive son. He gave his wife an exasperated look and motioned for her to "do something!"

Thankfully, Ma He's mother was quick to oblige.

"Ma He, if you and Xi Chen have finished eating, why don't you go outside?"

Ma He's persistent string of questions ended quickly as he looked to Xi Chen with an excited grin. It isn't often that your parents actually request that you spend time together.

But his mother holds her hand up, quick to add a word of caution. "But with all this talk about soldiers and Mongols being close by, I don't want you to go far. Understand?"

Ma He knows better than to disobey his mother. He nods and allows her a respectful, "Yes, mother." Ma He and Xi Chen stand and bow politely, moving toward the door and disappearing outside.

Hadji Ma maintains a disgruntled expression until his son is gone, then does his best to conceal a proud smile. Xi Chen's aunt, who was visiting, felt not a wisp of concern or animosity toward the youngsters. She smiled serenely, thinking happily about the wonderful marriage that the two would soon be celebrating.

With the sun still high in the sky, Ma He took Xi Chen by the hand and helped her onto his horse. They rode slowly across the broad meadow to a small thicket of trees, where the lad stopped his horse. He slipped to the ground and tied the animal to a jagged branch. Graciously, he helped Xi Chen to the ground. He pulled her into the shade of a gnarled old tree, far removed from the prying eyes of family.

"I sure would like to see that battle they were talking about," he confided earnestly to Xi Chen. "I've never seen a real battle before."

Xi Chen gave him an exasperated look. "And I don't ever want you to see a battle," she tells him, obviously fearful. "If something should ever happen to you, Ma He, I don't know what I'd do?"

Ma He leaned close to Xi Chen. "You're so practical," he whispered softly, brushing his lips against her cheek. "That's why I love you so much! But I truly do want to see that battle, Xi Chen."

She wrinkles her brow with a look of disapproval. But that doesn't stop him. "So far, the only thing I know about battles is what I've heard older people talking about or what I have read. I want to see the real thing! I'm sure you can understand my feelings, can't you? Nothing will happen to me. I promise. You'll see..."

His words came to an abrupt halt as a deep and distant rumble, like a rolling thunder beneath the earth, caused the ground to tremble. They both looked at each other, neither certain of what they were hearing.

Suddenly, a flock of birds exploded from a thicket nearby, startling them. Xi Chen clutched Ma He tightly, listening intently.

"What is it?" she whispered, her voice quivering.

The low rumble grew steadily louder.

"Maybe it's a storm," Ma He responded uneasily.

Xi Chen looked up at the sky. There was not a cloud in sight. "A storm?" she asked, looking into her lover's eyes, not quite believing he would mistake this deepening roar from below as a force of weather from above.

"Perhaps... from far away... and approaching," he ventured, still trying to sound optimistic and keep Xi Chen calm. But he too was concerned and didn't believe what he was saying.

The earth continued to move, the tremble turning to a distinct shaking. The branches and twigs of small bushes around them quivered as the ominous rumble gradually grew louder and louder.

Cautiously, Ma He and Xi Chen got to their feet, raising up high enough to peer over the top of the thicket.

To their amazement, they saw a massive army of ten thousand Chinese Imperial troops marching across the vast plain towards them, their trudging footsteps causing the ground beneath them to vibrate with a horrible growl.

Ma He and Xi Chen could barely believe their eyes. They both held their breath, unable to move. It was the most startling and intimidating thing they had ever witnessed.

Ma He's horse was spooked by the rumble of approaching soldiers. It began to twist against its tether, trying to wrench itself free. Ma He scrambled to his feet, diving toward the animal and grabbing the end of the tether.

"Hurry! We must go!" Ma He leaped upon the horse's back, pulling Xi Chen up behind him. He whirled the horse around.

"Where are we going?" Xi Chen asked. "Shouldn't we return to the village?"

"Just hang on tight," he told her with bold confidence. "I have an idea."

Ma He galloped his horse down the backside of the hill, away from the approaching troops, then expertly guided the animal into a twisting ravine, keeping them low and out of sight of the approaching army. When they emerge from the ravine, he urged his mount over the rugged terrain and into a rocky gorge that continued to shelter them from view. Xi Chen clutches Ma He tightly, pressing her face against his back and prayed that her Ma He knew what he was doing.

When they emerged from the mouth of the gorge, they unexpectedly came face to face with a ragged contingent of Mongol warriors.

Ma He gave a hard yank on the reins, whirling the horse around sharply. Surprised, the animal rose up on its rear hooves and flailed its front legs wildly. The animal then wrenched back, losing its footing. Ma He and Xi Chen are thrown back, sprawling on the ground. They scrambled to their feet, ready to run, but were quickly surrounded by the Mongol warriors.

The two youngsters were unceremoniously led into the enemy's chaotic camp. Ma He guessed their total number to be under a thousand. He could see they were ill equipped to do battle, especially against the superior force of the Imperial army that was moving steadily toward them.

Ma He and Xi Chen were dragged toward a cluster of men near the top of a steep hill that was surrounded by large boulders. As they approached, they could see a burly Mongol Chieftain shouting at his men, attempting to bolster their courage. The Chieftain was named Chi Li Bu Hua. He was the notorious leader of the rebellious Mongol tribes.

"The Chinese are cowards!" Chi Li Bu Hua shouted, shaking his fist in the air. "They will scatter like sheep before our swords! You will fight them to the death."

The Chieftain saw the two young captives being led toward him. He stopped shouting, looking at them, amused.

"And what are these?" he asks. "Spies?"

Ma He, unafraid, stands up to the Mongol leader.

"We're not part of your war."

Xi Chen pleads with Chi Li Bu Hua, "Please, I beg you, let us go free."

Chi Li Bu Hua turned his attention to the lovely young girl and approached her. Ma He tried to leap forward, but is pulled back by those who restrained him. "Stay away from her!" he shouted. Chi Li Bu Hua turned toward him, smiling at the brash outburst.

"So, you're ready to fight, are you?" he hissed, mocking the impetuous lad.

"I'll fight you, if I have to!" Ma He barked back, showing the Chieftain no fear whatsoever.

Smiling, Chi Li Bu Hua answered, "I'm sure you would."

A Mongol Commander shouted from the rim of the hill. "They're coming!"

Chi Li Bu Hua nodded, then returned his gaze to Ma He. "But today we have another enemy. Would you like to see?"

He grabbed Ma He roughly by the arm and led him toward the promontory that overlooked the broad valley below.

Ma He tried to pull away. "I've already seen them."

The Mongol Chieftain considers Ma He's grim expression. As they near the edge of the ridge, Ma He saw the pale and frightened faces of the Mongol Commanders concealed behind boulders near the edge.

Chi Li Bu Hua stopped short, eyes wide, as the terrifyingly awesome sight of ten thousand Chinese Imperial troops came into his view. He took a moment to comprehend the enormous threat before him, and then put on a face of courage, turning to address his men with bold authority.

"It seems their fear has caused them to send more helpless sheep to the slaughter than they can afford," he tells his Commanders with feigned bravado.

One apprehensive Commander wasn't so sure. "But, Sir, we can never defeat their numbers." Chi Li Bu Hua nodded in agreement.

"You're right, Commander. They leave us only two choices. We can either fight and die... or surrender." Chi Li Bu Hua turned to his men.

"What shall we choose?"

Ma He brashly interrupted. "There is a third choice."

The Chieftain turned to face the young lad, amused by his reckless outburst. "And what would that be?" he asked with unmasked skepticism.

"Demand peace." Ma He told him simply. "It may save your life."

Chi Li Bu Hua stared in silent disbelief at Ma He. After a long moment, he exploded in harsh, guttural laughter. He slapped Ma He on the shoulder roughly.

"Thank you, my young idealist. But today... I think we will fight and die." The Chieftain drew his sword and held it high for everyone to see, then announced boldly to his disheveled collection of rag-tag warriors, "Prepare to slaughter the enemy!"

As the Mongol soldiers drew their swords, spears and other forms of crude weaponry, a chill of fear and desperation ran through their tattered ranks. Chief Chi Li Bu Hua did not seem to notice. He turned to his Commanders.

"Disperse our warriors. Strike in small groups at their flanks. Give them no large target. If we are overrun, retreat to the villages."

Chi Li Bu Hua then turned to Ma He. "Here's a lesson for you boy. Never show fear. If you do, the battle is already lost."

The Mongol chief then headed off to lead his men. Ma He shouted after him, "I'm not afraid!"

Chi Li Bu Hua stop's, then turns to Ma He and grins. "Then you are probably the only one here who isn't."

The charismatic Chieftain waded into the churning mass of Mongol warriors, raised his sword high, stirring the men with his growing show of fierceness.

"Kill the oppressors!" he roared. "Slaughter them and take no prisoners!"

The Mongol warriors raised their swords and crude bows over their heads, shaking their fists and defiantly screaming oaths of allegiance to their fearless Chief.

Horses snorted, twisting with fear, loudly stomping their hooves on the ground in violent agitation. The mounted warriors quickly whipped themselves and their animals into a fighting frenzy.

Ma He desperately searched the throng of shouting fighters for Xi Chen, but didn't see her. He shouted her name as loudly as he could, but his voice was drowned out as Chief Chi Li Bu Hua screamed another command. "Disperse and charge their flanks! Leave no living soul!"

The Mongol army of frenzied warrior's, charged off in many directions like a scattering of savage ants.

Xi Chen flailed helplessly amid the surge of moving humanity, searching vainly for her love. She screamed into the din. "Ma He! Ma He!"

Ma He heard her tiny voice in the clatter and roar of soldiers driven by fear and dread. He spun around, desperately searching for her, then suddenly glimpsed her hair amid the throng of dirty, ragged, sweating men.

"Xi Chen!" he screamed at her. "Over here!"

They moved toward each other, weaving through the surging bodies of warriors and weapons, hands extended. As the soldiers dissipated, charging off into battle, Ma He and Xi Chen fell into each other's arms and embraced tightly.

Before he could utter a word, Ma He saw a horse running free, twirling helplessly in the confusion. In one swift motion, he grabbed the reins and struggled to calm the frenzied animal. He then lifted Xi Chen onto the horse's back and leaped on with her. Ma He dug his heels into the horse's flanks. The frightened steed responded with a wild whinny, then charged ahead, galloping strongly towards the ridge.

On the valley floor, two Chinese Commanders looked nervously at General Ho. Screaming bands of Mongol warriors were charging at them from all sides. Even though the Chinese troops far outnumbered the Mongols, the ferocious attack from all directions made the Mongols seem a much greater threat than they really were.

The old General, experienced in war, watched the approaching hordes calmly. He raised his hand to signal that the Chinese soldiers should stand firm and not break ranks.

The imperial troops held their positions as instructed, anxiously clutching their weapons, as they waited nervously for the signal to begin fighting.

The horse carrying Ma He and Xi Chen came to a stop on the ridge. They stared at the soldiers and Mongols converging below them. Massive carnage was about to unfold.

General Ho held his hand high, stiff and unflinching. Not a single Chinese soldier moved, even though the Mongol hoards were nearly upon them. The stench of sweat and fear filled the air.

As the savage Mongol bands were about to engulf the Chinese troops who were frozen like marble statues, General Ho suddenly dropped his arm. The Chinese soldiers abruptly came to life and exploded toward the Mongols, with flying spears and slashing swords.

A murderous barrage of rocket-arrows fired at almost point blank range, cut down dozens of startled Mongol horsemen before they could react. Then, another dense cluster of rocket-arrows slammed into the earth amid the charging warriors, causing a huge explosion of dirt and rocks.

As fragmented groups of Mongol's begin to retreat, Chinese cannon batteries fired a series of deadly volleys. The fallen and wounded were swarmed by the Chinese troops and quickly dispatched by sword and spear. Four thousand Chinese soldiers on horseback charged into the now swirling maelstrom, scattering the remaining Mongol's like panicked sheep.

Seeing his men scatter, Chief Chi Li Bu Hua turned to his nearest Commander.

"Ride to the villages! We will seize the houses and wait in hiding. When the troops come, we will take them by surprise."

Not waiting for a response, Chi Li Bu Hua wheeled his horse around and galloped off. The Commander hesitated for just a moment, then waved for his men to follow.

Ma He and Xi Chen could see the warriors scattering to the hills. They both realized what that meant .

"We must get to the village and warn everyone!" Ma He shouted. Xi Chen gripped Ma He as tightly as she could. He kicked the horse's flanks and they charged off together like a whirlwind.

In the village, Ma He's father, Hadji Ma, stepped from his house and squinted toward the horse that raced toward him from the far distance. A cloud of smoke and dust darkened the horizon. He immediately recognized that something was terribly wrong.

As the galloping horse grew closer, he could see that it was Ma He and Xi Chen, racing to get home as fast as they could. In order to save time,

Ma He took a shortcut, forcing the horse to jump a stone fence, then raced at breakneck speed across the meadow.

Hadji Ma saw Mongol riders beginning to appear in the cloud of dust not far behind Ma He and Xi Chen. The horse planted stiff forelegs in the hard dirt, its haunches dropping nearly to the ground. Ma He tumbled off, followed by Xi Chen, both sprawling awkwardly at Hadji Ma's feet. "Get inside!" he shouted at them.

As Ma He and Xi Chen scrambled through the front door, Hadji Ma paused just outside, seeing hundreds of Mongol horsemen filling the meadow. Suddenly, the harsh "woosh" of an arrow sailed past his head and buried its sharp point in the door. Not waiting a second longer he jumped inside, slamming the door shut and latching it from the inside.

Outside, Mongol horsemen began swarming into the village. Frantic villagers ran from their homes, hoping to escape the sudden, unexpected, invasion. But there was no time or opportunity. They were cut down in their tracks or carried off as slaves.

In Hadji Ma's house, Ma He and his brother desperately raced to cover the windows with anything that was solid.

"The Mongols will show us no mercy," he shouts to his wife and siblings, while helping to push a heavy wooden box into a window opening.

"It's much worse than that," Ma He called back, while bracing a chair against the front door. "Chinese soldiers, thousands of them, are coming for the Mongols."

"If we're trapped between them," Ma He's brother added sourly, "we'll be slaughtered like dogs!"

Without hesitation, Hadji Ma made a quick decision. "Ma He! Take your mother and Xi Chen and ride into the Stone Forest. Hide there until it's safe."

But Ma He didn't want to leave, protesting. Hadji Ma shouts at him again, "Do it, my son! Take both of them now! Your brother and I will protect the house."

"They will kill you," Ma He protested. "Do as I say, NOW!"

Ma He grabbed the hands of his mother and Xi Chen and pulled them toward the rear of the house. But his mother didn't want to leave. She screamed to her husband, desperately begging to stay.

But Ma He kept moving. He led his mother and Xi Chen out the back door toward several frantic horses, tied to the trees just outside. He pushed them up onto the backs of two small horses, then leaped onto the back of a larger stallion for himself. As all three galloped away, six Mongol warriors converged on the house.

The front door crashed open. Hadji Ma grabbed a knife and quickly turned to face the intruder. But an arrow fired at close range slammed into his chest, killing him instantly.

Ma He's brother saw his father on the floor in a widening pool of blood. In a blind rage, he charged through the open front door, searching for his father's killer.

Seeing the Mongol who fired the arrow, he charged at him, dragging him from his horse, sinking a knife blade deep into the man's chest. He then scrambled to his feet and turned to take on the next warrior. But it was too late. Before he could even raise his knife, another mounted Mongol was upon him. With one mighty swipe of his sword, the Mongol brutally cut off the head of Ma He's brother.

But Ma He was spared the sight of his father and brother being slaughtered. He was riding as fast as he could, just as his father had ordered, leading his mother and Xi Chen safely into the narrow canyons and gorges that would afford them a place to hide. As they worked their way up along a difficult switchback trail, Xi Chen's horse slipped, wrenching sideways. It's hooves flailed helplessly. The animal rolled onto its back, throwing Xi Chen to the ground.

Ma He leaped from his horse and rushed to Xi Chen's side as she struggled to her feet.

"Are you alright?"

"It's nothing. Just my arm," she stammered. "I think I cut it." Xi Chen collapsed on the ground, then tried again to regain her footing. But Ma He could see that she had suffered a long bloody scrape. He held her down, telling her, "Wait. Wait, Xi Chen… let me wrap your wound."

"I'll be alright," Xi Chen protested. "We must keep going."

Ma He's mother dismounts and approached them with a look of concern. "She's right, Ma He. We can take care of it later. We must not stop."

They heard a sound, turning to see a half-dozen Mongol warriors standing just a few feet away, their spears and swords held menacingly ready. A tall Mongol approached with his sword drawn. Ma He looked as though he was ready to bolt.

"Don't run," the warrior shouted, "or we'll have to kill you."

Ma He grew incensed, screaming wildly as he lunged at the Mongol with his sword held high.

Xi Chen called out, "Ma He… NO!"

But it was late. Ma He had already made his move and was committed to the attack. But before he could get to the warrior, two other Mongols grabbed his arms, wrenching him back and holding him tightly. A third warrior drew back the arrow in his bow and aimed it directly at Ma He's heart.

Ma He looked defiantly at the warrior who was about to shoot him, sneering, "You don't have the courage!"

Angrily, the Mongol pulled his arrow back further, ready to send it on its deadly course. But in an instant, Ma He's mother reacted instinctively, diving toward her son. The Mongol released the arrow, striking Ma He's mother in the neck, killing her instantly. Her lifeless body was sent spinning by the impact of the arrow and fell at Ma He's feet.

Xi Chen screamed. In a rage, Ma He struggled to break free, but the hands of his captors held him firmly. "I'll kill you! I'll kill you!" he screamed.

The Mongol who fired the arrow, watched Ma He struggling, admiring the boy's fierce courage and anger. He pulled out a dagger and threw it on the ground at Me He's feet.

"If it's revenge you want," he hissed, "then come ahead."

The Mongol raised his huge sword, telling his compatriots to "Let him go."

When Ma He was released, he instantly grabbed for the knife on the ground, whirling angrily to face his challenger. He took a defensive, half-crouch position, prepared to fight. But the smaller blade in his hand was no match for the imposing sword the Mongol warrior wielded. Ma He glared at the man with a vicious hatred.

The Mongol warrior saw his advantage clearly, raising his sword to strike. But then, he sensed something. His eyes shifted slightly to the side and his cold expression melted into fear.

Ma He was puzzled by this hesitation. He turned slowly to see a line of Chinese troops directly behind him, blocking their path of escape from the gorge. Their swords were drawn. Their arrows were aimed and ready to fly. A Chinese Commander stepped toward them.

The Mongol warriors were frozen in fear. "Drop your weapons!" the Chinese officer demanded forcefully. "You are now prisoners of the Chinese Imperial Army."

"We're not part of their rebellion," Ma He pleads. "We're from the…"

But the Chinese Commander wouldn't let him continue, cutting him off with a sharp motion of his hand. "Not with them?" he said, mocking Ma He. "And what is that weapon in your hand? Something for my amusement?"

Ma He dropped the dagger, trying to explain, "He gave it to me. To fight him."

"Ahhh yes, a boy with imagination," the officer said, mocking him again. "I like that!" He turned coldly to his troops and ordered them to, "Seize all of them. Bind them and take their weapons."

The troops quickly grabbed the Mongol warriors, Ma He and Xi Chen, tying their hands behind their backs. Then, they looped ropes around their necks, linking them all together.

Ma He couldn't believe this. "But I'm a Muslim," he angrily protested. "I'm not a Mongol!"

The Commander was not persuaded. "Tell it to Buddha," he snarled, motioning for his troops to lead the prisoners away. Desperately, Ma He struggled to look back toward his mother's body lying in the dirt. But he was violently wrenched forward by the rope around his neck and forced to stumble away.


General Ho rode onto the field of battle, proudly inspecting the carnage that surrounded him. Men and animals lay motionless in tangled heaps, their faces frozen into twisted masks of death. He smiled proudly at the grisly scene, then casually turned his horse away.

Mongol prisoners were herded together into one large area. Most were wounded and bleeding badly. Their moans and cries were like one grotesque chorus of agony.

The Chinese Commander who captured Ma He roughly pulled the rope from around the boy's neck and shoved him toward the other prisoners. Ma He stumbled to his knees, unable to free himself from the ropes that still bound his hands behind his back.

When Ma He was able to struggle to his feet and look around, he was shocked by what he saw. Most of the prisoners had ragged, bloody wounds. They sprawled helplessly in the dust, begging for water and mercy. But Chinese guards were not willing to offer either.

He quickly looked around for Xi Chen and was happy to see her several yards away. Her hands had been unbound, but she was being forced toward a group of Mongol women captives that was further away. Ma He called out her name and tried to push his way toward her. When Xi Chen saw him, she cried out, rushing forward. She threw her arms around his neck, sobbing hysterically.

However, Ma He has no time for tears. "Stop crying and listen," he told her firmly. "Untie my hands, quickly."

When she heard his words, she quickly smothered her tears, sliding her hands down his back, fumbling with the ropes.

Nearby, General Ho began an inspection tour of his prisoners. He slowly rode around the large circle of Mongols that had been captured, followed closely by several of his Commanders. When he saw Ma He

42

and Xi Chen mixed in with the others, he became curious. He stopped his horse a short distance away to watch. After pointing out the youngsters to his Commanders, he urged his horse forward through the Mongol rabble and stopped in front of the young couple. When Xi Chen saw the General, she paused for a moment, looking into his eyes. Then, surreptitiously, she continued trying to untie Ma He's bonds.

"Would you like some help?" General Ho asked her with a cutting sarcasm.

A Chinese guard cracked a large leather whip. Its tendrils wrapped around the legs of the two young lovers, yanking them off their feet. As they sprawled in the dirt, their legs tangled together, the guards and Commanders laughed with cruel delight. General Ho stared blankly at them.

Ma He angrily struggled to his feet, shouting at General Ho. "You have no right to treat us this way! We are not your enemy!"

"Who are you then?" the general asked calmly.

"We are Muslim," Ma He replied, continuing to show no fear of the imperial officer.

"Well, Muslim boy," General Ho told him with a brazen smile, "you may not be my enemy, but you are my prisoner."

Ho glared at the helpless boy, backing his horse away, then turned to rejoin his entourage of Commanders.


On the Ming flagship, Odoric sets his pen down and leans back, trying to rest. The pain in his chest is worsening, despite his efforts to ignore the throbbing ache inside.

He slowly takes a sip of tea, which has now become cold with neglect. He closes his eyes for a few moments and tries to summon new strength.

Outside, he can still hear the far away rumble of cannons being fired and hopes the tide of battle is beginning to turn. Maybe Zheng He's flagship, won't be lost after all, he ventures hopefully to himself.

Feeling slightly refreshed by this positive thought, he opens his eyes, puts pen to paper, and once again tries to focus his memory on what happened next...


Odoric was on his way to Beijing, happily riding in King Zhu Di's royal carriage, which itself was quite a pleasant surprise. He thought for sure that he'd be relegated to a wagon with some of the servants. But there he was, riding along across the sprawling Chinese plain in the elaborate carriage of a province king.

He had been told that the reason the king allowed him to ride in the royal carriage was because he wanted the two of them to become better acquainted. He learned later it was mostly because the king was anxious to add a little variety and excitement to his long journey, which up until that point had been boring and uneventful.

The king had also invited two of his associates to ride along with them. High Administrator Wong and Monk Dao Yan, sat across from Odoric so that they too could ask questions if they so choose.

It was very fortuitous that Monk Dao Yan was invited, as he, surprisingly, was able to speak a little Italian. He was a pleasant man, in his thirties and could, like Odoric, be described as having a stature that was somewhat plump.

Odoric learned from the friendly Monk that ever since Marco Polo traveled to China a century earlier and took the two Italian friars with him, Christianity had been able to establish a small foothold in China. Over the years, Dao Yan, though a devout Buddhist had become intrigued by this foreign religion and the people who had traveled such a great distance to bring it to his country.

Most of the religious travelers, like Friar Odoric, were Italian. So, gradually, Dao Yan had made it his business to acquire a working knowledge of the Italian language in order to more easily communicate with the Christian representatives he encountered. Odoric was only the most recent in a long line of religious messengers who had traveled by sea or over the Silk Road to China hoping to spread the teaching of Jesus Christ.

Dao Yan's explanation of why he had attempted to learn the Italian language was very similar to the one Chu-ji had provided. But, given the intellectual difference between the two men, the Chinese Monk's proficiency was much greater than that of the friendly mountain guide.

The other gentleman riding in the King's carriage was introduced with the lofty title of High Administrator Wong. He was very different from the friendly Buddhist Monk. For one thing, he was quite a bit older, perhaps in his fifties or early sixties. He was tall, very thin and possessed sharp, penetrating eyes. He never smiled and as far as Odoric could tell, he had a perpetually sour disposition. These two royal assistants were as disparate as the proverbial night and day.

When the province king invited Odoric to ask him a few questions he was more than happy to comply. Thankfully, the friendly monk was present to help with the needed translation.

"Will it be possible for me to start a mission in your capital city of Beijing?" Odoric ventured cautiously, curious as to how any question he might ask would be received.

Zhu Di looked to Monk Dao Yan for the translation. Once he understood the inquiry, he smiled and nodded his head, approvingly.

"Yes, off course. We Chinese believe there are many pathways to heaven. Personally, I follow the teachings of Lord Buddha, but even here, in this southern area of China through which we are now traveling, there are many who follow the teaching's of the prophet Mohammed."

Administrator Wong shifted uncomfortably in his seat and commented dourly under his breath, "They're infidels! All infidels! Anyone who would follow that fake prophet, Mohammed, is nothing but an infidel himself, plain and simple!"

Dao Yan raised his eyebrow and reluctantly gave Odoric the translation of what had been said. However, in an effort to protect Odoric's sensibilities, it was a somewhat edited version that eliminated any overt or offensive prejudice. Some time would pass before Odoric would finally get an accurate rendition of Wong's true feelings toward Muslims.

Before Odoric could follow with yet another question, Commander Tan ordered the carriage to stop. He looked within, acknowledging the king with respect.

"I'm sorry to interrupt, Sire, but several of my scouts have reported seeing Mongol soldiers in the area. I suggest that we stop for the night so that my men can check the way ahead and make certain that it's safe."

With barely a pause, King Zhu Di raised his hand to signal that no further explanation was required, nodding his approval. "As you wish, Commander," he replied. "As you wish."

Chapter Two

---

BECOMING A EUNUCH

The following day, Zhu Di's royal entourage encountered General Ho's army and the column of Mongol prisoners he was escorting back to Nanking. While still some distance apart, the two groups sat silent and still, waiting with great patience for emissaries from each to approach.

The province king motioned with a slight flick of his finger that Commander Tan should go forward and meet with the senior imperial representative. Tan gave Zhu Di a slight nod, and immediately rode forward at a measured and steady gait to make the required greeting.

Observing the ritual, I gave Dao Yan a curious look and leaned forward.

"Who are they?" I asked softly, more than a little frightened at seeing such a large army of men with its prisoners looming so close.

King Zhu Di must have known what I was asking for he provided the answer before Dao Yan could speak.

"This is our great Imperial Army. The man in front, the one who has forgotten how to smile, is General Ho, Senior Officer for my father, the emperor."

I couldn't believe what I was hearing. "Your father is the Emperor of China?" I gasped. I'm sure that Dao Yan was well aware of my astonished look.

Zhu Di smiled broadly and began to laugh.

"Yes, that's how I became king. And, as king of the Northern Province, I outrank the man with no smile."

I looked out the carriage window, chilled by General Ho's stern, unsmiling visage.

"I don't believe he's very happy about that." Zhu Di chuckled. "I'm sure he isn't."

General Ho, accompanied by Commander Chu, plodded slowly forward to meet with Commander Tan and six province soldiers who stood out brightly in their elaborate red uniforms. As all the riders came face to face and paused their mounts, Commander Tan acknowledged the general with a casual salute.

"King Zhu Di sends his greetings," he stated in a flat, cold monotone. "He requests that you identify yourself and your mission."

As King Zhu Di had observed, General Ho wasn't at all pleased. He shifted in his saddle and replied dourly.

"Your King knows precisely who I am, Commander. I am General Ho, Senior Officer of Emperor Hungwu's army. Yesterday I defeated an uprising of Mongol rebels who were trying to steal the emperor's land. We killed hundreds. The rest are my prisoners."

Ho turned and motioned towards the prisoners who were huddled together on the ground, surrounded by guards.

"Now, if your king has no objection, I would like to continue my journey. I'm under strict orders from the emperor to deliver these prisoners to Nanking."

"My king will expect the customary courtesies," Commander Tan told General Ho without hesitation.

"Of course," Ho replied with an edge of sarcasm.

As Commander Tan and his soldier escorts returned to King Zhu Di's caravan, Commander Chu studied the face of General Ho, aware that he was obviously bitter.

"You know this King?" he asked cautiously.

General Ho's words snapped out sharply, barely concealing his distaste.

"We have met. He's one of the emperor's unruly sons. He and his brothers were all given royal titles and put in charge of the outer provinces."

"What are these 'customary courtesies' he speaks of?" Commander Chu asked.

"It's their pathetic idea of tradition," Ho growled. "Now I must share my prisoners with this upstart nobody. I would call it theft."

Commander Chu turned to watch Commander Tan approach Zhu Di's carriage.

"Is he a troublemaker?" he asked.

"They're all troublemakers, Commander. Each one has ambitions to become the next emperor."

General Ho suddenly reined in his horse, turning to Commander Chu.

"Let them take their prisoners. All but the Muslim boy. I want him for myself."

General Ho yanked hard on the reins, pulling the head of his horse around. He heeled the animal in the ribs, galloping back toward his troops.

Later, as King Zhu Di prepared to make a formal inspection of General Ho's prisoners, I was, surprisingly, invited to join him. With Dao Yan still translating, I thanked the province king for the invitation and let him know how much I considered the opportunity a very great honor.

Inwardly, however, I was frightened. The thought of having to come face-to-face with Mongol prisoners was something that I really wasn't anxious to do.

As soon as Zhu Di's small entourage started moving towards Ho's column, I began fingering my wooden cross and tried to stick as close to Monk Dao Yan as I possibly could. If any trouble developed, I reasoned, it might be safer if I knew what was going on and I felt confident that he would tell me.

General Ho had his men assemble the prisoners so Zhu Di could more easily look them over before making his selection. Zhu Di slowly walked his horse around the collection of bedraggled prisoners. He made slight motions with his hand, indicating his selections. Dao Yan and I followed him, remaining a respectful distance behind.

But then abruptly, one of the prisoners moved toward me, reaching out and begging me for water. My first thought was that he may have noticed that I wasn't Chinese and perhaps believed that I might have more compassion for him. But as soon as he started begging, one of General Ho's soldiers rushed forward and laid a lash across the man's face, drawing blood. I was shocked. All the man was trying to do was get a little water. Ho's soldier then lashed the man hard across his face again and shoved him back into line.

I felt that such cruel treatment was unacceptable and immediately looked to Dao Yan for an explanation. But all he did was softly place a finger to his lips, signaling that I should not say or do anything.

I began to have serious second thoughts about what I was getting myself into. I squeezed the cross tightly between my fingers and silently prayed for the poor man. He had two ragged streaks of blood across his face.

While Zhu Di was still on the far side of the group of prisoners making his selections, Commander Chu took two soldiers and waded into the mass of wounded Mongols on the opposite side. General Ho had ordered him to remove Ma He and that's exactly what he intended to do.

Without saying a word, one of Ho's men grabbed the boy by the arm and unceremoniously dragged him away. When Xi Chen saw what was happening, she immediately gripped Ma He's other arm and wouldn't let go.

"Take your hands off him!" she shrieked, loudly, "Let him go!"

The other soldier slapped Xi Chen across the face with a powerful blow, knocking her to the ground. Ma He and several of the prisoners shoved the two guards back, helping Xi Chen to her feet. They gently brushed the dirt off the stinging bruise on her cheek.

"What are you doing?" Ma He growled angrily at Commander Chu. "Leave us alone!"

But Commander Chu was not to be deterred. He quickly ordered two additional soldiers to step in and remove the boy. Armed with leather whips, they waded into the prisoners and began lashing out furiously at the prisoners who were trying to block their path.

More prisoners joined the fray, trying to protect Ma He and Xi Chen. They crowded the soldiers, shoving hard against them, unafraid of the whips they wielded.

As more prisoners pushed forward, Xi Chen became more incensed, kicking wildly at the soldiers, surprising them with her fury.

"Leave us alone!" she screamed. "Leave us alone!"

Spontaneously, the prisoners took up her chant. "Leave us alone! Leave us alone!" their voices growing louder with each haunting repetition of the challenge.

"Leave us alone! Leave us alone!"

Hearing the rising commotion, King Zhu Di whirled around to face General Ho.

"Can't your men maintain order, General?" He spit his words out angrily.

General Ho looked toward the noisy disturbance with great concern. Whatever was going on was not making him look good in the eyes of the province king.

"It's nothing, Your Majesty," he offered sharply. "I'm certain it is nothing but a minor disturbance. My men will take care of it immediately."

Ho quickly tried to smooth over Zhu Di's harsh criticism by offering him an uninjured prisoner standing close by.

"This is a very fit fellow, Sire," he gushed. He ordered the man be pulled from the group. "As you can see, there's not a scratch on him. Why don't you take him? I think he's the strongest of the lot."

But then... another shriek from Xi Chen cut like a knife through the rising commotion. Zhu Di, growing more curious and upset, fixed General Ho with an unrelenting gaze.

"I wish to see what all this noise is about, General. Lead the way. Now!"

As they approached the fracas, Zhu Di was shocked to see the two young prisoners surrounded by soldiers. Wounded and injured prisoners fought to protect them, shoving the soldiers back.

Three soldiers wrestled Ma He to the ground. Xi Chen leaped onto the back of one soldier, kicking and screaming frantically, beating on him with her fists.

Seeing General Ho approaching with Zhu Di, Commander Chu panicked, snapping to attention. He quickly ordered his men to do the same, but his voice was lost in the skirmish.

But Zhu Di's voice rose up amid the din, roaring above the fray. "Release the boy! Release him at once!"

The startled soldiers hurriedly untangled themselves from Ma He and struggled to their feet. Upon seeing the province king and their irritated general, they immediately released their hold on Ma He and looked down in shame.

Xi Chen helped Ma He back to his feet, clutching his arm tightly.

"Who are you?" Zhu Di asked, remaining resolute and calm, so as not to aggravate an already unpleasant situation. "Why are you and this young girl being held with these Mongol prisoners?"

Before Ma He could answer, General Ho spoke up loudly. "He's no one, Your Majesty. A troublemaker we picked up along the way. Look at him. He's a weakling. Sick and frail. I would never think to insult you with so poor a prize."

Ho then pointed to his soldiers, issuing a curt command.

"Remove the boy at once! I don't wish for the king to strain his eyes on so worthless a package."

The soldiers seized Ma He by the arms. But Xi Chen gripped Ma He's arm tightly, refusing to let go. She began screeching as fiercely as before.

"STOP!" Zhu Di's voice thundered over them. "Don't move the boy."

The soldiers hesitated, looking with confusion at General Ho, uncertain who it was they should obey?

General Ho dismounted in frustration. He grabbed the arm of a prisoner, pushing him toward Zhu Di.

"Your Majesty... Let me offer you ten of my finest prisoners. Strong and healthy ones. Leave this worthless young rebel to me."

Ho turned to the soldiers standing closest to him. "Find the healthiest and strongest prisoners. Bring them here at once."

More than a dozen imperial soldiers began pushing wounded and injured Mongol prisoners off to the side, searching for those who looked most fit. But Zhu Di held up his hand to end the charade.

"No. I will take the boy." A sudden silence fell over the restless crowd of soldiers and prisoners.

General Ho stared in silence, unable to summon a response that would allow him to maintain even a modicum of authority and respect among his men.

Zhu Di stepped toward him. "But..." he said, with a voice as calm and certain as a soft summer wind, "...if you insist, I will also accept the ten healthy prisoners that you have so generously offered."

General Ho had no choice. He had made the offer and now was obliged to honor it. Reluctantly, he clapped his hands together. A dozen soldiers pushed their way into the ranks of the wounded and forcibly separated Ma He from the girl.

Xi Chen screamed even louder than she had previously. "Ma He! Don't leave me!"

Then suddenly, she spun around and scrambled toward Zhu Di, reaching up to him with outstretched hands.

"Take me! Take me!"

Zhu Di looked down at her with a stoic face untouched by any sign of emotion or empathy

"Not the girl. I have enough women."

Without hesitation, two soldiers dragged Xi Chen away from Zhu Di's horse and pushed her back into the huddled cluster of prisoners. Zhu Di had demonstrated his superiority and rank, leaving General Ho diminished in the eyes of his men. With brazen confidence and a rigid countenance, Zhu Di turned his horse away and trotted off, never giving General Ho another glance.

I sat upon my horse in silence. I pulled Dao Yan's sleeve and whispered in his ear.

"Can't we do something?" I asked, knowing full well that it was not within my power to become involved.

Again, Dao Yan silently put a finger to his lips and then followed this with a helpless shrug.

"There are some Chinese ways," he whispered, "which are probably difficult for you to understand. But, if it truly is God's will, as you say, then this young innocent girl will most surely be protected."

Ma He was thrown into a crude open wagon with the other selected prisoners. With tears streaming down her face, Xi Chen could do nothing but watch. Two soldiers continued to grip her upper arms, restraining her.

Suddenly, she ripped off her jade necklace and held it out for Ma He to see.

"Ma He!" she screamed. "Take my necklace!"

When the young lad attempted to stand up, several soldiers pushed him back down roughly.

I despised having to watch this, but there was nothing I could do. If I tried to intercede, I would surely have been restrained and possibly punished.

But then, without realizing it, my good judgment was abruptly overruled by my intensifying righteous anger.

I awkwardly dismounted my horse, walking directly to the young girl. Surprisingly, none of the soldiers stopped me. Perhaps they thought I was a person of importance or authority and therefore hesitated to break an unspoken protocol by interfering with my actions. In any case, I was able to approach her. She turned to look at me through her tears, not sure who I was. I held out my hand.

"Let me have the necklace," I told her in my native Italian. "I will take your necklace to him."

I knew she didn't understand what I was saying, but she must have sensed what my intention was. After a moment of silent recognition, she gently handed me the necklace. I nodded with a comforting smile..."Grazi." And in response to this small gesture and unfamiliar words, a torrent of grateful tears burst from her eyes.

I gently touched her head, trying to offer her some comfort. Then I walked back toward the wagon of prisoners with the necklace. Guards and prisoners alike stepped aside, watching me with curious eyes. No one attempted to stop me.

General Ho observed my small demonstration of kindness with spiteful indifference. He turned his horse around and issued an order to Commander Chu.

"Prepare to move the troops."

When I approached the wagon, a churlish uniformed guard moved to block my path. I simply gazed at him with calm and unthreatening eyes. The tension of the moment melted and he also stepped aside.

I handed the necklace to Ma He, who accepted it with humble gratitude. When I looked into the boy's eyes, I detected an immediate rapport between us. It was, I must admit, an undeniable connection I hadn't expected.

"Hold this close," I told him with a gentle smile. "It will lead you back to her."

Ma He did not understand my specific words, but he clearly grasped the meaning that I expressed. With clarity in his eyes, he gave me a respectful nod. The prisoner wagons began to move forward, amid shouted commands from King Zhu Di's uniformed soldiers on horseback.

I stepped back and watched Ma He as his eyes strained to find Xi Chen in the crowd of prisoners. As the wagon rumbled past the Mongol prisoners, Xi Chen glimpsed Ma He. She struggled against the hands that restrained her, but couldn't break free. With tears streaming down her cheek, she called his name, her faint voice lost amid the sound of wooden wheels crunching on the brittle earth.

Ma He held the necklace up above his head, hoping that she could see it. They desperately watched each other for as long as they could, until the swirling cloud of dust made seeing each other impossible.

I crossed myself and prayed to God that everything would work out for the best. Somehow, deep inside my heart... I knew it would.


When we arrived at Zhu Di's northern palace in Beijing, I was truly excited about finally beginning my great Chinese adventure. I was already making friends and becoming familiar with some of the oriental ways. But what happened next to the Muslim lad, Ma He, was beyond all my wildest expectations. If I hadn't been there to see it for myself, I never would have believed it.

Upon Zhu Di's arrival at his palace, he immediately held a conference with several of his senior palace officials. And surprisingly, he invited me to attend.

"Welcome to my humble palace," Zhu Di sang out when he saw his Chief Eunuch bring me into his spacious throne room.

"Humble" hardly described it. I was completely taken aback when I saw Zhu Di's collection of ornately carved furniture, exquisite gold and silver decor, stunning silk tapestries and thick decorative carpets. There was also a magnificent and stunning collection of Ming vases.

"Thank you for seeing me, Your Majesty," I stammered, unable to keep my eyes from wandering around the grandiose surroundings. "I know your time is very precious."

"All life is precious." Zhu Di responded smiling, knowing that I was sufficiently impressed.

"Indeed it is," I agreed, trying my best to concentrate on what Zhu Di was saying by way of Dao Yan's rapidly sputtered translations.

"You are settled and comfortable?" the king asked with great politeness. He was seemingly quite sincere.

"Dao Yan has been very helpful," I responded, turning to acknowledge the king's monk sitting close by. "I am quite comfortable, thank you."

I then hesitated for a moment and must have frowned, because Zhu Di, who was watching me carefully, was quick to comment on it.

"What is it that seems to be troubling you?" he asked.

"The boy," I replied cautiously, "the one among the Mongol prisoners?"

"The Muslim?"

"Yes."

"He's strong and well fed," Zhu Di replied. "He will be fine. Your concern, friar, is quite heartening."

I looked to Dao Yan, trying to discern if he was keeping pace with the translation of my words. Then, hesitantly, I ventured a more perilous question.

"Perhaps... he could be released?"

Zhu Di sat back in his expansive chair, obviously surprised. "Free him?"

"Yes..." I said, my voice becoming unintentionally tentative.

"This young captive was among our Mongol enemies," he firmly stated through tightened lips. "He very well could be a great danger to us."

It was clear I had crossed a line of royal protocol by questioning the king. But now that I had taken the leap, there was no advantage in backing down.

"But he is innocent," I told Zhu Di, trying to keep my demeanor and voice as unthreatening as I could.

Zhu Di studied me for a long moment, his eyes squinting. It was as if he was trying to see into my soul.

After a very long silence, he asked, "Of this you are certain?"

"In my heart, Your Majesty, I am certain."

Zhu Di thought about this for a long moment, then turned to Chang, his Chief Eunuch. "Bring the Muslim boy to me."

For the next several minutes King Zhu Di asked me about where I lived in Italy. Then, he surprised me by asking if I knew Marco Polo? Not wanting to embarrass him, I hesitated in my stumbling explanation that Marco Polo and his family visited China over a hundred years ago and that I wasn't quite that old.

After a somewhat clumsy translation, Monk Dao Yan managed to cleverly shift the conversation to another subject. He explained to Zhu Di that I had hopes of starting a small mission in Beijing.

While Zhu Di and I continued our conversation, Chief Eunuch Chang and two lesser eunuch servants hurried to the prison to fetch Ma He. When they arrived, they swung open a heavy wooden door which led to a large dark chamber.

A shaft of dusty light illuminated the Mongol prisoners who were huddled inside. Among the ragged, dirty men, the bright, youthful eyes of Ma He peered toward the light with hopeful expectation.

Minutes later, the large gold doors of Zhu Di's palace swung open and Ma He was escorted in. He gazed around at the unexpected opulence, just as I had done a short while before. It was like nothing the naïve young lad had ever seen.

I could tell that he was surprised to see me there. When our eyes met, neither of us dared speak. Chang led Ma He before the king. Ma He lowered his eyes humbly in respect. But I could tell that he was not intimidated by Zhu Di or by the great opulence that surrounded him.

"So, my young friend," Zhu Di said with an uncharacteristic smile, "apparently you have someone here who trusts in you."

Ma He flashed a quick glance in my direction but said nothing.

"He doesn't feel you are an enemy. Shall I believe him?"

Standing straight and tall, Ma He responded evenly to the province king. "I wouldn't assume to tell you what to believe. Each man must believe only what is in his heart."

Zhu Di was surprised at the young lad's profound response.

Suddenly, the door to the king's chamber again swung open and Commander Tan entered. He cast a curious glance in my direction. No doubt, he didn't expect to find me there either. And when he saw Ma He, he seemed even more puzzled.

Zhu Di turned sharply to acknowledge his presence. "Yes, Commander?"

"I'm sorry to interrupt, Your Majesty, but I bring urgent news."

Commander Tan's eyes shifted once more to me... and then to Ma He, unsure if he should continue. Zhu Di saw his hesitation and waved his hand for him to continue.

"And.."

Reluctantly, Commander Tan continued. "General Ho's troops have been attacked."

Zhu Di stiffened in his chair. "Attacked? By whom?"

"The Mongol Chieftain Chi Li Bu Hua. He raided them in the night and freed the remainder of the Mongol prisoners. They have rejoined their rebel leader."

Zhu Di was clearly disturbed by this news. He shook his head with disappointment. But I also detected a hidden pleasure at hearing that General Ho had encountered trouble.

My gaze immediately went to Ma He. I'm certain he was concerned about what may have happened to Xi Chen during the raid. A worried expression pulled at his face.

Zhu Di continued with a steady voice. "I'm sure the general will wear this shame for a long time," he told Commander Tan, the hint of a smile playing on is lips. "Send him a brief message of consolation... and be sure to thank him for the prisoners he provided us."

Commander Tan suppressed his own smug grin and bowed graciously. "Yes, Your Majesty."

Commander Tan turned to go. But Zhu Di couldn't resist adding another sly comment. "And please tell him that we still have 'our' prisoners."

Commander Tan offered Zhu Di another nod, then quickly retreated from the room. When the doors closed, King Zhu Di immediately turned his attention back to Ma He. "That was an interesting development, don't you think?"

Ma He nodded his agreement, a clash of excitement and trepidation running through his heart.

"Anyone can be triumphant one day," Ma He told Zhu Di, "and defeated the next."

Zhu Di smiled at the young man's wisdom. Then, Ma He added, "We are all made vulnerable by pride."

"Your thoughts flow from your mouth with such ease," Chief Eunuch Chang gushed, astonished at the way the Muslim lad spoke.

"He's young and inexperienced," I quickly explained, immediately hoping that I hadn't overstepped my bounds.

Surprisingly, King Zhu Di smiled upon hearing the translation.

"But wise already." Zhu Di squinted at Ma He. A smile followed.

"Young man, I think I would like for you to join my royal court as a servant."

Ma He struggled to restrain his excitement at this unexpected invitation. I offered Zhu Di a respectful bow, letting him know how grateful I was for his decision.

It wasn't long before Dao Yan and I were, walking down a cobblestone street on our way to see Ma He's initiation as a royal servant. The monk could tell that I was quite excited about the Muslim lad's good fortune.

"To be a servant in the royal court," I gushed happily, "is really quite an honor, isn't it?"

Dao Yan hesitated a moment before answering, but then confirmed, "Yes, it is quite an honor."

"I think it's just wonderful for him!" I again allowed happily. "The boy is very smart. I could tell that when I first saw him. Something in his eyes tells me he has wisdom that is far beyond his years."

After walking for several minutes without speaking, Dao Yan turned to me and asked me if I "understood."

I was puzzled by this odd question and tried to find some logic in its brevity. "I understand it will mean a great deal of responsibility for the boy."

Dao Yan hesitated, looking for the right words, then attempted to ask again... "But do you understand that he'll have..."

I interrupted him excitedly, feeling that I had grasped what he was trying to say. "Oh yes...yes. Of course. That he'll have to work hard and be loyal and..."

Dao Yan raised his hand, abruptly interrupting me. "...And that he will have to become a eunuch."

"A eunuch?" I stammered, not quite sure I understood. I pondered this with furrowed brow, sorting my way through this new information. Then... "You mean?"

"Yes. He must be..."

I cut him off sharply, the word flying from my lips. "Castrated?"

Dao Yan shrugged casually, as if this were perfectly normal. We both grew silent, continuing to walk, each absorbed in our own thoughts. Finally after a few moments, Dao Yan broke the awkward silence.

"It is Chinese custom."

"It's barbaric," I snapped, obviously upset. "Why must they do that?" I demanded, bristling at the thought of such inhumane treatment. "Why would anyone ever think that kind of thing is necessary?"

Dao Yan's countenance remained calm. His voice was soft and certain. "He will have many duties within the royal court..."

Still perturbed, I interrupted him again. "Yes, yes... I understand that, but..."

Dao Yan abruptly stopped walking and turned to me, looking directly into my eyes.

"The king has many concubines, my friend."

My response came more slowly this time. "Yes... I know."

"The royal servants must protect the chastity and purity of the Ladies-in-Waiting within the royal court."

"Of course. Yes, of course..." I mumbled, trying my best to anticipate what he was trying to say.

"At all times... the fidelity of the king's concubines and ladies must be preserved. And therefore, no uncastrated male, apart from the king himself, is ever permitted to enter the imperial harem."

The cloud was lifted from my mind. I finally grasped what my friend was telling me. I sighed heavily. There are times when the reality of the world is most difficult to accept. In my heart I secretly held out the hope that perhaps, in this one instance, protocol and tradition could be somehow overlooked.

"The king wouldn't need to worry about Ma He," I argued. "He's already madly in love with the young girl, Xi Chen."

"Love is not the issue," Dan Yan offered before turning and continuing to walk.

"But they just can't!" I protested again. "It will destroy any chance for a life with the one he loves."

Dao Yan looked at me skeptically. "The one who was being held with the Mongol prisoners?"

I nodded.

"It's unlikely that she's still alive."

"But we don't know that for certain," I argued. "She could still be alive. She may have escaped."

"He should forget her," Dao Yan stated simply, without a breath of irony or regret. "There is no choice in the matter."


Chief Eunuch Chang escorted Ma He down a long dark alley that led to the building where his castration ceremony would take place. Ma He was unaware of what was soon to befall him. He had only been told that he was going to be a royal servant for King Zhu Di.

A cold drizzle was falling. Both Ma He and Chang walked with cautious steps, trying to avoid losing their footing on the wet cobblestones. Ma He noticed that Chang maintained a perpetual scowl on his face. He wondered why Chang seemed so unhappy.

"Perhaps it's the cold rain," he thought to himself, as they walked together in silence.

Ma He carried with him several rolled garments, which he had been told he would have to wear during the ceremony. He held them close to his chest in an effort to keep them dry.

Chang and Ma He entered a large wooden door, which led them into a courtyard surrounded by several dismal gray buildings. Chang pointed the way to another door across the courtyard. They had to scurry across the wide expanse as the rain began to fall even harder.

Chang led Ma He through a long narrow building, into a cold, stark room with very little illumination. Even though the light was dim, Ma He could see numerous pallets lining each side of the room and each pallet was covered with a thin woven mat.

Almost a dozen young boys, all in their late teens, were lying on the mats. Curiously, some seemed to be doubled over in pain, while others lay stretched out flat on their backs. Most of them stared blankly at the dark ceiling.

Ma He became somewhat anxious when he noticed that many of the boys were moaning softly. He also noticed crimson stains on the thin sheets that covered the lower halves of their bodies, but naively didn't associate their condition with the fate that would soon await him.

As the door opened, a dozen older servants turned to stare at Ma He, now standing in the doorway, wet and shivering with cold.

Chief Eunuch Chang waved in their direction and issued a curt command. "Prepare him."

The giggling eunuchs immediately converged on Ma He and began to remove his damp outer garments.

"You're a very fortunate boy," Chang told Ma He with a scowl. "If you worked as a servant for me, I'd have you scrubbing pots all day."

An effeminate eunuch named Wang flitted around the Muslim lad and pushed at him with delicate fingers. "That's all he's good for. Scrubbing pots."

"I'm not anyone's slave," Ma He told Chang forcefully. "I serve only Mohammed."

Chang suddenly pulled Ma He close to him, gripping the back of his neck tightly. He spoke with a harsh whisper into his ear.

"Listen, my young flower. You are here to serve the king. Your only loyalty is to him and his wishes. And I... will tell you... his wishes."

He shoved Ma He away and turned to the others.

"Have him ready in one hour."

Chang then turned with an exaggerated flourish and scurried from the room. The other eunuchs giggled and imitated Chang's flamboyant gestures.

"So," Wang screeched in a tremulous, high-pitched voice, "you are the next lucky one. Did you beg them to let you become a eunuch?"

Ma He didn't understand.

"A what?" The term "eunuch" tumbled through his mind. It sounded vaguely familiar but he had no real understanding of its meaning.

"I had to plead with them," Wang said mockingly. "Oh, please! Save me from my wretched life! Make me half a man, so I'll be whole."

The effeminate servant continued to giggle annoyingly. Ma He tried to move away from him, but the other eunuchs blocked his way.

"What are you talking about?" he asked in a defiant voice. "I am going to be a royal servant to King Zhu Di."

Wang giggled again.

"Yes, and to be a royal servant for the king, you must be a eunuch."

Ma He was confused.

"I don't know what that is."

Wang motioned to several boys who were standing nearby. They coyly opened their robes and exposed their disfigured nakedness, chuckling among themselves.

Ma He stared in silent shock. A horrible realization flooded over him.

"And you are going to be next!" Wang giggled to the delight of his fellow eunuchs.

Ma He panicked and bolted for the door. The eunuchs grabbed his arms and pulled him down. Then, they forcefully restrained him and tied his flailing arms to his side so he couldn't move.

Ma He's eyes' were wide with fear.

When the eunuchs got him dressed in the purple garments he was carrying, other robed eunuchs guided him to the Ch'ang Tzu, a small dark building just outside the western gate of the Tzu Chin Palace. He was bound so tightly he couldn't move either of his arms.

The rain had now stopped, but Ma He trembled with fear. A damp sweat coated his face.

As the eunuchs escorted Ma He inside the Ch'ang Tzu, their long shadows stretched eerily out in front of them. When the heavy wooden door closed with a loud thud, their shadows were suddenly swallowed up by the unexpected darkness. Only a few small candles and torches illuminated the interior of this sacred ceremonial room.

Two servants silently approached Ma He and removed his arms from the cloth bonds, gripping his wrists tightly so that he could not break free. They dressed him in an ornate gold and purple robe that matched the robes worn by the other attending eunuchs.

Ma He grew dizzy with fear, his body tense with a growing morbid anxiety. The eunuchs lifted him off his feet and carried him to the k'ang, a ceremonial table located in the center of the room. Even in the semi-darkness, Ma He could glimpse darker stains of blood visible on its surface.

Ma He continued to tremble and quiver, turning his head to the right and left, struggling to see what was going to happen to him next. A hard lump of fear stuck in his throat, choking back all ability to speak.

The eunuchs then pulled open Ma He's ceremonial robe and washed his private parts with a hot pepper-water. As steam from the water raised like a cloud from Ma He's genitals his mouth flew open in wrenching agony.

He tried to scream, but what emerged from his throat sounded more like the rasp of a long dry wind.

Suddenly, a loud gong echoed through the dark chamber. The specialist who would perform the ritual, known as the tao tzu chiang, stepped from the shadows with a disturbingly serene smile. Immediately, the eunuchs pulled Ma He's ankles apart and secured his legs. Then, with swift movements born of repeated ceremonial tradition, they secured his arms and abdomen firmly to the k'ang.

The specialist then began to chant. Slowly, he withdrew a large curved blade from the darkness. Candlelight glinted off the razor sharp edge of the blade as the tao tzu chiang held it up to the light.

Ma He grew frantic, straining at the bonds that held him. He struggled to lift himself up, his face turning red from the effort. But no matter how much he struggled, the eunuch servants held him firmly to the ceremonial k'ang.

Ma He again opened his mouth to scream. But, as before, only the raspy sound of a sharp hiss emerged.

One of the ceremonial servants forced a well-worn wooden stick between Ma He's teeth. He bit down hard on the piece of wood, then spit it away, sickened by the taste of blood, sweat and saliva from others who had gone before.

With the same serene smile on his face, the specialist parted the boy's robe then gently touched the ultra-sharp edge of the blade with his finger. Even this very slight touch drew blood. Slowly, the specialist raised the blade over Ma He's groin, then paused to look deep into his eyes.

"Will you regret it, or not?" he asked, still smiling.

Before the Muslim lad could answer, the door flew open with a crash and the room was suddenly illuminated by a burst of daylight from outside. An imposing shadow fell upon all of them. All eyes turned as King Zhu Di unexpectedly strode into the room.

"Stop!" he shouted, his voice booming in the chamber.

The king walked directly to the ceremonial table and looked down at the frightened boy tied there. He then shocked everyone in attendance by stating with unruffled authority, "Everyone leave. I will perform this ceremony myself."

No one moved. Zhu Di slowly turned his gaze to the eunuchs and ceremonial servants. A direct command exploded from him.

"All of you leave. Now!"

The eunuchs and servants trembled, afraid to breath. Nothing like this had ever happened before.

"At once!" Zhu Di ordered again, leaving no doubt as to the seriousness of his order.

After offering a slight bow, the eunuchs and ceremonial servants quickly turned away rapidly and filed out of the room without looking back. Zhu Di then turned to the tao tzu chiang.

"And you as well."

"But, Your Majesty," the specialist argued, "perhaps I should give you some instructions as to... This is a very delicate..."

Zhu Di cut him off harshly. "I've seen it done many times."

King Zhu Di took the blade.

"I am well aware of how to separate a man from his manhood."

Zhu Di looked into Ma He's eyes. He saw nothing but terror and dread. The king touched Ma He's shoulder with surprising gentleness, attempting to calm him. He then turned again to the specialist who hadn't moved. He spoke each word with a conclusive finality.

"I... told you... to get OUT!"

The specialist still hesitated, his lower jaw trembling as he tried to find words of protest.

"Leave!" Zhu Di whirled around to face the specialist, brandishing the blade threateningly. "Or I will personally see you join these eunuchs as one of them."

Bowing his head, the specialist stepped back two steps, then reluctantly turned and departed. The heavy wooden doors closed with an ominous thud behind him.

A silence filled the void as the echo from the door was swallowed by the dank, shadowy darkness.

Zhu Di didn't hesitate. He raised the blade over Ma He's groin.

"I trust you, Ma He," Zhu Di told him in deep sincerity. "I trust your instincts... and I trust your loyalty."

With startling suddenness, he swung the blade downward, stopping just short of the Me He's genitals. The boy gasped, shaking uncontrollably, a tear squeezing from the corner of each eye. But the sharp blade hovered there, like a humming bird floating in air, a harsh light flashing and sparkling off its deadly surface.

"But...do _you_... trust _me_?" Zhu Di asked, speaking each word with undeniable clarity.

Ma He exhaled in relief, as sweat and tears flowed in a torrent down his face. Forcing a sound from deep in his throat, he squeezed out a barely audible reply.

"Yes."

Chapter Three

---

THE MIRACLE

I need to rest. The cloth that covers my chest wound is now soaked with blood. Why am I still bleeding? If it doesn't stop soon, I'm sure I will have no blood left within me. Do I have a fever? Feeling my brow, I don't think so. My chest does throb with pain, but what should I expect? I was struck with a spear.

Thank God my wooden cross was able to stop the sharp point of the spear from going any deeper or I wouldn't be here to write about it. Was it a true divine intervention? Or a "Deus ex machina" fabricated in my own fervid and desperate imagination? For the time being, I will opt for divinity and soothe myself with that comfort.

I wonder when Zheng He will get back to his Flagship, if he does make it back at all? No no no, I can't think like that. The cannons have stopped firing outside, or at least, I can't hear them anymore. No one has come into my cabin to kill me, so that must mean the battle is won. I can't allow my mind to think otherwise.

My mind is spinning. Where am I? Do I have enough paper? I hope so.

Where are the servants? I don't want them to stay away forever. I need more tea. Are they going to just let me lie here without checking on me until I die?

I must stop thinking like this. Start writing again. That's what I need to do. Get it down on paper. Don't forget anything. It's important that the world knows everything that happened to Zheng He and all that he has accomplished.

And so, I must pick up my pen. My thoughts are rivers. And the ink flows like warm blood onto the page...


When, as a young man, Ma He became a favored servant in Zhu Di's royal court, the province king changed his name. He would no longer be referred to as Ma He. From that day forward he was to be known as Zheng He.

I'm not certain why Zhu Di chose the name Zheng for his new servant, but in Chinese the name means "prudent." I can only surmise that the king felt the young Muslim lad, even in his bold pronouncements and reckless bravado, exhibited a certain manifestation of discretion, caution and prudence. Or perhaps it was a random selection, simply lifted from a list of miscellaneous servant names to help distinguish one from the other. I will never know, for I never asked.

But one thing I did discover was how Zhu Di came to be king of the northern province.

Ten years before Zheng He was chosen to be Zhu Di's servant, the future king's destiny was placed firmly on an irreversible course. It was then that Zhu Di's father, the first Ming Emperor, Zhu Yuanzhang, died.

He had five sons and each had been given the title of province king. They were all independent and maintained strong control over each of their own particular outer provinces. China's large northern province of Han was given to Zhu Di, who located his capital city at Beijing.

Zhu Yuanzhang was also known by his dynastic title as Emperor Hong-wu. When he died, each of his sons hoped that he would be chosen emperor. Instead, imperial officials selected Zhu Yun-wen, a young man who was the eldest son of Zhu Di's oldest brother, who had also recently died.

All the brothers, including Zhu Di, were furious at the obvious affront. They felt the imperial officials at Nanking had forced Yun-wen upon them. None of them could stomach Zhu Yun-wen and argued strongly that he was much too weak and ineffective, lacking the experience needed to govern as emperor. In their mind, he should never have been chosen for the most exalted position of power in the land.

Emperor Zhu Yun-wen knew of the bitter feelings that were held by his uncles and had always been wary of the strength and influence enjoyed by them in the outer provinces. To be more correct, it was

Zhu Yun-wen's imperial ministers who were most wary of the province kings. Their power and influence stemmed directly from their ability to keep this young, and easily influenced, ruler on the throne. Consequently, they did everything they could to undercut the power of the province kings, so none would become powerful enough to overthrow the emperor.

Following King Zhu Di's interruption of Zheng He's castration ceremony, word spread through the palace like a harsh wind. Everyone said the king had spared the Muslim lad from the blade. But did he really trust Zheng He enough to spare him? Or was it merely a cruel rumor concocted by the other eunuchs? Speculation was rampant. No one was certain. Not even I was sure.

But it was quite intriguing that after an extended period of recovery, Zheng He did become King Zhu Di's most trusted and loyal servant in the royal court.

Some asked why I didn't know the truth, since Zheng He and I were very close friends? The answer is simple. Zheng He lived inside the palace and I did not. I began my small mission in Beijing and served there for several years. But in those early years, Zheng He and I rarely saw each other.

But I do recall one significant day, perhaps a full decade later, when Zheng He was in his late twenties. I was walking through the marketplace when I nearly ran into him as I was turning a corner.

"Sorry," he said, not even recognizing me. He was about to hurry away when I suddenly realized who he was.

"Zheng He? Is that you?"

He stopped and turned. A look came over into his eyes, like the dawn of a new day. A brilliant smile spread across his face, which was now fuller and chiseled like a man's. He was no longer an innocent boy.

"Friar?" He rushed back and gave me an enthusiastic embrace. I looked him over carefully and could see that he had grown into a strong and very handsome man.

"How are you?" I gushed, thrilled by the prospect of seeing him after so many years.

"I am well," he responded happily. "And you? I hear your mission is thriving."

"Yes, it does serve a purpose," I replied with a smile. "A good purpose."

"Come, walk with me, I'm late," he urged, patting me good-naturedly on the back. "I must return to the palace to confer with the King Zhu Di and his advisors."

We talked while walking hastily toward the gate. Since it was the first time I had seen him in almost ten years, I was curious if I could easily detect whether or not he was a eunuch.

"You seem to walk well enough," I ventured cautiously, while trying to keep up.

"And why shouldn't I?" he responded casually.

"No reason."

I tried again.

"And your hair grows full and thick, like the trees of the northern forest."

"I'm healthy," Zheng He answered, undoubtedly curious as to why I was making so many strange observations.

"And you look strong," I continued. "I wouldn't have known you by your voice."

"I'm not a boy now, Friar," he told me without slowing down. "It's been many years."

"It has been," I agreed. "Too many years."

Then I noticed Xi Chen's necklace still hanging from his neck.

"I see you still have..."  I let the words trail off, but looked directly at the necklace.

Zheng He touched it and smiled to himself, his thoughts obviously turning to Xi Chen.

"I think of her every day," he admitted. "And I miss her greatly.  If only..."

He looked off and his smile faded.  I wanted to fill the awkward silence, tempted to ask him what he was thinking.  But I hesitated too long and then, in the blink of an eye, the moment had passed.

Zheng He turned to me, allowing his enthusiasm to rise once again and fill the void.

"I will come to your mission sometime, so we can talk.  Is it agreed?"

"I would love to talk with you, don't make me wait for such a long time."

"I must go," he sang out cheerily, as he hurried off toward the palace. His delighted voice echoed in my mind long after he had disappeared around the corner.  But so did his sadness.


Later that same day, when I returned to my mission and mentioned to a friend that I had just run into Zheng He, the first thing he asked me was if I could tell whether or not he was a eunuch.

My answer was simple... and true.  "He was as I remembered him to be, only taller and older."

"No, no," my friend complained, "that isn't what I mean? I want to know how his features looked and what his voice sounded like. All the eunuchs that I know have delicate features with high little voices, like cats and chattering birds. Was Zheng He like that?"

I chuckled to myself. "He wasn't anything like that. His voice sounded strong, like thunder beneath the sea, and his features were not delicate at all. He's developed into a very tall and rugged looking young man."

"So, seeing him," my friend asked, obviously perplexed, "you say he looked just like he did before?"

"No. As I said... taller, stronger and older."

My friend shook his head. It appeared he was not hearing what he wanted to hear.

"With Zheng He's position as the king's favorite servant," he reasoned, "there's no way he would be able to work in Zhu Di's royal court if he wasn't a eunuch. But, from what you tell me, he doesn't look or sound like a man who's been castrated?"

"Who's to say if he is, or isn't?" I countered. "I consider Zheng He to be my friend. And that will never change."


Zhu Di was now in his late thirties. As with Zheng He, the king had lost any appearance of youthful innocence. He now had the solid maturity and weathered experience of a true leader etched into his face.

As the king sat on his royal throne and prepared to meet with his military advisors, Zheng He stood off to one side and assumed the role of Zhu Di's trusted advisor and confidant, as well as servant.

Chief Eunuch Chang, now showing his age, maintained his usual position to the rear of Zhu Di's throne. Chang was jealous and not at all happy with the special position of trust that Zheng He held with the king.

On this particular day... I believe it was the summer of 1402... a select group of military commanders and high officials had gathered for their weekly meeting with the province king. Also in attendance were Commander Tan and High Administrator Wong.

Sitting off to the side, with a haughty attitude of casual indifference, sat Zhu Di's number two son, Prince Han. Although barely in his twenties, the angry young man was totally convinced he knew more than his father about absolutely everything.

Absent from the meeting was Crown Prince, Zhu Bao Zhi, the king's first born. He cared nothing about affairs of state. He was overweight, fastidious, and had a terrible fancy for pretty clothes. Since he viewed boredom as the greatest curse one can endure, it was not unusual for him to avoid these tedious meetings.

Commander Tan rose from his chair. The room grew tensely quiet. The Commander paused to study a parchment that had been delivered to him less than a minute earlier by messenger. When he felt he had everyone's attention, he handed the parchment back and sent the messenger away with a dismissive flick of his finger.

"I have received some very disturbing information," he reported solemnly to Zhu Di.

"Well, Commander, you've certainly disturbed me many times before," the king responded, smiling. "Just get on with it."

Hooking his thumbs into his broad black belt, Commander Tan stood as tall as his modest frame could manage and delivered the message in an inappropriately booming voice.

"Your brother, Prince Ning, demands the return of lands in the northern province, claiming they are his alone. We have reason to believe he has gathered a large Mongol force and is planning to attack."

No longer smiling, Zhu Di got straight to his feet and began pacing the floor. Prince Han watched with great interest, as he privately enjoyed his father's discomfort.

"My own brother plans to attack ME?" Zhu Di bellowed, then asked a question.

"What do you make of this?

Prince Han jumped to his feet to offer a response.

"It does seem to me..."

But Zhu Di quickly raised his hand to silence his son.

"Han, I wasn't asking you for your opinion, I was asking Zheng He." He then turned to his trusted servant.

"Give me your opinion, please."

Prince Han was cut deeply by this obvious insult. As he retook his seat, he leveled a cold gaze at Zheng He and grew petulantly mute.

Zheng He didn't hesitate.

"In the Koran, Sire, the prophet Mohammed..."

Next it was High Administrator Wong who leaped to his feet and interrupted the royal servant.

"I'm sick and tired of your talking about Mohammed," he shrieked. "You're always quoting from his book of lies. Mohammed is a fraud. Lord Buddha is the light of this world, if you would only..."

"SILENCE!" King Zhu Di shouted at Wong. "I cannot hear Zheng He's reply if you are making loud noises."

Stung by the sharp rebuke, Wong also retreated to his seat, and, much like Prince Han, continued to glower.

Zhu Di turned again to his favored servant.

"Zheng He, please continue."

"I was only saying, Your Majesty, that if Prince Ning is willing to risk eternal damnation by attacking his own brother, then he must be incapable of clear thinking. A ruler incapable of clear thinking cannot, and will not, prevail."

Zhu Di looked sternly at both Wong and Commander Tan.

"Commander Tan?"

Commander Tan immediately came to attention.

"Your Majesty?"

"My clear thinking tells me we should prepare the troops for battle. We'll make our defense at the Great Wall."

Commander Tan bowed to Zhu Di and strode briskly from the room.


Later that same afternoon, High Administrator Wong stood by the window in his office brooding, as he observed the palace square below. Prince Han had joined him earlier and was now circling the room with agitated energy.

"I don't like this eunuch Zheng He," Wong complained sourly to the young prince. "He has way too much influence with your father."

"Why would my father want to listen to him?" Han whined, throwing his arms into the air in mock despair.

"Because your father is a fool," Wong responded, angrily. "This is a bad omen for us, Han. If a common eunuch can have such influence with the king, our destiny is sealed."

"He's nothing but a lowly servant," Han offered, hoping that what he was saying was true. "There's no power in his words."

Wong turned from the window to face Han.

"But the army is marching to war, Prince Han, because of what that servant had to say."

Han countered.

"He's only one person."

"Yes," Wong agreed, "he is only one person, but the number of eunuch servants is growing every day. There are hundreds now. Soon there will be thousands. It's getting totally out of hand."

"Then we must stop them," Prince Han bellowed, again throwing his arms into the air in exasperation.

"If we don't," Wong predicted, "at the first chance, they will seize power with their dainty little fingers and twist our plans to dust while we sleep."

Just seven days later, near the Great Wall, Mongol Chief Chi Li Bu Hua stared silently into the early morning mist, sitting upon his majestic white horse. He looked striking with his flowing mane of long, black hair. His creased face had been well seasoned by the harsh sun and smoke of battle.

Next to him, also on horseback, was Commander Tu, the chief's senior military officer. They both gazed across the broad valley toward Prince Ning's large Mongol army stretched out along the long slope of a grassy hill.

Chi Li Bu Hua and Commander Tu nudged their horses past a large contingent of Mongol soldiers who busied themselves cleaning their bows and spears, in preparation for battle. Dozens of gray-clad servants, both men and women, were bent over large steaming kettles, serving food to the last of Ning's army.

Chi Li Bu Hua motioned to an officer nearby, who hurried to him.

"Pack up the camp," he told the officer curtly. "Prepare to have the men advance across the Wall."

The officer nodded and quickly began moving through the area, spreading the word for the men to pack up and prepare for engagement.

In less than an hour, Chi Li Bu Hua and Commander Tu had traversed the valley to a small rise, not far from the huge stone edifice. It was still early. The sun was only now beginning to show itself over the far horizon, but had yet to burn away the mist that hung like a deep shroud over the entire landscape.

The thick mist partially obscured several large portions of the Wall, which snaked its way over hills and into deep valleys as far as the eye could see. It was eerily quiet. The only sound was the muted snorting of horses and their soft, nervous stomping of hooves on the ground.

"It's quiet," Commander Tu whispered to Chi Li Bu Hua softly.

"Yes," the Mongol Chief agreed. "Too quiet."

"Prince Ning's advisors told us this part of the Wall would be undefended," Tu whispered again.

"The Prince is not here to feel the sting of death, nor taste the blood of battle," Chi Li Bu Hua sneered.

Commander Tu motioned towards the unmanned Wall. There was not a stirring of life anywhere along its expanse.

"But there's no one to fight. I'm certain we can move deep into the province before we will encounter any troops. We can then take them by surprise and slaughter them in their sleep as we go."

Chi Li Bu Hua didn't blink or take his eyes from the Wall. He listened very carefully to the strange silence that hung in the thick mist.

"There are no birds," he whispered, almost to himself.

"What?"

"The birds," Chi Li Bu Hua said once more, almost with reverence. "Do you hear them?"

Commander Tu listened, but he could hear no sound at all. Behind them, the Mongol army of Prince Ning began to stir as it prepared to move. But at the Wall, there was only silence.

Commander Tu whispered back to the chief, "No. I hear nothing."

Chi Li Bu Hua looked at Tu and nodded slowly, confirming the thought that was now growing in his commander's own mind.

"The blackbird always sings, whether the world is wrapped in fog or rain, or dead of night."

Commander Tu was not impressed with the Mongol Chief's odd assessment of the situation.

"I mean no disrespect, but I don't think we should let 'birds' inform our military judgment. If you are reluctant to do so, I will proceed forward myself and confirm our safe passage."

Commander Tu softly nudged his horse and the animal began to move forward. But then the animal itself abruptly halted, nervously shying. Tu squinted toward the Great Wall in growing disbelief.

As if by magic, Zhu Di's massive army of twenty thousand soldiers suddenly appeared before them from the mist. All along the stone rim, as far as the eye could see, spears, arrows, cannons and crude fire rockets were now pointed directly at the Mongol army of Prince Ning.

As the mist began to lift like a curtain, Chief Chi Li Bu Hua and Commander Tu could now see thousands of troops revealed on the far hills beyond the Great Wall. It was a stunning, unexpected sight, so overwhelming in its power that the Mongol soldiers could hardly find the strength to breathe.

Chi Li Bu Hua exhaled quietly. This seasoned warrior was not one to panic. Instead, his words carried the tone wry sarcasm. "This," he said, "is a disturbingly familiar situation."

On top of the Great Wall, Prince Han and Commander Tan stood on a high parapet. They gazed at the Mongol army before them, which was comparatively small by comparison to the massive force that was emerging from the mist.

"We could crush them all within minutes," Commander Tan said confidently.

Prince Han smiled with twisted amusement.

"Good. It will mean more Mongol blood to enrich our soil."

Across the valley, Commander Tu returned to Chi Li Bu Hua's side. His face was ashen.

"They are twenty times our size," he gasped, obviously terrified.

But Chi Li Bu Hua was not deterred.

"I'm not about to sacrifice my men for a petty quarrel between brothers. Send out an emissary and request a conference with King Zhu Di. I would like to meet this clever province king myself."

Commander Tu had no courage or bravado left to engage in debate. He quickly whirled his steed around and galloped back to the ranks of Mongol soldiers.

Later, as the morning mist merged into darkened clouds, Chief Chi Li Bu Hua and Commander Tu slowly rode toward the Great Wall to meet with King Zhu Di. Commander Tu was extremely nervous, feeling the damp pall of sweat on his neck and back. Fear etched his face like a grotesque mask.

On top of the Wall, a Mongol emissary stood silently beside Zhu Di. Zheng He, Commander Tan and Prince Han stood nearby, watching the two Mongol officers approach.

Commander Tan smiled to himself. "I smell surrender in the air."

But Prince Han wasn't so sure. "Or a trick."

Zheng He looked closely at the two riders with an increasing glimmer of recognition.

At the base of the Wall, Chief Chi Li Bu Hua and Commander Tu slowly climbed the stone stairs to the top of the Wall. When the Mongol Chieftain appeared, Zheng He gasped to himself. He clearly recognized the man who had now come into view.

Chi Li Bu Hua bowed respectfully to King Zhu Di as they came face to face.

"I'm honored, Your Majesty," he said with a subtly mocking tone and an exaggerated bow.

Chi Li Bu Hua then cast an eye around the group gathered behind Zhu Di and studied each of them. When his eyes met Zheng He's, the Chief instantly recognized the feisty young Muslim lad who was now a grown man, and smiled to himself.

Wasting no time, Zhu Di addressed the Mongol Chief sternly.

"You are wise to recognize the futility of your position."

"I don't disagree," Chi Li Bu Hua said. "I'm a warrior of many years," he allowed, cleverly maintaining the sly smile on his face. "I know a difficult battle when I see it."

"When faced with death or surrender," Zhu Di stated firmly, "the reasonable choice between the two is apparent."

Commander Tan was getting anxious. "Shall we proceed?"

Chief Chi Li Bu Hua bowed again to Zhu Di and then unexpectedly stated, "I have a demand."

This utterance stopped Zhu Di and Commander Tan cold. But now it was Zheng He who was smiling. He was well acquainted with this ploy.

Zhu Di stared at Chi Li Bu Hua for a long moment, eyes locked and unmoving. Then, responded firmly.

"You are not in a position to make a demand. A fool's tongue could lead you to destruction. But, if you are so reckless... you may speak."

Chi Li Bu Hua again bowed to Zhu Di, with an even deeper, lower, more exaggerated gesture.

"I demand... peace," he stated simply, with only the tiniest hint of an insincere smile on his lips.

Zhu Di managed to conceal his surprise and let the words soak in. He then turned and began pacing in a small circle, considering this strange negotiation.

Chi Li Bu Hua and Zheng He privately shared a knowing smile while Zhu Di continued his restless pacing. The Mongol warrior closed his eyes for a brief instant and gave Zheng He a sincere nod of gratitude.

Zhu Di heaved a sigh and spun on his heel, returning to his position before Chi Li Bu Hua. Commander Tan wanted no part of any ridiculous peace offer. He could barely restrain his disgust at this charade of compromise.

"Your Majesty, I must object."

Zhu Di raised his hand to silence him, then looked directly at the Mongol Chieftain.

"I accept."

Commander Tan and Prince Han were shocked, but Zhu Di continued before they could protest formally.

"But, I also have a demand."

Chi Li Bu Hua was not at all surprised. He expected nothing less from a leader as astute as King Zhu Di.

"As a diplomatic courtesy, you must provide me with a large number of male and female servants," Zhu Di told him. He paused for dramatic effect, enjoying this fascinating game of war and peace. "Preferably... those who are the very favorites of my brother, Prince Ning."

Chi Li Bu Hua smiled slyly at Zhu Di's words, impressed by the irony of it. He was beginning to really like this province king.


Later that same afternoon, everyone was in place for the impromptu ceremony. Zhu Di's ceremonial throne had been brought to the battlefield, so he could receive the Mongol Chieftain with regal authority. As he sat quietly, waiting for Chief Chi Li Bu Hua to arrive, Zheng He stood at his usual position by Zhu Di's side.

Commander Tan and Prince Han, also standing close by, watched with stern faces as two long columns of Zhu Di's soldiers formed a broad pathway, which led directly to the province king. Monk Dao Yan and I were also present to witness this unusual ceremony.

The first to arrive were Chi Li Bu Hua and Commander Tu, both on horseback. They walked their horses slowly down the long phalanx of armed soldiers toward King Zhu Di. They were followed by a long column of servants, who were required to pass by Zhu Di for his review and selection.

When the Mongol Chief approached Zhu Di, he dismounted and took up a position next to Zhu Di's throne, opposite Zheng He.

As forty male and female servants prepared to pass in front of the province king for his selection, Zhu Di became slightly irritated.

"And these are all?"

Chief Chi Li Bu Hua quickly assured Zhu Di of their special importance. "These are the most precious to your brother. He will miss them greatly."

This pleased Zhu Di. With a subtle flick of his finger, he began selecting the servants who seemed most pleasing to him. If a particular servant was not to his liking, he simply motioned with a disparaging wave of his hand and they moved on.

As he watched this process, Zheng He began to sense something. He studied the line of servants carefully as they moved slowly toward him.

Suddenly, he caught a brief glimpse of flowing hair and familiar shining eyes. His heart began to race. As he strained to see, Xi Chen abruptly came into view. The exquisitely beautiful young woman took small steps, her head bowed humbly as she approached.

Zheng He clutched the necklace around his neck. Chi Li Bu Hua took particular notice of this and quickly realized that Zheng He was bursting with pent up excitement. He followed Zheng He's riveted gaze directly to the lovely Xi Chen.

Xi Chen stepped before Zhu Di and shyly stared at the ground. The king paid little notice and motioned for her to pass by.

Zheng He could not restrain himself. He was about to leap forward and call out, when Chi Li Bu Hua leaned toward the king and pointed out Xi Chen.

"This one is Prince Ning's personal favorite," he told Zhu Di smiling.

Zhu Di nodded and grinned with great appreciation, then motioned for the guards to pull Xi Chen from the line and add her to his growing collection.

I observed what had just unfolded and was quite pleased and happy for Zheng He. I knew he must be churning with delight and wanting to cry out to the love of his life, but somehow he managed to control himself, remaining silent. His eyes, however, never left Xi Chen as she was led away with the other servants who were now going to join Zhu Di's royal household.

As the procession continued, I saw Zheng He turn to the Mongol Chieftain and nod with heartfelt gratitude for his gracious gesture of kindness.

Zhu Di took little heed of the drama that unfolded right in front of him, continuing to make his final selections among the remaining servants.

When his selections were complete, Zhu Di turned to Chi Li Bu Hua.

"I have another demand, my friend."

Chi Li Bu Hua was not surprised. "Of course you do," he said, smiling.

"I ask your pledge that you will take your men and go peacefully, and never again swear allegiance to my brother, Prince Ning."

"And if I don't?" Chi Li Bu Hua asked, a glimmer of amusement in his eyes.

"I will, unfortunately, be forced to slaughter you and all of your army."

The engaging smile never left Chi Li Bu Hua's lips.

"Then I have no choice, do I?" Chief Chi Li Bu Hua bowed deeply to Zhu Di. "Consider it done."

It was abundantly clear to all those present that these two adversaries now shared a strong mutual respect.


As Zhu Di's army marched down the long valley heading back to Beijing, he rode comfortably in his royal carriage escorted by a large contingent of armed guards. Zheng He and I rode together on horseback, enjoying the end of a very fine day.

Zheng He smiled broadly. I don't think I'd ever seen him so happy in his whole life. We had hardly begun our return journey, when he turned and asked me, "Friar, is it possible, when we return to Beijing..."

I hastily interrupted. "I'd be happy to arrange it." I already knew what he was going to ask. Only a fool could not.

He looked at me with genuine surprise. "You'll arrange it? How do you know what I was going to ask?"

"Please, my son. Do you really think I walk this earth with my eyes closed?" And then I assured him, "You will meet with Xi Chen within the week. I promise."

He rode on beside me, grinning from ear to ear for the entire journey. His happiness was truly contagious.

As soon as we arrived back to Beijing, I arranged for Xi Chen and Zheng He to meet secretly in Zhu Di's royal rose garden. It was a clear night. The moon was full and it bathed the garden pathways and floral patterns with a soft beautiful glow.

As Zheng He and I waited in the shadows of a sprawling willow tree for Xi Chen to arrive, my friend was so nervous he couldn't stand still. He paced continuously. I tried to get him to calm down, but nothing I could do or say would help.

"What if she doesn't come?" he whispered softly as he continued to pace

"She will come." I told him calmly, trying to build his confidence.

"Maybe she couldn't slip away," he worried again. "They may have locked her in."

"You must calm yourself," I cautioned, "or your tongue will be tripping over your words."

But that didn't stem his anxiety. "She many not know me," he worried again. "It's been so long."

Then, as if by magic, the silhouette of Xi Chen appeared nearby, the moonlight clearly outlining her delicate form.

Zheng He was spellbound.

Now that the two lovers were about to be together again, I thought it best that I step further back into the shadows so that my presence did not inhibit them.

For a moment, Zheng He remained frozen, unable to move. I suppose he was afraid that if he dared approach her, she would turn to mist before his eyes.

But then, as if commanded by the same internal voice, they moved from the shadows toward each other, stopping only an arm's length apart. Their simultaneous breathing was like a rising and falling wind, warm and moist.

Xi Chen spoke first, her voice tiny and fragile.

"Ma He? Is it really you?"

Without answering, he pulled his love close and embraced her with the painful force of lost years and stolen moments. Both immediately became overwhelmed with tears of joy.

"I was so afraid that I'd never see you again," Zheng He whispered softly with tears streaming down his face.

Xi Chen drew back and tenderly touched his cheek, while studying his face.

"I waited for you, Ma He," she told him, beginning to cry. "I knew that someday, somehow, Allah would bring me back to you"

"And I waited for you, my little flower," he responded lovingly, while gently brushing tears from her eyes. "I dreamed of you every night and I loved you for..."

"Ten years," Xi Chen interrupted.

"A thousand years!" Zheng He corrected.

She kissed him passionately, overflowing with an emotion that had been trapped inside her for so long. But then suddenly, she pulled away, feeling faint. Zheng He held her tightly in his arms to keep her from collapsing.

When she regained her composure, she put her arms around his neck again and let her lips brush across his cheek.

"Do you remember the vow we made to each other?" she cooed softly.

Zheng He held her face in his hands and smiled.

"I told you that I would love you, forever."

"And I promised to remain faithful only to you," she replied, pressing her cheek tightly against his, "and that no other man would ever..."

Zheng He pulled her even closer to him and began smothering her words, caressing her face with tearful kisses.

"I love you," he gushed, over and over, "I love you, Xi Chen, I love you."

Suddenly, Zheng He heard a sound in the garden and pulled away. He tried to see where the sound came from as he looked around fearfully.

"What it is?" Xi Chen gasped.

"We must be careful," he whispered quietly. "We can't be seen together."

"But why?" Xi Chen whispered back. "We've waited for so long."

"It's because I'm..."

Zheng He hesitated, as he searched for a way to explain.

"You're what?" she asked, not understanding his hesitancy.

"I'm a trusted servant of King Zhu Di's royal court," he ventured cautiously. "I'm expected to have only one allegiance. And that is to the king."

"But what about us?" Xi Chen asked, as she looked deep into his eyes searching for answers.

"We must meet in secret," he responded carefully. But when he saw the disappointment in her eyes he quickly added "...at least for now."

Zheng He again embraced Xi Chen and held her close in the safety of his arms. Her tears continued to fall, but now they were tears of sadness, instead of joy.

In Zhu Di's bedchamber, his wife, Xu, circled him with a watchful eye and then took a seat at his side.

"You did well, my husband," she told him, smiling. She motioned for a servant to bring her some tea. "You have defeated your arrogant brother and made peace with the Mongols."

"But I still must rule in the shadow of my insolent nephew," he complained. "He's nothing more than a spoiled child posing as emperor."

Xu accepted a cup of tea from the servant and waited patiently until her husband received his tea as well. Then, she reached out and tenderly caressed her husband's hand.

"His favor with the people will soon fade away, Zhu Di. You'll see. Your time to rule the empire will come."

"Not soon enough, I fear," he groused, while taking a sip of the steaming tea. "Not soon enough."

At the same time in Nanking, Emperor Zhu Yun-wen marched into his throne room at the palace and uneasily took a seat. He was a young man in his early twenties. He was rather thin and mousy-looking and maintained a perpetual scowl on his face. His elaborate throne nearly swallowed him in its opulence and made him appear less significant and even physically smaller than he actually was.

A Senior Minister began reading a report to Zhu Yun-wen from a scroll. His monotone droned on and on, reciting facts and numbers. The young ruler, obviously bored, paid little attention.

Twelve other Ministers and several servants were also present for the daily assembly. They, however, paid close attention to what the Senior Minister was reading. After several minutes Zhu Yun-wen waved with irritation at his Senior Minister, demanding that he stop.

"There are too many words," he complained. "Just summarize your report."

The Senior Minister bowed then rolled up the scroll and spoke directly to the young emperor.

"The servants of your uncle, Prince Ning, were then surrendered to King Zhu Di. The Mongol leader, Chi Li Bu Hua, whom your uncle trusted so dearly, accepted defeat in the name of Prince Ning, and also in your name, Emperor Zhu Yun-wen."

"Is that all?" Zhu Yun-wen asked flatly, still bored by this formal recitation of facts already known.

"Yes. That is the report, Your majesty." But then he felt compelled to add, "Something must be done to stop Zhu Di. We feel this victory over Prince Ning has made him much too strong."

Zhu Yun-wen stared straight ahead, unconvinced.

"Too strong? Why do you say that? All he did was step on a few dirty Mongols?"

"But he also stole your uncle's servants," the Senior Minister added, pouring fuel on the fire.

Zhu Yun-wen jumped up and pointed a bony finger at the imperial official.

"Enough! I will handle Zhu Di in my own way."

But the Senior Minister was not about to back down.

"It is our opinion, Sire, that you should do so quickly, before his annoyance becomes a threat."

Zhu Yun-wen in no mood for ultimatums from those who he commanded. "Did I ask for your opinion?"

Unfazed by the emperor's rebuke, the Senior Minister turned to the other Ministers, as if to silently seek their tacit consent, then turned back to Zhu Yun-wen.

"We recommend that you weaken his power from within."

"And how, Senior Minister, shall I accomplish this subtle task? Should I insult him? Should I send him gifts of rotted food? Or maybe, you think I should torture him with bad advice?"

Refusing to be taunted by Zhu Yun-wen's snide, sarcastic remarks, the Senior Minister replied in a calm voice. "You simply remove each stone in the foundation of his house, and it will soon crush him."

Emperor Zhu Yun-wen stared blankly, not understanding the metaphor being constructed by his Senior Minister.

"I have no patience with your puzzling symbols and confusing talk of houses and stones," he shouted, wrapping his imperial robe tightly around his thin frame. With a royal pout he mumbled, "Speak to me straight... or not at all"

"Remove his strongest leg, Sire, and he shall fall."

Emperor Zhu Yun-wen heaved an impatient sigh, still plagued by these euphemisms. "His strongest leg? What leg are you speaking of?"

The Senior Minister stepped close to the throne, leaning toward the petulant ruler, speaking with soft confidence into his ear. "Commander Tan, the leader of Zhu Di's army. Destroy him... and the power of Zhu Di will crumble."


In Beijing, King Zhu Di slumped upon his own royal throne in discontent. He had just received a report that Imperial Ministers were coming for an unscheduled visit and it troubled him.

"Coming here?" the king asked High Administrator Wong, who had just brought him the news.

"Yes, Your Majesty. Two of the Emperor's Imperial Ministers will arrive today from Nanking."

"Why would my nephew send his Ministers here? Now?" Zhu Di asked, trying to assess his nephew's true motive. Zheng He, as always, was at his side, attentive and alert. The king looked to him, hoping for some guidance.

Prince Han began to circle the room restlessly, like a caged animal. He didn't like what he had just heard.

High Administrator Wong shrugged. "A diplomatic errand, perhaps, to discuss..."

But Zhu Di interrupted him.

"No, that's not it. The timing of this visit, so soon upon our defeat of Prince Ning troubles me."

Zheng He waited for the proper moment and then ventured his own advice. "Your Majesty, it is said that in order to obtain the golden pearl from the dragon, it is first necessary to slay the dragon while he sleeps."

Zheng He's comment made Prince Han angry. "What is this nonsense!" he shouted at Zheng He. "We don't need to hear your foolish poetry!"

The young prince rushed forward to address the crown.

"Father, Emperor Zhu Yun-wen is nothing more than a weak and silly tyrant. His Ministers will chastise and insult you with their lying tongues. I beg you, don't receive them with your graciousness. Turn them away."

But Zhu Di kept his gaze focused on Zheng He.

When Han saw his father wasn't listening to him, he turned to glare at his father's loyal servant.

"Why do you look to him? What does he know? He's just a lowly servant."

Ignoring his son, Zhu Di stood up and turned to face his royal staff with a knowing smile.

"Prepare to welcome our guests," he stated with calm assurance. "I will honor our Imperial visitors with a large banquet. Make all the arrangements."

Later that evening, King Zhu Di walked down the marble hall, stopping just outside the banquet room. A royal advisor greeted him with a polite bow and then conferred with him in hushed tones.

"The Emperor's Ministers have requested they be seated beside Commander Tan at the banquet."

Zhu Di nodded. "As they wish."

A large feast had been prepared for Zhu Di's Imperial guests. Dozens of servants scurried about the room, as they made preparations to serve the honored guests.

Guards in ornate uniforms stood at attention all around the perimeter of the room. Each had a sword at his side.

Everyone stood up respectfully as Zhu Di entered the room. He was seated at the head of the table beside Queen Xu. Prince Han sat at a separate table nearby, fidgeting and irritable.

I was offered a seat at a smaller table near the back of the large gathering, but close enough so I could observe everything as it unfolded.

A few moments later, the officers, dignitaries and members of the royal inner court entered the room and took seats in their assigned positions.

Zheng He, as usual, stood directly behind Zhu Di, attentive and watchful.

Several servant girls entered to serve the honored guests. Xi Chen was among them. They glided effortlessly around the table serving tea, floating like leaves on a soft wind, silent and lovely.

As Xi Chen neared Zheng He, their eyes met, but she quickly looked away as he had instructed her to do.

Commander Tan entered the room and was given a seat not far from Zhu Di. The province king acknowledged his senior military officer with a courteous nod.

As the two Imperial Ministers were escorted into the banquet hall, a hush fell over the crowd. Zhu Di offered them a small bow as well.

The Imperial Ministers returned Zhu Di's bow with one of their own, then were seated on either side of Commander Tan as they had requested.

While everyone was preparing to receive their meals, both of the Imperial Ministers surreptitiously slipped daggers from the folds in their sleeves.

Zhu Di silently observed this furtive behavior of the Ministers, but remained stoic, careful not to reveal that he had witnessed their diabolical preparations.

A few moments later, Zhu Di slowly got to his feet and placed his right hand lightly against his chest, as if he were about to speak. This gesture was a signal to the Royal Guards standing at attention throughout the room. Seeing the warning sign, they immediately became alert.

At that same moment, the two Imperial Ministers turned toward Commander Tan and raised their daggers. But before either could strike a fatal wound, four guards had rushed forward with swords drawn, plunging their sharp blades into the would-be assassins.

The two Ministers collapsed in a bloody heap on the table, startled expressions of shock still frozen upon their twisted faces.

Commander Tan looked on in horror as the attackers fell on either side of him, their crimson blood spreading across the table. He slumped in his chair, pale and breathless, realizing how close he had come to being assassinated.

Zhu Di calmly surveyed the carnage and then gave an order to his guards.

"Cut off their heads and return them to my nephew. Serve the rest to the dogs."

He then turned to Zheng He and smiled, thanking him for his greatly appreciated insight and advice. "No dragons have died tonight."

Chapter Four

---

OMEN OF THE BLUE ROOF TILES

At Zhu Yun-wen's palace in Nanking, the emperor was behaving like a small child. He gleefully chased a dog around the royal chambers, barking at the animal in his grating, high-pitched voice. Then, tiring of this ridiculous behavior, he flung himself onto his over-sized throne and laughed uncontrollably. His attendants looked on stoically, afraid to show their disdain for this foolish young man and his foolish antics.

The massive doors to the throne room suddenly swung open with a loud echoing thud. Zhu Yun-wen looked up with glassy eyes to see who was daring to interrupt his frivolity.

His Senior Minister strode into the room with heavy footsteps, carrying a large teak box. His face looked drawn and glum.

"What is this?" Zhu Yun-wen shouted at the Minister. "A gift to brighten my dismal day?"

The Senior Minister stopped before the emperor, but hesitated to speak. Impatient, Zhu Yun-wen began wiggling his fingers like a flock of fluttering birds, beckoning him to hurry.

"Well," he shrieked, "what is it?"

"It's a package from your uncle, Majesty."

Zhu Yun-wen responded mockingly.

"How lovely, how generous, how very kind. Perhaps Zhu Di is finally learning his place as my devoted benefactor."

Zhu Yun-wen waved his Senior Minister closer. "Come, come, open it. Let me have my prize."

The Minister slowly unlatched the box and turned it over. Two bloody severed heads tumbled onto the floor at the emperor's feet. He reacted with a startled yelp, as a lump of bile rose in his throat, effectively cutting off the pathetic whining sound from within.

Zhu Yun-wen's dog began scampering around the severed heads, barking and growling furiously. In a rage, Zhu Yun-wen kicked the dog and the animal went tumbling across the marble floor with a startled whimper. Red-faced with anger, the infuriated emperor shouted at his Senior Minister.

"Bring me General Ho! I will not endure this craven insult!" The minister started to reply, but Zhu Yun-wen interrupted him again. "Bring me the general, NOW!"

Having no choice, the Senior Minister whirled around and headed for the door. While he was leaving, Zhu Yun-wen continued his savage harangue, harshly spitting out words, his screechy voice battering the air.

"Tell him to take six hundred thousand Imperial troops to Beijing," he shouted, pointing a bony finger at the quickly retreating official, "and crush my uncle's kingdom! Do you hear me, Senior Minister? I want General Ho to burn everything to the ground! Then bring Zhu Di's bones to ME!"

A week later, in Beijing, Zhu Di conferred in private with Zheng He. It was quite obvious the province king was very anguished and troubled on this particular evening.

"My anger has created a firestorm," he confessed, walking in anxious circles about the room.

Zheng He rose from his chair and bowed respectfully.

"What lies ahead may be grave, Your Majesty, but I don't think that it's hopeless."

Zhu Di stopped pacing and offered his servant a dour prediction. "Optimism has led many a fool to a dusty death."

Zhu Di sighed heavily. His own words lay heavy upon his aching heart.

"There's no way to defend ourselves against General Ho's huge army," he told Zheng He. "He commands a thousand troops, times six hundred. My small army would be but a helpless insect under his mighty foot."

"But if you could have more troops," Zheng He suggested, trying to remain optimistic.

"How is that possible?" Zhu Di countered, throwing his arms into the air in desperation. "My eunuchs will not fight, and, as you well know, I am not a practitioner of magic."

Inspired by a thought, Zheng He was quick to reply.

"The Mongol Chieftain Chi Li Bu Hua owes you a great debt of gratitude, Sire. You honored his 'demand' for peace. It is not too soon for him to repay your charity by respecting your 'request' for war."

Zhu Di studied Zheng He for a moment. He admired his humble servant's keen intuition and tactical wisdom.

"But does he have enough men to make a difference in the outcome?" he asked, warming to the unexpected suggestion.

"The loyalty and devotion of his people is legendary," Zheng He replied firmly. "I have an instinct that Chi Li Bu Hua can procure more men than we could ever imagine."

Again, Zhu Di paused to consider his servant's words.

"Then you shall be the one to carry this message to him."

"Me?" Zheng He responded, obviously surprised.

"As my emissary, you're the only one I trust."

Zheng He realized he had no choice in the matter so bowed to his king graciously.

"I will do so, Sire... as you have instructed."


Later that same evening, Zheng He had arranged to meet secretly in the royal rose garden with Xi Chen. They sat together in the shadows, illuminated only by the warm glow of moonlight. Xi Chen cried softly.

"We just found each other," she whimpered, while dabbing a silk handkerchief at her eyes, "and now you tell me you're leaving me again?"

"I will return, my love. Please don't worry."

But Xi Chen wasn't convinced. "You promised me once before that we would never be apart..."

"We were children then, Xi Chen," he reminded her. "Long before I knew the true ways of the world."

Attempting to make her feel better, Zheng He pulled Xi Chen close and held her in a comforting embrace.

"I must deliver a message for the king," he whispered softly, "that is all. Then I will return to your arms forever. I give you my word."

Xi Chen looked into his eyes and searched for a reason to believe his promise. She then buried her face in his neck and hoped she could remain in his embrace forever.

The following morning, outside of Zhu Di's palace, Zheng He prepared his horse for travel. He tightened the saddle cinch expertly and then easily swung himself up into the saddle. His youthful days of riding across plains and mountains had served him well. It was a skill he had not forgotten.

When I heard that my good friend was leaving, I made certain that I was present to see him off. I handed him a small pouch before he left, sending him off with a warm smile and best wishes.

"Food for your journey," I told him, "and a spiritual talisman to protect you."

"Allah will protect me," he replied serenely, happily returning my smile.

"Allah, Lord Buddha and Christ Jesus will all watch over you," I added. "You are blessed with a great abundance of spiritual comfort."

Zheng He accepted the pouch with gratitude, then with a nod and another smile, nudged his horse and headed for the city gate. Immediately, the contingent of mounted royal guards fell into formation behind him. The hooves of their horses clacked loudly on the courtyard cobblestones as they rode away.

A three-day journey across the Mongolian Steppes brought Zheng He and his contingent of royal guards to the palace of Chief Chi Li Bu Hua. The edifice was not nearly as splendid as Zhu Di's palace in Beijing, but its crude interior had a certain elemental, primitive charm that was free of artifice and false grandeur.

Inside, the Mongol Chieftain rowdily entertained an attractive young woman in his private quarters. He had a delightful time grabbing at her and kissing her whenever she would allow him.

And she thoroughly enjoyed the chieftain's playful advances as well, coyly pulling away, teasing him with her flirtatious eyes and melodious laughter. He was about to pull her close again, when his personal servant entered and interrupted the raucous frivolity.

"Sir, an emissary has arrived from Beijing." But Chi Li Bu Hua didn't want to be bothered.

"Tell him to wait," he shouted. "Better yet, tell him to go away!"

The chieftain laughed again and growled playfully at the young woman, while she squirmed on his lap with great delight.

But Chi Li Bu Hua's servant did not move, instead he maintained his dogged persistence. "He bears a message from King Zhu Di. He said to tell you that his name is Zheng He."

This caught Chi Li Bu Hua by complete surprise. He abruptly pushed the woman off his lap onto the floor.

"Zheng He? Zheng He is here? Well, then, bring him to me. And be quick about it!"

The servant nodded and departed. Chi Li Bu Hua quickly and unceremoniously waved the young woman away. Perturbed by this unexpected dismissal, she made no effort to conceal her displeasure. He smacked her playfully on the rear and with a hearty laugh once again waved her away. She made a spiteful face at him, but found herself unable to resist his roguish charm, grinning broadly over her shoulder as she left.

Chi Li Bu Hua assumed a regal posture in his favorite chair, attempting to create the appearance of official decorum. But realizing what a silly sham this was, he gave up the charade and slouched casually, legs askew.

When Zheng He entered a moment later, Chi Li Bu Hua forgot all pretense and appearances, leaping to his feet and rushing over to roughly embrace his old friend, slapping him on the back and jostling him.

"Ahhh, my young diplomat! What have you come to 'demand' from me now?"

Laughing at his own joke, Chi Li Bu Hua hugged Zheng He good-naturedly, bringing a smile to the royal servant's lips.

"This time I bring only a request, from His Majesty, King Zhu Di," Zheng He replied, attempting to introduce a tone of seriousness.

"A request, is it?" Chi Li Bu Hua thought about this, feigning a look of mock concern. "Request is such a heavy word to carry. Does it portend evil and calamity? Must I be seated for this?"

Zheng He looked at the casual furniture scattered about, motioning to a pair of leather hassocks. "Perhaps we should both sit."

When they were finally situated, Zheng He leaned toward Chi Li Bu Hua, attempting to look and sound more earnest. "The King has provoked the wrath of Emperor Zhu Yun-wen."

Chi Li Bu Hua simply shrugged, doing his best to keep the mood light-hearted.

"That ridiculous little worm is so easily provoked," he joked, then once again turned mischievous. "What did Zhu Di do? Point out the ugly truth of Zhu Yun-wen's questionable ancestry?"

Zheng He started to lose his patience with the chieftain's light banter.

"He beheaded two of Zhu Yun-wen's Senior Ministers and had them delivered to his door."

This left Chi Li Bu Hua speechless for only a brief moment. Then... he burst out with a boisterous laugh.

"That's the spirit!" he laughed heartily. "What a wonderful thing for Zhu Di to do!"

"They were assassins," Zheng He added, still not smiling.

"No doubt! And infrequent bathers as well, I'm sure," Chi Li Bu Hua added, while laughing uproariously.

"They had come under false pretenses," Zheng He told him firmly, refusing to take part in the chief's frivolous responses. "They came to murder the Commander of our army."

This remark caused Chi Li Bu Hua to finally grow silent, a concerned look on his face.

"These are dark times indeed, my friend. So, what course of action do you presume his devious nephew will take now?"

"He's sending his entire six-hundred thousand man army to destroy Beijing and kill Zhu Di."

"Has he no sense of humor?" Chi Li Bu Hua asked, again trying his best to wrest some wit from the absurdity of all this violence. "It's only two heads, from two ministers. Nothing will change."

Chi Li Bu Hua suddenly leaped up and began to pace the floor, something wild stirring within him.

"Zhu Di's army is no match for Zhu Yun-wen's Imperial legions. Now he must realize how I felt. Like a small feisty mouse facing an enraged tiger."

"That is why King Zhu Di has requested that you and your army join forces with him against Emperor Zhu Yun-wen."

Chi Li Bu Hua stopped his pacing and whirled around to face Zheng He.

"Accchhh!" he growled. "And then we would be two mice against the tiger! More for him to eat! There is no virtue in such a foolish pursuit. Our two armies combined would still be but a shadow of Zhu Yun-wen's huge force."

"But what if there were three?" Zheng He suggested.

"What?" the Chief asked, "Three armies?"

"Yes."

"Where could you possibly find another?"

"The army of Prince Ning," Zheng He replied with caution.

Chi Li Bu Hua stared at him in silence as he digested this curious suggestion. Then, suddenly, his response erupted like an explosion.

"HA!" he sneered. "Prince Ning wouldn't even sacrifice his own army to fight his brother. That's why he sent me, and my men. We were disposable."

Chi Li Bu Hua paced the room, rolling all this around in his mind. Then, he turned and looked hard at Zheng He.

"Tell me... what makes you think he would send his precious troops in service to Zhu Di?" He scoffed and walked in another quick circle, gesticulating with his arms, growing more agitated.

"And who would even be so bold... so insane!... to ask such a preposterous favor?"

"Zhu Di himself," Zheng He responded. "He's on his way to Prince Ning's palace now to make that very request."

Chi Li Bu Hua stopped pacing. All his energy subsided as he realized what had been set in motion.

"He'd better watch his head," Ch Li Bu Hua warned.

"King Zhu Di is accompanied by his Royal Guard," Zheng He countered quickly.

"Then they should all watch their heads."


King Zhu Di's carriage rumbled toward Prince Ning's palace accompanied both at the front and rear by a large contingent of armed Royal Guards. The carriage rolled to a stop at Ning's palace gate. High Administrator Wong was dispatched to greet the Head Palace Guard.

"Please inform Prince Ning that his brother, King Zhu Di, has arrived," the old administrator intoned solemnly.

There was a tense moment of indecision by the Palace Guard. Wong stared him down with a cold scowl. "Well? Shall I do it myself?"

Shaken from his indecision, the Guard hurried off to make the requested announcement. Wong clutched both his arthritic hands together, twisting the fingers nervously. He looked back toward Zhu Di's carriage, trying to summon a weak smile of confidence, but failing.

At this moment, no one was certain what the outcome of this reckless gamble might be. But at the Mongol palace, Chi Li Bu Hua had begun to formulate his own interpretation of what Prince Ning's reaction might be. And if he might be willing to risk his own head in such a foolhardy enterprise.

"If I were to accept," he mused carefully to Zheng He, "then we would have three mice challenging the savage tiger. It's still a suicidal plan. There is no way we could possibly win against the beast. What would we do? Command him to lie down? Maybe we could tell the tiger to remain sweet and still? Or perhaps, ask him not to bite?"

After a moment, Zheng He offered his own thoughts.

"The tiger is large and sometimes clumsy. The mice are small, but determined and fierce."

Now it was Zheng He's turn to pace about as he verbally began to create a stunning scenario using the chief's own metaphor.

"The mice would move quickly, running in circles around the big clumsy tiger. They would never stop their relentless pummeling. While one slept, the other two would continue to provoke and prod. Soon the tiger would grow exhausted by the continuous and

91

unpredictable attacks, always turning its head this way and that way... unsure from which direction the next assault would come. Confused and dazed, he would eventually stumble and fall. And then... the mice would pounce together, devouring their weakened rival."

Chi Li Bu Hua stared wide-eyed at Zheng He, amazed by his elaborately colorful tale.

"Ah-HAA!" he bellowed, sarcastically. "Did you dream up that fantastic tale in your own mind?"

"My grandfather fought alongside the great Kublai Khan," Zheng He told him evenly. "His tales of daring battles were well told, and I was a good listener."

Chi Li Bu Hua was beginning to see the logic in Zheng He's words. "It is a brilliant strategy, Zheng He, one that may well work. But will that fool Ning be wise enough to recognize its brilliance?"

The corridors of Prince Ning's palace were dark and cold. Zhu Di and Wong were escorted past a number of armed guards and a few curious observers. Large ornately decorated doors were swung open wide, revealing Prince Ning sitting regally upon his ornately decorated throne.

He glowered harshly at his brother, Zhu Di, and the High Administrator who stood nervously at his side. Tension filled the chamber as a heavy silence descended on them all.

But there was no tension at Chi Li Bu Hua's palace. The Mongol chieftain sat opposite Zheng He at a massive wooden table. He leaned forward, eyes glimmering with questions driven by years of experience and wisdom.

"I cannot believe that Prince Ning will ever agree to such a reckless venture," Chi Li Bu Hua stated. "Especially with a brother he despises so."

Zheng He's reply was direct and to the point, revealing a piece of the puzzle that had not yet been divulged. "A proposition will be put forth to Prince Ning. A proposition that he will not be able to refuse."

Chi Li Bu Hua smiled broadly. It was dawning on him that Zheng He had conceived this plan with great care and thought.

There were no royal courtesies extended between King Zhu Di and his brother, Prince Ning. All common civility and diplomacy were dispensed with. The only concern was the business at hand. Prince Ning leaned forward, the tone in his voice coldly dispassionate.

"And so, my brother... why have you chosen to pay me this unexpected visit?"

Zhu Di was about to respond when he glimpsed Commander Tu among the officers gathered around the prince. "I would like to speak with my brother, in private," Zhu Di stated firmly.

Commander Tu didn't move. And neither did the other officers and royal advisors.

"Alone!" Zhu Di demanded, his voice booming in the stone chamber.

Commander Tu stepped forward, addressing Prince Ning.

"That's not advisable, Sire. It wouldn't be safe."

"No, it isn't advisable," Zhu Di shot back. "And it isn't prudent. And it most definitely wouldn't be safe. But it is what will be!"

There was another uncomfortable pause as Prince Ning considered his options. Finally, he waved away his military protectors.

"Leave us." And looking directly at Commander Tu, the prince added, "All of you."

Commander Tu tried once again to object. "But, Your Majesty,"

"My brother and I will talk in private," Ning stated firmly and waved them away.

Commander Tu had no option. He bowed and reluctantly left the room with several of Prince Ning's ministers, officers and advisors. High Administrator Wong hesitated a moment, unsure if he should leave Zhu Di alone with his brother. But Zhu Di nodded his assent.

When the doors of the throne room were closed, Ning stood and spoke sharply to his brother.

"This is a reckless thing you do, coming here," Ning hissed. "After stealing all my best servants. Unless, of course, you've come to return them."

"I've come to make a request," Zhu Di told Ning sternly, unwilling to engage in political pretense.

"Of ME?" the prince replied sarcastically. "Now humor is your game."

But Zhu Di shows no amusement, remaining stone-faced. "I've come to issue a demand. Our dangerous nephew continues his charade as emperor..."

Prince Ning interrupted him curtly. "He was placed on the throne by public proclamation and certified by Imperial Council."

"They were all deceived," Zhu Di responded angrily. "It's a brash mockery of power and you know it! He should not be emperor."

"Perhaps," Prince Ning allowed cautiously, "but it's none of my concern."

"It is now," Zhu Di grumbled angrily. "Zhu Yun-wen gathers his troops to march upon Beijing."

Ning shifted uncomfortably on his throne. "That isn't my quarrel. My stronghold is here. What happens in Beijing is your problem."

"But if he should taste victory over me, I think you know that you will be next."

Prince Ning laughed. But it was uneasy laughter, born of insecurity and doubt. "That's ridiculous. Why would he want to attack me? I've done nothing to him."

"You have an army. Someday you could be a threat. That is enough for him." Zhu Di moved uncomfortably close to his brother, pressing a stiff finger into his chest for emphasis. "Zhu Yun-wen's only desire is to remain in power. At any cost. He would sacrifice you without hesitation."

Ning looked deep into his brother's eyes, troubled by these disturbing thoughts. Zhu Di pressed on with his demands. "I want your army to join mine in defense against this mad offspring of ours."

"Our two armies are no match for his," Ning shot back, seeking some way to avoid becoming embroiled in Zhu Di's dangerous proposal.

But Zhu Di already had a response to that concern. "We will also be joined by the Mongol Chieftain, Chi Li Bu Hua."

Prince Ning sat straight up, his face red with anger. "He's a cowardly scoundrel!" Ning spit the words out bitterly, still seething over Chi Li Bu Hua's recent defection. "That man is useless! He is a tyrant. You can't trust him!"

Zhu Di let his brother take a breath and then calmly presented his most convincing argument. "But he does have ten thousand warriors."

Still, Ning was not convinced. "He will run away at the slightest provocation."

"He will fight to the end if I ask him," Zhu Di countered forcefully.

Ning got up from his throne and started pacing restlessly, as he thought about what his brother wanted him to do. Finally, he turned to Zhu Di, his face livid with anger.

"NO! NO!" he shouted. "Not me! You're not going to get me, involved in 'your' problem. Not with my army! Not against my own nephew!"

Zhu Di moved around his obstinate brother, like a hawk circling its prey. Then, suddenly, without warning, Zhu Di lunged and grabbed Prince Ning by the throat. He shoved him back onto his throne, choking him with one hand and putting a sharp knife to his throat with the other.

"Listen to me, little brother. I'm tired of all your whining lies and pathetic excuses. You <u>will</u> join forces with me or I'll cut off your head and mount it on a stake for all to see!"

Ning's face began to turn red as he desperately gasped for breath. Zhu Di tightened his grip. An ugly sound of fear and panic gurgled up from somewhere within his brother's constricted larynx.

"Think fast," Zhu Di warned him. "I will not tolerate any lengthy consideration."

The king pressed his blade against Ning's throat. A thin line of blood appeared... and then, red rivulets began trickling toward his chest like small crimson rivers.

"Agree to fight beside me little brother or die a coward's death."

Ning desperately struggled to nod his affirmation, as tears and sweat mingled in his eyes. Zhu Di released his grip and shoved Ning away contemptuously. He glared down at his pathetic brother, who whimpered while clutching at his bleeding neck.

"You've made a wise choice." Zhu Di wiped a broad smear of damp, glistening blood on Prince Ning's royal raiment. "Today I let you live. Don't disappointment me tomorrow."


At the Mongol palace, Chi Li Bu Hua sat across from Zheng He, still musing about the details of this proposition. "If Prince Ning accepts, I have but one concern."

"What is that?" Zheng He asked, "Achieving victory?"

"No. Our victory is assured. Otherwise I would not agree to this madness. What troubles me is that I made a pledge to Zhu Di to never again align myself with Prince Ning. And, as you know... I am a man of my word."

"You will be joining forces with Zhu Di," Zheng He quickly assured the Chief, "not with Prince Ning. Zhu Di will strike his own agreement with the prince. They are separate. Have no worry. Your pledge is firm."

After a brief moment, Chi Li Bu Hua grinned.

"You are a juggler of fine points, my friend."

Then the chieftain rose to his feet, motioning to Zheng He. "Come... let's have some tea."

They moved to a cushioned alcove where tea was waiting. Both took a seat. The chieftain eyed Zheng He intently as he tried to decide whether to ask a question that had long been on his mind. Finally, he threw caution to the wind. "So, my friend... is it true that you are a eunuch?"

Zheng He reflected no surprise at the inquiry. Not even a blink of the eye. "Why do you ask?"

The chief shrugged. "You're a servant in the royal court of Zhu Di. All men who are in such a position, as I understand it, must be eunuchs. So therefore, I assumed..."

Chi Li Bu Hua smiled innocently, shrugging his shoulders. "But all eunuchs I have known are sweet and delicate souls, like flowers, with tittering voices that aggravate, and silly prancing ways. They are also small and fragile, while you are bold and strong, like a dragon."

Zheng He didn't respond, deepening the mystery for Chi Li Bu Hua. His expression remained pleasantly vacant and therefore impossible to interpret. The chieftain studied this fascinating young man, then added...

"Though, I must say, you do have a gentle, thoughtful side. A smooth, soft nature... like silk. Perhaps you are a silk dragon. Gentility and courage combined."

The chieftain gave Zheng He a questioning look, but maintained a twinkle in his eye, wondering if perhaps he had struck the incredible truth in describing his friend. But, as before, Zheng He simply smiled faintly and revealed nothing.

Chi Li Bu Hua took a sip of his tea and answered his own question.

"Accchh! It doesn't matter to me if you're a eunuch or a god! You are a man nonetheless."

Chi Li Bu Hua chugged the last of his tea, got to his feet and started pacing, thoroughly enjoying his own loquacious pontification. He waved his empty teacup at Zheng He as he continued.

"Besides, any man would be better off without that annoying encumbrance. Nothing to waggle about, getting in the way. Nothing to hang there, limply begging forgiveness. Nothing to vex us all our waking hours, taunting the ladies and terrifying other men. And think of it! There would be no need to ever compare, question or appraise if it's too big, or too small? No more struggling to stand at attention, trumpeting its false glory with disingenuous pride."

Chi Li Bu Hua looked at Zheng He to see if he was enjoying this creative rambling. When the royal servant smiled and waved for him to continue, he did.

"Besides, it hardens like stone at the most inopportune times, making sleep an uncomfortable proposition at best. Yes, I think we would be better off without it, freeing us from needless distraction, and finally affording us the glorious luxury of concentration. Without it we would possess what every woman desires in a man, a passionate disposition without that annoying protuberance to plague them with the burden of children."

Chi Li Bu Hua again turned to Zheng He and looked for his approval.

This time, Zheng He did not sit mute. He quickly pointed out a few errors in the chieftain's clever description of a eunuch's sexual paraphernalia.

"It's obvious, my friend, you are unaware that becoming a eunuch does not necessarily mean a male must have his 'annoying protuberance', as you describe it, removed, in order to work in the king's royal court. That's not true at all. It is true, however, that all male servants must be castrated, so they cannot create children. But that usually means their testicles are removed, or damaged, so they cannot produce sperm. So most eunuch servants do, in fact, retain their 'annoying protuberances'. And this enables them to sexually dally with other eunuchs, or, as is often the case, have frequent evening rendezvous with the king's personal concubines."

Chi Li Bu Hua was incredulous. "I've never heard of such a thing."

"Oh, yes," Zheng He continued. "You would be quite surprised at all the illicit scampering about that goes on after dark. If one is out late on honest business, it's almost impossible not to be overrun by a crowd of eunuchs flitting from one tryst to another."

Chi Li Bu Hua shook his head, dazzled by the wealth of arcane information that has been imparted.

"I am most grateful for you sharing your knowledge on such matters. But, in any case, it doesn't matter to me, what type of eunuch you are, or even if you are a eunuch? You are still my friend. And always will be."

Zheng He smiled and nodded his appreciation to Chi Li Bu Hua for his wonderfully entertaining monolog on a male's 'protuberance'... but most important, for his generous pledge of unconditional friendship."


One week later in Beijing, Monk Dao Yan made his way through a driving rainstorm to the unpretentious building that housed Zhu Di's private quarters. The wind was blowing so hard it had begun to rip tiles from the king's rooftop. One of the tiles shattered at Dao Yan's feet. He halted abruptly to look at the broken pieces with some trepidation, then carefully stepped over them and moved on.

When Dao Yan arrived at Zhu Di's residence, Chief Eunuch Wang led him into the king's private chamber as the harsh wind continued to howl outside. He found Zhu Di sitting in a chair beside a small fire, attempting to fend off the dank chill that had enveloped the room.

Dao Yan noticed that Zheng He was also present, standing near the king, attentive and quietly observant as always.

It had become obvious to the monk that Chief Eunuch Wang was envious of Zheng He's position as a member of Zhu Di's Inner Court. He had noticed the Chief Eunuch glaring at Zheng He unpleasantly on many occasions. But Wang always bowed courteously to the king as custom required, said nothing and quickly exited the room.

"Dao Yan," the king greeted him with a gracious wave, "I'm so grateful you have come to me on such a foul night. Please come join me by the fire."

The Monk nodded his appreciation and took an empty seat close to the warmth of the flames.

"It's no discomfort, Your Majesty," he allowed politely. "I'm pleased to be here."

Zhu Di sat in silence for a few moments, thinking, while staring glumly into the dancing flames.

Dao Yan wondered if something was wrong and cautiously ventured a question.

"Is something troubling you, Sire?"

"I haven't been able to sleep," he acknowledged softly, obviously worried.

Just then, a clattering of tiles could be heard blowing from the roof.

"Did you hear that noise?" Zhu Di asked. "Listen?"

Suddenly, there was a loud rumble of thunder, quickly followed by the harsh clattering of more tiles and a few soft crashes, as some of the clay tiles were sent spiraling to the ground.

Zhu Di continued. "Tiles are being blown from my roof, Dao Yan. I'm certain it's a very bad sign."

Dao Yan looked up toward the roof above them.

"It is an omen, Your Majesty. But perhaps..."

But Zhu Di interrupted him. "We can never defeat this emperor, even with our three armies joined. It's a foolish notion driven only by my selfish pride."

More thunder and clattering could clearly be heard above.

"Listen! There it is again! I'm sure it's a message from Lord Buddha that we will not prevail."

Dao Yan considered what King Zhu Di had just said, and saw a chance to bid for peace.

"Perhaps, Sire, this presents an opportunity to reconsider your course of action. Surrender and peace, though sometimes undesirable in its dire circumstance, may be the wise path to choose."

Another gust of wind and devilish clattering of tiles could be heard from above. The two men looked nervously toward the ominous sound. Zheng He remained silent at his position in the shadows, his eyes calmly observing both Zhu Di and Monk Dao Yan.

"They plague me like stampeding horses!" Zhu Di moaned. "How can I sacrifice my people without a struggle? They look to me for strength."

Zhu Di hung his head, staring at the flickering light from the fire that danced on the stone floor. His burden of responsibility was becoming heavier each day, weighed down by a growing fear and superstition.

Feeling sympathy for the troubled king, Dao Yan reached out and gently touched Zhu Di's head with his fingers, hoping that this gesture would offer some solace.

"I will leave you, Your Majesty, to allow you time for contemplation. I'm certain Lord Buddha will guide your decision."

Dao Yan got up from his chair and bowed slightly. Then, with a quick glance toward Zheng He, took his leave into the stormy night.

When the Monk had left, Zheng He stepped toward Zhu Di, who remained sitting silently in his chair.

"If I may, Your Majesty," he started softly, "I propose that you may have misread the signs."

Zhu Di raised his head and looked up at Zheng He with puzzlement.

"Misread the signs?" he asked, slightly annoyed. "These cursed tiles continue to leave my roof even as we speak! The signs cannot be more obvious!"

"Your blue tiles, Sire, are being blown away," Zheng He explained, "so that there will be space for new yellow tiles. Only the emperor is allowed to cover his roof with yellow tiles."

Zheng He stood silent for a moment, allowing Zhu Di time to grasp the logic of this argument. And then he added, "You see... it is not an omen of impending doom, Sire. It is an omen of your impending victory. I am sure of it."

Zhu Di abruptly found himself overwhelmed with emotion. He reached out and clutched Zheng He's arm with a mighty grip. As tears of relief slipped from the corners of Zhu Di's eyes, he whispered gratefully, "Yes, Zheng He. My victory."


Later that same night, Zheng He and Xi Chen took advantage of the foul weather to meet again in the garden. This time, they chose a wooden storage shed near the back of the garden in which to hold their secret rendezvous. The wind had slackened somewhat, but the rain continued to fall in torrents. One small candle provided a faint light for them, reducing the risk that they would be discovered.

Even in the dim light, it was clear to Zheng He that Xi Chen was deeply troubled by something. Not wanting to pressure her with annoying questions, he chose instead to sit quietly for a few moments and wait for her to reveal what was on her mind. After a long period of silence, she finally spoke.

"You're going to be in great danger, Ma He," she began, her voice trembling slightly. "The army of General Ho is so huge."

Zheng He slipped around her soft, delicate body, holding her close to his chest.

"My name used to be Ma He, but now it's Zheng He."

Xi Chen turned to look into his eyes, incredulous. "I've heard people calling you Zheng He and wondered why? You don't answer to the name Ma He anymore? Why is that?"

When I was asked to be a servant in Zhu Di's royal court, I became the king's personal property. Zheng means 'prudent' in Chinese. For some reason, he must have felt that I was, indeed, prudent. So he changed my name to Zheng He. There is nothing I can do about it. He is my king."

He turned to look at her eyes, which now seemed saddened by this revelation. "Will it be so hard for you to call me Zheng He? Whether Ma He or Zheng He, I'm still the same person who loves you."

Xi Chen thought about this for a long moment, then forced a halfhearted smile. "You're right. It doesn't matter what people call you. But you will always be Ma He to me. And I will never stop worrying about your safety."

Zheng He took her face in his hands and started covering her neck and cheek with little kisses. This was his way of demonstrating that there wasn't anything for her to worry about. But kisses and embraces had little effect on Xi Chen on this rainy evening. She abruptly pulled away, obviously irritated.

"Stop it, Ma He... or Zheng He... or whatever your name is," she said sharply, holding his two hands in hers so that he couldn't continue the caresses. "This is serious! Now's not the time to be playing with me like a helpless little kitten. I am frightfully worried about losing you again. Maybe this time, forever!"

"You're getting yourself upset about nothing. This battle will just be another battle. I have seen many."

Xi Chen turned her back on him and pouted. "But this may be the last battle you will see. And this time you may not come back to me. Now that I have you, I can't bear to lose you again."

Zheng He grew impatient with all this sad talk. He was so delighted to finally be alone with Xi Chen in the darkness with the rain beating down outside. He had no interest in depressing talk of what could go wrong. He leaned closer and whispered seductively in her ear.

"I will come back to you, because my trust is in Allah. It is HE, who will deliver me back to you."

Zheng He gently fondled Xi Chen's breast, softly kissing her ear. Dismayed, she pushed him away.

"You're impossible," she complained angrily. "You're no different than when we were children. Always playing games!"

"We're alone, Xi Chen. We're together. I don't want to talk of death and battles. I want to love you and kiss you, just like I did when you were my Little Flower."

Xi Chen turned back to Zheng He, touching his cheek tenderly with one finger, gazing longingly into his strong dark eyes.

"You haven't called me Little Flower for a very long time. It reminds me of how things were between us before everything changed."

Zheng He stroked her hair, lovingly. "Yes, many things have changed, Xi Chen. But loving you isn't one of them. I still want desperately to make love to you."

Her eyes widened at this bold statement. "You want to make love to me?"

"With all my heart..." He hesitated, the words trapped in his throat. "But we can't..."

"If you care for me as you say..."

Zheng He put his finger to her lips, stopping her.

"We can't because... we are both servants to Zhu Di. It is not allowed."

"But King Zhu Di doesn't even know that I exist!" she protested. "And it is not his concern. Our love is between us. It has nothing to do with the king."

"I wish it were that simple, Xi Chen. But as servants in the palace, we are not allowed..."

Tears filled her eyes. "You care more about this king than about us," she said, a terrible throb of intense pain filling her soul.

She pulled herself from his arms and struggled to get to her feet. Zheng He grabbed her by the wrist, pulling her back down. "Wait, Xi Chen..."

"No!" She shouted, suddenly slapping him hard across the face.

Stunned, Zheng He released his grip, staring into her eyes, confused by the harsh reaction.

With a painful whimper, Xi Chen leaped to her feet and dashed out into the rain and away in the night.

Zheng He touched his burning cheek. He felt the sharp sting of Xi Chen's hand in the very depths of his heart.

At the king's palace, Commander Tan entered the throne room and walked directly towards Zhu Di with great purpose. He hated to interrupt the ruler's meeting with his advisors, but what he had to report was of extreme importance.

Prince Han circled Tan suspiciously, casting a sour look of concern at High Administrator Wong.

Commander Tan bowed to Zhu Di. "Excuse the interruption, Your Majesty, but there are reports that the emperor's army is only four day's march from our city gates."

Zhu Di clicked his tongue confidently, unfazed by this news. "We are prepared. Please alert Commander Tu and Prince Ning. I want them here at once. Zheng He will review our strategy for confronting the enemy."

Commander Tan gave Zheng He a curious look, surprised at the level of authority being delegated to this servant.

Prince Han was also taken aback. He stepped toward Zhu Di, strongly registering his objection. "But, father... how can you?... He is but a lowly servant."

Zhu Di cut him off with a wave of his hand. "Zheng He will act as my military liaison. And he will be as fully authorized as an officer in my army."

Prince Han stood in stunned silence. Such a radical decision seemed uncharacteristic even for his father.

Zhu Di ignored his son's shocked reaction, turning his attention instead to Commander Tan.

"Cheng He's instructions of engagement will be followed precisely to the letter. Do I make myself absolutely clear, Commander?"

"Yes, Your Majesty," Commander Tan responded with a reluctant bow.

"Father, I think that..." Prince Han attempted to interject. But his words were immediately severed by Zhu Di.

"I want you to remain here at the palace."

"But, father, I must..." Zhu Di raised his hand, cutting him off sharply once again. "If Zhu Yun-wen's army defeats us, I want you to destroy the palace. Burn it to the ground, so that theirs is an empty victory. I'm depending on you to do this, my son. Do you understand me?"

Prince Han nodded with reluctance.

As the last day of summer drew to a close, General Ho arrayed his massive, six-hundred-thousand-man army on the battlefield outside of Beijing. He was anxious to meet Zhu Di's meager forces face-to-face, so he could annihilate them quickly and receive the expected accolades from his emperor. However, much to the general's amazement and chagrin, Zhu Di's army was nowhere to be seen.

"What is it with this cowardly king?" Ho growled to his officers. "Does he wish only to hide in his palace like a mouse and await death? This spineless monarch makes it much too easy for us."

An Imperial Officer stepped forward, asking General Ho what plan of action he would like to take.

The General gave his officer a stern look. "I'm going to do what I should have done two weeks ago. I'm going to attack Zhu Di's palace at Beijing."

This caught the officer off balance. "Attack the palace?"

"Yes. In the morning. At first light. I'm tired of just sitting here on an empty battlefield, waiting for him to reveal himself. Perhaps our imminent approach will rouse these cowards from their slumber and inspire a desperate defense. What a shame it would be if we didn't get an opportunity to slaughter at least a few thousand of them in tribute to our glorious emperor."

It never crossed General Ho's mind that Zhu Di might be intending to unleash some extraordinary battle strategy that could prove troublesome to his army. He was quite certain there was no way the king's puny forces could do anything but delay the tragic inevitable.

But on that very evening, after almost two weeks of waiting... everything changed.

General Ho's soldiers slept soundly in their tents. Fires had burned to embers and were now glowing softly in the silent darkness.

A few sentries guarded the perimeter, but at this late hour, most were on the verge of dozing off.

One sentry noticed that the shadowy hills seemed to be undulating softly, rising and falling like waves. He stared at the outline of oscillating hills and blinked his eyes, trying to clear his head, thinking that his lack of sleep was creating the curious vision.

Suddenly, silently, not far away, a lone knife slit the throat of a sentry who dozed at his post. As his lifeless body was lowered to the ground, Zheng He motioned for fifty of his men to slip quietly into the unguarded area and steal toward a row of more than one hundred tents.

Stealthily, the men slipped into the tents with their knives, spears and axes to begin their brutal slaughter. Little was heard except for a few soft moans of pain and the occasional thud of an axe being buried deep into the backs and chests of Ho's sleeping soldiers. Then, like a silent wind, Zheng He and his men slipped away, darkness covering their retreat.

The next morning, ten senior officers were lined up inside General Ho's tent, victims of his fury.

"Who's responsible for this?" he bellowed.

The officers stood frozen, afraid to move.

"Speak up!" General Ho screamed.

Still, none of them spoke.

"Three hundred of my troops were killed!" General Ho thundered. "And no one has any idea who was responsible?"

The imperial general walked up to each of the trembling officers and gave him a withering look.

"If this EVER happens again," he threatened, "one of you will lose your HEAD!"

General Ho started to walk away. The men relaxed, thinking they had escaped any more chastisement. But then, unexpectedly, the general spun around and strode back to them.

"Double the guard," he snarled. "Dig more defensive trenches. And gentlemen, whatever you do... no one sleeps!
If we are surprised again, one of you will lose his head."

There was no more talk from General Ho about invading Beijing.

That afternoon, thousands upon thousands of the general's troops were put to work digging defensive trenches. Up and down the line, nervous officers shouted a continuous litany of orders to their men.

"If I see any of you sleeping tonight, I'll personally take your head as a trophy!" the general exclaimed with constant regularity.

That night, General Ho's men remained wide awake in their newly dug trenches, weapons at the ready, waiting expectantly for Zhu Di's attack.

Officers moved among the men all night long shouting commands. "Stay awake! Stay alert! The province king is out there. He's coming! Be ready for him!"

Zhu Di was most certainly out there, but he was not coming. While General Ho's men struggled to stay awake, Zhu Di's men were enjoying a good night's rest. While the men slept, Zhu Di and Zheng He talked about the previous night's activity.

"You did well." Zhu Di grinned. "Our men are sleeping like babies, while our enemy waits for an attack that will never come."

Zheng He also grinned. "General Ho's troops are going to have many sleepless nights, Your Majesty. I suggest we wait three or four nights, then strike at them from the rear, where they have no trenches."

"Just be careful," the province king warned. "There's no need to be hasty. The one thing we have on our side is time. Let's use it wisely to our best advantage."

Four nights later, the forces of General Ho were totally exhausted. As Zheng He had predicted, far to the rear of the imperial forces, no trenches had been dug, but there were numerous guards. Unfortunately for them, they were so exhausted that they could barely stand on their feet.

An officer passed among them issuing orders. "Take turns sleeping if you have to," he shouted in a voice made hoarse by exhaustion. "But somebody must always remain awake."

"They won't come here," one soldier moaned, leaning heavily on his bow for support. "The battle lines are far away. Please, Sir, we need to sleep."

"NO!" The officer rebuked him harshly. "You will remain awake! I'm not going to lose my head just because a bunch of weaklings think they need to sleep!"

"But, Sir!" the man begged.

"DO AS I SAY!" the officer screamed, and slapped the soldier across the face. "Stay awake and you have a chance to continue living. Sleep... and you will sleep forever!"

It was another long and torturous night for General Ho's troops. The camp was silent, except for a constant grumbling that could be heard among the soldiers. Off in the distance, periodic shouts of officers could be heard, extolling their men to push themselves further, harder, longer.

The men did their best to remain awake, but it soon became an impossible situation. Many fell asleep on their feet, still holding their weapons. Those, who managed to remain awake, did so out of shear, unnatural determination. But most of the men stared blankly out into the pitch-black darkness, their minds no longer able to function normally.

Two soldiers slapped each other's faces in a desperate attempt to comply with General Ho's orders.

"Hit me harder," one man begged the other. But his fatigued comrade was of little help. "I can't stay awake, myself," he confessed. "I must sleep. Just for a few minutes." Gradually, both men allowed their eyes to close, overcome by total exhaustion.

Just before first light, the heads of the two sleeping men were jerked back violently and their throats cut. Blood gushed out in thick ugly streams, quickly staining the ground at the men's feet.

Chi Li Bu Hua's warriors draped in dark animal skins and cloaked in furs, moved like invisible spirits through the massive camp, slaying with silent efficiency. When an alarm was finally sounded, it was too late. As before, almost all of Chi Li Bu Hua's men were able to slip away into the misty darkness and vanish like phantoms.

General Ho was filled with uncontrolled rage. He lined up his surviving officers and threatened all of them with their lives.

"I warned you" he screamed, "and now you're going to pay."

A frightened officer stepped forward and offered a quick bow to General Ho.

"General, I beg you, my men must sleep. There's no way they can..."

Without saying a word, General Ho pulled a large blade from a scabbard at his waist and swung it with lethal precision. In an instant, the officer's head was sliced from his body and fell to the ground in front of the others. Ho kicked the man's severed head across the muddy earth, leaving a bloody trail behind it.

The terrified officers stepped back from the crazed general, eyeing his bloody sword.

"All right," Ho growled, ominously. "Who's going to disobey my orders next?"

The cowering officers were frozen in sheer terror.

"Return to your posts," General Ho hissed. "And cherish your heads. For if another soldier dies tomorrow, your own head will follow him in tribute."

The following morning, massive search parties were sent out on horseback to comb the hills and valleys for signs of Zhu Di's elusive army.

Suddenly, a scout appeared from a canyon and shouted for everyone to follow. "I think I have found them! This way! This way!"

Immediately, officers shouted frantic orders. Nearly five hundred sleepy-eyed soldiers dutifully followed on horseback, most so tired that they struggled with great difficulty to keep from falling from their mounts.

As the ragged contingent of General Ho's soldiers entered the canyon, three figures observed them from a cluster of rocks on a distant high ledge. Zheng He, King Zhu Di and Chief Chi Li Bu Hua were pleased at how easily their trap had been set.

Chu Li Bu Hua laughed softly to himself. "They have no idea that they are riding into a dead-end canyon. It would be so easy to slaughter them. Too easy."

King Zhu Di nodded. "When they return empty handed General Ho will do it for us."

"Yes, yes," Chi Li Bu Hua said with cruel irony. "I'm sure he will have them boiled in oil for wasting their day in empty pursuit."

Zheng He's strategy was working even better than he had expected. "General Ho is hoping we will confront him directly in a mighty battle. But that would not be to our advantage. We must take his army apart piece by piece."

Chi Li Bu Hua laughed. "Like being nibbled to death by ducks."

"We will strike from the other direction tonight," Cheng He said. "They are at the end of their tether. The mice are about to devour the tiger."


Later that evening, the five remaining imperial officers made their reports to a disgruntled General Ho.

"We looked everywhere," one officer stated with certainty. "There can be no doubt, general. Your remarkable army has frightened King Zhu Di's pathetic forces into hiding."

General Ho glared at the officer, not so easily fooled. "An empty canyon does not necessarily signify a victory. It can be easily seen as a failure on the part of you and your men to accomplish your mission." General Ho grasped the handle of his sword. The officer trembled.

But at that moment, a soldier approached General Ho, bowing with deference. He held a message in his shaking fingers. General Ho took the paper and quickly read it. Angered, he crumpled the message and threw into the faces of the startled officers.

"Our emperor has just issued me an ultimatum," he announced with a displeased hiss. "He has stated that I must find and destroy King Zhu Di... or I will personally suffer the consequences."

General Ho moved a step closer to his frightened officers. They could see that his hand was wrapped tightly around the handle of his long sword. "I don't like it when the emperor threatens ME!" he roared. "King Zhu Di is making a fool of us... but I will be the one who must pay. Do any of you realize what that means?"

The earth rumbled beneath their feet. General Ho looked off, a shadow of deep concern darkening his face. The officers turned to look toward the distant horizon.

Suddenly, chaos enveloped them. A frantic voice arose from the ranks of soldiers as they began to scatter in every direction. "It's King Zhu Di! He's attacking!"

General Ho and his officers rushed to their horses and quickly mounted. They galloped toward the distant sound of thundering cannons, past the rows of tents and staggering soldiers. In the distance, they could see the unmistakable glow of burning fires.

When General Ho and the officers arrived at the top of a broad hill, they encountered the staggering aftermath of a battle that had already ended.

Scattered before them were the dead and dying bodies of more than two thousand imperial soldiers. Wounded horses flailed helplessly on the ground amid the smoking tents and bloody soldiers.

General Ho saw very few enemy dead scattered among the ravaged corpses of his own men. He leaped from his horse and withdrew his sword, the long blade still stained with the dried blood of his officer.

"Who's in charge here?" he screamed, spinning around, eyes scanning the twisted bodies. But no answer came from the horrible tableau of carnage.

General Ho stumbled through the wounded and the dead, searching for anyone with a pulse who would accept responsibility for this catastrophe.

"I want to know who's in charge!" he screamed hoarsely.

A bleeding officer staggered forward, clutching a gaping wound. "Everyone was awake, Sir," he stammered. "Everyone was prepared."

"Then how did they surprise you?"

"They didn't surprise us, sir. They just... overwhelmed us."

General Ho embraced a façade of extreme calm, measuring his words precisely, biting them off crisply between gritted teeth.

"They... overwhelmed you. We still have five hundred thousand troops... and King Zhu Di 'overwhelmed' you with his pathetic little group of stumbling oafs? Is that what you are telling me?"

The wounded officer winced in pain, clutching his wound desperately, trying to stem the flow of blood. He managed to nod and squeeze out a grating whisper. "Yes, sir."

What came next was so sudden and rapid that it was barely visible to the naked eye. General Ho raised his sword and slashed with devastating power and brutality, cleanly severing the officer's head with a single cut.

He picked up the officer's bloody head, dangling it by the hair and holding it up high for all to see. "This is what he has done to us!" he screamed. "I want Zhu Di's head! I want you to bring me the head of the king!"

At nightfall, Zhu Di held a conference with all of his close supporters in his command tent. Commander Tan, Monk Dao Yan, Zheng He, Chi Li Bu Hua, Prince Ning and a number of his senior military officers were all present.

I had also been invited to join them on the battlefield and was allowed to be present at this critical gathering.

"I'm extremely pleased that everything has been going so well," Zhu Di told them with enthusiasm. "Thanks to some very clever tactical maneuvers conceived by Chieftain Chi Li Bu Hua and Zheng He, we have been able to elude General Ho's forces for more than two months, while exacting a heavy toll on his vast army. If our estimates are correct, we have decimated nearly half of the general's fighting force."

Zhu Di turned to Zheng He, motioning to him with great appreciation. "It's obvious that Zheng He's battle plans have been working even better than we could imagine."

He paused, becoming solemn. "But now the time has come for us to teach General Ho a final lesson." He turned to Zheng He, motioning for him to come to his side. "Zheng He, would you now please describe to everyone how we intend to deliver our final, decisive assault."

Zheng He nodded gratefully and approached a large map that had been suspended from the inner wall of the tent.

"Tomorrow, General Ho will finally get his wish," Zheng He began, smiling. "We will confront him on the field of battle."

While describing the action to be taken, Zheng He pointed out specific locations on the map and indicated the tactical movements that would take place at each one.

"Half of King Zhu Di's army will align themselves here on the far ridge. Half of the warriors under Chief Chi Li Bu Hua's command will gather here... to the north of the valley and half of the men under the command of Prince Ning will position themselves on the south side, here."

Zheng He turned to face those gathered before him. They leaned forward, anxious to see the next step of the assault plan unfold.

"When General Ho sees the contingent of soldiers lined up on the ridge, I'm quite certain he will be so anxious to get his hands on us that he will blindly go on the attack."

The men stirred with excitement, beginning to see a strange logic taking shape is this curious strategy.

"As this frontal assault begins, our three armies, which are, as you recall, at half strength... will slowly fall back feigning defeat."

Another stirring of excited murmurs among the men.

"But you must take special care," Zhu Di warned, "that your troops make it appear absolutely real. Unfortunately, many may be killed in the fighting. But that is the price we must pay for ultimate victory."

Zhu Di stepped over to the map. "I'll be located here, on this slight rise. Upon my signal, you will retreat steadily and deliberately into this large gorge... here. Zheng He will be waiting on the high ground above with the remaining half of our soldiers."

Zheng He continued. "When General Ho's forces follow our retreating army into the gorge, we will be waiting for him. Commander Tan will position the other half of Zhu Di's troops, here, up high, on this side of the gorge."

He turned to the Mongol Chieftain Chi Li Bu Hua. "Your senior officer, Commander Tu, will position the other half of your troops, also in concealed positions, up high, on this other side of the gorge."

Chi Li Bu Hua nodded his agreement. "I believe we can handle that," he said with a broad smile, prompting laughter from the others.

Zheng He then looked to the King's rebellious brother. "And Prince Ning... the positioning of your army is the most critical of all. When General Ho's troops are deep inside the canyon, your army must move into position here, at the mouth of the canyon, and block any possible retreat."

Prince Ning nodded. "I will be pleased to seal their fate."

"As you can see, from the top of the canyon wall, we will be in a perfect position to send a steady rain of death and destruction upon the remainder of General Ho's troops. For him, there will be no escape. There will be no place to run. No place to hide! General Ho and his imperial army will be soundly defeated."

A heavy silence fell over the group of men as they considered the daring strategy. No one spoke. There was barely a breath taken. Finally, it was Zhu Di who broke the silence.

"On the map, everything looks easy. On the field of battle, I assure you, it will be quite different. General Ho still has many more troops than we have... and therefore we must logically conclude that he continues to have a serious advantage over us."

When I heard Zhu Di say this, I could contain myself no longer and loudly spoke up. I leaped to my feet and gave a cursory bow toward the king.

"Begging your pardon, Sire, but I'm afraid I must disagree"

A nervous murmur was heard among the men. Zhu Di looked perplexed at my unexpected interruption, but also amused.

"You disagree?" he asked, having no idea what it was I was about to challenge.

"Yes, Your Majesty," I said respectfully, allowing a wide grin to spread across my face. "I believe it is <u>we</u> who have the advantage."

Everyone in the room began looking at me like I was crazy.

"Is that so?" King Zhu Di said with a small grin, anxious to hear my observation.

"May I remind you, Sire, that we have, not one, but THREE prophets on our side; Lord Buddha, Mohammed and Christ Jesus. From my perspective, I'd say we have a three-to-one advantage over General Ho."

Everyone began to laugh uproariously at my brash, but absolutely accurate, statement. Even Prince Ning broke his normally foul countenance and grinned broadly. Eventually he was even heard laughing and repeating my words to others.

I do know for certain that King Zhu Di must have enjoyed what I said, for he good-naturedly slapped me on the back and immediately called for the servants to "bring us wine!"

And they did. Much wine.

By first light, the three smaller armies had taken their appointed positions on the battlefield. Cannons had been rolled into place and thousands of rocket arrows loaded into their launchers. To the rear, supply wagons filled with extra water and ammunition waited for the command to be brought forward.

With flags flying and thousands of armed men positioned on horseback, Zhu Di's troops were fully prepared to face the imperial forces of General Ho in one, final, life and death struggle for victory.

General Ho had been alerted by one of his scouts just before daybreak that the army of King Zhu Di was approaching over the eastern ridge. The general quickly ordered his massive forces to assemble and prepare for battle. The moment that he had been anticipating so long was nearly upon him. He relished the idea of finally facing Zhu Di's inferior forces... and decimating them.

General Ho watched from a small hill overlooking the battlefield. All preparations had been completed.

"We have him now," General Ho crowed with cruel delight. "There's no way for him to escape me now. I swear before Lord Buddha that this province king will crawl to me on his knees and beg for mercy before the day is through."

A senior officer halted his mount before General Ho and saluted smartly. "Sir! They await us on the far hill. May I order the charge?"

Ho stared across the valley, pleased at the destiny he envisioned for himself on this day. "Let their blood flow. Do it now!"

The senior officer motioned to the ranks. A moment later, fifty trumpets could be heard loudly heralding the start of the momentous assault. Before the trumpets had faded, a dozen imperial officers shouted, "Forward!" and General Ho's huge imperial army began to move like a massive sprawling beast.

With flags whipping in the breeze, horses and men charged across the muddy earth. Chariots were brutally shaken by the rough terrain. The warriors held bows and spears at the ready, prepared to engage and annihilate the enemy.


Zhu Di sat upon his handsome horse at the front of his own lines, waiting patiently for the approaching hoards. Chief Chi Li Bu Hua and Prince Ning, also on horses, watched from vantage points with their own armies. The earth shook below as thundering horses and chariots rumbled steadily toward them.

Zhu Di sat still as a stone, filled with a calmness he had not felt for a long time. "Wait for my signal," he ordered with soft assurance.

Finally, just before the imperial army was upon them, Zhu Di screamed the command they were waiting for... "ATTACK!"

The two armies came together in one, cataclysmic clash of men and animals. The noise was deafening as thousands of shouting men were thrust together in a monumental struggle for survival.

While the men engaged in vicious hand-to-hand combat, cannons fired heavy balls of steel at point blank range. Arrows filled the sky. Swords clashed upon swords. Blood cascaded from thousands of horrible, gaping wounds. The screams of men, mortally wounded and maimed, filled the smoke thickened air.

Hundreds of chariots and wagons were set ablaze by a steady rain of fire arrows. The flames quickly spread to the dead carcasses of both men and animals. This growing conflagration caused a noxious smell that permeated the nostrils of those still living and fighting for their lives.

After an extended period of vicious life-or-death combat, Zhu Di issued the second command his army had been waiting to hear.

"FALL BACK!" he screamed, as loudly as he could, while two signalmen waved large red flags that could easily be seen by Zhu Di's forces on the battlefield.

"FALL BACK! FALL BACK!" could be heard repeatedly, as the three small armies, slowly, but purposefully, began to give ground to General Ho's imperial forces. Wagons, chariots and horses turned and began to retreat toward the rocky gorge in the distance.

Watching the battle from his sheltered vantage point on the hill, General Ho and his senior officers could see Zhu Di's large flags waving and his forces falling back.

General Ho's senior commander watched this sudden turn with smug excitement. "Congratulations, general! The king's army is already retreating! Look at them! The victory is yours!"

General Ho could also see what was happening and roared his hearty approval. "The victory is mine, Commander! And the army of Zhu Di will be wiped from the face of the earth!"

Another officer stepped forward and shouted his support as well. "Let's drink a toast, General. To victory!"

"I'll give you better than a toast," General Ho roared back, thrusting his fist into the air. "I make a solemn vow. Before this day is through, I shall personally cut the head from Zhu Di's body!"

The officers raised their own clinched fists and shouted allegiance to the seemingly victorious general.


Zhu Di's forces had nearly filled the rocky gorge, trying desperately to fend off the attacking army of General Ho. From Zheng He's position on the upper slopes of the canyon, he had an expansive vantage point from which to view the two clashing armies as they pushed deeper into the canyon below.

He felt the nervous anticipation of the soldiers around him, raising his hand as a cautionary gesture. "Wait..." he warned them. "Let's not be overly hasty. We must be certain they are deep within the canyon walls before we close the door behind them"

Six archers stood in position nearby, arrows perched precariously in their bows, waiting tensely for the signal. Zheng He slowly raised his arm, waiting. Then, at the perfect moment, he brought his arm down with a powerful flourish.

"NOW!" he screamed.

The archers ignited the tips of their fire arrows and shot them high into the sky. The six feathered missiles arched gracefully across the canyon, leaving a trail of ominous smoke across the sky. It's as though the clouds are being slashed open, Zheng He thought to himself, and death is about to rain down upon the evil and the unjust.

In the wake of the menacing signal, a murderous barrage of arrows and cannon fire poured down upon General Ho's troops from both sides of the steep canyon walls. Equality ruled the conflagration. Soldiers, horses, servants, slaves and imperial officers... all suffered the same devastating fate.

Before General Ho's troops could attempt a frantic retreat, Prince Ning's army had moved into position and boxed them in, effectively sealing their fate. The slaughter went on for nearly three hours. When it was over, little was left of General Ho's once invincible Imperial army.

Zheng He, King Zhu Di and Chieftain Chi Li Bu Hua gazed down at the terrible carnage below.

"Those who are still alive have scattered like frightened birds to the wind," Chi Li Bu Hua noted without irony.

Zheng He nodded. "They no longer have the will to fight."

"Shall we hunt them down?" the chieftain asked Zhu Di.

"Let them run. Their loyalty has been compromised. Soon they will be begging to join with us."

The Mongol chieftain turned to Zheng He and slapped his shoulder with proud gusto.

"You were right, my friend. The vicious little mice have eaten the tiger."

"Only the tiger's shadow," Zhu Di corrected. "We are not finished. We must now march on Nanking. The tiger himself is in hiding."


Indeed, when Emperor Zhu Yun-wen learned the news of his army's devastating defeat, he retreated into hiding, consumed by panic and dread. There was no question what would happen now. Zhu Di would be coming for him and he knew it.

"Guards!" he screamed, running frantically through the palace halls. "Fortify the palace. I demand you protect me with your lives!"

The terrified emperor spied a group of guards and servants huddled together in a darkened corridor. They had already heard the terrible news of the slaughter and word was spreading like a wildfire through the palace.

Zhu Yun-wen pushed his way into the group, frantically shouting commands. "You must protect me," he demanded. "It is your responsibility to the throne. To ME!" No one moved.

"Protect me... or I'll have you KILLED!"

No one responded. They had lost all interest in helping a leader who had lost his authority... and his sanity.

"Did you hear me?" he screamed. "Save me! Or you will DIE!"

No one moved. One by one the guards and servants turned away, disappearing down the darkened corridor, leaving the emperor alone to face his demons.

"You will all be punished!" he shouted. His words echoed back to him. "I WILL DESTROY ALL OF YOU!"

He crouched against the stone wall, shrinking to his knees, tears of apprehension and regret washing his cheeks.


Outside the city gates of Nanking, Zhu Di sat on his glorious white stallion with the rigid pride of a conquering hero. He slowly turned and issued an order to General Ho.

"Open the city gates, general. Or the siege of Nanking will rest on your head."

The impressive quartet of Zhu Di, Zheng He, Chi Li Bu Hua and Prince Ning watched with muted gratification as the defeated general struggled by himself to push open the heavy gates to Nanking.

"Save the city," Zhu Di shouted to his men, "but burn Zhu Yun-wen's palace to the ground!"

The three armies surged forward through the widening portal, shouting and yelling with pent-up rage and seething vengeance. They stormed onto the palace grounds and sent thousands upon thousands of flaming fire arrows into Emperor Zhu Yun-wen's private sanctuary.

Inside the palace, the raging fire spread quickly from curtains and lines to anything that would burn. Zhu Yun-wen, now virtually alone, ran through the rising smoke and flames screaming empty threats to servants and ministers who were no longer there. All of them had long abandoned him, finally seeking freedom from his senseless tyranny.

"If you don't save me," he continued shouting, "I'll have all of you killed! I warn you! Save me or you will die!"

Completely insane now, Zhu Yun-wen sought safety in the false security of his throne room. Within minutes he was consumed by the righteous flames of victory.


At a joyous celebration held in a provisional palace in Nanking, Zhu Di was crowned Third Ming Emperor of China.

After the formal celebrations had been completed, Zhu Di happily invited Zheng He, Commander Tan, Monk Dao Yan and me to a private gathering, so we could relax together and ruminate on our recent victory. The room was small and much less formal than Zhu Di's beautiful throne room in Beijing. But since the palace had been destroyed, at his direct order, he had no choice but to make do with whatever temporary quarters he could find there.

As the new emperor looked around at his unsatisfactory surroundings, he shook his head sadly. "It's not much to look at," he acknowledged, "but at least we're alive."

All those in attendance muttered their firm agreement with this positive observation.

"I must admit Friar Odoric was correct. Buddha, Mohammed and Jesus did give us the advantage we needed."

Everyone smiled, laughed and clapped spontaneously, including me. When the silence once again enveloped us, Zhu Di offered a more serious commitment.

"Under my rein as Third Ming Emperor, you can be assured that all people of China will be encouraged to practice their own religion... without limitation or persecution."

There was an audible affirmation from those present. Then, wishing to make a comment, Commander Tan rose to his feet and bowed politely.

"Please excuse me for interrupting, Your Majesty, but I'd like to know what you plan to do about Zhu Yun-wen's burned palace? I don't believe these temporary accommodations are at all suitable for the new emperor of China."

"They may not be suitable," Zhu Di agreed, smiling, "but I'm afraid we'll have to put up with them for the time being. I plan to leave Zhu Yun-wen's palace just as it is... so it will remind others of my fearful retribution should they entertain any thought of plotting against me."

The room sat heavy for a long moment as this threat penetrated the hearts of each man. Then, as if letting in a soft breeze of relief, Zhu Di burst into laughter at his portentous words. Within an instant the weighty gloom departed and the new emperor was joined in lighthearted laughter by Commander Tan, followed by Zheng He and all the others as well.

When the merriment subsided, Zheng He stepped from his position just off to the side of Zhu Di's throne and bowed.

"Since you plan to stay here in Nanking, Sire, perhaps I should arrange for your servant staff to be transferred from Beijing to Nanking. I'm not sure how loyal Zhu Yun-wen's staff will be in serving you."

Zhu Di readily agreed. "You're probably right. Please see to it at once. There's no need for us to endure poor service if we don't have to."


Three weeks later, after most of the servants had been transferred from Beijing to Nanking, Zhu Di took a leisurely stroll through one of his newly acquired gardens. With him was a young concubine who held tightly to the emperor's arm while showering him with utmost attention.

Zhu Di loved the attention that this younger woman gave him and he had a marvelous time showing her the beautiful flowers and carefully sculpted bushes that grew in colorful profusion within the imperial enclosure.

"Zhu Yun-wen was a wasteful and disingenuous little pest," he told the young concubine, not bothering to hide the contempt he felt for his departed nephew. "But he did know how to tend a garden. I can't believe these blossoms flourish with such life."

The young woman holding onto Zhu Di's arm gazed into his eyes.

"Perhaps," she giggled, happily, "it's because there is now a new emperor to fill them with hope." He swallowed this obvious flattery as if it were a sweet dessert.

As Zhu Di stopped to smell a particularly fragrant rose, his eye unexpectedly caught sight of Zheng He sitting with another young woman in a secluded area of the garden.

Surprised, Zhu Di turned to his concubine and requested that she wait for him while he handled a momentary task.

The two servants, who always trailed the emperor wherever he went, dutifully followed Zhu Di down a narrow pathway. The emperor paused, hesitating a moment, observing Zheng He from a distance. But now his gaze was drawn to the lovely woman at his servant's side.

Zheng He was sitting with Xi Chen, who had just arrived the night before from Beijing. It was the first time the two had seen each other since Zheng He left to participate in the great battle. Believing that the garden was seldom used, Zheng He had chosen this secluded area to hold their secret rendezvous.

Unaware that Zhu Di was watching, Zheng He took Xi Chen's hand and looked deeply into her eyes. "This will be our new home," he told her softly, as he devoured her incredible beauty. "You will see, my love, everything will be different now that Zhu Di is emperor."

And at this very instant, Xi Chen caught a glimpse of Zhu Di approaching through the maze of flowers and shrubs. Her voice caught in her throat.

Seeing her startled expression, Zheng He whirled around to find Zhu Di and the two servants almost upon them. Zheng He quickly released Xi Chen's hand and leaped to his feet, his heart beating fast.

He bowed graciously. "Your Majesty!" he sang out. "What a very pleasant surprise."

Zhu Di looked beyond Zheng He, unable to keep his eyes off Xi Chen's exceptional beauty.

"Yes, I should say," he sighed, exhaling happily. "This is a very pleasant surprise. And who might this delightful creature be?"

"Uh... she is one of your pantry servants, Your Majesty. I was, ahhh, just acquainting her with palace etiquette."

"And her name?"

"Oh, her name? Her name is..."

She offered Zhu Di a courteous bow, smiling with sweet innocence. "Xi Chen, your Majesty."

"Ah, yes... Xi Chen. The morning sun. And you are as lovely as any sunrise."

Zheng He watched this exchange, disturbed by the emperor's fascination.

Without taking his eyes from Xi Chen, emperor Zhu Di made a slight motion with his hand. "Zheng He, you may go."

Zheng He hesitated, surprised. "Sire?"

Zhu Di finally turned to Zheng He. "You're dismissed. There's much work to be done in preparation for my meeting with the ministers. Please see to it."

Zheng He and Xi Chen exchanged subtle glances of concern. But Zheng He had no choice but to follow this direct order. He bowed to Zhu Di and then backed away a few steps. With one last longing glance at Xi Chen, he turned and departed the garden.

As Zheng He walked down the small pathway, away from Zhu Di and the woman he loved, he felt as if his very life was being sucked from him. When he passed Zhu Di's concubine, still waiting impatiently beside the garden path, he never gave her a glance.

When Zheng He got to the edge of the garden, he stopped and looked back toward the emperor and Xi Chen. Zhu Di had now seated himself next to her on the bench.

After a painful moment, Zheng He turned and walked from the garden, unable to bear the pain of watching.

The next day, in a dignified but simple ceremony, Emperor Zhu Di conferred various honors upon all his close friends.

"Monk Dao Yan," he intoned, solemnly, "let it be known from this day forward, that you shall be addressed formally as High Consul."

Dao Yan rose to his feet, bowed to Zhu Di, then turned and accepted the applause from all those present. After waiting a suitable period for the applause to subside, the new High Consul bowed gratefully to his emperor and seated himself.

"Also let it be known, that from this day forward, my trusted servant, Zheng He, shall hold the official title of Chief Eunuch and shall be addressed as such."

But Zheng He's mind was not on the ceremony. All sound had ceased to penetrate his mind. He could think of nothing but Xi Chen. So when he saw everyone gazing at him and clapping, he wasn't sure what was happening.

Instinctively, Zheng He bowed politely, looking at the emperor, wondering what Zhu Di had just conferred upon him.

118

Then, as the applause died down, Zhu Di honored Zheng He further by providing him with an unexpected gift.

"For you many years of loyal and faithful service, Zheng He, I have decided to provide you a personal servant of your very own."

A large number of the guests began to applaud until Zhu Di raised his hand to indicate he was not yet finished. The emperor then motioned to a young man who had been standing off to one side to please step forward.

"Zheng He! I'd like to present Ma Huan. Like you, he is also a follower of Islam. I hope that he will provide you with as many years of faithful service as you have provided me."

While Zheng He smiled and acknowledged more applause from those around him, several servants sitting together in the farthest reaches of the room began to complain among themselves.

"How can the emperor give Zheng He the title of Chief Eunuch?" one whispered to another. "Some say he isn't even a eunuch."

Another servant leaned over and let the others know his own assessment. "He must be a eunuch," he whispered back more loudly than he should have. "Otherwise Zhu Di would never trust him to be near his concubines."

Several people sitting nearby looked around curiously when they heard the whispers emanating from the back of the room. They glared at the servants, causing the eunuchs to fall into a petulant silence.

Looking to Commander Tan, Emperor Zhu Di announced, "For your many years of loyal and faithful service, it is with great personal pleasure that I elevate your rank to that of Full General!"

Commander Tan beamed with pride, standing and bowing graciously. The room of guests exploded with applause for the popular officer.

"From this day forward," he continued, "General Tan shall be the senior military officer in my imperial army."

Again, there was more enthusiastic applause, which General Tan amiably acknowledged. But Zhu Di was not finished. "Just in case you wondered, General Tan, you won't have to worry about General Ho anymore. I've demoted him to the rank of corporal and sent him to a garrison that is located so far away that he'll die of old age before he can find his way back"

Everyone had a hearty laugh at Zhu Di's joke, including General Tan. "Your wisdom knows no bounds, Your Majesty. From the bottom of my heart, I thank you."

As General Tan returned to his seat, Zhu Di called upon High Administrator Wong, who was sitting near the center of the audience beside Prince Han.

"High Administrator Wong? Would you please stand?"

Wong slowly rose to his feet wondering if he was about to face a promotion or a demotion. Or perhaps just a joke at his expense?

"You've been with me ever since I was a boy," Zhu Di began. "My own father, Emperor Hung-Wu, assigned you to me to help with my upbringing. For providing me with so many years of faithful service, I shall give you a reward as well."

Zhu Di paused for a moment and smiled broadly at the audience, delighting in the anticipation that filled the room. "From this day forward, as a member of my imperial staff, you shall be given the newly created title, Minister of Protocol."

The guests responded with great enthusiasm, applauding enthusiastically. Wong bowed deeply, acknowledging the accolade with only a pleased grin.

Zhu Di then turned and walked up the two wide steps back to his throne, fluffed his imperial robe dramatically and took his seat. While servants busied themselves making sure the long robe flowed nicely down the throne steps, Prince Han, obviously disturbed, pulled anxiously on Wong's robe.

"He can't be finished!" the young prince complained. "I haven't received any acknowledgement."

Wong leaned over and discretely whispered for him to "remain silent." But Han was in no mood for silence

"No!" he whispered loudly. "I won't remain silent. It's not fair. I helped him become emperor. I deserve to have something!"

Several of the guests who were sitting close by became irritated at Han's loud whispering and turned around to stare at the brash prince. Refusing to be intimidated, Han stared right back, making a spoiled face.

"What are you looking at?" he hissed. "Turn around."

Settled comfortably on his new throne, Zhu Di addressed his imperial subjects once again.

"Before we finish, my friends, I would like to make a special announcement."

The guests began to buzz with excitement again, thoroughly enjoying all the surprising announcements.

"Dao Yan, our newly appointed High Consul, informed me about a magnificent vision he recently had. In that vision, he was told that I, Emperor Zhu Di, had been given a 'Mandate from Heaven'!"

Hearing this unexpected pronouncement, those in the room began whispering excitedly among themselves. Han pulled on Minister Wong's sleeve again, but this time didn't bother to speak in hushed tones.

"What's he talking about? I haven't heard anything about a 'Mandate'!"

Annoyed at the young man's continued interruptions, Wong brashly chastised him. "Listen and you may find out!"

Ignoring the slight disruption being caused by Prince Han, Zhu Di continued.

"In response to this heaven-sent 'Mandate', I intend to build an enormous fleet of ships."

The crowd buzzed with excitement. Zhu Di raised his hand to quiet them so he could finish.

"This magnificent fleet will carry envoys to the far corners of the world, so we can establish trade with a large number of foreign countries. I sincerely hope and pray that because of this increased trade, our great Chinese people will enjoy many years of uncommon wealth and prosperity."

Zhu Di, again, paused for dramatic affect, knowing full well that his latest statement would assuredly cause another round of excited whispering. He was not disappointed.

"I'm quite certain, my friends, that with my 'Mandate from Heaven', the name of Zhu Di, Third Ming Emperor of China, will never be lost on the pages of time."

The guests applauded with polite enthusiasm at this grand announcement. But some began to wonder if their new emperor had possibly begun to adopt a magnified perception of his own importance.

As for Zheng He, his mind still churned with worry. All he could think about was Zhu Di discovering him with Xi Chen in the garden the previous day. What would he do if the emperor became as entranced by this lovely woman as he was?


The next day, Zhu Di's royal entourage busied themselves trying to get moved into the burned-out palace. As a steady stream of servants and porters carried in thousands of pieces of furniture and artwork, the new emperor supervised the activity with glowing pride. His wife, Empress Xu, stood by his side, happily approving some items with a small nod and rejecting others with a slight shake of her head.

"If you rebuilt the palace," she told her husband, "then our treasures might find a more pleasant home."

"No," Zhu Di disagreed, "it shall remain in this wretched condition as a reminder of the great cost that was paid to achieve our victory."

"But it reeks of ashes and smoke," she quickly complained. "And I can't sleep."

"The price of ambition." He told her, just as his eyes fell on a large teak chest being carried in by two servants.

"Not that!" he scolded. "It's much too ugly. Give it to Wong. I'm sure he will appreciate its 'unique' appearance."

The two servants nodded, turned around and carried the chest back out the door.

Zheng He entered the palace carrying some large scrolls. Zhu Di motioned for him to come to him.

"Zheng He," he asked casually, "may we speak?"

"Yes, Sire, of course," Zheng He replied, bowing.

"I would like for you to select several new Ladies-in-Waiting for my Inner Court," he told his Chief Eunuch with a casual tone.

Zheng He gave Empress Xu a quick, uneasy glance. But she seemed completely unperturbed by her husband's request.

"Certainly, Your Majesty," Zheng He responded. Then as he turned to go, Zhu Di added another request.

"I would like for you to include Xi Chen. She's such a lovely creature."

Shocked, Zheng He hesitated for just a moment, then nodded his assent. "I shall carry out your wishes, Majesty."

Clearly devastated by Zhu Di's request, Zheng He turned away slowly, his troubled reaction not unnoticed by Empress Xu. Zhu Di, however, was completely oblivious to his new Chief Eunuch's obvious pain. He waved pleasantly to Zheng He as he left the room.

For the rest of the day, Zheng He wandered aimlessly in the burned ruins of the palace, unable to bring himself to carry out Zhu Di's wishes.

"I can't do it," he moaned unhappily to himself. "Not Xi Chen. Not the only woman I've ever loved. Zhu Di will be able to do anything that he wants with her. There is no way that I can allow that."


Later that day, Zheng He came to visit me in the small room I was provided while I struggled to create a new small mission in Nanking. We sat together for more than an hour, drinking tea, while he told me everything he was feeling and agonized over his terrible plight.

"I will go to Zhu Di," I volunteered, "and explain to him that you and Xi Chen have known each other and have loved each other for a very long time. Zhu Di is a reasonable man. I'm sure he will understand."

But Zheng He wouldn't agree to this. "I'm afraid it's you who doesn't understand, friar," he told me dejectedly. "Xi Chen and I are servants.   And we are both servants to Emperor Zhu Di.  It is our solemn duty to do only as the emperor wishes."

"But that's not fair," I tried to argue. "Surely Zhu Di will listen to reason."

"Fairness and reason have little to do with this.  As much as I appreciate your good intentions," Zheng He told me, "I simply can't let you tell the emperor about Xi Chen and me."

Zheng He put his hand on my shoulder. "I do love Xi Chen," he told me sadly. "I love her more than anything in this world.  But I have no choice.  I am Zhu Di's servant.  And I am bound by duty to carry out the wishes of my emperor."

"What are you going to do?" I asked, seeing no way out of this difficult predicament.

"I'm going to find Xi Chen and tell her what has happened. I want to make her aware of the situation before she hears it from someone else."


That same evening Zheng He arranged to meet secretly with Xi Chen in one of the Imperial Gardens.  He told her as gently as he could that Zhu Di wanted her to work for him in his private quarters as an Imperial Lady-in-Waiting.

Xi Chen looked deeply into her love's eyes.  Many questions troubled her mind.  "If I must work within the emperor's private quarters, will I be subject to his personal requests?"

Zheng He hesitated answering Xi Chen, but he knew he must.
"I'm afraid so."

"But I have promised to remain faithful only to you," she whispered softly. "How can I keep my sacred vow?"

Zheng He somberly reflected on what Xi Chen had just asked him, then squeezed her hand tightly.

"To escape the cat," he responded, trying bravely to smile, "a bird must flit from place to place, never pausing to rest, always aware of the..."

Xi Chen cut him off sharply.  "I don't want to hear your riddles and poetry, Zheng He! I want to hear your heart, beating as one, next to mine.  Don't fill me with advice. Fill me with your love."

Torn by conflicting emotions of anger and desire, she embraced Zheng He tightly and washed his cheek with her tears.

Holding each other in the fading light of the garden, Zheng He sobbed softly to the only woman he's ever loved, "What are we going to do, Xi Chen?  What are we going to do?"

Chapter Five

---

## CHOOSING AN ADMIRAL

I was exhausted. I felt like I had been writing for days. Fortunately, the pain in my chest was not growing worse. But it continued to throb with the same terrible intensity making it extremely uncomfortable to remain in an upright position for very long.

I continued to remind myself how fortunate I was that the cross around my neck deflected the weapon's blow, otherwise no words would flow from my pen and the story would never be told."

Two Chinese servants poked their heads in to see if I was still alive. Surprised to see me look up, fully awake and aware, they entered the cabin, changed my bandages and then replaced my cold tea with a fresh pot that was hot.

After exchanging furtive glances with each other, they bowed slightly and backed out of my cabin.

After resting a few more moments and taking an invigorating sip of the tea, I did feel better and a little stronger. I tried to refocus my mind on the unfolding story, putting my pen to the paper.

When Minister of Protocol Wong received the hideous piece of furniture from Zhu Di, he was not at all happy, correctly interpreting it as an insult. He angrily slammed the lid of the large teak chest shut and turned to glower at Prince Han.

"What is this? A joke of some sort? Zhu Di taunts me with a cruel and useless gift."

"My father is not the same," Han replied, offering the old minister a casual shrug.

"He's worse," Wong countered loudly, almost shouting. "Already this power has clutched his heart and made him mad with pride."

"Perhaps you misjudge his intent," Han offered weakly, not really wanting to defend his father's obvious intent.

"An ugly box of no purpose?" Wong shouted, railing angrily. "It's not a gift. It's an insult. To let us know our place!"

"Our place?" Han questioned, surprised the Minister of Protocol had included him in the personal slight.

"Yes!" Wong said, stepping close to Han and jabbing a gnarled finger into the young man's chest.

"Though you are his son, you are still no more than a servant here. His beloved Zheng He holds greater rank than you... and a favored place at his side."

Wong's words cut Han deeply, causing a sharp surge of bitterness to well up from deep inside.


Thankfully, Zhu Di didn't pursue Xi Chen immediately. He already had his wife, Empress Xu, and more than a hundred beautiful concubines and lady servants to cater to his every whim. Most of these females were foreign, for Zhu Di loved women of all exotic derivations. Among them were Koreans, a few Japanese and even a number of Malaysian beauties. Only a few of his Ladies-in-Waiting were Chinese. Although Xi Chen was born in China, she looked somewhat alien, which perhaps was one of the reasons he was so attracted to her. It would be a matter of time before Zhu Di would turn his attention to the newly discovered Muslim beauty. And Zheng He knew it.


Several months later, Zhu Di had moved all of his large entourage of family, friends, government employees and eunuch servants from Beijing to his new imperial capital at Nanking.

One of the first things he did was order a large force of workers to begin rebuilding some of the government buildings and living quarters that had been destroyed during the attack on the city. But he directed that nothing should be done to rebuild Zhu Yun-wen's once beautiful palace. He had firmly decided that it should remain as a blackened reminder of his nephew's reign.

Xi Chen slipped easily into the daily routine of serving Zhu Di at his imperial court. The emperor made no advances on her right away. As was his manner, he liked to first become friends with the ladies who served him in order to determine who he thought might be appropriate subjects of a more special, long-term relationship. Consequently, it was perfectly normal for Xi Chen to be on hand to serve when the new emperor called everyone together.

Under an ornately decorated gazebo, positioned in what was once Zhu Yun-wen's largest rose garden, Zhu Di presided over a select group of government officials, civil servants, family and friends. Also in attendance were his closest friends; Zheng He, High Consul Dao Yan and General Tan. I was also invited, although it always surprised me that Zhu Di would request a foreigner to attend his special functions. But, like Crown Prince, Zhu Bao Zhi, I was never one to turn down a royal invitation.

Minister of Protocol Wong, who was also considered an "outsider," was among those invited as well, as was Zhu Di's impetuous number two son, Han. Wong didn't really care whether he would be invited or not. But for Prince Han, it was quite a different matter. Han was clearly delighted that his father had chosen to allow his presence at what promised to be a very historic announcement.

Xi Chen was also present at this special function to help serve Zhu Di and his impressive gathering of guests. She was joined by numerous other lady servants who moved quietly about the outdoor area making certain the guests were served their fill of sweet-smelling rice cakes and Jasmine tea.


There was a lot of excited small talk among the invited guests as they anxiously awaited the arrival of the new Ming emperor. Zhu Di had promised to provide them with information about his plans to build a huge fleet. Consequently, everyone that afternoon was anxious to hear what he might have to say.

Building such a fleet was not an entirely new idea. His own father, Hung-wu, the first Ming emperor, built several ocean going vessels and sent them out with envoys to various foreign countries. Of course, establishing contact with other lands and cultures had many benefits. But the most important reason for this kind of maritime expansionism was to counteract the ambiguous and less-than-satisfactory image that China had in the eyes of the world.

The previous Mongol ruler, Kublai Khan, had developed an unsavory reputation far and wide for invading and conquering his neighbors. As could be expected, this caused many foreign rulers to be openly suspicious and hesitant to deal with Chinese officials and their representatives. Consequently, during Hung-wu's thirty-one year reign, he struggled vainly to let his neighbors know that the Imperial Ming could be trusted. He desperately wanted the world to know that he and his countrymen were not interested in a policy of destruction.

To further this policy of benevolence, Emperor Hung-wu sent one hundred and three envoys to foreign countries that bordered China. They were armed only with a message of goodwill and friendship. Thanks to Hung-wu's efforts, the negative image developed by the previous Mongol Dynasty was eventually overcome to a large degree.

This practice of sending out envoys to foreign countries was not only popular with other foreign rulers, it was also quite popular at home. As a young boy, when Zhu Di was growing up in Nanking, he was keenly aware that his father's practice of sending out envoys was widely supported by the various Ming officials and civil servants of his court.

Now that he was emperor himself he knew quite well that many of these same officials and civil servants, who once supported his father, were now grumbling and complaining behind his back over the illegal way they perceived that he had succeeded to the throne. In order to assuage what he thought was their unjustified criticism, and to prove that he was a worthy successor, Zhu Di decided to initiate his father's once-popular practice of sending out envoys.

"If my father received an abundance of praise for sending out a few envoys in a few ships," he reasoned, "I will send out thousands of envoys in a huge armada of ships. Those misguided Ming officials and civil servants who dare to question my legitimacy and authority will no longer have a valid reason to complain."

It was within this framework of historical background and reasoning that Zhu Di called for the meeting in the garden.

A servant struck a large metal cymbal. The new emperor made his dramatic entrance into the garden, followed by members of his personal staff. All the guests immediately fell silent. Zhu Di took his seat in an impressively over-sized, red lacquered chair. The imperial ruler was no fool. He made certain his chair was placed directly in front of his distinguished guests, elevated slightly so that he could easily see all of his invited guests and be seen by them in return. Situated on either side of Zhu Di's impressive chair were two beautifully sculpted cranes. Each one was nearly five feet tall and crafted entirely of gold. The cranes were a dramatic symbol of his expected long life as emperor.

When Zhu Di was comfortably seated, he wasted no time in getting right to the point. "I've heard talk in Nanking that there are those who believe I assumed the throne without following the proper and honorable procedures."

He looked in the direction of the imperial administrators and civil servants, leveling his gaze at those who he knew were responsible for perpetrating this erroneous impression. Each of them adopted a blank, stoic expression, attempting to avoid any acknowledgment of Zhu Di's accusative glare. "I will not tolerate the spread of these false rumors."

Having sent a clear message, he returned his attention to the larger crowd of faces before him. "To demonstrate my commitment to an even greater imperial rule, I will build and launch hundreds of ships that will carry thousands of envoys and Ming representatives to the far corners of the world."

The audience gasped at this announcement and began to applaud. Zhu Di held up his hand, quieting their enthusiastic reaction.

"I shall send these ships to the far corners of the world. They will be filled with magnificent Chinese treasures... silk, jade, silver and gold. Other rulers of the world will see for themselves the greatness of our Chinese people and the benevolence of its new Ming ruler. Beginning today, we will not only change our nation. We will change the world!"

Those in the polite audience leaped to their feet and cheered Zhu Di with wild appreciation. This time, Zhu Di made no attempt to stop them.

The imperial administrators and civil servants, whom Zhu Di had pointedly singled out earlier, slowly rose to their feet with a distinctly muted reception for the emperor's impressive announcement.

Prince Han unexpectedly jumped to his feet, summoning a boisterous voice to make a brash offer.

"Father! I would like to be the first to volunteer for your magnificent project. If you would allow me to lead your great fleet of ships, I would consider it a very great honor!"

Taken aback by his son's reckless offer, Zhu Di was caught off guard. He could only provide a forced, crooked smile. Most felt sympathy for the emperor. They could see that he was clearly embarrassed by his son's unorthodox request.

While the emperor searched for some way out of this awkward predicament, the guests could do nothing but shift nervously in their seats and wait for the moment to pass.

Not wishing to embarrass his son any more than necessary, Zhu Di nervously cleared his throat, offered Han a weak "Thank you, I will give it my consideration," and motioned for him to take his seat.

Prince Han stepped back, unsatisfied by his father's response. But he was well aware that there was nothing more he could or should do. He nodded with feigned politeness and slowly slumped into his chair, attempting to conceal his disappointment.

"After the fleet is constructed," Zhu Di continued, "I also plan to build a new palace at our previous home in Beijing."

There was another collective stirring among the guests, followed by another round of spontaneous applause. Zhu Di raised his hand once again, gesturing for the guests to withhold their enthusiasm. They had not heard everything yet.

"I can assure you, my friends, the palace I intend to build will be unique and resplendent in every way. Anyone who comes to visit will marvel at the incredible strength, creativity, intelligence and talent of our great people. I assure you, your emperor will soon be known and respected throughout the world as a wise and benevolent ruler."

Zhu Di completed his dramatic statement, then nodded graciously to his guests, indicating that it was now acceptable for them to once again show their appreciation and respect with applause. And they did, with even more enthusiasm than before. The applause continued for several long minutes, preventing Prince Han or anyone else from interrupting or registering protest to the plan.

Han tried to overcome his earlier indiscretion by clapping his hands louder and with more enthusiasm than everyone else. There was, however, no change in Minister Wong's dour expression. His lackluster response was indicative of his general, unsupportive position for anything that Zhu Di proposed or attempted to accomplish.

It was no surprise that Zheng He, General Tan, Dao Yan and I cheered our royal benefactor with exceptional gusto. We all knew that the two magnificent projects the new emperor had just announced would do wonders for both the people of China and its benevolent ruler.

Zhu Di smiled broadly at the adulation he was receiving and happily motioned for his Ladies-in-Waiting to begin serving the guests more rice cakes and tea. As the ladies moved around the garden area, Xi Chen made certain she was not in line to serve Zheng He. She feared that even her slightest attention to Zheng He would betray her feelings of intimate desire.


She busied herself on the far side of the reception area, serving other high-ranking Ming officials and their friends. But despite her efforts to concentrate only on the work at hand, she could not resist sneaking a look at her handsome lover. Even though their last two meetings in the garden had been strained, they both loved each other dearly. Neither of them wanted these periodic disagreements to interfere with their deep and abiding feelings for one another.

But, they also were afraid to reveal their true feelings to anyone around them. Both Zheng He and Xi Chen knew that if emperor Zhu Di became aware that they had been involved in a prior relationship and that, indeed, they were actually in love, the situation could quickly worsen.

Xi Chen smiled pleasantly when she offered some refreshment to me. I acknowledged her smile by offering a slight nod in return, partially to thank her for the refreshment, but mostly to let her know how pleased I was at the discretion she was exhibiting in not betraying her true feelings for Zheng He.

While everyone excitedly discussed Zhu Di's incredibly ambitious announcement, Minister Wong, surprisingly, stepped to Zhu Di's side and offered him a bit of false flattery.

"That's quite an impressive undertaking you've described, Your Majesty."

But Zhu Di was not fooled. "Yes," he replied smiling. "It's an undertaking to put the world in awe. Perhaps, Minister Wong, you should help engage our best ship designers, and safe keep their brilliant plans within your new chest."

Zhu Di then gave Wong a caustically wry smile, merging his apparent confidence with a not-so-subtle insult. Wong could only smile faintly and nod weakly, as he felt what little power he had diminish.

Then, as the old minister turned to go, Zhu Di added, "Oh, Minister Wong... Please schedule nautical examinations for all of our qualified men."

Wong didn't understand. "Qualified, Sire? Such as officers and, uh..."

"Officers, yes..." Zhu Di repeated. Then added, "as well as citizens and servants. We will find out who is the most suited to lead my great naval expedition."

Wong stared in silence at the emperor, his mouth slightly agape, and then nodded his reluctant acknowledgement.

Several weeks later, a large number of young men filed into a cavernous building that had been set aside especially for the examinations. Officers, ministers and administrators were directed to long benches and tables on the right of the center aisle.

The eunuchs entered, each one carrying a clay jar in his hands. These jars contained their private parts, known as "pao." The eunuchs were directed to a nearby table where monks and other officials would open each jar and examine the contents. They would then direct the eunuchs to long benches and tables on the left side.

Zheng He entered, uneasily clutching his pao jar. He found a spot in line with the rest of the eunuchs. When it was his turn to approach the table, the Officer took the clay jar from him and handed it to High Consul Dao Yan for examination.

The friendly monk looked at Zheng He for a long moment, gently holding the jar, and then, unexpectedly, handed it back to him without opening it. He then nodded for Zhu Di's favorite servant to be seated on the left side of the room with the other eunuchs.

Chief Eunuch Wang noticed the special treatment that was afforded Zheng He with suspicious interest. He continued to watch with a sour expression as Zheng He took his seat and placed his pao jar on the table in front of him, waiting quietly for the examinations to begin.

When the day arrived for Emperor Zhu Di to make his announcement of the individual he had chosen to lead his mighty expedition, a large crowd gathered in the Palace Square. They awaited the emperor's arrival with much anticipation.

A loud clash of symbols dramatically announced his arrival. The imperial ruler appeared with a grand flourish and then took his seat on a raised platform above the crowd. With him was his wife, Empress Xu, his new Minister of Protocol, Wong, second son, Prince Han, and General Tan. As customary, Zheng He stood at the emperor's side.

Zhu Di's imperial representatives were given seats of importance near the emperor's raised platform. I was present as well, positioned not far from the raised platform that had been reserved for the emperor's special guests and other representatives of authority.

Out of the corner of my eye, I caught sight of Xi Chen, peering from a doorway of the palace. She was desperately trying to see what was going on, but was also being careful not to be glimpsed by anyone outside of the palace.

As Zhu Di stood and raised his arm, the large throng immediately grew silent. "My good friends," he intoned solemnly, "the man I select to supervise the design and construction of our great Ming fleet, must be an outstanding man. A man of unique vision."

Prince Han smiled arrogantly to himself, assured his father would select him for this great honor.

"I intend to take a personal interest in all phases of this great effort," he continued. "Therefore, the man I select must be someone I trust completely. Someone I've worked with closely in the past."

Prince Han glanced with haughty assurance to Minister Wong, growing ever confident that he would be the one selected.

"The results of the examinations," Zhu Di said with bold confidence, "have confirmed my selection."

Prince Han began to grow worried. He had not taken the examinations, assuming that his position as the emperor's son would excuse him from engaging in such trivial procedurals. His eyes darted towards Wong, hoping to see an expression of reassurance. But Wong turned his eyes away, making Han even more nervous.

Emperor Zhu Di picked up a scroll from the table beside him and unfurled it with another exaggerated flourish. He motioned for two servants to hold the scroll in place before him, so he could read.

"As Third Ming Emperor," he began, "I do hereby proclaim, on this tenth day of June, in the Year of the Rabbit, that the man I have chosen to supervise the design and construction of the great Ming fleet is..." He paused dramatically to look out over the crowd of expectant faces, clearly savoring the tense moment. "My trusted confidant, military officer and loyal servant, San-pao t'ai-chien, respectfully known as Zheng He."

Zheng He was stunned by the announcement, not certain if he had heard correctly.

Prince Han was in total shock. He had already taken a half step forward, certain his name was going to be called. But when he heard Zheng He's name echoing instead, he rocked back on his feet and physically slumped as the words sunk in.

A surprised rumble and murmur began rolling through the crowd as heads turned and voices began to question what they had just heard.

Xi Chen gasped and clutched her breast. She, too, couldn't believe what she had just heard. She didn't know whether to squeal with delight or burst into tears. Many of the eunuchs in attendance began to applaud. Others, who felt slighted or jealous, quickly grumbled at the unexpected announcement.

Zheng He stepped forward and respectfully bowed his appreciation to Emperor Zhu Di. "Your Majesty, I most humbly accept this great honor."

Without saying another word, he graciously returned to his place of authority beside the imperial throne.

As many in the prestigious gathering continued to applaud politely, Prince Han fumed with anger in his seat. The very core of his pride and self-esteem had clearly been injured.

Following the ceremony, Prince Han met with Minister Wong in his private chamber. Still furious, he angrily smashed a vase against the wall, then whirled around and grabbed a chair. With a pained growl, he threw it as hard as he could across the room, where it landed with a loud crash.

Wong winced at the violent gesture and resultant clatter, but still managed to remain calm. He was careful not to admonish the young prince about his brash actions, for fear of stirring even further demonstrations of anger.

"How could he do that?" Han shouted irately, slamming his fist down on Wong's desk. Papers flew in all directions. "Zheng He is but a lowly servant! A foreigner! He's not even a follower of Lord Buddha!"

"Worse yet," Wong added, unintentionally fueling Han's resentment, "he's a eunuch!"

"I'm his son," Han wailed again. "I'm a prince! I should have been chosen."

He swept his arm across a nearby table, sending goblets, candlesticks and plates clattering to the floor. Again Wong struggled to ignore Han's irrational behavior and instead focus on what he perceived as a much broader problem.

"This gives them a dangerous strength," Wong cautioned solemnly, looking at the bigger picture.

But Han was only interested in himself. "Why do you go on about the damned eunuchs?" he complained bitterly. "What about ME?"

Wong took a seat behind his desk, which was now in total disarray. "They are a greater threat than you know, my young prince. With their growing numbers and their power, they will soon eclipse any influence you imagine you might have."

But Prince Han didn't want to believe this. "That's unlikely," he scoffed, throwing his arms in the air for effect.

But Wong was resolute. The threat was clear to him.

"You've seen it yourself," he told Han. "They already have the run of the palace. They influence policy, interfere with imperial law, and even have access to the royal concubines."

All this talk made the prince nervous. He started to pace, trying to calm himself. "Which is of little consequence," he muttered, trying hard to convince himself. "Since they no longer have the tools required for lustful pursuits, they present no threat to the emperor."

"Not so," Wong stated with a casual wave. "They can still pleasure the emperor's ladies-in-waiting in a number of other inventive ways. And, I might add, without the creation of unwelcome children to betray their illicit dalliance."

Han stopped pacing and returned to Wong's desk, clearly surprised at what the elder minister was revealing to him.

"Do they all do this?" Han inquired curiously.

"All who desire it," Wong confided dourly. "It's a clear presumption of their growing power."

Han couldn't believe what he was hearing. "You say the women actually..."

"Enjoy it? Oh, yes!" Wong interrupted. There was almost a squeal of delight in his high thin voice. A crooked little smile, slyly devious in nature, disrupted his normally grim expression. "Most partake quite happily I should say." He turned to Han, a harsh seriousness returning. "Oh, you may think it is a very small warning. But I promise you, it is one that could ultimately topple our control of imperial authority."


That evening, in the servant's quarters, Xi Chen sat by herself looking out a small window noticeably lost in thought. Another Lady-In-Waiting named Mai-Li, who was her friend, observed her sitting alone and went to her.

"Is something wrong?"

Xi Chen snapped out of her unhappy reverie, unaware that anyone had been watching her.

"No, nothing."

Mai-Li did not believe her.

"But such sadness, Xi Chen, there must be something wrong. Please tell me."

Just at that moment, Wang, the distractingly flighty eunuch, entered the room like a small tornado and began collecting teapots and cups wherever he could find them. He pretended to immerse himself in his hyperactive chores, secretly eavesdropping on their conversation.

"It's just that I..." Xi Chen hesitated.

"What?" Mai-Li asked, taking a seat beside her. "What troubles you so?"

Wang smirked and offered a catty remark.

"She's mooning over Zheng He."

Mai-Li was shocked. "Zheng He?"

"I'm just worried for him," Xi Chen confessed.

"Don't fret," Wong offered eagerly. "He couldn't have any more good fortune thrust upon him if Lord Buddha were his father."

Mai-Li agreed and turned to Xi Chen.

"That is true, you know. He's been awarded the highest rank among his peers."

"But there are those, Mai-Li, who speak harshly of him," Xi Chen worried.

Wang put his nose in the air and extravagantly waved Xi Chen's comment away. "It's jealousy and envy, that's all it is."

"But they say he's a eunuch," Xi Chen gushed, "and speak of it as if it's a curse."

"It's more than a curse," Wang agreed gleefully, "it's a privilege. All of the male servants in the emperor's Inner Court are eunuchs. Everyone knows it's required."

"But I don't understand," Xi Chen stammered. "What does it mean?"

Wang made a silly mocking face. "Are you playing with me?"

"No, truly, I don't know. I thought it was just another name for male servant, but..."

Wang cut her off prissily. "Oh, my... you <u>are</u> such a sweet and innocent child."

"Wang, please," Mai-Li said, trying to caution him.

But Wang would not be dissuaded. "You Muslim girls are so naïve."

Mai-Li stood up. "I'll explain," she interjected.

But Wang ignored her, exclaiming sarcastically, "We're sooo lucky! They cut off our..."

"Wang! That's enough!" Mai-Li demanded sharply, glaring at him. "I'll tell her. Not you. It's none of your business."

But Wang was having too much fun. He would not stop. He quickly swung one hand down on the other, like a blade.

"WHACK!" he exclaimed loudly. "And it's all over."

Mai-Li stepped toward Wang, raising her voice. "Go find something to do! Stop bothering us."

The effeminate servant rolled his eyes, waved his hands like fluttering wings, grabbed up a handful of teapots and cups and scurried from the room.

When he was gone, Xi Chen turned to Mai-Li and asked her cautiously, "What did he mean?"

Mai-Li wasn't sure how to proceed. She searched for the right words, not wanting to confuse or worry Xi Chen more than she already was.

"The male servants..." she began hesitantly, and then stopped. After a moment of thought, she started again. "The emperor has many concubines, Xi Chen,"

"Yes, I know. The Ladies-in-Waiting. Like you and me."

Mai-Li nodded, continuing. "And our chastity must be protected. It is most precious."

"To whom," Xi Chen asked, still not understanding fully.

"The emperor."

Xi Chen looked puzzled. "The emperor?"

"And so," Mai-Li continued, again cautiously, "all his male servants are... castrated."

"Castrated?" Xi Chen whispered softly, not understanding.

Mal-Li took a deep breath before explaining to Xi Chen what she knew she didn't want her to hear. "Their pao... their treasure... their private parts, are severed."

Xi Chen gasped in horror at the thought. Her mind began spinning at the consequences. As she realized what it meant for her and Zheng He, she burst into tears.

"No, no!" she sobbed. "It's not true!"

Mai-Li tried to console her. "Listen to me, Xi Chen, there's no reason to fear. It has long been known around the palace that Zheng He was spared by Zhu Di."

Xi Chen looked at Mai-Li with tears streaming down her face. She struggled to make sense of this, afraid to let hope replace her growing sense of dread. She rubbed the tears from her eyes and stammered, "What do you mean when you say... he was spared?"

"It is said that Zheng He is a eunuch in name only," she explained. "Many believe that Zhu Di so trusted him to be faithful and true, that he exempted him from the terrible curse of castration."

Xi Chen wanted to believe what Mai-Li was telling her, but it didn't seem to make sense. "How do you, know this?" she asked hesitantly.

"I have heard it many times from the eunuchs themselves," Mai-Li said, trying to lift Xi Chen's hopes.

But Xi Chen still wasn't convinced. "Can it really be true?"

Mai-Li looked around the room to make sure they were alone, then whispered very softly to Xi Chen. "I know it for certain. When the examinations were given to determine who would supervise the building of the fleet, all the eunuchs being tested were required to present their pao in a jar for inspection to prove that they are indeed eunuchs."

Mai-Li paused for a second to catch her breath, nervously checking around once more to be sure they were alone.

"But the emperor did not require Zheng He's jar to be opened and inspected. Wang observed this himself."

"But why?" Xi Chen asked.

"There can be only one reason," Mai-Li told her with great confidence. "Because his pao was not in it."

As the full impact of the logic struck Xi Chen, a huge wave of relief washed over her. She collapsed against Mai-Li and began sobbing uncontrollably. A torrent of tears flowed from her eyes, but this time they were tears of joy.


Zheng He wasted no time in getting started on the glorious task he had been assigned. Thankfully, he invited me to help, which I was most willing to do. Joining us at the Fukien Shipyard was Zheng He's new personal servant, Ma Huan, who was also anxious to begin the work at hand.

The shipyard was located about twenty miles south of Nanking, directly on the Yangtze River. The room we were assigned to work in was mostly empty, except for three wooden desks and several small drafting tables.

When Zheng He sat down at his new desk for the very first time, he ran his hands over the imperfect finish and thought about the magnitude of the tasks that lay before him.

"This isn't going to be easy," he worried out loud to Ma Huan as he assessed the situation. "I'm sure Zhu Di will expect us to build the fleet quickly and I don't even know where to start."

"Where does the emperor want the ships to go?" I asked. "How far must they be expected to sail?"

"That's a good question," he answered honestly, pondering the possibilities. "I'm not sure if he even knows yet."

"If he doesn't know," I responded with logic, "then who would know? Perhaps it's a question for you to consider. Pull the answer from the heavens."

Zheng He thought about this bold suggestion. Then, he stammered, "I'm sure Zhu Di would want the fleet to visit all the known countries in this part of the world... and perhaps even beyond."

"Beyond! Now see there. That is truly inspired thinking," I said, filled with delight by his answer. "and why do you think he wants to send so many ships? Hundreds, he said."

Zheng He considered this thoughtfully, beginning to enjoy this process of exploration. "So he can demonstrate to the rest of the world the power and strength of the imperial Ming."

I gave him a skeptical look and a small shrug of the shoulders.

"Come now, friar. It's a wonderful idea. You shouldn't cast doubt on the emperor's proposal. The fleet will establish trade with a large number of foreign countries. It will be a very good thing for the people. You will see."

"Yes," I grumbled, still unsure. "But which people in particular? The emperor. But who else?"

Zheng He chose to ignore my rude remark and I couldn't blame him. He had been selected by the emperor to do an important job and, knowing him the way I did, I was certain he would give it the best of his ability.

Not wanting to waste any more time arguing over the merits or true purpose of Emperor Zhu Di's project, Zheng He turned to Ma Huan.

"Ma Huan... what we need to do more than anything else is to gather information. I want you to start organizing a team to collect facts and ideas and suggestions that will be helpful to us in accomplishing our great task." He thought a moment more, and then raised one rigid finger, as if to signal a sudden inspiration. "Perhaps you should go along with them. I'll ask General Tan to provide your teams with some type of military escort."

"Who do you want me to talk to?" Ma Huan asked, quickly warming to the task.

"Talk to statesmen, government officials, foreign traders and travelers wherever you can. Also talk to ship captains and seamen. Talk with anybody you can find who has any kind of information or knowledge about a foreign country, its ruler, its people, their customs." His words poured out with a burst of excitement. "And talk to the men who build the ships. Ask them how it is best done. What makes a ship stronger and swifter upon the high seas? Collect whatever knowledge you can and bring it back to me here at the shipyard."

"Isn't that going to require a great expense?" Ma Huan asked, knowing that sending out so many people to do so much certainly would come at a dear cost.

"You don't need to worry about the expense!" Zheng He countered. "If you think you'll need a thousand teams, get them together. I'm certain Emperor Zhu Di will stand behind my decision. We need this quickly. Our goal is to create the greatest armada of ships possible for the emperor."

Zheng He whirled around to me, becoming even more excited by his plan. "Why don't you start collecting maps, friar?"

I didn't mind doing what Zheng He had suggested, we certainly did need maps following Zheng He's suggestion. But it seemed logical that, since Ma Huan would be traveling a great deal, he should also be collecting maps. That would mean we would both be doing the same thing.

"Perhaps Ma Huan should collect the maps during his travels," I suggested. I shrugged, a bit embarrassed. I didn't want him to think that I was simply trying to get out of work. I tried to explain further. "The same people he'll be talking to will also have maps. Don't misunderstand. I'd be more than happy to..."

Zheng He laughed at my awkward attempt at an explanation. "Friar Odoric... have no fear. I would never think you were trying to shirk a duty or obligation. And, yes... I believe you are correct. That's a very good idea."

He turned to Ma Huan with a big grin. "And so, Ma Huan, now you have even greater responsibilities. Doesn't that make you feel honored?"

Ma Huan nodded hesitantly, beginning to feel somewhat overwhelmed by all the work before him, but also pleased that Zheng He had entrusted him with such far-ranging duties.

"I'll still be your expert," I told Zheng He with a sincere smile and a friendly chuckle. "I just think I can be more useful, if I stay fairly close to you here at the shipyard."

"Alright," Zheng He said agreeably. "There are probably many things you can help me with here while we wait for Ma Huan and his teams of assistants to return."

He turned to his servant. "I've given you much work to do, Ma Huan. Do you think you can carry this great burden or should I find you additional help?"

Ma Huan smiled proudly and offered Zheng He an eager bow. "I know it won't be easy but I'm very good at organizing things. I'm certain I will be able to get you everything you'll need."


Within a week, armed with letters from Zheng He and Emperor Zhu Di, Ma Huan and a dozen ten-man teams left Nanking on their fact-finding journey. Twenty armed soldiers accompanied each group.

They divided the country into regions, with each group covering one area. For more than four months the teams talked with various individuals, recording reams of pertinent data and information on foreign travel.

When they returned to the shipyards, Ma Huan brought back so many wooden chests filled with papers, maps, books and charts that it all nearly filled one entire large room.

"You did an excellent job," Zheng He exclaimed happily to his young servant as he gazed at the huge stacks of material. "Now, all we have to do is go through everything you have learned and see what will be useful to us."

Ma Huan smiled broadly. "Oh, but I have already taken the liberty to do that."

Zheng He looked at Ma Huan with puzzlement. "Do what?"

"Catalogue and organize all the information that we gathered. We have recorded everything in these volumes."

Ma Huan held up a thick unbound volume of pages, and then handed it to Zheng He.

Zheng He couldn't believe what his young servant had done. He casually leafed through the pages. "You are saying that these volumes contain what we need to know about all the countries in this part of the world? The rulers of each country... what each country has to trade, their strengths, their weaknesses, how far away they are from our country... with maps, navigational charts and...?" Zheng He's words trailed off as he looked through the pages.

Ma Huan didn't want to appear boastful, but he had done a very good job. And he knew it.

"In addition, I have provided the details of the weather at various times of year, likely currents that may be encountered in the seas surrounding them and how friendly, or unfriendly, the people are in each country. It's all there just as you requested."

Zheng He dropped into his chair, unable to believe his servant had already completed so much work.

"I want you to take some time for yourself, Ma Huan," he said with extreme gratitude. "You deserve it."

Ma Huan bowed to his master. "You're most generous. But I'm afraid there is still much work to be done. You need me here.

Zheng He shifted uncomfortably in his chair. He knew that Ma Huan was right. They would need to begin work immediately.

Zheng He rose from his chair, moving to a large flat table. More than a dozen sketches and drawings of ships were stacked, one upon the other.

"I want to show you something, Ma Huan." He shuffled through the sketches, displaying them to his servant. "While you were gone, Friar Odoric and I collected together the best ship designers and draftsmen we could find. We had them prepare several sets of plans for different sizes and types of ships."

Zheng He pointed to the sketch that now lay on top of the stack. It featured an impressively colorful painting of a magnificent ship. "This one is called a Baochuan! It will be our Treasure Ship."

Ma Huan was amazed at the incredible design and precise detail in the painting. It was one of the most beautiful things he'd ever seen.

"How large is it?" he gasped. "I don't think I've ever seen a ship that big before."

Zheng He gave me a smile, amused by his servant's reaction. "You haven't seen another ship this large," Zheng He boasted, "because nothing has ever been built to match the Baochuan's size and strength."

Zheng He picked up a rosewood stick, pointing out the features of the proposed ship. "She will be four hundred and thirty feet long, from bow to stern. She'll have three wide, watertight decks that will transport treasures and trade goods. As you can see, the Baochuan will also feature three, Ming-style pagoda's and have nine large masts and sails."

"How wide will the ship be?" Ma Huan asked, trying to calculate in his mind how wide he believed it should be to carry that immense sail area.

"Slightly less than one hundred feet," Zheng He said proudly. "Ninety four feet to be exact. Having such a wide beam will not only allow the Baochuan to be stable in a fair breeze, it will also enable us to have an extremely shallow draft. That will allow us to enter small bays and rivers, even if they aren't particularly deep."

Ma Huan lifted a corner of the drawing, trying to get a look at the next rendering.

"Are all the ships going to be this large?" Ma Huan asked still dazzled by the size of the Baochuan.

"No. Not all," Zheng He said, laughing. He slid the next painting to the top of the pile. "This one, for example, is called a Machuan. It's a horse transport. As you can see, we've designed it so that it's somewhat smaller in size and more appropriate to its purpose."

"It doesn't look much smaller to me," Ma Huan observed happily with a twinkle in his eye.

"If we don't have any further changes in the design," Zheng He said, "the Machuan will be three hundred and twenty feet long and about eighty four feet wide. As you can see, she'll be carrying eight masts and sails, instead of nine, like the Treasure Ship. But it will be very useful because we will need a lot of four-legged animals to carry the many soldiers and pull all our wagons."

"How many horses will each of these ships carry?" Ma Huan asked curiously, growing more fascinated by all these new revelations.

"Each one would carry approximately five hundred horses," Zheng He replied.

Ma Huan shook his head. "I mean no disrespect, but I don't think I'd want to sail on one of those."

"Why not? She'll be a very sturdy ship?"

Ma Huan wrinkled his nose and made a strange face. "With all those horses on one ship, I'm certain there's going to be, shall we say... a very 'memorable' odor."

Zheng He chuckled at this. Ma Huan continued, "If it pleases you, Sir, I would much rather be assigned to one of those beautiful Treasure Ships. I think they will be much more comfortable."

"I doubt we'll be going anywhere, Ma Huan," I said. "All we're supposed to do is design and build the ships, then help the emperor decide where to send them."

Ma Huan looked disenchanted at this news. He was obviously hoping for an opportunity to see the world and experience new adventures.

Zheng He sensed Ma Huan's disappointment. He quickly changed the subject, hoping to boost his young servant's enthusiasm once more. "Would you like to see the other ship designs?"

"There are more?" Ma Huan asked, his excitement revived. "Yes! I would love to see them."

Without hesitation, Zheng He revealed yet another painting.

"This third ship is called a Liangchaun. It will be used as the fleet's main transport for all our provisions. She'll be two hundred and eighty feet long and about eighty feet wide. As you can see, there are only seven masts with sails."

He presented another elaborate painting. "And this Tsochaun. It is even smaller and will be used for personnel transport. It's just two hundred and forty feet in length and seventy-five feet wide. With six masts and sails, she'll be carrying less sail area than the Liangchaun."

Ma Huan ran his finger across the drawing, mesmerized. "I can't believe you've designed so many ships, Sir. And do you plan to actually build all of them?"

"I don't see why not," Zheng He said. "Every one of them will be needed."

Zheng He searched through the many drawings and sketches, finally finding the colorful illustration he was looking for. He carefully spread it out before Ma Huan.

"I also want to build this small five-masted warship. It would be very maneuverable. We will probably construct more than a hundred of these ships. If we're going to protect the armada from attack, we will need to have enough ships to carry an appropriate number of soldiers and armament."

At this point, I spoke up. "Zheng He had all of these ships designed so they could be built here at the Fukien shipyards using construction techniques that are already familiar. In that way, we won't have to waste time attempting to create new methods and materials."

"Even these big treasure ships?" Ma Huan asked.

"Yes. Even the big treasure ships," Zheng He replied, slapping his young servant's shoulder amiably.

"So... When do we begin?" Ma Huan said with great excitement and energy.

Both Zheng He and I gave the young man big smiles, pleased to see such wonderful eagerness.

"We have already begun," Zheng He exclaimed proudly.

"At this very moment," I said, "ten thousand men are cutting down an entire forest of teak trees."


In the mountain forests, the giant trees were harvested and then hauled overland by elephant and oxen to the sea. It was there that dozens of the huge logs were chained together and floated up the Yangtze to the shipyard.

Once the construction began, Zheng He was required to make periodic visits to the emperor in Nanking at least once every month. Zhu Di wanted to be kept informed of every detail. But each time, before Zheng He could deliver his report, the emperor always asked him the same two questions.

"Is everything still on schedule?" he would inquire. "Do you have everything you need?"

Equally predictable, Zheng He always gave him the same two answers when asked.

"We are on schedule, Your Majesty," he would confide while bowing deeply. "And you've provided me with much more than I ever anticipated needing. Your infinite generosity is most heartening."

As a diplomatic gesture, Zheng He usually offered to scale things back a little, so there wouldn't be such a large drain on the imperial finances. But Zhu Di's reply would always be, "Nonsense! A large fleet is exactly what I need. Especially if I'm going to use it to impress the rest of the world!"

It had become a ritual between them and they both enjoyed playing this game. Zhu Di would often add for good measure, "You worry about getting the fleet built, Zheng He. Let me worry about paying all the costs."


One month later, when Zheng He arrived for his meeting with Zhu Di, they once more engaged in this traditional exchange. But then, Zheng He made the error of giving voice to a new observation. "I've noticed, Sire, there are a number of palace officials and civil servants who have expressed concern about the amount of money you are spending on the ships."

Unfortunately, Zhu Di was not in a particularly pleasant mood that day. He pounded both fists on the arms of his chair, his face turning red with anger.

"Who are they to criticize?" he shouted. "They can rot in hell and suffer the anguish of damnation!"

Any time the emperor heard a rumbling of dissension or a rumor of complaints about one of his ventures, it made him angry. "They have no right to question me!" he thundered angrily. He leaped up from his throne and began to pace the floor. After several long moments, he was able to regain his composure. He collapsed into his throne, slouching there in irritable disenchantment.

"Such talk is traitorous," he hissed, obviously still upset. "It's a direct insult to the crown and a direct insult to the people. I know there is such talk. I've heard it before many times. But I cannot manage to discover who is perpetrating this poisonous thinking."

Zhu Di continues to grumble to himself, the words lost under his breath. Zheng He now deeply regretted having brought the subject up and disturbing his emperor so.

"Do you know how I'm paying for the fleet?" the emperor asked with new clarity. "Do you have any idea where the money is coming from?"

Struggling to come up with a logical response, Zheng He nervously cleared his throat, stalling for time, hoping that inspiration or wisdom would suddenly descend upon him. He finally decided to take the high road and honestly claim his ignorance on the matter.

"No, Your Majesty... I don't know how you're paying for the fleet. Nor is it my place to ask. Such information, I'm sure, is strictly confidential."

"Well, I'm going to tell you anyway," Zhu Di growled without a moment of hesitation. "That way, you will never have to wonder or speculate about it again."

"There's no need for you to tell me anything, Sire..."

Zhu Di raised his hand to silence Zheng He. Then, after filling his lungs with an invigorating breath, he began.

"One hundred years ago, during the time of the Mongol dynasty, Genghis Khan conquered a large portion of our southern Shantung and northern Ankui provinces. The Great Khan drove out the original inhabitants and turned the land into a large hunting preserve for himself. No one has been allowed to settle in the area since."

Zhu Di paused to take a sip of tea from the porcelain cup at his elbow.

"When my father came to power, this extremely fertile region remained under our control. It was used exclusively by my family and by a few important Ming officials. I'm now selling portions of this land, which officially belongs to me, to finance the building of the fleet. When the fleet is finished and ready to sail, I'll have to sell even more of my land to fund its operation. No finances of the Ming dynasty are being used now... nor will they ever be used in the future. This quest... this dream of exploring beyond our horizons... is my own. And therefore, I will bear the expense of its realization."


Zheng He was stunned. He had no idea that the emperor was financing this ambitious venture by himself. Most people assumed that any grand projects undertaken by the seat of power were funded entirely by the coffers of government. This was what Zheng He believed as well.

"Perhaps I should inform others of your very great and benevolent sacrifice, Sire," Zheng He suggested, hoping to atone for his thoughtless assumption.

Zhu Di sat back on his throne and scowled, casting his eyes upward as he rejected this idea. "No, I think not. Those small-minded fools who run around the palace spewing lies, will just continue to do so regardless. Once they knew I was spending my own money, they would surely concoct some other insane conspiracy as my motivation. All they would accomplish is to upset my stomach."

The thought of stomach pains made him wince. He sat straight up, gently rubbing his ribs, one eyebrow arched curiously. "Should all the civil servants and officials band together, uniting against my policies, they would surely cause problems. But it would do nothing but bring irreparable harm to the people. I know that what I'm doing is right, Zheng He. Building this fleet and sending it out to represent the people of China is the very best thing I can do. Believe me... I wouldn't be spending my very own money if I wasn't absolutely confident."

A silence descended on them both. The emperor stared at the shafts of dusty sunlight that filtered through some small transom high above.

Zheng He fidgeted uneasily. "Is there something more you wish from me, Majesty?"

Emperor Zhu Di raised his eyes, slowly emerging from his reverie. "When you return next month, I would like you to bring all of your completed drawings to me. I think it would be commendable for me to at least see what I'm paying for."

Zheng He bowed and turned to go. But Zhu Di's voice stopped him in his tracks. "Oh... and one other thing. I would like to have the fleet constructed and ready to launch no later than the summer after next."

"That would be... within the next twenty-four months, Sire." Zheng He said, surprised by the shortened timetable.

Zhu Di raised his eyebrow, a faint smile on his lips. "And you won't disappoint me, will you?" He spoke the words with a soft kindness, yet they still carried the power and force of a direct order.

"No, Sire," said Zheng He, "I will never disappoint you. That is my solemn vow."


When Zheng He stepped outside the sunlight caused him to blink furiously, raising an arm to shield his eyes from the bright orb above. Ma Huan waited for him by a carriage, along with a small contingent of mounted soldiers.

"I trust you had an excellent conference with the emperor," he said with a smile, fully expecting a positive response. But instead he was met by an uncustomary silence. He opened the door to the carriage.

"Is the emperor pleased with what you've accomplished thus far?" he ventured, hoping to stir a response. Zheng He took a seat in the carriage and gazed at Ma Huan for a long time before finally answering.

"He has given me two impossible deadlines." His voice was flat and without joy, as if a heavy cloud had wrapped itself around him. "All the construction designs must be completed with the month and brought to him. And..." His voice dropped yet another octave, emphasizing the burden that he felt. "We must be ready to sail in twenty-four months."

"But that's impossible!" Ma Huan exclaimed. "There's too much work yet to be done!"

"This is something you and I both know full well," Zheng He said with a sigh. "Unfortunately, our emperor is not of the same mind."


Two months later, there were now thousands of workers at the Fukien shipyards, splitting logs, laying keels, scraping, sawing, and hammering furiously. Huge timbers were raised into place with ropes and pulleys. It was noisy and dusty, and the work went on continuously throughout the night and day.

Zheng He, Ma Huan and I still had our desks in the large shipyard drafting room. However, we had now been joined by many other workers, causing the space to become cramped and cluttered. More than fifty professional draftsmen had been  crowded into the room with us.

One evening, after a particularly long stretch of non-stop work, I watched Zheng He rub his eyes one evening. I worried that he was putting in too many long hours on this demanding venture. I was certain that it wasn't good for his health.

"You need to take a break?" I suggested, hoping he would listen. "Why don't you go back to Nanking for a few days? You could visit Xi Chen. It will do you good to get away for awhile."

Zheng He shook his head. "I wish I could, friar, but there's too much work that still needs to be done."

Ma Huan joined in with his own words of encouragement. "I think the friar's right. You've been working from early morning until long after the sun has set... every day, every night, for many months. If you don't rest soon, you may find yourself resting for eternity. And then the friar and I would have to take charge of building the ships. Do you really want to see that happen?  It would be a catastrophe!"

Zheng He managed a smile at this. He knew that Ma Huan was correct, but he could not bring himself to abandon the effort, even for a few days to rejuvenate his body and soul.

He struggled to his feet and approached a table covered with papers. He grabbed a handful of documents, holding them up.

"Deciding how many soldiers we'll need... how many envoys we should take with us... how much food... how many animals and wagons and gifts we'll need. All this must be done. If I leave, even for a week... it won't happen," he complained gruffly.

I was not about to give up my effort to convince him. "All this work is not going anywhere," I told him sternly. "It will be waiting for you when you return."

He dropped the papers on his desk, then turned to face both Ma Huan and me.

"How much time do we have left?" he asked. "Sixteen months? Eighteen months at most?" Exhausted, he slumped down into his chair. "The time is so short. I must stay right here until we're finished."

Zheng He searched through the personal belongings on his desk, finally retrieving a letter. "Ma Huan, there is something you can do for me. Would you please take my carriage to Nanking and deliver this letter to Xi Chen?"

"Perhaps you should deliver it yourself... in person," Ma Huan suggested. "I'm sure she'd much rather have you deliver it than me."

"Tell her that I promise to see her next month when I deliver my report to the emperor." He paused. For a moment it seemed as if he was about to reconsider his decision.

"Tell her..." He hesitated, then with a flushed face and flustered demeanor, he told Ma Huan, "Oh... you know what to tell her."

The awkward moment was abruptly interrupted by a tremendous crash outside, followed by a chorus of screams and shouting voices. We rushed outside, looking out from our vantage point on the second floor staircase to the construction yard below. A large portion of the wood framing and scaffolding that surrounded the skeletal frame of one huge treasure ship had collapsed onto six workers, crushing them. Many others had been thrown to the ground and were injured and bleeding badly.

Zheng He turned to us with a look of great concern. "This is why I cannot leave. Friar, please go to them and offer your prayers for their salvation."

I was already on my way to the scene of this horrible tragedy before Zheng He's final words were even spoken.

Three days later, Ma Huan was finally able to deliver Zheng He's letter to Xi Chen. When he handed it to her, she immediately went into the garden and opened it in private. She trembled as she read it.

"I miss you, my dearest little flower," the note began, "and I love you desperately. My heart is with you every moment of every day. But at this time, my duty is to serve the emperor."

Xi Chen put the letter down for a moment, considering the words she had just read. "He's more in love with the emperor than he is with me," she thought, then pushed the words from her mind. She forced herself to continue reading.

"As you are aware, Zhu Di has given me a very great honor. I must do my best to see that the design and construction of his fleet is carried out successfully and on time. I pray to Allah, that someday soon we'll be able to have the precious life together that we've both longed for and dreamed of. Yours in love, forever, Zheng He."

Xi Chen kissed the letter and wished it had been longer, but any piece of news from the man she loved was to be cherished and read many times, over and over.

But then, the troublesome little thoughts she always tried to keep hidden bubbled up again from somewhere deep inside her consciousness.

"I'm glad that Zheng He had his servant bring me this letter," she mused to herself, "but I need more than just a letter from him, I need..."

But the thought was too hurtful, so she chased it from her mind. "The man I love is Zheng He," she said to herself, closing her eyes and picturing what he looked like. "Zheng He really does want to make love to me. I know that. Because, he told me so himself."

Xi Chen shook her head again, not wanting to give any consideration to this painful thought. But it always came back. "The only reason he doesn't make love to me is because he can't. That's the real reason. He can't because..."

Xi Chen thought about what Mai-Li had told her. "She said he really wasn't a eunuch. She had proof. And if he isn't, then why won't he make love to me?" This terrible doubt always came back to taunt her and torment her. It would twist her dreams of something beautiful into a nightmare of doubt and despair.

While Xi Chen struggled with her jumble of thoughts, reading the note over and over, Zhu Di unexpectedly passed by and saw her sitting alone in the garden. Wanting to surprise her, he motioned for his two eunuch servants to wait where they were.

Xi Chen didn't notice Zhu Di until he was almost directly in front of her. Embarrassed, she discretely tried to hide Zheng He's letter in the fold of her robe. She got to her feet and made a show of bowing deeply.

Fortunately, Zhu Di did not notice her conceal the letter or her embarrassment. As before, during their first meeting, he was completely captivated by her remarkable beauty.

"Will you honor me with your presence, fair lady?" he asked. "I'd like to sit with you for a few moments and enjoy your company."

Xi Chen gathered her composure and smiled as sweetly as she could.

"It is I, Your Majesty, who am honored."

Zhu Di then took Xi Chen's hand and found a seat next to her on the bench.

"You are called Xi Chen, if I remember correctly," Zhu Di said pleasantly, never taking his eyes off the lovely creature beside him. "Morning Sun." He said the words slowly and with reverence, nearly a whisper. "And can you tell me how you received such a delightful name."

"It's a name that was given to me by my grandmother, Sire," she responded. "I'm not sure, but I suspect I was born early in the day and so named."

"Yes," Zhu Di agreed, smiling, "and it fits you well. The early morning sun shines daily with radiant beauty, just as your own beauty shines and illuminates those around you."

Xi Chen blushed and lowered her eyes. "You flatter me with your eloquence, Your Majesty. I'm embarrassed."

Zhu Di then took both of her hands in his and held them tenderly. "You must allow me to spend more time with you, my dear. I'd like to get to know you better. In fact, I'd like to get to know you better than you know yourself."

Xi Chen looked into Zhu Di's eyes, trying not to reveal how nervous he made her feel. "Your wish is my command, Majesty."

Zhu Di smiled inwardly, satisfied that his encounter with the Xi Chen was going exactly as he'd hoped. "Well, then, it's settled!" he said merrily. "I must leave you now, but I promise I'll be seeing you again... very soon."

With that, Zhu Di squeezed Xi Chen's hands and left the garden, trailed by his two servants.

Xi Chen wasn't sure if she would laugh or cry. She knew that having the emperor take a personal interest in his servants and ladies was quite uncommon. In fact, it was considered a very special and much sought-after honor. But she didn't want the emperor to notice her. At least... she didn't think she did.

Her thoughts were spinning in circles now. The emperor did go out of his way to compliment her. Exceedingly. He was not like Zheng He at all, who often just complained about how she behaved. She loved Zheng He terribly. That she was sure of. And she had promised him that she would never, ever allow the emperor to touch her. But now...

What in the world was she thinking? The emperor only stumbled upon her in the garden by accident. It would never happen again. She didn't want it to ever happen again. Zheng He was the only man she loved and she would never love anyone else. She told herself over and over, repeating the words in her mind. The only man I love and the only man I'll ever love.


Zhu Di was late. His wife awaited him. As he rushed up the outside steps to her living quarters, he dismissed his servants with a wave of the hand. They halted outside the door and made no attempt to follow him into the empress's private quarters.

As Zhu Di swept into his wife's room, all the ladies attending her silently rose to their feet and retreated behind a large decorative screen located on the far side of the room.

Empress Xu gave her husband a cross look as he slumped wearily into a nearby chair without even saying hello.

"You're late," she snapped. "You know I don't like to be kept waiting."

"I've been engaged in a very busy schedule," he countered, testily. "Surely you're aware of my great number of duties and responsibilities?"

"Duties and responsibilities, indeed," she hissed, not intimidated by his curt demeanor. "You were probably detained by one of your ladies, as they like to be called. Most are nothing but harlots, who make a fool of you with their fake pretensions of love."

Zhu Di disliked it when his wife insulted his concubines and lady servants. He sat bolt upright in his chair and pointed an accusing finger at her.

"I've heard enough!" The angry sound of his voice startled the female servants hiding behind the screen. "I will not have you speaking disrespectfully about ladies of the court."

Before Empress Xu could respond, he continued railing, never even pausing to take a breath. "How can you claim to be jealous?" he shouted. "Haven't I allowed you to bear our two sons? Isn't it 'you' who has been given this great honor? You are the empress, woman! Be satisfied with that glory!"

Empress Xu had stirred her husband's anger and she now wished she hadn't been so unwise. But it was hard for her to restrain her own resentment. The way Zhu Di conducted himself with the lady servants and concubines always made her terribly jealous. She tried to ignore it. After all, Chinese rulers had always kept a large harem of women to cater to their every personal whim. That's the way it had always been. It was... tradition. Chinese rulers believed that making love to a large number of different women brought them a long life, abundant strength and very good health. This was a very old and well-established Chinese custom. But it also was a custom that Empress Xu never approved of.

"Yes, Zhu Di," she retorted, "I _am_ the empress. And, as empress, I do not intend to sit idly by and keep my feelings silent."

She knew from past arguments that she'd better stop, because things would only get worse if she continued. Immediately, she changed her approach, softening her tone.

"I don't like to think of you sleeping with another woman," she cooed softly, touching him gently. "You're my husband, Zhu Di. I have feelings. Don't my feelings count?"

Zhu Di shrugged her hand off his arm, as if trying to chase away an annoying insect that buzzed around him.

Empress Xu moved behind her husband's chair and slowly put her arms around his shoulders. "What's happened to us, Zhu Di?" she purred, still trying to make amends. "I feel like we're always arguing with each other. We shouldn't, you know."

He glanced over his shoulder at her, but said nothing, still resisting her friendly advances.

"I'm just jealous of all the time you spend with the other ladies. That's normal isn't it? I can't help it. Why can't we enjoy each other the way we used to when we were young?"

"When we were young," he said, "I was not emperor. I was but a young and inexperienced Province King. Things were simple then. Now that I'm emperor, things are much more complicated. Everything's different. I have many more responsibilities to the people."

The empress moved in front of Zhu Di's chair, so she could look him in the eye. His intransigence had not helped to soften her anger. She pointed a bejeweled finger in his face, no longer worried about restraining her true feelings.

"First, my very important husband," she said sharply, "you have a responsibility to _me_. I am your wife. I demand to be treated with courtesy and respect."

Empress Xu put her hands on his chair and leaned over so her face was close to his. "I will not stand in line behind your ladies and concubines begging for your attention!"

Zhu Di didn't like to be lectured to by anyone, much less the empress. Nor did he appreciate anyone shaking a finger in his face. He grabbed the arms of his chair and pushed himself to his feet, almost knocking Empress Xu over. He spun back around to her and pointed a finger in her face.

"YOU may be my wife." he shouted, "but I am EMPEROR! As emperor, I do not have to subject myself to the ranting and raving of a woman possessed with petty selfishness."

He pushed past his wife and headed for the door.

"Petty selfishness?" Empress Xu shouted at her husband as he neared the door. "How dare you accuse me of being selfish? Just because I want to spend more time with you."

Zhu Di whirled around at the door.

"It's not the same between us, woman!" he shouted. "I don't know if it will ever be the same again! You must try to conduct yourself..."

But he never had the opportunity to finish. Empress Xu picked up a silver tray and hurled it at him with all her strength. Zhu Di saw the object coming and dodged behind the door. The tray and its contents clattered loudly, smashing on the floor.

The two servants waiting just outside quickly fell in line behind the retreating emperor. Their stiff bearing and expressionless faces betrayed no awareness or acknowledgement of the unpleasant incident.

The servants had to hurry to keep up. Zhu Di was fuming and walking at a very fast pace across the wide courtyard. He wasn't sure where he was going, but he refused to waste any more time with this totally selfish woman.

He walked briskly through an elaborately decorative moon gate, then across a second large courtyard, continuing to take great strides as he went. Gradually his anger began to subside and his pace slowed, much to the appreciation of his trailing servants.

With his mind no longer consumed by angry thoughts, he started thinking about the lovely lady servant he met in the garden less than an hour before.

"What a beautiful creature she was," he thought to himself, as he slowly began to relax. "I know she is simply one of my lady servants, but why haven't I taken notice of her before? She really is amazingly lovely."

A new thought came to mind, one that he wished he had considered sooner. "As soon as I entertain this week's list of ladies," he decided magnanimously, "I will add Xi Chen's name to the list. She will be a wonderful new adventure for next week."

A smile crept over Zhu Di's face and he discovered he couldn't stop himself from laughing. I wish all my decisions were that easy. Life would be wonderful."

The trailing servants were totally perplexed, as to why Zhu Di's dour mood had suddenly changed so dramatically for the better?

Since construction of the Ming fleet was now underway, Zhu Di knew that it wouldn't be long before he'd have to choose someone to lead the first expedition. He asked his two closest confidants, General Tan and High Consul Dao Yan, plus Minister of Protocol Wong and other imperial advisors, to put together a list of potential candidates. He told them that he would make his choice from the list of candidates they recommended.

When Prince Han heard what was going on, he went straight to Minister Wong's office, bent on pressuring him to put his name on the list.

Wong was not cooperative. "I can't just add your name to the list," he argued, "for no good reason."

Han didn't like the sound of that. He shook his fist in the old man's face, hoping to coerce him into changing his mind. "You CAN add my name," he threatened loudly, "and you WILL! I'm as qualified as anyone else."

Wong didn't like to be threatened. He rose from behind his desk and crossed the room, pretending to busy himself with some inconsequential activity. In truth, he was trying to distance himself from the impetuous prince.

"Your father wanted a list of older, more experienced men," Wong suggested. He looked for something amid the clutter on a table. "Whoever is chosen to be admiral of the fleet must have a certain status and position."

"I have status and position," Han yelled at Wong. He grabbed him by the robe and whirled him around, scattering papers everywhere. "I'm a PRINCE!"

Wong stared at him with cold confidence. "Yes, you are a prince," Wong agreed, making an attempt to retrieve some of the papers from the floor, "but you don't have the proper experience. That only comes with age and wisdom. You lack both."

Han grabbed Wong by the front of his robe. "I don't care about proper experience. That is merely an excuse for denying me the respect I deserve. I want you to put my name on your list. Now!"

Wong gently peeled Prince Han's fingers from his robe, pushing them away. "All right. I'll add your name. But there is no guarantee that you'll be chosen."

Han headed for the door. "You just submit my name," he told Wong haughtily. "My destiny will fulfill itself."

At the shipyard, thousands of workers were busy laying the keels of more than a hundred ships. The disaster that had struck more than a week ago was now behind them. As a shipyard supervisor peered through a window watching the activity below, he caught sight of Zheng He coming up the outside stairway towards him.

"Damned eunuch," he grumbled to a nearby assistant. "They're no better than filthy monkeys."

As Zheng He entered the room, the supervisor's gruff scowl instantly turned into a big insincere grin.

"Welcome," he sang out happily. "We are so pleased that you have returned, Zheng He."

Even though the supervisor offered a quick bow, Zheng He was not fooled. He knew the man did not respect him, but chose not to make an issue of it.

"I've heard the work is progressing well," he told the supervisor calmly, doing his best to appear friendly.

"Most definitely," the supervisor responded merrily, continuing to smile while motioning grandly toward the shipyard below. "As you can see, the vessels are taking shape."

Zheng He kept up the charade. "Excellent," he said cheerily. "I believe I shall inspect them more closely."

Now, there was nothing the supervisor could do but nod with feigned delight. "Of course."

"There will be additional wood by week's end," Zheng He advised the disgruntled official as he turned back towards the door. "We must hasten our schedule."

As Zheng He descended down the stairs and headed into the vast shipyard below, the supervisor's gracious smile once again turned to an ugly sneer.

That evening, in the servant's quarters at Zhu Di's palace, Xi Chen and Mai-Li sat and talked about their life as servants. As often happened, Xi Chen steered their conversation to Zheng He. She complained that he never had the time or opportunity to visit her anymore. His constant work at the imperial shipyards had become his only activity.

"He seems more faithful to the emperor and his ships than to me," she moaned sadly.

"Men are quite fickle," Mai-Li agreed.

Wang abruptly entered the room. He seemed strangely stoic and unfriendly. This uncustomary behavior surprised both the young women.

Wang stopped a few steps from Xi Chen and pointed his finger directly at her. "The emperor has requested you."

"Me?" Xi Chen gasped, unable to catch her breath.

"Yes... you. Now. And it is wise not to be late."


When Xi Chen arrived at the emperor's private bedchamber, she opened the door very slowly and peered inside. Her frightened eyes slowly scanned the room. She could see very little in the darkened chamber. Then, she detected the shadowy silhouette of Zhu Di sitting on a large sofa decorated with beautiful silk pillows. He motioned to her.

"Come," he said smiling, beckoning for her to enter.

When Xi Chen closed the door, she discovered that she and the emperor were alone.

"Where are your other lady servants, Your Majesty?" she asked cautiously. "I seem to be the only one here."

"I thought if we were alone, Xi Chen, it might give us an opportunity to know each other better. To have others around would only serve as an unnecessary distraction."

She bowed and forced a weak smile, not wanting Zhu Di to know how nervous she was. "I hope I'll be able to provide you with proper service."

As Xi Chen prepared to serve the emperor a cup of hot tea, he abruptly took the pot of tea from her hand and set it on a nearby table. He then gently guided her to the sofa next to him.

"There's no need to worry about providing me with service, pretty lady," Zhu Di explained, while rearranging some of the silk pillows. "I'd just like for you to sit here with me for awhile, so we can talk."

Xi Chen was used to being around Zhu Di in the role of a servant, but sitting beside him as a personal guest proved to be a distinctly unsettling experience for her.

"What would you like to talk about, Majesty?" she asked, hoping to keep the conversation light and impersonal. "Anything in particular?"

"No, nothing I can think of," Zhu Di responded with marked nonchalance. "I'm just looking for an excuse to spend an evening alone with you so that I might enjoy your exceptional beauty."

Xi Chen blushed and lowered her eyes, pretending she was embarrassed. But deep down, she began to worry about what might be coming next. She did what she could to remain calm so Zhu Di wouldn't know what she was thinking.

"Your Majesty," she cooed. "You flatter me. I'm sure you have many lady servants and concubines who are much more attractive than me. I'm almost thirty years old!"

Zhu Di had to laugh at that. "Trust me, my dear," he gushed. "None are more attractive than you. And besides, I like a woman with maturity and experience. They, at least, have had the chance to develop some common sense."

Xi Chen smiled demurely at the emperor. "In that case, Your Majesty, you may not object if I ask you about your new fleet of ships. Is construction of the vessels progressing satisfactorily?"

Zhu Di was taken aback by Xi Chen's interest in his fleet. None of his other ladies or concubines... not even his wife, the empress... had ever inquired about the projects that he had undertaken.

"Why I can't believe you'd be interested in such a thing," Zhu Di gasped, still in a state of surprise. After regaining his composure, he sat up proudly and attempted to answer her question with imperial dignity. "It's progressing quite satisfactorily. Thank you for asking."

Zhu Di decided to have a little fun with his newly found beauty, encouraging her to comment further.

"Is there anything else you'd like to know about the fleet? You may ask me anything you'd like."

Xi Chen didn't realize the emperor was teasing. She thought for a moment, then asked another question.

"Please forgive me, Sire, but several times, while I've been serving guests, I've overheard you speaking with your advisors, trying to decide on who you should select to lead your fleet."

Zhu Di was again taken aback at the lady's unabridged forthrightness.

"Don't tell me you have a suggestion?" he gasped with mock appreciation. Xi Chen detected the tone of sarcasm in his voice.

"I'm afraid, Sire, that perhaps I've asked too much. I must apologize for being so forward."

But Zhu Di was now amused and had no intention of letting her off the hook.

"Oh, no, fair lady," he retorted happily, "I've received dozens of names for consideration. One more from you can't hurt."

Xi Chen was clearly apprehensive, but knew she couldn't retreat at this point. "Well, Sire," she began slowly, "I was thinking that your servant, Zheng He, would make an excellent candidate. Have you ever thought about him? He seems to be extremely qualified."

He stared at her for a long moment, curious at her great interest in Zheng He. "And please tell me... do you know what his qualifications might be?"

Once more, Xi Chen suspected she may have overstepped her bounds. "I'm embarrassed, Your Majesty," she pleaded, lowering her eyes as she looked away. "It's not my place to offer the emperor a suggestion about anything. Please accept my most humble apology."

"Oh, no! Please!" he said, while gently stroking her cheek so that she would turn back to him. "I would truly like to know why you think my servant, Zheng He, is qualified to receive such an honor."

"Well," Xi Chen ventured cautiously, "I heard from others that he speaks several languages. Chinese, of course, and Persian. I understand, possibly even a little Arabic. This would serve him well in sailing to foreign nations."

She hesitated a moment to see what Zhu Di's response might be. When she saw him smile and motion for her to continue, she took a relieved breath and pressed forward.

"And Zheng He is obviously well versed in the design and construction of ships, Your Majesty, since it is he whom you have put in charge of that magnificent undertaking."

"Is there more?" Zhu Di asked, still maintaining his smile. And still quite amazed that this lovely lady servant was being so forthright. "I'd like nothing more than for you to continue."

Becoming less concerned whether or not Zhu Di was teasing or serious, Xi Chen continued her inquiry, gaining more and more confidence by the minute.

"Well, as you know, Sire, he is a practicing Muslim and quite knowledgeable in the ways of Islam."

"Is that so?" Zhu Di responded, doing his best to sound earnest while at the same time egging her on.

"He's also familiar with the teachings of Lord Buddha!" she exclaimed enthusiastically. "I would think, Sire, that the man you choose to represent your magnificent fleet must be well versed in the religions of many people, especially those with whom he might come in contact during the long voyage. In my opinion, Majesty, this knowledge could prove to be quite valuable when negotiating trade agreements with envoys and leaders of foreign countries."

Zhu Di sat back on the sofa and stared in amazement at the beautiful looking lady sitting next to him. Not bothering to ask for Xi Chen to serve him more tea, he poured a cup for himself.

Encouraged, Xi Chen eagerly added another statement. "And what I think is most important, from what I have personally observed, your servant Zheng He is extremely loyal to you."

Zhu Di took a small sip of tea before responding. "Yes, Zheng He has proven to be an extremely loyal servant, Xi Chen. I quite agree and I also want to thank you for your suggestion. But now, if you don't mind, I'd like for you to fetch me more tea. With all this talk about Zheng He, mine seems to have grown cold."

A month later, Zheng He, Ma Huan and I were again at our shipyard office busily going over lists of people who had been assigned to take part in the first expedition. The room was now overflowing with draftsmen and technicians who continued to work in lengthening shifts.

In the shipyard, more than one hundred vessels could be seen in various stages of construction. Like the draftsmen, thousands of workers toiled around the clock, hammering, sawing, painting, caulking and fitting. It was dirty and noisy work that never ceased.

Just that morning, Zheng He had received another list of new workers from the emperor. But the shipyard was already overflowing with laborers and craftsmen.

"I hope this is the final list we get," Zheng He groused, exhausted and irritable from lack of sleep. "If Zhu Di tries to add one more person to our work force, I don't know where we'll put him."

Ma Huan had a duplicate copy of the list. That way they could double check the names and make certain no one was left behind.

"Sir, if you'll read the names on your list," Ma Huan suggested, "I'll check my list to make certain we're correct."

Zheng He took a deep breath, then nodded his agreement and began. "Seven imperial eunuchs, as ambassadors," he intoned. "Ten junior eunuchs, as assistant ambassadors. Fifty-three eunuch chamberlains, ninety-two senior military directors..."

Ma Huan interrupted. "How many, Sir?"

Zheng He sighed heavily, obviously annoyed by the interruption.

"Ninety-three!" he spat out testily. "Have you got it?"

"Yes, Sir! Ninety-three!"

Zheng He continued. "Two chief military directors, one senior secretary of the revenue ministry, two masters of ceremony..."

Ma Huan interrupted again. "Sir? What does a master of ceremony do?"

Ma Huan's constant interruptions were getting on Zheng He's nerves. "I don't know!" he snapped. "Maybe they're supposed to maintain protocol. May I continue?"

Ma Huan realized it might be better if he kept his questions to himself.

Again, Zheng He began again. "One master meteorologist, four assistant meteorologists, one hundred and twenty-eight medical officers, plus the officials and envoys we recorded earlier."

"You mean...? Are you talking about the twenty-six thousand, eight hundred and three, military officers and sailors we've already counted and assigned to ships?" Ma Huan asked, hating to go back on his vow of silence, but really needing to know.

It was a valid question and Zheng He knew it.

"That's right!" he responded with civility. "There's no need in breaking down those twenty-six thousand again. We've already listed them as military officers and soldiers, reservists, cooks, purveyors, clerks, technicians, sailors, carpenters and interpreters."

"Doesn't that number also include the one hundred merchants who are going along to help make the proper selection of foreign goods?" Ma Huan asked.

Trying to make amends for becoming angry with Ma Huan earlier, Zheng He gave him a warm smile and congratulated him on being so alert. "Yes, you are correct. I'm glad you remembered."

Pleased to see that Zheng He was no longer as irritable, I jumped in to offer my own assessment of the situation.

"As you said, Zheng He, if the emperor comes up with any more names, I don't know where you're going to put them."

"Maybe we better go over the list again," Zheng He surprisingly suggested, even while yawning at the same time. "We can never be too careful."

As far as Ma Huan was concerned, that was a terrible idea. "Sir, we've gone over the list at least four times. Please don't tell me we must do it yet again."

Both men were tired and short-tempered. I could feel trouble brewing. "If I've made a mistake, Ma Huan," Zheng He snapped angrily, "...and several hundred people are left behind, I will be the one who will carry the burden of this egregious oversight, not you!"

"Alright!" I interjected, quickly. "There's no need getting on each other's nerves now. In two or three months the fleet will be ready to set sail and we will all be able to get our lives back to normal." And then added, "Unless the rumor I've heard is true."

"What rumor?" Zheng He asked casually without looking up, already going over Zhu Di's latest list another time.

Ma Huan was also curious. "Yes, friar, what rumor are you talking about?"

I tried to be diplomatic. "Well, I heard from very reliable sources that Zhu Di was going to add Zheng He's name to the list of those who might lead the voyages."

Zheng He looked up. "There is a list?"

"Why yes. Of course. A roster of possible candidates qualified to lead the fleet."

Zheng He couldn't believe what he was hearing. "And I am on this roster? That's crazy. The emperor would never choose a servant to lead the fleet. Where did you hear such a thing?"

I shrugged, grinning from ear to ear. "And I suppose he would never select a servant to oversee the design and construction of the fleet either?"

Suddenly, the possibility became a reality to Zheng He.

I shrugged innocently. "I don't know that it's true. I only know what I have heard."


Prince Han had heard the same rumor about Zheng He. He was not at all happy. The first thing he did was rush to Wong's chamber, barging in without an invitation.

"Did you put Zheng He's name on your list of qualified recommendations?" he yelled, seething with anger.

Wong grew immediately defensive. "Of course not! Why would I do such a thing?"

"I just heard that Zheng He was being considered," Han snarled.

Wong gathered his wits and went on the offensive.

"Your father has his own list, Prince Han. And I have mine. I assure you..."

Han didn't let him finish. "You've got to do something, Wong! Do you hear me? Zheng He can't be selected to lead the fleet!"

The very thought of Zheng He leading the prestigious Ming fleet made the prince furious. He pounded his fists on Wong's desk like a spoiled child. He spun around, walked in dizzy circles, then returned to Wong.

"It would be bad enough," he shouted, "to have a servant lead the fleet. But Zheng He is a 'eunuch' servant. And a Muslim eunuch servant at that! He's not even a servant of the Buddhist faith!"

"Can we be certain that Zheng He is actually a eunuch?" Wong countered, trying to deflect Han's criticism. "Rumors still persist."

Han was incredulous. "My father wouldn't have selected Zheng He to be Chief 'Eunuch,' if he weren't actually a 'eunuch'! Would he? I think my father is insane, but I don't think he's THAT insane."

Wong shrugged. "I agree. But still, one can never be sure. There was reason to believe, many years ago, that your father made an exception in Zheng He's case. You must remember, this took place when you were still but a child."

Han leaned across Wong's desk and poked his finger into the old gentleman's chest.

"I want you to force my father to tell you the truth, Minister Wong! You can do it! If he admits Zheng He is not a eunuch, then the servant lives a lie. He can't walk around with the fancy title 'Chief Eunuch'!"

Becoming calmer now, Prince Han began to unfold his own twisted strategy. "On the other hand, if he admits that he is a eunuch, then no palace official or civil servant will support him as a representative of the people of China. Either way, discrediting Zheng He will only make it easier for my father to choose me. Make him tell you the truth, Minister Wong. You can do it!"

Wong discretely and firmly pushed the young man's finger away from his chest.

"My dear boy," he stated earnestly, "you're old enough to know that nobody makes the emperor do anything that he does not choose to do. Now, if you'll please excuse me, I have duties I must attend to."


During a casual social gathering several weeks later, Zhu Di entertained General Tan and Monk Dao Yan for several hours in one of the imperial gardens. The three old friends sat sipping tea, while discussing the emperor's favorite project.

"The construction of your Ming fleet seems to be on schedule," General Tan suggested, knowing his comment would please Zhu Di. "I saw Zheng He the other day and he told me he remains confident he can have the ships ready to sail on time."

Zhu Di was obviously pleased to hear the news.

"My servant is doing a marvelous job," he allowed, "just as I knew he would. I've told him that I want the fleet ready for its maiden sail by the beginning of the summer near Shanghai."

"Will all the sailors and officers be properly trained by then?" the general asked, fully aware that proper training is the key to any successful armada.

"Zheng He is way ahead of you, General," Zhu Di confided, happily. "He tells me that he has arranged for the different ship's officers to take the fleet on a leisurely voyage to the south, down to the Min River in Fukien province. During this extended period, which should last anywhere from four to eight weeks, Zheng He expects that he and the officers will be able to work out any problems which might arise with the ships or the men."

"I never cease to be amazed at your servant's superior good sense and intellect. May I congratulate you, Sire, on putting such a capable person in charge of getting your fleet ready to sail."

Zhu Di beamed with pride and provided his two friends with some additional information. "At the end of this maiden sailing period, if all the ships are still in fine working order, I told Zheng He I wanted everyone to be on board ready to set sail on the first major voyage from Shanghai in December or early January."

"That sounds marvelous," Dao Yan concurred happily, slapping the table with an open hand..

Zhu Di smiled at Dao Yan's enthusiasm. "Zheng He has also informed me that such a date should coincide quite favorably with the annual monsoon season."

"I'll bet you're excited!" Dao Yan gushed again, his smile almost as large as the emperors.

General Tan interrupted. "Summer is only four weeks away, Your Majesty. May I ask if you've chosen someone to lead the fleet?"

Zhu Di took a sip of tea before answering. "I'm leaning towards several candidates," he confided casually. "Do you have any suggestions?"

General Tan responded quickly. "The High Consul and I both believe very strongly that you should select your servant, Zheng He. In our humble opinion, Sire, he's by far the most qualified."

Zhu Di pretended to be surprised. "Really? And why do you say that?"

Now, it was Dao Yan who spoke up. "Because he's extremely resourceful, Your Majesty, and I'm sure you're well aware that he speaks several languages fluently."

At this point Zhu Di held up his hand and stopped his High Consul's effusive rhetoric. "I don't wish to be rude, my friend, but I think I've heard all this before... and from a source far lovelier to the eye. I'll make my selection in a few days. In the meantime, why don't we have the ladies bring us something refreshing to drink. Do you agree?

They did, indeed.


Several days later, Prince Han was getting desperate. He went to his father's quarters so he could have a private, face-to-face meeting with him. His plan was to convince his father of his own unique qualifications.

"When you first announced your intention to build the fleet," Han began quietly, "I hope you remember, it was I, Prince Han, your second son, who first offered to lead your great armada of ships."

Zhu Di squirmed in his seat at the uncomfortable memory, immediately realizing what his impetuous son was leading up to. "I remember," he countered tentatively, trying to decide how to best tell his son that he was not going to be chosen.

"I don't want you to be offended by what I'm about to tell you, my son, but, in my mind, you're still a young man. To my way of thinking, you still... how shall I say this?... lack certain areas of experience."

"Experience!" Han shouted. "Haven't I fought side-by-side with you in your military campaigns? Haven't I proved to you, over and over, my utmost loyalty and bravery?"

Zhu Di didn't like the tone of his son's booming voice, but was determined not to become involved in another nasty confrontation with him.

"There's no question of your loyalty to me or of your bravery on the field of battle, but the man I choose to lead the Ming fleet must have a certain maturity. Such maturity, Han, is only gained by years of experience, working with all types of people."

When Han started to interrupt, Zhu Di stopped him. "I don't want you to be disheartened. It may very well be possible for you to have a position on some future expedition. I would most happily consider that."

Han was extremely disappointed at his father's reluctance to choose him for the honor, but knew better than to press his case further. He decided to change his approach.

"If you refuse to choose me, father, then I want you to consider choosing your old friend, Minister Wong. You say that I don't have the proper experience? Well, Minister Wong has more than enough experience. Would you do that for me? I think Minister Wong would make an excellent choice."

Zhu Di sat back in his chair, wishing his son would simply drop the subject. But he knew this was unlikely to happen.

"Minister Wong _is_ being considered," he said. But Prince Han could tell that his father's words were spoken without conviction.

Just the idea that his father might select Zheng He for the prestigious position was more than he could take. The civility he had managed to demonstrate up to this point evaporated in a flash.

He jumped up from his chair and angrily started pacing the room, agitated. Zhu Di knew that his son could be just as volatile as he was. He watched the frustrated young man pacing nervously, worried about what might be coming next.

"I've heard rumors," Han began, his breath coming in short spurts, "that you're actually considering Zheng He for this important honor. Is it true?"

Zhu Di gazed at his son with unblinking eyes, then spoke with quiet certainty. "I may be. Do you have an objection?"

Han immediately rushed toward him, standing defiantly in front of his father, his fists clenched in tight balls.

"The man's a lowly servant, father!" he shrieked. "Surely you're not going to honor someone of such inferior standing?"

Zhu Di maintained a steady demeanor. "I haven't made my decision, but when I do, I expect to have your full support. Do I make myself clear?"

Prince Han knew that he had stepped over the line. He turned on his heels and walked to the door. He paused there, then turned. His face was red with bitterness. "If you do select him, father, I will be certain that you are insane. And it will doom you to failure."

Prince Han slammed the door to his father's residence, walking into the night.

Several days later, Zheng He and I were enjoying a sunny walk together within the walls of the Nanking palace. I told him that I thought it was a miracle the way he had been able to get the emperor's fleet built on time.

"It was hard work, friar," he told me simply as we walked slowly together across a broad courtyard. "And we never lost sight of his vision."

"Your vision was certainly true, Zheng He," I said, "and it's an accomplishment of which you should be very proud."

"I am proud, but too much pride can lead to..."

I cut him off. "Stop, Zheng He", I cautioned. "Parables and lessons are my calling. 'You' are the student."

Zheng He smiled at my genial admonition, saying nothing to dispute it.

As we walked along, I became vexed by a question I had wanted to ask, but had heretofore been afraid to broach.

"Now that you're finished with the fleet," I ventured, "you must be anxious to see Xi Chen."

My question must have bothered him somewhat, because he seemed hesitant to give me an answer.

"In time," he finally told me softly.

I pressed on. "But you've been away for many months."

"There are some things I do not hasten to discover, friar," he told me with an edge to his voice. "Now if you would just drop the subject, I would be forever grateful."

I was surprised at his response. We continued our pleasant walk together, but in silence.

At the Fukien shipyards, Zheng He continued to push himself. He made certain that every single detail was checked and double-checked. While he was consumed with making sure the ships were ready to sail, everyone else was consumed with wanting to know who Zhu Di would select to lead the magnificent fleet. The much-awaited announcement was expected at any time.

Two days later, while Zheng He, Ma Huan and I were going over the final preparations for the maiden voyage, two couriers unexpectedly arrived at the shipyard with a message for Zheng He. He was to accompany them back to Nanking. Zhu Di wanted him to be present for his upcoming announcement.

When Zheng He asked the messengers to wait outside for a few minutes, I immediately clapped him on the back and sang out happily. "That's it, my friend! You're either going to be removed from your position... or put in charge of the entire fleet."

Zheng He grinned broadly and shook his head mockingly. "At the present time, I would welcome being removed from my honorable position."

I stuck out my hand, offering my congratulations. Zheng He laughed and gave my hand a good shake. But he still wasn't convinced that he'd be the one chosen.

"I appreciate your kind thoughts, friar, but I honestly don't think there's a chance in the world Zhu Di would chose a servant for such a prestigious honor. I don't want you and Ma Huan to be disappointed when I'm not selected."

Ma Huan, however, was as optimistic as I was. "Can we go with you to Nanking, Sir? I'd like to be present when you receive the good news."

Zheng He relented. "Why not? When we receive the news, whatever it is, we'll receive it together." But then, he added his disclaimer. "I still think you're both going to be disappointed!"

When we arrived at the palace, we were immediately ushered into Zhu Di's quarters and surprisingly, found both Prince Han and Minister Wong already there. They were in the midst of a heated discussion, attempting to dissuade Zhu Di from picking a mere servant for the honored position of fleet commander.

Zheng He couldn't help but overhear several of their rude remarks and felt he had arrived at a very bad time. After bowing respectfully, he suggested that maybe he should come back later.

"Nonsense!" Zhu Di sang out happily, while motioning for his servant to enter. "I requested your presence and I'm delighted that you're here. Prince Han and Minister Wong were just discussing your qualifications."

Prince Han and Wong gave a perfunctory nod in Zheng He's direction, but it was evident they were reluctant to acknowledge his presence.

"Zheng He!" Zhu Di shouted again, happily, "I'd like for you to describe the type of man whom 'you' think should lead the expedition."

Without hesitating, Zheng He immediately offered an appraisal of the qualifications he thought the candidate should have, never once looking at his two detractors. When he finished, Emperor Zhu Di clapped his hands together enthusiastically. "Marvelous! You've just described yourself. I'll make my official selection tomorrow."

That night, Zhu Di informed his wife that he would be choosing a concubine for the evening. He requested that Xi Chen be brought to him. Because the following day would be such an important day, he decided he should reward himself by having an intimate encounter with the irresistible Muslim beauty.

When she arrived, the emperor made a determined effort not to rush things. He wanted to purposefully take his time so he could savor every aspect of what promised to be a very titillating sexual experience.

He knew, of course, that all he had to do was issue his lady servant a command and she would be obliged to carry out his most personal desires. But, ordering a lady to make love to him was not his manner, especially a lady as sophisticated and alluring as Xi Chen.

He much preferred having the encounter develop naturally into an honest expression of love, preceded by several hours of pleasant conversation. Only then, after they had grown to know each another and the fragrant candles had begun to burn low, would Zhu Di allow himself to become engaged in the less refined aspects of human sexual activity.

While Xi Chen served wine to her host, Zhu Di began putting his plan into action, engaging her in small talk.

"I'm sure you're aware, fair lady, that I must make a very important decision tomorrow."

"Oh?" Xi Chen responded pretending not to know what the emperor was talking about. "What kind of a decision do you plan to make, Sire?"

"A decision that Prince Han would like me to make in his favor," Zhu Di replied, attempting to be coy.

"Prince Han, Your Majesty? He's a very nice young man. What would he have you do?"

"He would have me choose him to lead our great Ming fleet."

"Prince Han?" she questioned, continuing with the obvious ruse and pretending to be shocked. "Isn't he a little young for such an important position?"

Xi Chen then coyly acted as if she'd made a mistake by saying something negative about a member of the imperial family. "Oh, I'm terribly sorry, Your Majesty," she begged, trying to sound overly-sincere. "I shouldn't have said that. I'm sure Prince Han would make a wonderful leader of the fleet."

"Maybe you shouldn't have said it, Xi Chen," Zhu Di replied, with an exaggerated scowl, "but I'm afraid it's true. I also have grave doubts about the maturity and leadership qualities of my number two son. He would like to be my selection, but I just can't bring myself to give him the honor."

Xi Chen slipped around behind Zhu Di and started gently rubbing his neck and shoulders. The emperor closed his eyes for a moment, so he could enjoy the soothing touch of her delicate fingers. As Xi Chen's fingers worked their magic, she asked Zhu Di if he was thinking about choosing anyone else? With his eyes still closed he responded, casually.

"I've thought about my Minister of Protocol Wong. He's been a friend of the family ever since I was a boy, but he's old and, unfortunately, not someone whom I feel I could completely trust."

Xi Chen continued rubbing Zhu Di's neck and shoulders, listening. When the emperor paused and made no additional comments, she cautiously offered one of her own.

"And Zheng He, Your Majesty? Is he not being considered?"

Zhu Di opened his eyes and responded to Xi Chen coyly.

"You can rest assured, pretty one, my most talented servant is being very seriously considered."

Xi Chen wanted to say something more in support of Zheng He, but she hesitated, afraid to say too much. Her gentle massage continued, becoming more soothing to the emperor.

"May I again suggest, Your Majesty, no one is more knowledgeable about the fleet than your servant Zheng He. It was he who helped design the ships..."

Zhu Di opened his eyes and turned to her. He then pulled her face close to his and gave her a sweet kiss on the lips to prevent her from saying anything further.

Xi Chen trembled, shocked that the emperor had just kissed her. But she accepted his playful show of affection with a warm smile, then gently turned his head forward and continued massaging his neck. After Zhu Di closed his eyes yet again, she daringly ventured another comment.

"Also, Your Majesty," she began again, "in knowing the wishes of both Buddha and Mohammed, Zheng He is in a..."

This time Zhu Di pulled Xi Chen close with a forceful hand and whispered into her ear. "You've told me before that your selection is Zheng He. Tonight, sweet lady, my selection is you."

Xi Chen anticipated what would happen next. But she also knew that she was expected to be receptive to the emperor's advances. But every fiber in her body fought to resist. She wanted to bolt from the room and never look back, but she knew that she didn't dare.

The sacred vow she had taken with Zheng He was still very real to her. Xi Chen had promised she would never allow another man to touch her, not even if that man was the emperor. But now she was alone with the emperor in his private bedroom and he was beginning to make some serious sexual advances.

Nervously, Xi Chen kissed Zhu Di lightly on the cheek, laughed playfully, then got him to turn back around, so she could continue rubbing his neck and shoulders.

She had been waiting and praying for a long time that she might once again feel totally satisfied as a woman. There had never been anyone, even in the deepest recesses of her heart, who she had wanted to make love to other than Zheng He. But now, the man who was kissing and whispering in her ear was not the man of her dreams.

She watched, slightly terrified, as Zhu Di got up from the lounge, took her by the hand and deliberately began leading her into his private bedroom.

"I can't do it!" the voice in her mind screamed. "I promised Zheng He I would never make love to anyone but him!"

"Your Majesty..." she begged suddenly, pulling away. "You must give me a little time. It's not that I find you unattractive. It's just that affairs of the heart must be tended to with care. Like a beautiful rose, they must be allowed to blossom, slowly, over time."

She then gave Zhu Di a quick sisterly peck on the cheek and began gathering her things. Rejected by a lady of his court was not only unusual, it was totally unprecedented. It was something that Zhu Di had never before encountered, not even as a young king.

But instead of being angry or insulted, he found himself amused and even more intrigued by this most unusual lady.

Two eunuch servants appeared from behind a decorated screen on the far side of the room and quietly stepped in front of the doorway, effectively blocking Xi Chen's path.

She stopped, holding her breath, waiting to see what would happen next. Much to her relief, the emperor gave the servants a casual wave and Xi Chen was allowed to pass.


The next day, in a lavish ceremony at the palace, Zhu Di announced the decision everyone was waiting to hear.

"Following great deliberation," he intoned seriously, "and after a lengthy spiritual communion guided by our revered Lord Buddha, I am pleased to announce who I have selected to command my new Ming fleet."

When the stirring of excitement finally died down, Zhu Di announced to everyone, "I have chosen my close friend and faithful servant, Zheng He!"

Several loud gasps could be heard from the distinguished gathering, along with a smattering of scattered applause.

Xi Chen also gasped, covering her mouth with her hands to stifle the delighted shriek that wanted to escape.

Prince Han stiffened, his face immediately clouded by a dark brooding shadow. He stared numbly. The only emotion he could feel was a churning need for vengeance deep in the pit of his stomach.

Zheng He remained at attention, respectful and noble. He couldn't believe the emperor had chosen him, but he forced himself not to let any emotion show, one way or the other.

Zhu Di continued. "Let it be known that it is he, San-pao T'ai-chen, who shall be in charge of my great armada of ships. From this day forward he shall be addressed as Lord Zheng He and shall lead my great armada with the formal title, Admiral of the Ming Fleet."

There was another round of somewhat restrained applause. General Tan and Minister Wong bowed with stiff politeness to Zheng He, as expected by imperial formality. When the applause faded down, Prince Han gritted his teeth and leaned close to his father so he could speak privately.

"Respectfully, father," he whispered, "you have made the greatest mistake of your life."

Then Prince Han strode angrily from the room, his face a bitter scowl. Empress Xu watched her son's departure with great concern, then stole a look at her husband, but said nothing.

Many of the guests and dignitaries approached Zheng He to offer their reluctant congratulations. Others stood back, grumbling to each other unhappily. The room was clearly divided in its opinion of the emperor's unexpected selection.

Prince Han was clearly beside himself with agitation. He waited outside in the square for the ceremony to end. When Minister Wong finally emerged from the palace, Han sought him out and intercepted him at once. His jaw was set with a determined thrust.

"This foul decision shall not escape retribution," he hissed to the elderly minister. "Mark my word."

Wong agreed. "There is already strong opposition among the ministers," he told the young prince, as the two of them walked hurriedly across the broad stone square. "Your father is risking rebellion from within his own court."

Inside Zhu Di's throne room, the polite congratulations continued unabated. Zheng He tried to accommodate all of his admirers with a comment or two, but was more interested in seeking out Xi Chen with his gaze. When their eyes finally met, she smiled at him with soft assurance, but withheld any sign of the passion and pain that was churning inside her.

After several more minutes, Zhu Di retired to his private chamber and invited Zheng He to join him. As he entered his quarters, he waved the servants out with a flick of his finger and they quickly departed.

Now alone with Zhu Di, the new Ming Admiral bowed deeply to the emperor before he spoke. "I am most honored, Your Majesty."

When Zhu Di offered him a seat close to his, Zheng He noticed something seemed to be wrong. A shadow had fallen upon the emperor's face, as if he was brooding about something. After such a wonderful celebration, Zheng He had no idea what the trouble might be. After a few moments, Zhu Di spoke directly to his Zheng He. "I fear Hui-Ti still lives."

Zheng He was surprised at the emperor's comment. "That is highly unlikely, Sire," he stammered. "The fire was..."

Zhu Di cut him off sharply. "No. The young fool remains in hiding. He's like a phantom in my dreams. He haunts me nightly."

Zheng He wanted to say something to reassure his friend, but Zhu Di raised his hand like a curtain, so that he might sit in silence.

After a few moments, he continued. "But this great fleet," Zhu Di said, "will certainly draw him out of hiding. He will be unable to resist such a blatant accomplishment without coming forth to claim what he so foolishly believes to be his own."

Zheng He stared at Zhu Di with concern. He feared the emperor was becoming demented by his twisted fixation with Hui-Ti. Zheng He was certain the young ruler had died in the flames and didn't feel Zhu Di had anything to worry about.

However, it was true that Emperor Hui-Ti's body was never discovered and because of this, some speculated he had escaped with his life. A few even believed that Hui-Ti would someday return to claim the throne as his own.

But Zheng He also knew Zhu Di's troops had completely surrounded the palace when it was burning. There was no possible way that Hui-Ti could have lived through the terrible inferno.

Rumors and speculation had a way of taking on a life of their own. Zheng He knew that well. Some had speculated that he was a eunuch, while others were certain he wasn't. No amount of rumor or speculation, could convince one side or the other of the truth.


The next morning, a group of dissenting ministers requested an urgent meeting in Wong's chamber. He was happy to host the gathering for he was certain they had come to register some sort of complaint against Zhu Di's selection of Zheng He as Admiral of the Fleet.

A minister named Du Wei, who was the oldest and who had known Wong for many years, offered Wong a slight bow before speaking.

"The eunuchs are growing in number and influence," he hissed angrily. "They are like weeds in our garden. Soon they will be out of control."

Wong, inwardly pleased, nodded, but said nothing.

A second minister, much younger, quickly added, "And now they have a hero to inspire them."

The third minister in the group, who didn't wish to be outdone, was quick to offer Wong a fake smile as he made his feelings known.

"They look to Zheng He as a glorious leader and endeavor to emulate him."

The first minister, Du Wei, then spoke again and added the most telling comment of all.

"We must halt this tide of rebellion before it drowns us all. Don't you agree?"


Late that same day, Minister Wong and his group of dissenting ministers paid an unannounced visit to Zhu Di. It was growing late. The emperor was sitting alone in his imperial chamber, slumped on his throne. His face was buried behind his hand as if he was asleep, or in some type of deep contemplation.

When a servant entered to announce Wong's arrival, Zhu Di, absorbed in his revere, didn't acknowledge his presence. The servant had to clear his throat, so the emperor would know he was in the room. After a moment, Zhu Di slid his fingers apart and peered out.

"Your Majesty, Minister of Protocol Wong, and three Imperial Ministers, bid an audience with you."

Slowly, Zhu Di motioned for him to bring them in.

As the servant left, Zhu Di's mind began stirring with thoughts, as he tried to consider why Wong and his friends were paying him this unexpected visit.

When the doors opened and Wong and the three ministers entered the throne room, Wong sternly waved at Zhu Di's servant to step aside and stay back. The small contingent of solemn men then marched sternly toward Zhu Di and didn't halt until they were directly in front of him. Each bowed with insincere politeness.

Wong, with a familiar scowl on his face, did not waste time with formalities.

"Sire, we have a critical grievance that we'd like to address."

"Yes, I'm quite sure you do," Zhu Di responded calmly, "And I'm anxious to hear it. But first, let me share with you something of interest."

Zhu Di's deviation displeased Wong and the ministers, but they had no choice but to remain silent and listen to what he was going to tell them.

"I've decided that Minister of Protocol Wong will join Lord Zheng He on the expedition as second in command."

This unexpected announcement completely stunned Wong and the ministers, as it took the wind out of their sails. Before they could respond, Zhu Di put them on their heels yet again.

"He will thereby assure the success of the expedition while personally representing all of your interests and concerns."

Zhu Di watched their response carefully. He was proud of his own clever move to subvert their obvious mission, and he secretly enjoyed their stunned silence.

"So now," Zhu Di asked smiling, "what is this grievance that you wish to air?"

Wong and the three ministers quickly exchanged uneasy glances among themselves, as they were unsure just how they should proceed. The youngest minister gathered his courage and pushed himself toward the front so he could speak directly with the emperor, but Du Wei, the oldest minister and Wong's friend, blocked his path and began to address Zhu Di in a forceful, yet measured tone.

"Sire, we do not want..."

But Wong stopped him from continuing. "We do not want to trouble you. The hour is late. We can address our concerns at another time."

Zhu Di didn't want to let them off that easy. "On the contrary," he said cheerfully. "Please. My eyes and ears are open. Trouble me."

More uneasy glances flashed among the three now uneasy ministers.

The youngest minister again tried to make a comment.

"We have a..."

Again Minister Wong raised his hand to silence the young minister, then took the lead.

"There are those among the Inner Court, Your Majesty, who have certain grievances on a variety of subjects. But since you are so deeply involved in many other, more important, issues, we'd like to spare your concern and endeavor to resolve these petty complaints amongst ourselves."

"How generous of you," Zhu Di crowed. He smiled at them again. It was quite obvious that outwitting his rebellious advisors gave him a great deal of satisfaction.

Chapter Six

_____

A JOYOUS BEGINNING

The next morning, Zheng He, Ma Huan and I were back in our shipyard office going over maps, checking routes and making final preparations for what promised to be a very historic voyage. Ma Huan asked the new Ming admiral about the assignment of "watches" on board the ships. It was something that hadn't even occurred to me, so I was very curious as to what he would say.

"There will be ten watches on each ship," Zheng He told him matter-of-factly. "Each watch will last for two hours and forty minutes."

Now it was Ma Huan who was even more curious than I was.

"Why did you select two hours and forty minutes?" he asked with a puzzled expression. "It seems like such an arbitrary amount of time."

"It's not arbitrary at all," Zheng He explained. "Sailors have been standing two hour and forty minute watches for many generations."

After looking through his desk, Zheng He retrieved three incense sticks.

"You know what these are don't you?" he asked, holding the sticks up.

"Sure. They're incense sticks. They're used in just about every one of our religious ceremonies."

"That's right. But what you probably didn't know is that these incense sticks burn at a very constant rate. It takes exactly two hours and forty minutes for one stick to be consumed. Consequently, if we burn one incense stick on each watch, we can pretty well be assured that our ship watches will start and end on time."

Ma Huan beamed. "That's ingenious. Brilliant." He took the three sticks from Zheng He and studied them closely. "Why did I not know this?"

"Probably," I interjected wryly, "because you never sat through a religious ceremony that lasted two hours and forty minutes."


As Fleet Admiral, Zheng He was in charge of all the soldiers and sailors that had been assigned to fleet duty. It was his responsibility to make sure the men were fully trained and physically prepared for the long voyage. As part of their training exercise, he had them compete with each other in various challenges on horseback.

Zheng He and Ma Huan watched from a tall bamboo tower as dozens of soldiers and sailors were put through complex military maneuvers on the field below. One group rode on horseback toward a small wooden target, attempting to hit it with arrows shot from a crossbow. Not so easy from the back of a galloping horse.

A second group, also on horseback, snatched spears from the ground and heaved them at another target as they galloped past it at a dead run. Most of their efforts were clumsy and unsuccessful, but one man, blessed with superb grace and agility, rode with such a fluid motion that it allowed him to hit the target nearly every time.

Zheng He took special notice of this man's unusual skill and pointed him out to Ma Huan.

"Who is that young officer? He rides like I did when I was his age."

Ma Huan's eyes searched the scroll he carried. "I believe his name is Zhang Ji." Then, he pointed excitedly. "Yes, yes... here it is! Lieutenant Zhang Ji. I was correct."

Zheng He smiled, impressed by Ma Huan's memory and his swift response. "Be sure that he's assigned to my flagship."

Ma Huan nodded his affirmation and made a note.


That same evening, at the emperor's residence, Empress Xu conversed with a female servant as she carefully arranged her elaborate roll of hair.

In a moment of great indiscretion, Empress Xu's young servant confided that she thought Xi Chen was in love with Zheng He.

Empress Xu looked back over her shoulder at the servant with surprise. "You say... she loves him?

"Oh, yes," the young servant agreed. "It's rumored, empress, that she has loved him for many years."

Empress Xu was eager to learn more. "Do they meet secretly?" she inquired.

"When possible, I understand. But it's most difficult."

Both women abruptly fell silent as Zhu Di entered the room and took a seat on a plush silk couch nearby. Empress Xu immediately dismissed the female servant with a subtle gesture.

"You appear very pleased, my husband," she announced with a pleasant smile. "And why not? Your great fleet is almost ready to set sail."

Zhu Di returned his wife's amiable smile with one of his own. "It is truly a night of celebration. Tomorrow the greatest fleet of ships the world has ever known will set sail for new lands."

"And so," Empress Xu responded with a scowl, "you will, no doubt, celebrate with your concubines."

Zhu Di shifted uneasily. "You resent this?"

She replied stoically, "It is your right."

"It is also custom and tradition," he scolded her firmly, proudly justifying his behavior. But then he noticed the troubled look on her face. He quickly changed his tactic, softening his voice and demeanor.

"Are you angry?" he asked sweetly.

"No, not at all," his wife lied. "You are Emperor. You can do as you wish."

Zhu Di wasn't certain if she was being truthful with him or merely trying to spin a web of confusion to keep him off balance. He took a firm stance, ignoring her probable manipulation. "And so I will," he announced proudly. "I've called for five of my favorite Ladies-in-Waiting, so that I may choose among them."

Empress Xu smiled knowingly, reflecting on her own secret thoughts. Zhu Di glimpsed a disturbingly strange look in her eyes, puzzled by it.

"What amuses you so," he asked, curious as to why she had become so cheerful in the face of his confidence.

"Oh, nothing," she lied again. "Only that you are so easy to predict."

"Me? Easy to predict? I don't believe so. My motives and private desires are quite elusive to the eye." He leaned toward her with bold certainty. "Anyone's eye."

Empress Xu smiled with a sly confidence, undeterred.

The door to their private residence swung open with a whoosh of warm air. Wang, the openly effeminate eunuch servant, escorted five concubines into the room. One of them was Xi Chen.

As they approached, Empress Xu's eyes never left Xi Chen, delighting in the secret knowledge that she now possessed.

The empress turned to Zhu Di.

"If you are such a puzzling mystery, my husband, then it will no doubt astonish you when I predict your selection."

Zhu Di shook his head, stood straight and announced firmly, "That's impossible."

The five women stopped before the emperor. They did their very best to avoid his direct gaze. Xi Chen huddled in the center of the group, attempting to shrink away and vanish.

When Xi Chen glanced up shyly, her eyes briefly met those of Empress Xu. The empress gave her a faint knowing smile.

Zhu Di was quick to put his wife to the test. "And so, my love," he asked, "where shall I find my pleasure tonight? Which will be my fortunate selection?"

Empress Xu leaned over, moved her lips close to her husband's ear and whispered to him, "You shall choose, the lovely flower in the center."

Zhu Di's face was immediately drained of its color, as his confidence withered. But he was not about to let his wife be correct. Despite his keen desire to have Xi Chen for the evening, he would rather trick his mate at her own brazen game than have to live with her obnoxious victory. His expression hardened into stern determination.

"You are wrong," he declared firmly with perverse obstinacy.

Zhu Di then nodded at the young dark-haired girl who stood at the end of the line, looking her directly in the eye.

"On the far left," he exclaimed. "She will be my pleasure tonight."

Empress Xu stared at him coldly for a long moment, then shrugged as she feigned only mild disappointment.

"You have confounded me again, dear husband. I bow to your eminence," she told him, unable to conceal her sarcastic smirk.

As Wang led the other four women away, Xi Chen quickly glanced at Empress Xu. With a subtle expression, she let the empress know that she understood what had just happened. She gave a little nod of gratitude. The empress responded with her own subtle nod of acknowledgement.

Zhu Di, still embroiled in his own mixed feelings of success and failure, was completely oblivious to this exchange.

Elsewhere in the palace, Prince Han was still highly agitated over Zheng He's selection as the Ming Admiral. Unable to quell his troubled thoughts, he paid a visit to Minister Wong's quarters.

As he circled the older minister, his devious mind began to work. "As number two in command, you are in a perfect position," he told Wong gleefully.

Wong could not agree more. "It does suit me, doesn't it?"

"You can plant the seeds of mistrust," Han continued. "You can cause my father to lose all faith in this cunning and manipulative eunuch."

Wong clearly relished his newly found position of authority. He posed haughtily, giving Han a look of audacious superiority. "If I do choose..."

Prince Han angrily cut him off. "What do you mean IF you choose? You must choose! It is your duty."

"Don't speak to me of duty," Wong objected, haughtily. "I now have total authority to decide what I shall do and what I shall not do. And I do not plan to squander it."

Han fretted about Wong's new show of confidence. "Are you being seduced by a false taste of power, Minister Wong? How can you be so easily turned?"

Wong slowly faced Han with a penetrating look. "Have no doubt, my young prince. I will destroy Zheng He. Prepare your gratitude."


Later that same evening, Zheng He took Ma Huan with him when he went to meet secretly with Xi Xhen. They paused just outside a chamber of the servant's quarters. The admiral turned to Ma Huan and whispered what he wanted him to do.

"Let no one enter. Do you understand? I trust you with this."

Ma Huan bowed.

"You have my solemn word."

Zheng He stepped inside the chamber and closed the door behind him. Ma Huan, as ordered, stood outside and kept a sharp eye out for anyone who might approach.

As Zheng He entered the dark chamber, his eyes carefully searched the shadows for his love. He noticed that shafts of moonlight slashed across the room from several high windows, creating numerous pools of illumination on the floor.

At first, Zheng He didn't see Xi Chen, but he heard her voice. "Why do you torture us so?"

He turned around to see Xi Chen's face, glowing softly in a nearby shaft of moonlight.

"Xi Chen." He whispered, moving toward her. But she had abruptly vanished. He looked around, his eyes searching the almost completely darkened room. Then, he saw her again, just a few feet away, shimmering in a different pool of golden moonlight.

"It has been an eternity," Xi Chen told him softly. With each day, my love..." But Zheng He stepped forward suddenly, cutting her off.

"Just tell me, Xi Chen... have you been with him?"

"As I promised you long ago," she answered softly, "I have always been faithful only to you. My love for you does not diminish. It only grows stronger."

Xi Chen then looked down sadly. "But he is emperor, my love, and with each day,"

Zheng He didn't want her to finish. "I give you my solemn pledge, Xi Chen... I will always protect you."

He turned away to look off into the shadows. With stern resolve, he told her, "I will never let him have you."

When he turned his gaze back to the soft pool of light, Xi Chen had disappeared yet again. He panicked. His eyes again scanned the murky darkness.

"Why must you always leave me?" Xi Chen whispered, as she slid into a closer pool of glowing moonlight.

"The ships are now finished," he told her, trying to think of something positive to say that would chase away her melancholy. "It's a magnificent fleet, Xi Chen, like no other in the world."

But his words made her even sadder. "Yes, and now the fleet sails. And you must go. Again, I will be alone."

Desperately, he tried to reassure her. "A man's life is an adventure, my love. He must not let the world write his story. He must write it himself."

She vanished in the shadows once more. But then, just as suddenly, she was in his arms, appearing as if by magic from the darkness.

"Oh, Zheng He," she murmured softly, her warm breath on his cheek. The two lovers embraced fervently.

"Make me part of it," she begged him. "Include me in your adventure."

She caressed Zheng He and then kissed him with great passion. He responded with forceful kisses of his own.

"My thirst for you cannot be quenched," Xi Chen gasped. "Desire burns my soul."

Her hand moved down his chest and across his stomach. She desperately began pulling at his clothing.

"Make love to me, my love," she gasped. "Possess me like we've always dreamed."

Zheng He was immediately torn by growing emotions. Here was the woman of his life, begging him to make love to her; yet, she belonged to Zhu Di and not to him.

Xi Chen's kisses grew more ardent and her hands became more insistent. Then, knowing what he must do, Zheng He abruptly pushed her away. He held her wrists tightly.

"No! I cannot," he told with a harsh voice.

Xi Chen looked deeply into his eyes and responded breathlessly. "There's no reason for you to resist, my love. I'm yours. You can take me. Take me now."

Then she surprised Zheng He when she whispered softly in his ear, "I know your secret."

Zheng He was shocked.

"My secret?"

He pulled away, confused.

Xi Chen clutched at him desperately, trying to pull him back to her. "No, Zheng He. Please!"

"I must go," he told her, brusquely.

"Don't leave me," she begged. "Please don't leave me."

Zheng He stopped at the door. "My heart will never leave you, Xi Chen. It will always be here for you."

He quickly stepped outside the chamber door, shutting it behind him. All hope and strength drained from Xi Chen's body. Her legs turned to air. Her head spun. She collapsed on the stone floor, sobbing.

Four months later, sea trials had been successfully completed and the Ming fleet assembled off the mouth of the Yangtze. Soldiers, sailors, servants, envoys, gifts, animals and supplies were all on board and prepared to take part in the elaborate departure ceremony.

Zhu Di and a large entourage of government officials, guests and servants had traveled to Shanghai from Nanking, so they could all be present for this unprecedented historic occasion.

Before watching the ships pass-in-review, Zhu Di offered prayers to the Goddess of Protection to make certain the fleet had a safe return. He then presided over a series of smaller ceremonies each attended by hundreds of special guests, state officials, ministers and civil servants.

When all the ceremonies had been completed, the emperor then led everyone to the mouth of the Yangtze River, where the huge fleet was assembled. They awaited Admiral Zheng He's signal for the gigantic fleet to pass-in-review.

Zhu Di, Empress Xu and the couple's two sons, along with Admiral Zheng He, Minister Wong and a large number of honored guests, took their places on the Reviewing Stand that had been constructed especially for the occasion on the bank of the river. Many other guests of lesser standing arranged themselves according to rank and government position on either side of the richly decorated imperial structure.

Zheng He took a seat in his place of honor next to Emperor Zhu Di. Empress Xu was already seated next to her husband on the other side. She smiled pleasantly to the Ming Admiral. He acknowledged her with a polite bow.

Zheng He was nervous and found it difficult to accept the fact that he was sitting on the Reviewing Stand as Admiral of the Ming Fleet. He was not there to provide services to others, but rather to take his place as an honored leader beside the Emperor and Empress.

As his eyes scanned up and down the huge bay, he was delighted the day had turned out so bright and sunny. This was Zhu Di's special day and he deserved to have it just as perfect as it turned out to be.

Thankfully, a fresh breeze was blowing down the bay. Zheng He knew this would make it easier for his ship captains to keep their vessels in proper alignment as they dramatically "passed-in-review" before Emperor Zhu Di and his honored guests.

Ironically, Zhu Di's favorite Lady-in-Waiting, Xi Chen, had been given the great honor to personally serve Empress Xu. This, quite naturally, put her in very close proximity to the Ming Admiral.

Since Zheng He had been away from Nanking conducting important sea trials for many weeks, the two had not seen each other since their troubling late night rendezvous nearly four-months earlier. Now that he was back for the historic ceremonies, today had been the first time the two lovers had actually even glimpsed one another since that dark evening. Obviously, this was yet another reason for Zheng He's extreme uneasiness.

As the event unfolded, Zheng He and Xi Chen were within touching distance of each other on several occasions. But neither made any attempt to communicate with the other, remaining completely remote and dispassionate. It wasn't for lack of true desire. They were much more concerned about betraying their feelings in public and feeding the rumors that were surely flying about the palace. They also were both uncertain as to how to respond following their last time together.

Empress Xu had not revealed anything she knew about the personal relationship between Zheng He and Xi Chen. She understood clearly that having this kind of special knowledge gave her a distinct edge of power and control over those around her... most prominently, the emperor. And, besides, she had no intention of disrupting her husband's very special day. The influence that she could potentially wield with the knowledge she possessed could wait for a more appropriate time.

When Zheng He saw that Zhu Di and his distinguished guests were properly seated, he nodded to his new servant, Ma Huan, who quickly signaled four other servants positioned nearby on the bank of the river. They, in turn, lit four small rockets, which immediately whooshed, skyward startling everyone as they burst overhead in beautiful cascading colors of red and blue.

On board the admiral's flagship, some three miles down the bay, Captain Su saw the colorful signal he had been waiting for and turned to his assistant officer.

"All right, lieutenant, that's our signal. Trim the sails and set a course past the Royal Reviewing Stand. Keep her as close to shore as possible. But, if you value your life, don't dare run us aground!"

Lieutenant Zhang Ji was at the helm and gave the captain a smile of confidence. "We will come so close, captain, the emperor will be able to smell our lamp oil and hear the beating of our hearts."

All eyes were on the huge fleet of ships as they began a slow turn down wind. Within minutes, over three hundred ships were turning with simultaneous grace, each taking their cue from Zheng He's massive flagship, which was positioned in the front of the line and leading the way.

Waiting at the very mouth of the river were the emperor and empress, accompanied by honored government officials and guests. Tens of thousands of other people had assembled on the shoreline, all wanting to be present for this momentous historic occasion. When they saw the huge ships turning, they all started cheering as one.

On the Reviewing Stand, Crown Prince Zhu Bao Zhi was cheering louder than anyone. This was exactly the type of celebration he lived for.

"Here they come!" he shouted happily, while waving to everyone he knew. "I can see them turning!"

The number of ships that Zheng He had assembled was unprecedented, both in size and strength and splendor. Three hundred and seventeen magnificent vessels, all under full sail, were riding the wind down the wide bay towards the emperor and his distinguished guests.

First to sail majestically past the Imperial Reviewing Stand were the magnificent Baochuan Treasure Ships. Sixty of these huge, nine-masted vessels sailed past in two, long columns, with each ship carrying an identifying number on its large front sail. Zheng He's flagship led the way, proudly displaying the number 'one' on its main sail.

Next to pass were the eight-masted Machuan. There were also sixty of these huge ships, and they, too, like the Baochuan Treasure Ships before, were arrayed in two long columns, each of them holding a steady line on the vessel in front.

These were followed closely by fifty, seven-masted, provision transports, called Liangchuan. Both on the main deck and two decks below, huge earthen jars were filled with a wide variety of food items for the men and animals. These slightly smaller vessels sailed past the Reviewing Stand dramatically arrayed in a spectacular three-column formation. Two ships followed at the rear, making a tremendous racket, with their cannons firing continually.

This dramatic, unexpected display of naval gunfire brought everyone in the crowd to their feet. Those who lined the shore clapped and shouted with robust enthusiasm, thoroughly enjoying the incredible display of Ming power and might.

Even a large number of dignitaries on the Imperial Reviewing Stand forgot about their reserved demeanor and suddenly found themselves on their feet, caught up in a spontaneous demonstration of patriotic fervor. Not surprisingly, Crown Prince Zhu Bao Zhi continued to clap and shout as loudly as he could. He even went a step further and began lighting strings of firecrackers, which he gleefully tossed into the nearby crowd just to see them jump.

Sailing behind the provision transports were the smaller, six-masted personnel transports called Tsochuan. Seventy-seven of these magnificent ships passed-in-review in a very tight formation, three abreast. Many of the men on the ships had taken up positions on the rail or high up in the rigging. They could be seen waving a proud salute to the emperor and his important guests as they passed.

Zheng He couldn't help but smile when he saw the Crown Prince, dressed up in his finest, throwing handfuls of firecrackers into the crowd, all the while laughing and waving joyfully to everyone. He knew this was the same young man who was always the first to come up with an excuse if he wanted to get out of a battle or dangerous assignment. But there was no doubt he could always be counted on to be present at every prestigious occasion or ceremony.

Bringing up the rear of this impressive Ming flotilla, was a truly, massive formation of five-masted warships, called Chanchuan. One hundred of these sturdy vessels, each heavily fortified with rocket launchers and short-barreled cannons, sailed past the Imperial Reviewing Stand with their rockets whooshing skyward and cannons blasting forth. It was truly an unprecedented demonstration of military might. The noisy, colorful, display of five-masted warships again brought the crowd to its feet, including all members of the normally stoic Imperial family.

Zhu Di happily clapped Zheng He on the back in an unusually spontaneous gesture of enthusiastic friendship.

"I've never seen anything like this in my whole life," the emperor shouted with the glee of a schoolboy. "You've exceeded my wildest expectations. I don't know how I'll ever be able to thank you, Zheng He!"

"You've already thanked me, Your Majesty," Zheng He replied graciously, "by honoring me with your trust. As Fleet Admiral, Sire, I'll do everything I can to see that you're not disappointed."

While Zhu Di and his guests happily offered toasts of success to Lord Zheng He and his men, Prince Han and Minister Wong slipped away behind the Reviewing Stand for a final, clandestine rendezvous. The obstinate young prince took this opportunity to once again threaten Wong, reminding him of what he was expected to do.

"We have agreed that you will disrupt the expedition, Minister Wong," he whispered. "It is up to you to see that Zheng He fails."

Wong was eager to do what he could to make certain the Ming admiral was not successful, but he didn't like to be ordered around by someone more than half his age. If Han had not been the emperor's son, Wong would not have been nearly so generous with his patience.

"Do you understand me?" Han sneered, rudely poking a finger in Wong's face.

Minister Wong gazed around to assure their privacy and then told Han in a high-pitched voice, "It will be my distinct pleasure, Prince Han, to do what I can to make Zheng He fail miserably. But when I return, I expect you to honor your part of this bargain. Do I make myself perfectly clear?"

"You don't need to worry about me, minister," Han replied brashly. "If Zheng He is deeply humiliated, I can assure you, you will be handsomely rewarded."

Everyone on the reviewing stand awaited the arrival of the admiral's private launch, which would soon take Zheng He and Minister Wong to the flagship.

Zheng He took this opportunity to slip away for a moment when he saw Xi Chen step into a small tent that contained the refreshments being distributed to the officials and invited guests. Ma Huan followed Zheng He and stood watch outside the tent to prevent interruption.

Inside the tent, Xi Chen took Zheng He's hands and held them to her breast. "Do you feel my heart beating like a frightened bird?" she asked him. "I'm so ashamed," she apologized softly, her voice trembling while she searched his eyes for some sign of what he might be thinking.

Zheng He brushed his lips against her cheek. "There's nothing to be ashamed for," he told her. "It has been a difficult time for both of us."

"But now you're leaving!" she sobbed, the deep hurt suddenly gushing forth so quickly she couldn't stop it. "I don't want things to be this way between us, Zheng He. Not when you're going away."

He then took her face in his hands and looked deeply into her eyes. "I love you, Xi Chen. I love you more than I've ever loved anyone in this whole world. You must know that. You must know that I'll always love you."

Xi Chen slipped her arms around his neck and kissed him passionately on the lips, trying to hold onto the moment, not ever wanting to let him go.

She pulled back, letting her lips linger softly on his cheek. "And I love you, my dearest, sweetest, Zheng He" she whispered, "more than you'll ever know."

Xi Chen kissed him again, then looked tearfully into his eyes. "Will I ever see you again?" she asked. "I feel as though you're always telling me goodbye. How do I know that this time it won't be forever?"

Zheng He shook his head. "It won't be forever, my love. If everything goes as planned, we'll be home again in less than two years."

"Two years?" she moaned with great sadness. "That is the same as forever. How can I bear to live without you for that long?"

Zheng He gave her another lingering kiss, then told her with full confidence, "Zhu Di will see that you're taken care of, my love." But the words caught in his throat. And Xi Chen tensed when she heard Zhu Di's name.

"I'll be back before you even realize I'm gone," he told her. "And then we will be together, just like we've always dreamed."

Zheng He took Xi Chen by the hand. He paused at the tent flap, peering out to be sure no one beside Ma Huan was outside. He gave Xi Chen a final kiss, then stepped out of the tent. Ma Huan and Zheng He moved quickly toward the gathered officials. In the distance, they could see the private launch from the flagship approaching.

During their brief rendezvous, neither Zheng He nor Xi Chen had dared mention their sacred vow of fidelity. Both knew deep inside that such a promise was no longer possible to keep. It was, unfortunately for them, subject to the very slightest whim of the emperor.

While the Ming fleet waited just outside the mouth of the wide bay, Zheng He, Minister Wong and Ma Huan, plus more than a dozen senior servants, boarded the admiral's beautiful teak launch and were rowed out to the flagship.

Once on board, Lord Zheng He, Admiral of the Ming Fleet, ordered a final cannon salute, which immediately triggered a fantastic display of fireworks on the shoreline. Amid this final round of cannons firing, fireworks blasting and thousands of excited people cheering from the shore, the mighty flagship led the glorious flotilla away from Shanghai and out into the South China Sea.

As the last of the ships disappeared over the horizon, Zhu Di, along with his family and guests, retreated to temporary quarters, which had been set up at Shanghai for the evening.

Speculation quickly spread throughout the emperor's harem about who would receive the great honor of sleeping with the emperor on this grand occasion. A keen competition had even developed among the eunuch servants. Each of them hoped that Zhu Di would choose the concubine that he had personally recommended. To be singled out in this way was a great honor for a eunuch and demonstrated a high level of trust by the emperor.

Empress Xu was not worried, however. She was quite certain that her husband would choose her and her alone. She reasoned that on such an historic occasion, it was only right that the emperor should sleep with his own wife.

Unfortunately, it was not to be. The very beautiful Xi Chen was the flower Zhu Di would choose to receive his special honor.

For Xi Chen, however, it was not an honor she sought, nor was it an honor she was anxious to receive.


As the Ming armada maintained a southerly course down the Chinese coast, Zheng He and I had a quiet dinner together in the admiral's dining room, which was located on the second deck of his four-story Admiral's Building. The dining room was richly decorated with many pieces of jade sculpture, more than a dozen beautiful paintings, and a marvelous collection of carved rosewood furniture.

The Building itself was part of a three-building complex, which sat squarely in the middle of the broad Treasure Ship. In front of the Admiral's Building was an equally impressive-looking three-story Ming structure called the Ceremonial Building. The first two floors consisted mostly of offices, but the third floor was an open cupola from which dignitaries could look down upon the large courtyard on the main deck below and easily view whatever was going on.

Just to the rear of the Admiral's Building was another three-story building that was also decorated in traditional Ming style. This structure, called the Envoy Building, housed more than a dozen ministers and trade envoys that had joined Zheng He on the expedition. It was in this building that Minister Wong was given a private suite. It wasn't nearly as nice as Zheng He's four-story complex, but given Wong's position as second-in-command, it was more than adequate.

Between the three buildings were two magnificent stone terraces, which featured finely decorated covered walkways on either side. When viewed close up, or even from a distance, Zheng He's mighty flagship looked like a floating Ming palace.

On this first night at sea, Zheng He was, surprisingly, in a very melancholy mood. Having just been put in charge of a whole fleet of ships and with an adventurous voyage before us, I would have thought he would have been overflowing with excitement.

"Life is strange," he told me sadly, while slowly sipping a glass of rice wine.

I wasn't sure exactly what feeling had overtaken him, but my instincts told me it had something to do with Xi Chen. His mind and heart were clearly far away from this ship and the men under his command.

Zheng He took another sip of his wine. "Here I am," he mused, his voice so soft I could barely hear him, "leading the greatest armada the world has ever known... and yet my heart is filled with sadness."

I thought maybe I should say something, but decided it would probably be better if I stayed silent and just listened.

"You know how fond I am of Xi Chen," he finally ventured, without looking up from his wine. "She's the only woman I've ever loved, friar, or ever will love for that matter. And yet, right now, I know that she may be in the bed of my emperor."

I touched the cross hanging from my neck, hoping it would impart some strength and wisdom to me. "She made a vow to you... and she promised to keep it." I said, trying to offer a positive view. "You told me so yourself."

He finally looked up and shook his head. "Yes, she made a vow to me, but keeping that solemn promise may be impossible for her."

Now I wished I hadn't spoken of the vow. "Don't torment yourself," I pleaded. "Turn loose of these feelings. Trust in the Father."

Tears began to stream down Zheng He's face. His voice came like a low wind, shaking and trembling. "I guess that's all I can do," he confessed. "As you say, I must leave it with the Father."

We sat together for quite a while after that, sipping our wine, silent, each of us absorbed in his own thoughts. Outside, a fresh breeze caused a steady stream of waves to slap against the Baochuan's large, flat bow. Slowly and inexorably, with the help of our twelve sails, we were pushed steadily forward with a pleasant, rolling motion.

Nothing more was said about Xi Chen by either of us. We simply sat there together, listening to the sounds of the sea and watching the fading daylight turn to lantern shadows, sliding slide back and forth across the wooden deck.

Zheng He had every right to be sad. I found out much later that two hours after we set sail, Xi Chen was summoned by four eunuch servants who escorted her directly to Zhu Di's private quarters.

The Ming Admiral had been gone for less than three hours and already Xi Chen was forced to face the arduous test of fidelity they both had feared.

As the eunuch servants turned to leave, Xi Chen wished she could go with them, but she knew that this time there would be no turning back. She had been very fortunate during her previous encounter with the emperor. Zhu Di had expected sexual favors from his lady servant. But when she refused, he had merely become amused. He knew that there would be many more opportunities and therefore didn't want to rush her, especially after her strangely stubborn refusal.

But on this night she knew that things would be much different. Zheng He was far away and could not protect her as he had promised.


Xi Chen bowed respectfully to Zhu Di when she entered the room. She waited nervously for him to take the first step. He accepted her show of polite deference, ignoring her obvious unease, then rose to his feet and took her by the hand, leading her directly to his bedchamber. He had no intention of wasting time on the couch this evening. There would be no lengthy sexual foreplay under the guise of casual conversation.

A eunuch serving within the royal chamber made a record of the emperor's selection for the evening and then departed, smiling toward the couple as they disappeared into the emperor's bedchamber. Now that Xi Chen's name was duly recorded, it became a permanent record of Zhu Di's daily activity. Such information could prove useful should a child be born as a result of the expected union.

Zhu Di was excited over the fleet's departure and the anticipated sexual adventure he was about to share with Xi Chen. There was no way he would ever allow her to slip through his fingers again.

Xi Chen was terrified, but also determined not to let the depth of her feelings show. As Zhu Di sat down beside her on the bed, two other female servants appeared from behind a decorative screen close by and served wine to the emperor and this evening's guest. They bowed respectfully and then retreated silently once again behind the hand-carved screen. They were gone, but still close at hand, hidden only by the thin rice paper and delicate wood frame.

Like Zheng He, Xi Chen was used to providing service and felt uneasy in the role of accepting it. After taking a few sips of the sweet tasting wine, the emperor took Xi Chen by the hand and gently began kissing her fingers one-by-one.

"Why did you run away from me?" he asked, surprising Xi Chen by his very direct question. "I felt terrible that you refused my advances on your previous visit."

"That was many months ago, Your Majesty," she cooed, hoping to slip past the embarrassing recollection of that moment. "I'm even surprised you remember."

"Oh, I remember, all right," he said, shaking his head slowly, a gloomy mask descending over his features. "How could I forget? It isn't often I get turned down by one of my lovely lady servants."

"I didn't really turn you down, Your Majesty," Xi Chen suggested, trying to think of something that wouldn't hurt his feelings. "It was just that, I'm a Lady-in-Waiting. It is my function to serve you in every way... but I didn't feel that I was worthy enough to receive your personal affection."

"Not worthy?" Zhu Di responded, shocked at her unexpected reply. "A flower of such grace and beauty, not worthy?"

Zhu Di was becoming even more fascinated by this Muslim beauty than he was before. "Xi Chen, my dearest," he whispered, his voice growing husky, "you must know that I find you extremely desirable."

Without waiting for a reply, he offered Xi Chen a sip of wine from his own goblet. She shyly wet her lips, licking the moist drop of wine with her delicate tongue. He set the goblet on the lacquered table next to the bed. Then he gently guided her body back upon the soft bed, making sure she was resting comfortably on several large silk pillows that seemed to enfold her like clouds.

Without saying a word, he started removing Xi Chen's clothes, piece-by-piece, slowly and seductively. She gasped slightly, breathing in the warm air. He began to lovingly kiss her breasts and thighs as each became exposed. There was no rush, no hurry, no frantic clutching and grabbing. Everything was done with care and grace... and, seemingly, with great affection.

As if on cue, soft music drifted from behind the beautiful screen and silky curtains, filling the room. Only one small candle flickered beside the bed, tossing its dancing light across the two lovers.

Xi Chen now lay naked on the bed. To see her fully exposed in the candlelight was almost more than Zhu Di could bear. He wanted to seize her in a mad rush of passion and thrust himself inside her body. But years of training and experience had taught him that it was much better to take his time and savor every delicious moment of the tantalizing conquest.

Slowly, Zhu Di removed his own silk robe and let it slide to the floor. He lay down, naked, beside her on the bed.

The moment had finally come that Xi Chen had long dreaded. In a few moments, she would lose her precious virginity... and there was nothing that she or Zheng He could do about it.

"My love!" she cried softly to herself, the words spinning through her mind, squeezing her heart. "You know I want to remain faithful to you. Please don't hate me for surrendering. I can resist no longer! I wanted only you. I waited for you, my love. I waited for so long. But now..."

A tear rolled down Xi Chen's face just as Zhu Di moved his body on top of her. As he became more aroused, he pressed her legs apart and thrust himself deep inside her trembling body. She whimpered softly, sucking in a rush of breath. The emperor drove himself deeper and deeper, again and again, relishing the conquest with a flagrant desire.

Then, instinctively, lost in the frenzy of a hot rush, Xi Chen began to thrust her hips to meet the pulsating movements of Zhu Di's body. She wasn't sure if her forceful gyrations were a vain attempt to push the emperor's clumsy weight away, or if it might be a disturbing carnal desire of her very own, escaping after too many years trapped within. But there was no doubt that now, suddenly, shockingly, an aching passion was bursting forth, screaming to be released from deep inside her.

Xi Chen dug her fingernails into Zhu Di's now sweating back, trying desperately to pull him even deeper into her. They undulated together, sweating and grunting, thrusting and thrashing toward a rhythmic crescendo of frenetic passion that neither of them had expected.

As a mighty wave of bliss engulfed them both, they clutched at each other, moaning and gasping for air, waiting for the unbelievable rush of passion to release its grip and subside.

Finally, Zhu Di rolled off of Xi Chen and lay stretched on his back, fighting to catch his breath. He was completely spent.

They both lay quietly for several minutes, attempting to recover from the strenuous encounter. Neither said a word. They both watched the shadows from the flickering candle, listening to the gentle strains of soft music that drifted through the room.

Xi Chen blinked back several tears, not knowing if they were tears of sadness for her beloved Zheng He or tears of joy for herself. But she was certain of one thing. Because of the intimate relationship she and the emperor had enjoyed, from this day forward she would be addressed formally as Honorable Lady.


Several days had passed and the overwhelming despair that Zheng He felt on that first night had largely subsided, replaced by more immediate concerns. He had accepted that there was nothing he could do about whatever was happening in Nanking, so instead he concentrated on those things he did have control over. That meant taking charge of the great armada of ships and fulfilling his destiny.

Before long he had become the man he was before, full of optimism and anxious to perform his duties to the best of his ability. He would do it for the glory of Emperor Zhu Di and the Imperial Ming Dynasty.

After morning prayers, which he enjoyed at a small private mosque located on the third floor of his Admiral's Building, Zheng He called for a meeting with Lt. Zhang Ji, Ma Huan, Captain Su, Minister Wong and several of the other senior flagship officers.

They gathered in the admiral's private office located on the first floor of the same building. He also asked me to join the meeting and I gratefully took a seat between Ma Huan and his Lieutenant Zhang Ji.

The Ming Admiral stood before a large navigational chart with a rosewood pointer, indicating on the chart where the fleet would be sailing next.

"We will continue on course to Champa and then to Java, where we will replenish our supplies and engage in diplomatic relations with their leaders. With fair winds we should be able to reach Palembang, here," he tapped the pointer on the map, then moved it to the next destination. "Then on to Siam, here. This should take approximately six months. We will then sail on around the coast of India."

Zheng He traced their planned route on the chart a second time, to help secure it in the minds of his officers.

"We will then journey on to the continent of Africa, which will be our final destination."

Wong was not impressed. He leaned toward several of the officers with a furrowed brow, looking grim. "His plans are exceedingly ambitious," he grumbled. "A bit too ambitious, I would say."

The officers moved closer to Wong, made curious by his critical assessment of Zheng He's plan. Wong seized upon their interest to add, "Our voyage is fraught with the potential for disastrous failure."

The officers were unsure why the Second-in-Command should be complaining so vehemently about their route. They stared at him with deep concern. Zheng He noticed the officer's private conversation and interjected. "Do you have an observation you'd like to share with us, Minister Wong?"

Caught off guard, Wong looked up and then grudgingly responded. "I was just commenting on your great ambition, Lord Zheng He."

Zheng He nodded, unconvinced of Wong's sincerity, but said nothing more. Unfortunately, the seeds of discontent had now been planted among the admiral's own officers.

After three weeks at sea, a strong typhoon blew into the South China Sea and tossed the large ships about like they were nothing but small pieces of wood. Sheets of rain slashed horizontally across the tossing waves, threatening to tear the sails from their masts and rip them to shreds.

Zheng He stood at a window of the ship's navigation room, located on the fourth-deck of the Admiral's Building. He watched the ferocity of the storm increase. From this vantage point, high over the main deck, the mountainous waves seemed to be growing larger every moment. The fierce wind howled and shrieked through the ship's rigging, blowing everything into the ocean that wasn't tied down. Each time a huge wave started to curl, the wind smashed off its top and covered the ocean surface with long streaks of frothy white foam.

Ma Huan saw Captain Su struggling up the outside stairs to the navigation room. He opened the door for him. The captain tumbled inside, soaked to the skin. He bowed to Zheng He and then revealed his troubled eyes.

"I'm sorry to bother you, Lord Zheng He, but the weather is getting worse. Some of the officers and men are becoming quite frightened. I think we should drop the remainder of our sails immediately."

Zheng He didn't look well. In fact, the rolling sea was making him feel quite ill. He nodded weakly, his face pale and cold. Lowering the sails sounded like an excellent idea, especially if it would help stabilize the vessel somewhat.

"There's no use risking the ships before we've even reached our first destination," he told Captain Su. "Maybe we should keep up one or two small sails at the bow and stern. That way we can continue to maintain some small measure of control over our steering. Signal the other ships to do the same."

Greatly relieved, Captain Su bowed and turned to leave. Zheng He stopped him.

"Has anyone seen the Deputy Envoy, Captain? I'd like to know how he's doing?"

"As far as I'm aware," Su responded, "Minister Wong remains in his cabin."

"Well, that's certainly understandable," Zheng He observed, wincing at his queasy stomach. "Let him remain there until we have emerged from this storm."

"Are you alright?" Captain Su asked, seeing the unsettled look in Zheng He's eyes.

"I could be doing better," Zheng He acknowledged bravely as he braced himself against another roll of the huge flagship. "But none of us must shirk his duty. You may carry on."

Unfortunately, the storm didn't weaken and Minister Wong was not in his cabin. As the crew struggled to get the sails down, the Deputy Envoy was busily moving among the men stoking their fears.

"This is a very bad omen," he warned one of the sailors, as he helped lash the sails to the main deck.

To another, he confided falsely, "Your admiral is weakened by his own fright. I know that he cringes in his cabin, while you must risk your life outside in this raging storm. We could all die out here while he trembles in safety."

When Captain Su went on deck to tell the crew of Zheng He's orders, Ma Huan followed to be of assistance. While moving among the crew, he overheard some of the negative admonitions being spread by Minister Wong. He immediately returned to the navigation room to take Zheng He a pot of hot tea and, more critically, report what he had heard.

"Sir, I've brought some tea for your stomach."

Zheng He was now slumped in a chair and looked grim.

"Is the storm growing worse?" he asked, after accepting the tea and taking a small sip.

Ma Huan nodded. "I don't believe it's getting any better."

The servant waited until Zheng He took another sip before cautiously continuing. "Sir, I have heard some disturbing rumors. Minister Wong has been sowing seeds of dissension among the crew."

Zheng He looked up, surprised. "Minister Wong? I thought he was in his cabin."

"Captain Su was incorrect. He's not in his cabin anymore."

"Where is he?"

"He is moving about the main deck feeding the crew's growing apprehension. He is encouraging them to turn against you."

Zheng He struggled to his feet.

"I must speak to them."

Ma Huan stopped him and gently guided him back down.

"You are much too ill, admiral. You must rest."

Zheng He waved him away. "My men are not resting, Ma Huan and neither must I."


With the thick low clouds from the growing storm, evening quickly turned to night. Thunder rumbled almost continuously amid the cascading flashes of lightning. A steady rain pounded the ship, pelting the men like stones from heaven.

Zheng He wrapped himself in a dark cloak and stepped out onto the main deck. As soon as the men saw him, they stopped what they were doing and turned to stare.

The Ming Admiral could hardly be heard over the howling storm. "We shall set a course for daylight!" he shouted as loudly as he could. "The new sun shall be ours for the taking!"

Minister Wong stood with the crew. "Words will not save us, Lord Zheng He," he shouted back. "We are besieged by the Goddess of Heaven. She has chosen for us to perish."

The superstitious men began to quake at Wong's dire prediction of doom. But Ma Huan found inspiration in what his admiral was saying and slipped away unseen.

Zheng He quickly answered Wong. "Do not listen to Minister Wong's harsh words! The hope is within you!"

A huge lantern in the forward part of the ship was positioned out of view behind a storage cabin. When the light burned softly in the lantern, the men were not aware of it.

Ma Huan turned the wick all the way up and watched as the flame rose and grew hot behind the thick glass lens. Then, he swung the big lamp around and turned it upward, so that its bright light began shining upon the large steering sail at the bow.

With the delicate movement of his fingers before the lens, the servant was able to manipulate the shadows and light upon the front sail.

Minister Wong was not aware of the light dancing on the sail as he continued to shout his displeasure with Zheng He's authority.

"If there was hope, we would see a sign. But there is no sign. There is only thunder above and a sea of death below."

Then, one by one, each man on the crew began to notice the flickering light that was now playing on the front sail. They stared in awe at the unusual display of brightness and shadows swirling on the broad canvas.

Wong saw that they were distracted. He turned to look behind him, puzzled by the unusual dancing light.

Zheng He smiled knowingly, quickly realizing that Ma Huan was the clever force behind the haunting apparition. And he didn't hesitate to take advantage of the situation.

"There is your sign!" he shouted to the men again. "The Goddess of Heaven speaks to us all! Her light will guide us to safety... and to a new day!"

Heartened, the men cheered loudly and began to work even harder at lowering the sails as instructed.

Minister Wong glared at Zheng He. He had also realized that it was a trick... but too late. The superstitious men had been infected by this bold inspiration and Wong had no viable counter-measure to unravel their belief.

Encouraged by the turn of events, Zheng He no longer felt as ill as he did before. He shouted once again to his men. "Our destiny is cast by this fine bright light!"

Just at that moment, lightning flashed, immediately followed by a loud crash of thunder. This coincidental display of dazzling light and crashing sound only seemed to further strengthen and confirm what Zheng He was saying.


Back in Nanking at the palace, the weather was equally foul. Lightning and thunder rattled across the large stone courtyard as Emperor Zhu Di prepared for bed. Empress Xu entered his private chamber and lit a candle next to his bed to chase away the chill. Zhu Di began staring into the flame. It was as if he saw something in flickering light that was invisible to others. His wife observed her husband staring at the flame light, a glimmer of excitement in his eyes.

"The flame fascinates you?" she commented.

Zhu Di smiled strangely, as if peering into the future.

"I will build a palace," he told her calmly.

"You have a palace."

Zhu Di shook his head. "A new one."

Empress Xu was surprised at first, then began to see the wisdom of it. "That would be most welcome. This charred and ashen rubble smothers me with its horrid past."

Zhu Di then turned from the flame and faced his wife.

"Not here on this desecrated ground. I will build it in Beijing, our home."

Zhu Di gestured grandly as his enthusiasm grew. "It will be like no other palace in the world. Indeed, it will reflect the wealth and greatness of all the Chinese people."

Empress Xu was not impressed. She had heard her husband make grand pronouncements before, only to be disappointed when they were not fulfilled. She turned away and started to gather her things, preparing to retire to her own bedchamber. Zhu Di picked up the flaming candle and followed her.

"It will be more than a palace," he continued, excitedly. "It will be a city!"

Empress Xu offered her husband no encouragement, countering his words. "There is already a city."

"It will be a city within a city," Zhu Di exclaimed, becoming more and more enthused as he described his new vision. "It will be so unique and rare that only those who have special consent may enter its gates. It will be known as the Forbidden City."

Empress Xu turned to face her husband, sighing deeply. "You taunt me with your madness. You already have the greatest fleet of ships, as well as an army of diplomats to rival that of any king or earthly god. Put your foolish dreams of a city to rest."

But Zhu Di ignored her admonition. "Tomorrow I will make an announcement."

"Then sleep now," she told him, nudging him gently back toward his bed. "In the morning your thoughts will be more rational."

Zhu Di sat upon his bed, staring with unblinking eyes into the future. With one quick breath, Empress Xu extinguished the candle her husband was holding.


The next day the late night storm had subsided. As the charred shell of the palace loomed in the background, Prince Han addressed a small group of rebellious imperial ministers who gathered around him.

"The fleet will not only fail," he warned, "but will collapse under the very weight of its own pretentious ambition."

"Do you have any report from Wong?" one minister asked.

"Even before they departed," Han replied, "Wong told me of dissension among the officers. The crew will not be far behind."

"And so what are we to do?" another minister asked.

"It's not this expedition that troubles me now," Han confided to the secretive gathering. "My father has a new curse to impose upon us. He desires to build a spectacular palace in Beijing. A 'Forbidden City' he calls it, with gates and walls to shield and nurture his growing madness."

"A city?" the first minister questioned, obviously shocked. "The cost would be enormous."

"Rightly so. We must put an end to his lunacy," Han told his followers. "And we must put an end to it now!"


When the huge storm had hit several weeks earlier, it scattered the Ming armada across more than a hundred li of open-ocean. Later, when the seas finally grew calm again, the ships had to struggle to find their proper place in the elaborate formation.

Communication within the vast fleet was difficult, but not so difficult as one might imagine. From the flagship's navigation center, officers directed the fleet's navigation and communication through a carefully developed system of lanterns, gongs, carrier pigeons and arrows.

At night, lanterns were used to send signals back and forth. During heavy fog, gongs were used. When the weather was clear, messages were written on small pieces of paper and tied to the legs of carrier pigeons or attached to the shaft of arrows that were launched across great expanses of water. In this way, direct communication was successfully carried out between the different-sized ships in the fleet.

As the great armada proceeded on its way to Champa, Zheng He had Ma Huan keep a detailed record of everything that happened on the entire voyage. For example, each day Ma Huan would keep a log that cited exactly where the fleet was headed, what course it was on, how long the fleet had been sailing on that course, the daily weather, the direction of the wind, the condition of the sea, and anything else that would be pertinent in the eyes of a sailor.

When we arrived at our destination, Ma Huan would also be asked to make a record of everything that happened both on shore and aboard ship. Zheng He had put a great deal of responsibility on his young servant. He expected him to keep detailed records of who Zheng He met with, the person's title and relative importance, the gifts that were presented to them on behalf of the Ming emperor, the gifts received in return, and the amount that was paid for fresh water and food. Everything that happened on the entire voyage was written down and accounted for.

Zheng He conducted a meeting with his senior officers every week. This became a permanent ritual beginning after the first week the fleet left Shanghai. Minister Wong was always invited to these meetings, but he usually found an excuse not to attend.

After the confrontation with Zheng He during the storm, it was highly unlikely that he would ever accept the admiral's weekly invitation. He always sent Zheng He his "regrets" through a personal assistant.


Lord Zheng He's flagship led the fleet into a large tropical bay lined with thousands upon thousands of tall coconut palms. These beautiful trees stretched in both directions as far as the eye could see.

Zheng He and I stood on the third-floor of the Ceremonial Building, in a room that was open on all four sides. We had affectionately dubbed it the "Penthouse" and spent as much time as possible there when the weather was pleasant. This room, situated high over the main deck but close to the bow, was an ideal location from which to view where the flagship was headed and, at the same time, where it had been.

After all the sails were lowered and our anchors set, Lieutenant Zhang Ji was sent ashore in Admiral Zheng He's private launch, along with a small contingent of Ming soldiers. His mission was to locate the local ruler and persuade him to come for a face-to-face meeting with Lord Zheng He on his flagship.

After a two-day trek, the lieutenant and his men found King Trang Su residing in a splendid palace. It didn't take Zhang Ji long to obtain an audience with the king. Within minutes he had easily convinced Trang Su that he should travel with him back to the coast to meet with Lord Zheng He and see the magnificent Ming armada he commanded.

When the Champa king arrived at the white sand beach, it was a site to behold. King Trang Su was riding on the back of a huge Indian elephant that had been gaily decorated with large quantities of silver bangles and ornaments. The king's seat, as well as the elephant's legs and head, were almost totally covered with the finely carved metal.

Closely following Trang Su and his elephant was an impressive entourage of one thousand soldiers and government officials. The soldiers were dressed in lightly colored shirts and pantaloons and each carried a simple-looking spear made of bamboo. The government officials all wore robes and headdresses, colored bright red, which made them, stand out from those without this special rank.

Following the soldiers and officials was a much larger group of curious spectators from the city and from the surrounding villages in the area. All together, nearly three thousand government officials, soldiers and villagers wandered down to the sandy beach to see for themselves the impressive armada of Chinese ships.

When they arrived, none could believe the sight that filled the large bay before them. They had expected to find no more than a few small ships. The king and his entourage were completely in awe of the amazing display that floated before them.

But while King Trang Su was impressed at seeing the Ming armada, he also felt apprehensive about putting himself at risk among so many Chinese foreigners. He knew that his own allotment of soldiers and officials was puny by comparison and wouldn't stand a chance should there be a confrontation between the two sides. But after much coaxing by Ma Huan and Lieutenant Zhang Ji, he finally agreed to join Admiral Zheng He on his flagship for the historic meeting.

Zheng He had arranged for three hundred Chinese officials, ministers and military officers to be present on the flagship when the Champa king arrived. Minister Wong, as required by protocol, was also invited to participate. Since he was Deputy Envoy and number two in command of the expedition, he had an obligation to stand with the Ming Admiral when he greeted a foreign dignitary. But Wong chose to send his "regrets" instead, refusing to have anything to do with the official ceremony.

Each Ming official was dressed in a colorful robe and each robe was a different color. The specific status or rank of an individual was reflected by the color of robe he wore.

All the officials were assembled on the Main Deck in front of the first Ming Pagoda. They stood in three long lines, waiting in the hot sun for King Trang Su and his entourage to board.

Zheng He arranged for the king and several of his senior official staff to ride from the beach to the flagship in his private launch. When they finally arrived and slowly climbed the steps to the Baochuan's huge main deck, each of the Champa visitors was again struck with awe at the incredible sight before them. Viewing the Baochuan from the beach was one thing, but actually walking up the steps to the wide Main deck was quite another. The sheer size and beauty of this amazingly large ship overwhelmed them, greatly exceeding their expectations.

When the king and his official entourage were properly seated in the front courtyard, between the beautiful, three-story Ceremonial Building on one side and Zheng He's larger, four-story Admiral's Building on the other, the Ming admiral began his formal speech of welcome.

"I, Lord Zheng He, Admiral of the Ming Fleet, welcome you on behalf of His Royal Highness, Zhu Di, the most benevolent and revered, Third Ming Emperor of China. We come in friendship and we come in peace. Our only goal is to establish a program of trade, which we sincerely hope and pray will be beneficial, not only for the people of China, but for the people of Champa as well."

Zheng He then nodded to Ma Huan, who clapped his hands loudly. Immediately, servants brought forward gifts which were distributed to the Champa king and the rest of his dignitaries.

Unknown to my friend, now caught up in the formal ceremony on the main deck, Minister Wong had ventured out of his cabin and had secretly taken up a position on the third deck of the Ceremonial Building. From this vantage point in the open penthouse, he and his servant could easily see and hear the formal proceedings unfolding below on the main deck.

Wong's servant, unfortunately, had to witness a steady stream of negative complaints from the irritated Deputy Envoy. "What a waste of money!" he complained, screwing up his face into an ugly scowl. "There's no reason whatsoever why we should offer such expensive gifts to these foreign infidels. Emperor Zhu Di must be out of his mind if he thinks these foreigners have anything we Chinese could ever want from them."

Wong's usually docile servant didn't care for these harsh remarks. Momentarily forgetting the decorum that normally goes along with his position, the servant reacted to Wong's barrage of complaints with a question of his own. "I don't mean to sound rude, Minister Wong," he burst forth, "but how can you be in the exalted position of second-in-command, if you don't support your emperor's program of foreign trade?"

Wong suddenly turned on his brash servant with a stern look. He couldn't believe that a servant, especially his own, would dare to question him. "I beg your pardon," he sneered harshly, sniffing the salt air with wounded indignation.

The servant had no intention of ameliorating his remarks. Indeed, he found a perverse joy in needling the cantankerous imperial official.

Having already breached official imperial etiquette, he threw caution to the wind and continued. "You always complain about Lord Zheng He and the way he runs the fleet. But I've noticed, on many occasions, the admiral has gone out of his way to be very friendly with you. What I don't understand, Minister Wong, is why you are always so angry and displeased with someone who has treated you so well."

The fire in Wong's soul began burning with an intense fury. He had never before been subjected to such gross insubordination in his life. He raised his trembling hand, seething with anger, pointing a bony finger at the brash servant. But the young man was not intimidated at all. The damage had been done. His only option now was to stand his ground and defend his position.

"I am a court official!" Wong barked with a hoarse quiver in his throat. "I was appointed years ago by the First Ming Emperor! And it was me... Minister Wong, who personally had the responsibility of seeing that the obstinate young prince, Zhu Di, was properly trained in the formalities and customs of government. It is quite obvious that I was successful in my teaching, since the pupil became king and is now EMPEROR!"

"And yet you are unhappy," the servant added, having risen well beyond fear. "Your pupil no longer needs, nor does he request, the services of his former teacher."

Wong couldn't believe that this attack from a mere servant was continuing. "Why you insolent... How dare you address me in such an insolent manner?"

"I do so for your own edification, Minister Wong. If you cannot support the ideas and beliefs of your emperor, the very man who you claim to have taught and nurtured since he was a child..."

"Enough!" Wong shouted. "That's quite enough from you! I have earned the right of respect. And you, as my servant, will show me that respect or I will see that you are severely punished for your foul and boorish behavior."

"My behavior is not in question, sir. It is your own that bears scrutiny for not supporting your admiral."

"That's because Zheng He is undeserving! He is nothing by a lowly EUNUCH SERVANT!" he shouted loudly. His screeching voice resonated across the deck of the flagship.

Below them, on the main deck, heads turned. Eyes searched above them for the voice that echoed like an raspy violin.

Minister Wong suddenly realized that his shouting had attracted the attention of all those gathered for the ceremony.

Admiral Zheng He gazed upward, glimpsing Wong and his servant standing in the open space of the penthouse. Wong angrily wrapped the flowing robe around his thin frame, once more retreating into a shell of stoic defiance. He glared down resentfully at Zheng He.

"I wish to return to my own cabin," he muttered to his servant.

"I don't believe the admiral has finished dispensing all the gifts," the servant commented flatly. "I believe it is customary protocol that you stay until the ceremony is over."

"Customary protocol does not apply to me," Wong stated arrogantly. "If you wish to keep your head, I suggest you follow." And with that, Wong turned and walked to his cabin. The servant did not follow. When he was seen the following day, he still had his dignity. And he still had his head.


When Zheng He finished dispensing the gifts and the official ceremony came to a close, King Trang Su formally invited the Ming admiral and his guests to join him at a banquet celebration in three days. He would host this grand banquet at his palace in the admiral's honor.

Zheng He graciously accepted the king's invitation. After the monarch and his official entourage had left, the admiral hurried off to his private shipboard Mosque to give sincere and heartfelt thanks to Mohammed and Allah. This first encounter with a new culture, a new country and a foreign ruler had gone much better than he had ever hoped.

As soon as he finished his prayers, Zheng He came to visit me in my modest cabin, which was located at the stern of the ship on the main deck. When he entered my cramped living space, he was still overflowing with excitement.

"Before the banquet we shall visit the king's palace and negotiate a program of trade," he gushed, his mind spinning with new ideas. But then he paused, his eyes clouding with a question. "Tell me... what was all the shouting about this afternoon? I thought I saw Minister Wong in the penthouse."

"Yes, it was Minister Wong," I told him. "I have no idea what he shouting. Perhaps his servant said something that angered him."

"That wouldn't be difficult to do," Zheng He agreed, a wry smile curling the corner of his mouth. "No matter what anyone says to him, it always seems to make him angry. Maybe his old age does not sit well with him."


During the festivities at the king's palace, the Champa ruler surprised Zheng He by offering him a very attractive woman as a personal gift. Not wanting to offend the foreign ruler by turning down his generous offer, he thought for a moment about offering the Champa woman to me. But when he saw the shocked look on my face, he quickly realized that probably would not be the correct course of action either.

While Lord Zheng He was trying to find a way out of his embarrassing predicament, Lieutenant Zhang Ji and his fellow officers tried to stifle their laughter and hide their amusement. It was quite obvious that King Trang Su had no idea that Zheng He was, according to official record, a eunuch.

Ma Huan was quite offended that the lieutenant and his friends were making jokes at his master's expense. "You shouldn't be making fun of Lord Zheng He," he mumbled to one of the officers beside Zhang Ji. "I don't think it is proper for you to mock the admiral. He is your commander aboard this vessel."

The officer grinned at Ma Huan. "We're just having a little fun, Ma Huan. No offense is meant to Zheng He."

"Lord Zheng He may not be a eunuch," Ma Huan said through gritted teeth. "I've heard that Xi Chen and Zheng He have a sacred vow of fidelity to each other. They wouldn't have such a sacred vow if he was a eunuch."

"It's a sacred vow of little merit, then," the officer taunted. "Everyone knows that Emperor Zhu Di can pluck that little flower anytime he wants."

Ma Huan angrily picked up his food and moved to another table in the banquet room. For the remainder of the evening, he sat alone, seething with anger at Lieutenant Zhang Ji and the other officers. Still their frivolity and crude joking continued, with whispered jibes and comments followed by bursts of raucous laughter.

Despite Zheng He's polite refusal of the king's gracious gift, the banquet was still considered a great success. There was much good will exchanged between the king and admiral. And a friendly rapport was established between all the Chinese officers and guests of the king.

Much to Lord Zheng He's delight, King Trang Su agreed to send several envoys to China so they could personally meet with Emperor Zhu Di and begin working out a program of mutual trade.

Two days later, amid a booming cannon salute to all the friendly people of Champa, Zheng He's huge Ming flagship led the fleet out of the bay and set a direct course for Java, which would be the second stop on the emperor's historic expedition.


At the emperor's palace in Nanking, day in and day out, Prince Han remained in a very ugly mood. He was thoroughly disgusted that he was forced to stay at home, while many of his close friends had been allowed to join the fleet as soldiers or members of the envoy staff. He was well aware that it was his father who denied him a place on the great expedition. This knowledge tortured him and Han's bitterness toward his father grew more intense with each passing day.

Whatever the emperor supported, Prince Han was sure to oppose. Several weeks previously, when he learned his father planned to build a new palace, he made certain to spread the word to his father's staunchest detractors. He was more than willing to let them know he was sympathetic to their way of thinking and would do whatever he could to support their views over those of his father.

Han's devious mind began to reason that if he could influence enough officials and civil servants to support him over his father, then, someday, he might even be able to mobilize them into a force powerful enough to overthrow the emperor himself.

With Minister Wong off on the expedition, Han remained busy doing whatever he could to cultivate these sympathetic government officials. He realized that his title of prince gave him a distinct advantage.

Many of the lower-level officials were more than willing to tolerate this young opportunist, hoping to curry favor close to the throne, knowing that someday he might actually realize his deviously lofty ambitions.

One of the officials who had lined up solidly behind Prince Han was a deceitful, middle-aged man named Yang. Yang was Zhu Di's official Minister of Rites. He was nearly as brutally ambitious as Prince Han. It was not surprising, therefore, that Yang should attach himself to this youngest member of the imperial family. After all, anytime one could brag that Prince Han was a close acquaintance, it seemed feasible to receive a boost in one's social standing. Therefore, in order to nurture his relationship with the prince, Yang pretended to agree with everything the wildly rebellious young man said, no matter how absurd.

But in truth, Yang was not a very helpful ally for Prince Han. He would do or say anything as long as the result would serve him well, even if it worked to the detriment of others.

If Prince Han decided he wanted to spread poisonous rumors throughout the palace, he would always seek out Yang as the conduit for his lies. It took very little time for word to be spread by Yang's friends and acquaintances. Yang secured this kind of rapid communication by promising his friends that he could get them an audience with a member of the imperial family.

When Yang then introduced his friends to Prince Han, the conversation would always turn to some political controversy. Yang would instigate things easily by ruffling feathers with harsh criticism of the emperor.

"Fighting nomadic Mongols was bad enough, but now Zhu Di has sent out this naval force to take on the entire world. Why would he do such a thing? Just so a few ignorant savages might be impressed that we Chinese know how to build ships?"

At first, Yang's friends were not certain whether they should laugh at this outlandish comment... or take him seriously. If they should laugh about the emperor in front of Prince Han, they worried it could jeopardize their position with the Imperial family.

But when Prince Han would then add his own degrading comments, it became clear that criticizing the emperor was acceptable. Before long, they were adding their own harsh condemnation of the emperor as well, mocking his fleet of ships and plans for expanding trade to different, unexplored countries.

"That's not the worst of it, Minister Yang," Prince Han would add boisterously. "My father has even arranged to shower these stupid savages with gifts! Can you believe it? He's literally giving them expensive Chinese treasures as gifts in exchange for their worthless trash."

"It's foolishness!" Yang would shout. And soon it became a mantra often echoed by Yang's friends.

Prince Han was quick to add seriously, "We must find a way to stop my father from throwing away our great Ming wealth on such wasteful misadventures."

It took no time at all for these new detractors to agree that spending money on Zhu Di's foolish adventures was bad for the people of China.

When the young prince was in their presence, many of the officials would often make foolish statements that they knew he wanted to hear.

But they wouldn't dare offer the same views in front of Emperor Zhu Di. Minister Yang and his friends could easily be described as brash and reckless, but they were not stupid.

Meanwhile, Zhu Di was blissfully unaware of the bitter and divisive grumbling that went on behind his back. Of course, he knew that his son was restless and unhappy, but he simply attributed this obstinate behavior to his relative youth and lack of experience. He rationalized that any reports of Prince Han's bad behavior were probably exaggerated or rooted in jealousy. He couldn't imagine that his son was nearly as bad or devious as some close to him had speculated.


As spring approached and winter was beginning to loosen its icy grip on Nanking. Zhu Di had loved this time of year since he was a boy. The budding flowers and new growth on trees always gave him a feeling of inspiration and confidence that was hard to explain. This newly awakening part of the year made him feel as if he could accomplish anything he wanted.

On this particular spring day, there was still a lingering bite to the air, but the warm sun, shining brightly through a cloudless sky, did wonders to help chase away the afternoon chill.

He strolled happily through one of his imperial gardens with Xi Chen, who was now his favorite Lady-in-Waiting. He led her to a marble bench located in a warm sunny area set some distance from any trees.

The two servants, who always followed Zhu Di at a discrete distance, automatically stopped when they saw him leading his lady servant to the marble bench. They quickly moved to take up positions nearby, beside a line of stately bamboo that sheltered one side of a small pond. The servants squatted on their haunches and waited, knowing that the emperor would spend a good deal of time visiting with Xi Chen in private.

Zhu Di and Xi Chen sat quietly together for a few moments, neither speaking, each soaking up the delicious warmth of the sun. Finally, impatient with the silence, it was she who initiated the conversation.

"The garden is so lovely this time of year," she told Zhu Di, dreamily. "I never tire of its changing beauty."

Zhu Di leaned over and kissed Xi Chen on the cheek.

"And I never tire of enjoying your beauty, he countered, whispering softly in her ear.

Xi Chen lowered her eyes. "Sire! You make me blush. I don't deserve such a compliment."

"You deserve much more than I can ever give you," Zhu Di exclaimed, shocking Xi Chen by the unexpected tone of his voice. "During the past four months, I have savored your beauty," he rhapsodized poetically. "And as I have tasted the delicious fruits of your love, my soul has soared like a bird."

Xi Chen couldn't believe what Zhu Di was telling her. She looked into his eyes and tried to decide if she should say anything in response. After a moment, she decided to remain silent, waiting for Zhu Di to continue.

"I feel as though I can accomplish anything I want," he told her. "Things I only dreamed of accomplishing when I was young."

"Your Majesty..." Xi Chen began. But Zhu Di quickly, yet gently, brought his finger to her lips.

"With you, Honorable Lady, I feel as though nothing in this world is impossible. Can you understand what I'm trying to say to you?"

Xi Chen looked away, afraid to know anything further about the feelings that were coursing through him. He took her hands and squeezed them firmly, but with a strange gentility.

"Now that the fleet is well on its way, Xi Chen, I've been thinking about starting a new project."

This sudden announcement took her by surprise. She hadn't expected him to veer away so abruptly from his heartfelt recitation of personal feelings. New project? What did this have to do with her? Of course, she had heard a rumor for several months that he planned to build a new palace in Beijing. But he had never said anything about it to her directly and she did not feel it was her place to ask.

"A new project, Your Majesty?" she asked, unsure if he wanted her to inquire or simply listen passively.

Zhu Di couldn't believe she didn't remember. "I mentioned it to you long ago... when I announced my plans for building the incredible armada of ships."

"Yes..." she said haltingly, pretending to recall. "Yes, I believe you did. I remember now."

"Of course you do. I said I wanted to build a new palace in Beijing. And it would be like no other palace in the world!"

She smiled at his exuberance, trying to appear interested. But in reality she found his enthusiasm for this new project oddly disturbing. Was it because he no longer seemed riveted by her beauty? That he had ceased to shower her with poetic compliments?

"When Lord Zheng He invites a foreign dignitary to visit us in Beijing," he said brightly, "I want this new palace to reflect the wealth and greatness of our Chinese people. But, I also want it to reflect the love, beauty and kindness of my most Honorable Lady, Xi Chen."

This last comment startled Xi Chen, striking out of the blue like a bolt of unexpected lightning. Her face turned red. She was clearly embarrassed by his words of flattery... and still reeling from the sudden change of direction that his thoughts had taken.

Not knowing what to say, she reached up and touched his cheek with her fingers. "You're such a good man, Your Majesty," she whispered, speaking to him from her heart. "I just don't understand why there are people in the palace who don't believe in your dreams of progress."

"Because they're fools!" Zhu Di growled, suddenly becoming agitated. "They are all just ignorant, shortsighted fools!"

Not wanting to sound excessively crass in front of his Honorable Lady, he caught himself and quickly softened.

"That's the kindest thing I can say about them, Xi Chen," he muttered, calming himself by taking a deep breath and then sighing. "Those who will visit us from foreign lands will bring with them many new ideas. And it's these new ideas that will enable our own people to grow and prosper... and to ultimately reach new heights for many generations to come. Do you understand what I'm saying?"

"What I do understand, Your Majesty," Xi Chen cooed, "is that you're a kind man, you're a good man, and you're very wise. I pray to Benevolent Allah, with all my heart, that all your wonderful dreams will someday come true!"

Zhu Di and Xi Chen stood up and continued their leisurely stroll through the garden, immediately followed by the two servants. They took several steps in silence. But the emperor could not restrain his excited rhetoric. He launched into a long and eloquent discourse on Zheng He and all the great things he would accomplish on his voyages.

But whenever Xi Chen heard Zheng He's name, she turned deeply, helplessly melancholy. In fact, every time anyone mentioned anything about the expedition or the Ming fleet, her heart began to long for the man she loved.

Many thoughts passed through her mind as they continued to stroll through the colorful flower gardens. "Zhu Di is truly a wonderful person," she mused silently to herself. "What is it that makes me want to cling so strongly to Zheng He? That first night in bed with Zhu Di stirred something within me that I don't think I'll ever forget. I want desperately to feel that same way with Zheng He. But if he won't make love to me..."

Her stream of thoughts and questions abruptly came to an end, stopped by this unanswerable question looming in the dark recesses of her mind. "Why do I continue to long for... to lust after... someone who refuses to return my great passion? I don't need to live in the past. If I could just rip this feeling from my heart."

Zhu Di suddenly stopped walking. "Xi Chen! You're not listening to a word I've been saying."

Startled, Xi Chen tried to hide her shame, taking hold of Zhu Di's arm and clinging to it.

"Yes I am, Your Majesty," she sang out brightly. "I was just thinking about... you! Please don't be angry with me. Tell me all about it again. Please?"

Several weeks later, General Tan requested permission to have an urgent meeting with the emperor. Zhu Di knew that whenever his general requested an urgent meeting, something unpleasant was about to happen. When the two were together, Tan bowed deeply then informed Zhu Di of a problem that never seemed to go away.

"I must apologize for once again bringing you bad news, Your Majesty. Another Mongol warlord has dared to steal your land. He managed to breach our defenses and break through a section of the Great Wall. He now occupies a small area of our Northern Province."

"Is there no rest from this madness?" Zhu Di howled, throwing his arms in the air in mock disgust. "The invader bastards never stop coming. Why don't they learn they will never win?"

"What do you wish for me to do?" General Tan asked, already knowing the answer.

"We'll do what we've always done, my friend. Defend the land with our lives. Prepare the troops for battle!"

Once again, huge Chinese cannons were brought forward to fire a withering barrage at the out-manned and out-gunned invading force. Those who managed to get through the first devastating onslaught were forced to face Zhu Di's deadly war wagons, each loaded with six clusters of rocket arrows.

When these weapons were launched, the attacking enemy had no chance of escape. Caught out in the open, both man and beast were cut down indiscriminately.

Even though General Tan was no longer a young man, he still relished the struggle of battle. Screams and cries of fighting men, swords clashing against swords, trumpets blaring, thousands of horses stomping and neighing in panic, flags and pennants snapping in a fresh breeze, the smell of freshly-fired gun powder; it all blended together into a montage of life and death he never grew tired of.

Zhu Di did not believe in leading his troops from the rear. In his estimation, only cowards behaved in that fashion. Consequently, he always set his command post close to the front lines. "So I can see what's going on," he told General Tan on more than one occasion.

"There's no way a commander can lead his troops," he liked to explain with great bravado, "if he's hiding like a rabbit in a hole."

Using a collection of colored flags, General Tan's military staff was able to send messages to the commander's in the field, informing them when they should attack, fall back, turn right or left, fire cannons, or initiate a rocket attack. Because of their ability to communicate with this array of colored flags near the front lines, Zhu Di and his generals could effectively and efficiently manipulate the entire battle.

During a lull in the battle, Zhu Di and General Tan retired to the emperor's tent to spend a few moments of quiet time together, sipping tea and reminiscing about their mutual friend, Lord Zheng He, who they now missed intensely.

"It doesn't seem the same without him," Tan lamented, sadly. "He's always been with us before."

"And guiding us with his exceptional wisdom," Zhu Di mused with a profound sadness. "The man is definitely one of a kind. I do miss his brilliance and courage."

General Tan nodded in agreement.

"You can be sure, Sire, Zheng He is performing his duty as your Fleet Admiral with the very same brilliance and courage he always brought to you on the field of battle."

Zhu Di took a sip of tea, continuing to think about his faithful servant.

"Sometimes, I wish I were with him," he unexpectedly admitted to Tan. "I would like to be out there on the open sea, watching the wind fill those mighty sails..."

General Tan chuckled softly, surprised by what the emperor was saying. He'd never heard Zhu Di confess anything like that before. "Your Majesty", I had no idea you even liked the sea."

Zhu Di looked up and smiled, secretly pleased that his senior general had been so astonished.

"All my life, I've dreamed of going to sea," he confessed. "But, like you, my lot is here, on land, fighting these thankless battles. Fortunately, almost all of them are against pathetically inferior foes."

After finishing the last of his tea, Zhu Di set down his cup, rose to his feet and stretched. General Tan quickly put down his own cup and followed the emperor toward the tent opening.

"We have our jobs to do, General," Zhu Di stated firmly, "and Zheng He has his. Why don't you and I see if we can't get this one finished quickly? I'm ready to go home!"

"As you wish, Your Majesty," Tan replied, offering his emperor a formal bow. "As you wish!"

When the battle was over and the Mongol invader sent scurrying back beyond the Wall, Zhu Di returned to his temporary palace at Nanking. On the first night of his return he held a quiet victory celebration with his closest friends, plus about fifty imperial officials who he was certain supported his policies.

During their simple candlelight supper together, a servant quietly entered, bowed to Zhu Di and handed him a message. After reading the note, the emperor rapped on the table with his gold chalice.

"Ladies and distinguished guests," he announced, merrily. "May I please have your attention?"

Zhu Di held up the note he'd just received so all could see it.

"A messenger has just brought me a correspondence from the distinguished ruler of Champa," he stated calmly, doing his best to contain his enthusiasm. "If you don't mind, I'd like to share what he has to say with you."

A rustle of excitement quickly filled the room. Zhu Di waited for everyone to settle down, then started reading the note.

"The ruler's name is Trang Su, and his official title is the King of Champa." He cleared his throat with great flair and then proceeded. "Here is what he has to say. 'I have recently been visited by honorable members of your Ming Fleet and was very favorably impressed. Your distinguished Fleet Admiral, Lord Zheng He, has suggested I send several envoys to Nanking for the grand purpose of negotiating a trade agreement between our two countries. You may expect a visit from several of my trade envoys within the near future.'"

Zhu Di smiled, and again, held up the note proudly.

"It's signed, and has the official seal of the exalted ruler of Champa, King Trang Su."

All the guests began to clap enthusiastically at the news. Everyone was anxious to congratulate Zhu Di, who was now beaming like a schoolboy.

Xi Chen, who was overseeing the small group of ladies serving the emperor and his guests, was overjoyed for Zhu Di's success. She was also secretly delighted that Zheng He's name had been mentioned.

The Ming emperor called for drinks all around and quickly offered a toast.

"I knew my idea for building a fleet was a good one," he announced happily. "This message from the King of Champa is the first proof of its success. Let's all drink a toast of appreciation to our good friend, Lord Zheng He, and the magnificent Ming fleet he now commands."

All the guests happily raised their goblets into the air.

"May their historic journey continue to be successful and may Lord Buddha protect all of them until they are safely home."

Zhu Di voraciously downed his goblet of wine and all the guests in the room quaffed theirs as well. Xi Chen and the other ladies hurried to refill all the now empty goblets.

The Honorable Lady beamed with pride, pleased that the emperor and his honored guests were toasting her beloved Zheng He.

Zhu Di and his guests had a marvelous time drinking and celebrating late into the night. But Xi Chen knew it wouldn't be over for her until the emperor finally pushed himself off her naked body sometime early the next morning, fully satiated with an excess of wine and lovemaking.

Chapter Seven

---

## SECRET REVEALED

I am growing weaker. The exertion of writing down all my memories has rendered my task nearly impossible.

I have no idea what is happening beyond the walls of my small, cramped cabin aboard the ship. There seems to be no sound coming from the vast world outside. No sound at all. What has happened to the cannons? Perhaps it is night and there has been a brief suspension of fighting.

I don't dare look at my chest. The pain is so severe. It aches and throbs continually, assuring me that I must still be alive. I can feel the blood pumping through my veins like hot lava.

I have a sudden craving for tea. But I'm afraid to move. I think I'll wait until the servants look in on me again. I'm sure they will soon. I hope they know that I am still breathing and in need of care.

But for now, I must write. If I stop, I feel that I will surely die from lack of purpose. My trembling hand raises the magical writing instrument, scratching the page with indelible remembrance.

The armada of ships left Champa and sailed onward toward Java. During the four-week voyage, Zheng He sent out several invitations to Minister Wong, requesting that he join him in his private suite. But on every occasion, the belligerent deputy envoy sent his "regrets" and stayed burrowed away in his own cabin.

Zheng He couldn't understand what Wong did to amuse himself during his forced isolation. He found out later that occasionally he would watch puppet shows performed by his servants. But most of the time he simply remained alone, bristling with resentment, waiting for the right moment to unleash his vengeful plan.

In Beijing, work had begun on Zhu Di's new palace. More than ten thousand craftsmen and stonemasons were brought to Beijing from all parts of the vast country and put to work building the emperor's 'dream' palace. Work hadn't progressed far enough for the imperial ruler to consider moving his official government from Nanking, but he did enjoy visiting his former capital city frequently to check on progress of the construction.

Whenever Zhu Di made the three-week journey to the north, protocol and custom dictated he should take along with him a large contingent of soldiers, eunuch servants, Ladies-in-Waiting, government officials and a host of Imperial advisors, whose presence was needed to keep everything running properly. It was necessary for Zhu Di to be kept informed on a daily basis about matters of political interest and diplomatic policy. It was also important for him to remain keenly aware of the heavenly alignment. For a superstitious person like Zhu Di, this was a critical knowledge that affected every aspect of his present activities and future decisions.

The list of things the emperor and his advisors had to worry about and keep track of was almost endless. For example, it was impossible for him to start on a long voyage without including those who would attend to the food and water wagons, both for men and animals. It was also necessary to bring along servants who would prepare the food for Zhu Di and his officials. Other servants were needed to wash the numerous changes of clothing that were required every day, not only by the emperor and the members of his immediate staff, but also for his many Imperial representatives, advisors and soldiers.

The soldiers were, perhaps, the greatest responsibility. Hundreds upon hundreds of brave warriors accompanied Zhu Di on his great Imperial voyages, along with their numerous weapons; swords, rocket arrows, cannons and ammunition. They were necessary, of course, to protect Zhu Di against any number of great travails and evil threats that might challenge him along the way. If Emperor Zhu Di decided to travel anywhere at any time, it always affected the lives and schedules of countless people.


On this particular trip, Zhu Di had been in Beijing for a little over a week. Work was progressing smoothly on his new palace and there were few problems requiring his immediate attention. Consequently, he decided it might be a good time for he and Xu Chen to share a quiet midday meal together.

Zhu Di selected an area in one of his newly planted gardens. It had a lovely, exquisitely decorated gazebo at its center. It was, he thought, a perfect location for them to share a peaceful rendezvous, without interruption.

"I'm glad you brought me with you to Beijing," Xi Chen told Zhu Di sweetly, the hint of a smile on her lips. "Your new palace is really growing."

"It's growing all right," Zhu Di agreed, returning her smile with an abrupt scowl as he looked around them with irritation. "But it is terribly noisy! I can't find a place that there isn't a damnable racket of construction."

"When you hear this great clamoring," Xi Chen said with a wry twinkle in her eyes, "you can be assured that your palace is a little bit closer to being completed."

He sat back with a humble shake of his head. "I guess you're right," Zhu Di allowed, his spirit brightening. "It is a comfort to know that we will soon be in our new home."

The Ming emperor eagerly separated several pieces of fish with his chopsticks, being careful to remove a bone that had been missed by the servants prior to his being served.

"I love fish," he admitted to his Honorable Lady, while pushing a big hunk of the delicate meat into his mouth. "I think I could eat fish every day."

"It is very good for your disposition," Xi Chen suggested, while picking up a much smaller piece of fish with her own two sticks. "And... I'm sure it keeps you healthy."

"After we eat," he announced happily, carefully plucking the fish's eye out with one of his elaborately decorated chopsticks, "I would like to give you a personal tour of my palace so you can see what has been completed thus far."

A servant stepped forward and refilled both their cups with tea, then silently withdrew, as silent and unobtrusive as an invisible spirit.

"Have you had any more news from the fleet, Your Majesty?" Xi Chen asked, hoping to sound as casual as possible. He didn't answer immediately. Xi Chen reached for another small piece of fish, wondering if she may have troubled him with her inquiry. Without appearing too obvious, she had hoped to glean a bit of news about Zheng He and the expedition.

Eventually, Zhu Di looked up and smiled. "Actually, I've had several pieces of news lately, my lady, and all of it good. Two new rulers have sent messages to me. Both have indicated they would like to start trading with us. What do you think of that?"

"Why, that's wonderful news," Xi Chen said, genuinely pleased. "I know it makes you very happy."

"Yes. It is wonderful news. I knew that a great many beneficial things would result from our fleet visiting foreign lands. But I had no idea we'd begin receiving messages from foreign rulers so soon... even before the fleet returned home. I must confess, such news has exceeded even my wildest expectations."

Xi Chen lovingly touched the emperor's hand. "I'm glad things are going well for you, Your Majesty. If anyone deserves to be rewarded, it is you."

Zhu Di took Xi Chen's hand in his and tenderly kissed her fingers. "Everything is going well for me, Xi Chen. And... if you promise to join me in my private chambers this evening, then all my dreams will be fulfilled."

Xi Chen gazed coyly into the emperor's eyes and smiled. She lowered her eyes discretely, subtly acknowledging that she was willing to acquiesce to his intimate desires.

The months crept by slowly, with Xi Chen beginning to enjoy her recognition as an Honorable Lady and Emperor Zhu Di regaining an enthusiasm for life that he hadn't felt in years. Things couldn't be going better for both of them. That is, until one evening when Prince Han got excessively drunk and revealed the dark secrets and disturbing thoughts that had been swirling around in his mind.

"I will not have you speaking lies about Zheng He," Zhu Di admonished his son sternly. "What you're telling me is simply not true!"

"They're not lies, father!" Han countered loudly, his voice rising. "You just don't want to hear the truth."

Zhu Di's face was flushed with anger. "You're always listening to Minister Wong," he shouted harshly, his hot breath beating against

Han's face. "I know he's the one behind all this! He never liked Zheng He from the first moment he set foot in the palace. You know that! His feelings are twisted and evil. You can't believe a word that old fool has told you!"

Prince Han threw his arms into the air with great flair, straining to dramatize his growing exasperation. "There you go again, defending Zheng He. All that lowly eunuch servant ever does is make a fool of you, father."

"SILENCE!" Zhu Di shouted, cutting him off like the swift blade of an axe. "I've had quite enough of this insolence. You have no idea what you're talking about!"

Han took a reckless gulp of wine and it dribbled from the corners of his mouth. He wiped the crimson liquid away with his sleeve. "Don't I? Your disreputable eunuch makes a fool of you every single day, father. And so does your so-called "Honorable Lady" Xi Chen."

This last accusation cut to the heart of Zhu Di like a sharp blade. But Han was not finished. He stabbed an accusing finger at his father's face. "She doesn't love you, father! She's in love with ZHENG HE! When you put him in charge of the fleet and sent him away, Xi Chen cried her eyes out. But now... since she can't have the one she truly loves... she pretends to care for you."

"ENOUGH!" Zhu Di shouted, angrily slapping his son's hand away.

"She mocks you in your own bed, father. But you're too blinded by lust and pride to see it!"

These last words pushed Zhu Di over the edge. It was more than he could take. He raised his goblet in a swift arc, splashing wine in his insolent son's face.

"How dare you speak to me that way!" he roared, unable to contain his rage any longer. "Get out of my sight! Get out! NOW!" Prince Han, also livid with emotion, threw his goblet to the floor with a loud clatter and stomped from the room like a spoiled child.

Zhu Di called after him, "I wish Zheng He were my son, instead of YOU!"

Prince Han slammed the doors shut at the end of the hall, leaving only a heavy echo as witness to his visit. Zhu Di slid down into his chair, his mind and heart racked by the weight of confusion.

Later that same evening, when Zhu Di joined his wife in her private chambers, he was still thinking about the terrible things his son had said. He dropped into an overstuffed chair and stared blankly into the darkened corners of the room. His wife took notice of his strange behavior, watching him with curious eyes.

"What is troubling you?" she asked. "Has something happened?"

After a long moment, Zhu Di looked up at her. "Not anything to be concerned about. I suppose that I am tired, that's all."

Empress Xu continued to study him, certain that he was not being honest with her. He felt her gaze. Heaving a sigh, he fixed his eyes upon her with great sincerity.

"Have you ever seen Zheng He and Xi Chen together?"

This unexpected inquiry surprised her. "That's an odd question," she said. "Of course I've seen them together. They're both our servants. Before Zheng He left on the great voyage, I would see them every day."

"That isn't what I mean," he said, shaking his head in frustration. "What I want to know is... have you ever seen them together? With each other... alone?"

Empress Xu began to sense what Zhu Di was getting at. Her personal servant had once confided in her that Xi Chen was in love with Zheng He. But the empress hadn't given this rumor any credence. Zheng He was, after all, a eunuch.

"What are you suggesting?" she asked, deciding it best to remain coy on the issue until she better understood her husband's interest in the matter.

Zhu Di waved his hand at her, casually dismissing the subject. "Nothing. Just forget it. Is there anything to eat?"

"Would you like a bowl of rice and fish?" she said flatly, her suspicion even further aroused by his sudden change of subject.

Empress Xu stood up and moved toward the door. "Where are you going?" Zhu Di asked, his voice again showing signs of irritation.

"To get you some rice and fish... to cure your hunger. Isn't that what you asked for?"

"But we have servants for that," he complained, the edge in his voice still evident. "Let them do it!"

"Why don't you just sit and rest?" she said with a calm and even tone. "It makes me happy to serve you. I'll be back with your meal in a short while."


At sea, Zheng He's flagship was now leading the Ming fleet across a vast area of open-ocean. The admiral had already completed successful meetings with the rulers of Champa, Java, Palembang, Siam and Calicut and was now on a more difficult and treacherous leg of their long journey, sailing toward the continent of Africa. As a fair breeze pushed the massive armada westward, Zheng He, Ma Huan and I spent a great deal of time together in the admiral's quarters. We spent many hours discussing the progress we'd made to date and any problems we might expect to face in the future.

We were heading into the vast unknown reaches of the Western Ocean and I could tell that Zheng He was becoming more and more concerned by the unknown waters that lay ahead.

"What troubles you?" I asked softly, letting him take his time in answering.

"I'm worried, friar," he confessed. "Up until this point we have sailed close to land, always keeping the shoreline within sight. But now, we have launched ourselves into a broad expanse of open and uncharted sea. What lies before us is anyone's guess."

"We shall be fine," I countered with a comforting voice, attempting to quiet his restless soul. "As long as the floating arrow in our compass points the way, we will find the landfall we seek."

Ma Huan found the compass of little comfort. What if the direction it showed was incorrect? What if this mysterious device somehow malfunctioned and led them astray, into a never-ending sea with no horizon?

"Sir..." he ventured nervously, "How long do you think it will take us to reach Africa? A month? Two months?"

"That's why I'm beginning to feel nervous," he admitted frankly, pouring himself another cup of tea. "I don't really know. Ever since we left Calicut on the Indian coast, we've been sailing on the same course, a little south of due west. All the ship captains we have talked with before our voyage said to stay steady on this course. Eventually, if we keep in this direction, we will encounter the great continent of Africa."

"Well, that would seem a reassuring endorsement," I said buoyantly, trying to raise his spirits up. "Everyone has said we will find it if we stay on course. And so there it is. We will!"

Zheng He waved his half-full cup at me, as if dismissing my optimism. "That may be true. But if I remember correctly, none of the ship captains could tell us exactly how long we would have to sail. Each of them sailed a slightly different route and most of them turned around and returned home before reaching landfall. I made certain we laid in all the supplies we needed to reach Calicut. But we can't roam the seas endlessly. There is a limit."

When Ma Huan saw me pick up my small wooden cross and place my lips upon it, his face darkened with a shadow of worry. "I wish you wouldn't do that," he begged, giving me a pleading frown. "Every time you kiss that little cross, I know something is not right."

"I'm sorry it upsets you," I told him sincerely. I replaced the crucifix beneath my tunic, out of sight. "I do it without thinking what others might feel," I said, giving him a sheepish shrug.

Zheng He paid little heed to our exchange, staring off into the distance, obviously deep in thought. Abruptly, he began speaking again, as if we had never interrupted him.

"For most of the crew," he said, still staring off somewhere else, "this is their first time at sea. As long as we were sailing near land and could glimpse the familiar comfort of trees and earth and rock, they had little concern for their safety."

He stood up, pacing restlessly now. "But now that we've been sailing for nearly three weeks across an infinite sea, their eyes are filled with a growing fear."

Surprisingly, it was now Ma Huan who tried to add a remarkably fresh and optimistic voice to the darkening conversation. "Perhaps we could help them by showing them there is nothing to fear."

I sensed what he was getting at and moaned loudly, throwing my arms up in a helpless gesture. "Ma Huan... please tell me you aren't planning to shine another light upon the sail."

Ma Huan grinned and shrugged with carefree exuberance. "It worked before! It could work again."

"No more fancy tricks," I howled. "The men need to believe... not be deceived."

None of this vigorous exchange penetrated Zheng He's awareness. He continued to stare off, contemplating the many challenges he must confront and pitifully few solutions he possessed to resolve them.

As this was happening, outside on the deck, our worst fears were becoming a reality. As Zheng He had suspected, members of the crew were growing more worried by the moment. Some hid their fears behind aggressive bravado, while others retreated within themselves. But most voiced their concern openly.

"We've sailed on this course for weeks now," one seaman groused to his shipmate, "and I haven't seen a wisp of land. Not once."

His friend was quick to agree. "I say the admiral has lost his way and is afraid to admit it."

"If that's so," a third seaman chimed in with a morose grumble, "then we're all as good as dead."

Having left his cabin in pursuit of some fresh sea air, Minister Wong happened upon the sailors and overheard their complaints. But it wasn't simply by accident that Wong found himself wandering among the men.

Earlier, several other seamen had secretly requested to meet with him. They wanted the minister to know of their growing fear that the armada of ships had now become lost in uncharted seas. Their initial burst of confidence in Admiral Zheng He on the day the armada set sail from China was now being steadily eroded as each week passed.

When Wong heard these sentiments of unrest, it stirred his soul to action. If he was going to honor Prince Han's request, this would be the best time to do it.

And now, as he walked the deck, he heard even more grave rumblings of discontent. He needed to seize upon their growing apprehension and manipulate it to his own ends.

When the grousing crewmen saw Deputy Envoy Wong, they instinctively stopped talking and offered him a bow as a sign of respect. The largest of the three men, also the oldest, finally gathered his courage and stepped forward to address the minister.

"Honorable minister, I beseech your indulgence. I have a direct question I would like to put to you."

Wong smiled with crooked lips, an expression that nearly grew into a cocky sneer. "Then speak. I am here to help resolve whatever concerns you may have."

The hulking sailor nodded with respect, unaware of Wong's petulant attitude. "I... that is 'we'... were wondering if you might know when we are expected to reach landfall?"

But Wong had no intention of assuaging their mounting uncertainty. "If I were you," he muttered with a rhythmic arrogance, "I'd be very worried. Very worried indeed."

Another man stepped forward. "What do you mean? Why do you say that?"

"I'm hesitant to do so," Wong lied, without even blinking, "but I feel I must warn all of you, this admiral doesn't care about your welfare. His only concern is how to increase his own personal power and wealth."

There was an explosion of restless muttering among the crewmen, surprised by Wong's unexpected comments. Finally, the large sailor who had first ventured a question dared to ask what everyone else was thinking. "How can the admiral possibly gain wealth from this expedition? This great quest was undertaken in service to the emperor. Wealth has nothing to do with it."

"Wealth has everything to do with it!" Wong snapped curtly at the sailors, delighted that he could so easily poison their thinking.

"The only reason Zheng He has accepted this position of unearned leadership is so that he might fill his pockets with the wealth of other countries."

More angry muttering ensued from the crewman gathered around Wong.

"How can he do that?" a lone voice called from the crowd of sailors. "Whatever treasures we acquire on this voyage will go directly to the emperor."

"Yes, that's right," another sailor blurted out. "And it will be preserved for the glory of China." Many of the other sailors cheered this sentiment, but their voices had now become less enthusiastic, subdued by doubt.

But Wong had no conscience whatsoever, continuing with his recitation of lies. "This admiral would risk all our lives so that he might reach Africa, then load our ships with rare and costly treasures and, once home, secretly conceal many of these treasures in his own keeping. For his own grand schemes and wealth."

"How do you know this?" the large sailor challenged Wong, bristling with disgust. "Where do you come by such foul and troubling news?"

"It is well known among those close to him," Wong replied with haughty pride. "Zheng He is allowed to keep one third of all the wealth he returns to the emperor. It is his reward. Of course, this is something he does not wish the men of his fleet to know, for it is all of you who are taking the greatest risk. And 'for what?' I ask you. So that you may have the privilege of suffering endlessly on this eternal voyage?"

The things Wong was saying astounded the sailors. They were literally stunned into silence. All but one man, who became surly and growled, "You are telling us that the admiral is risking our lives in order to gain greater wealth for himself? That is absurd!"

But another young seaman wasn't so sure. "Honorable, Minister... I have known Lord Zheng He since he was a eunuch servant for the emperor. I don't believe he could ever do something that dreadful."

"But he is not a eunuch!" Wong roared. "That is but another foul lie that Zheng He has perpetuated amongst you."

A chorus of grumbling voices arouse from the sailors now crowded around Wong on the deck, some accusatory, others simply torn by anger and confusion.

Wong raised his hand to stop the growing cacophony.

"Take my advice...!" he shouted above the din, then lowered his voice to a crafty and confidential whisper as the sailors fell into silence so they could hear him. "If you are wise, you will spread the word to your shipmates throughout the fleet. Make them aware of the deception and lies and thievery. Every day that the admiral keeps us on this wayward course brings us closer to catastrophe."

And once the seed of unrest was planted, the word spread like wildfire from man to man, ship to ship. The men used every means of communication available to alert their comrades. Signal lanterns flashed their news from one ship to the next. Messages tied to arrows flew through the misty air to their recipients, like birds on wing. But, ironically, the use of real birds was roundly discouraged by all, for the carrier pigeons could easily be intercepted by a ship's officer, who would then alert the admiral of the poisonous rumors being spread.


While the damage to Zheng He's good reputation continued to grow throughout the fleet, Zhu Di was beginning to suffer his own tribulations in Nanking. Not only had Prince Han greatly upset his father by telling him of Xi Chen's love for Zheng He, he had also launched an insidious and unrelenting campaign to stir up trouble in every quarter of the palace.

Thanks to the nefarious and truly sinister activities of Han, the number of Zhu Di's dissenters grew larger each day. Minister of Rites Yang, Finance Minister Wa, and the Assistant Finance Minister Jing, could now be counted on to fully support the ambitious prince. And of these three, Minister Wa was by far the most vocal. "Every time I think of all the wealth that is being wasted," he would howl like a man possessed with wild spirits, "it makes me wretch putrid bile from my soul!"

Han reveled in this melodramatic behavior by Minister Wa, knowing full well that it stirred the anger of others.

Another ploy Han liked to use when talking with the renegade ministers was to lower his voice when he was about to tell them something serious. "Someday, gentlemen," he would whisper with an ominous growl, "in the not too distant future, I intend to gather my loyal friends together and overthrow the crown. Then, I assure you, there will no longer be unnecessary fighting of border Mongols and no more wasting money on useless expeditions to backward nations."

Assistant Finance Minister Jing was quick to grow excited when he heard Han's boastful words. "If you promise that you won't back down, Honorable Prince," Jing announced, "you can rest assured we will all support your policies."

Han loved to hear that the ministers were with him. "I appreciate 'your' support, gentlemen," he would tell them, attempting to sound humble and sincere. "But please remember, I'll also need the support of all your friends and associates. Convince them to support me and I'll make certain your cooperation is handsomely rewarded."

All three ministers were pleased with these secret meetings they shared with the prince. They had, at last, found a member of the imperial family who believed the way they did.

Later, after Prince Han had dismissed the ministers from his presence, Zhu Di had occasion to meet with his Minister of Finance Wa. But this time, Wa presented a completely different perspective. He groveled in the presence of the emperor, exhibiting great deference, demonstrating his utmost cooperation and respect.

"Your Highness," he gushed, sweeping into Zhu Di's office with a smile that stretched from ear to ear, "I think it is absolutely wonderful the way your army has so bravely defended the country against the Mongols. I want you to know, Sire, that I strongly support your military initiatives in every possible way."

Zhu Di nodded in response to Wa's highly exaggerated effervescence. He gazed at the minister with a cool suspicion, fully aware that Wa was unlikely to support his policies. But this was no time to reveal his doubts.

"I'm glad to hear, Minister Wa, that I have your full support."

Minister Wa bowed deeply for a long moment, hoping to ingratiate himself even further in the eyes of the imperial ruler.

"At the risk of appearing too effusive," Wa said while smiling amiably, "I must congratulate you again on your decision to build the fleet. What a magnificent way to promote trade and good will with foreign countries. I must say, Your Majesty, you are a man of great wisdom."

Zhu Di wished he could believe all the praise that flowed from the lips of Minister Wa. But from the reports he'd received from his trusted confidants, his best choice was to remain highly skeptical of such obvious adoration.

Several close friends had reported seeing Minister Wa with Prince Han on several occasions. This, coupled with the fact that Minister Wa's reputation was already of questionable integrity, did not give Zhu Di confidence in the wildly flattering compliments that he espoused.

"You're most generous, Minister Wa," Zhu Di said, allowing only a slight sarcasm in his voice. "I trust you will let all of your friends, supporters and acquaintances know that you are in complete support of all my programs."

"You have my humble assurances, Sire," Wa gushed, continuing to grovel. "You have my most humble assurances."

Zhu Di had refrained from inviting Xi Chen to his private quarters following the disturbing encounter he'd experienced with his son. And since Xi Chen knew nothing about the incident, she wasn't particularly concerned that it had been so long since Zhu Di had chosen to invite her to spend the evening with him. She was, however, becoming curious as to why he had allowed their relationship to cool. It was, therefore, a very pleasant surprise when an invitation from Zhu Di was soon delivered to her.

That evening, when Xi Chen arrived at the door of Zhu Di's private quarters, two eunuch servants offered her their customary bow, as she passed by and went inside. A third servant, who was supposed to write down the name of Zhu Di's selection for the evening, was preoccupied with looking through some papers and didn't see who had just passed by him and entered. He looked up when he heard the door close.

"Who was that? Who did the emperor choose?" he asked the others. "I must make the notation."

The guard at the door replied casually, "Honorable Lady, Xi Chen."

"Xi Chen?" he exclaimed, scribbling her name down with a curious shake of his head. "We haven't seen her for nearly a month! I wonder why he hasn't called for her until now?"

The other guard smiled slyly. "Our emperor has always liked a little variety. Can you blame him?"

The servant at the table also smiled and spoke up. "I don't blame him. But then, I wouldn't know, would I?"

They all laughed at this irony. "He does seem to like non-Chinese girls best. They've always been his favorite!"

"But Xi Chen is Chinese," the servant with the book offered.

"Yes, I know," the table servant agreed, "but she looks very different... only part-Chinese. And Zhu Di usually prefers women from Korea and Malaysia. Just Look at his concubines. Only two are Chinese."

The guard at the door grew tired of this petty banter. "Did you write her name down?"

Annoyed, the servant at the table held up his book and shook it in the guard's face. "Yes, I wrote it down. Right there. Honorable Lady, Xi Chen. Do you want to inspect it?"


Zhu Di's private quarters were illuminated by the soft light of candles that had been placed at strategic points around the room and near the bed. The soft strains of a stringed instrument emanated from behind the decorative screen on the far side of the room.

Xi Chen and Zhu Di lay upon the soft bedcovers, their bodies exposed to the flickering candlelight. Neither spoke. Xi Chen felt that something was wrong. The emperor seemed subdued, restrained, as if a heavy cloud floated around him.

"Are you angry with me?" she asked tentatively, almost afraid to broach the subject.

Zhu Di feigned surprise. "Mad at you? Of course not. Why would you even suggest such a thing?"

Xi Chen slid closer and kissed Zhu Di on the cheek.    But he remained stoic and unresponsive.

"You haven't invited me to spend the night with you for weeks," she said. "And now that I'm here..." She left the rest unspoken, but he clearly understood her sadness and disappointment.

Finally, he turned to her. "Yes... well, I've been extremely busy, Xi Chen. You know, as emperor, I have many obligations."

Xi Chen lay back on the bed, staring at the ceiling.  Her naked upturned breasts were clearly visible in the flickering light from the candles, presenting him with an undulating temptation.

But Zhu Di remained on his back, saying nothing and not moving. The silence between them was deafening in its impact.  Neither spoke as the music floated over them like a warm blanket.

Zhu Di was unsure how to proceed.  After gathering his nerve, he ventured a cautious question.  "Xi Chen...?"

"Yes, Your Majesty?"

"I want to ask you something."

Xi Chen waited, but his initial statement was followed by the hollow sound of silence.  Now she was certain that something wasn't right.

"What is bothering you, Your Majesty?" she asked gently, trying to open the door so that he might comfortably step through and confide in her.

Finally, and with great hesitation, Zhu Di let the words come. "My son, Prince Han," he began...

"Yes, Your Majesty?"

Zhu Di looked at her with troubled eyes, afraid she might tell him something that he didn't want to hear.  Abruptly losing his nerve, he quickly rolled his body on top of her so that they now lay face-to-face, their naked skin touching from head to foot.

"It's nothing at all," he whispered softly, venturing an awkward smile. He gave her a long, passionate, soulful kiss.

Then, as their mouths drew apart, he looked into her eyes. "I just wanted to let you know how much I missed being inside of you."

Xi Chen pulled the emperor close to her breasts, pushing insistently against him with her thighs.  Now rigid with excitement, he inserted his manhood into her waiting velvet softness.  She wished she could be more responsive to his sudden desire, but somehow everything seemed different this time.  She stared blankly at the dancing shadows on the ceiling, lost in a rolling sea bereft of emotion.  She floated on the tumultuous crest of this swirling wave without ever being aware of the storm that battered her.

Far away, in the middle of the Western Ocean, the Ming fleet remained on a slow but steady due-west course toward the coast of Africa. This sea was calm. No storm tore at the sails. No wind pummeled the masts and rigging.

Zheng He had no idea how much further they would have to go before sighting land. The dissatisfied grumbling of the crew grew worse every day. And to make matters worse, the admiral had been beset by a troubling illness that had confined him to his bed.

The fleet's senior physician visited Zheng He often, trying to find some medicinal cure. Ma Huan did what he could to care for him, but with each sunrise the sickness only grew worse.

"I don't think you are getting any better, Sir," he moaned regretfully. "You are burning up with fever."

"I feel like living death," Zheng He muttered hoarsely. He reached around him, grasping at the air. "Is there anything cool to drink?"

There was an abrupt knock at the door of the admiral's cabin. Ma Huan opened it. Minister Wong stood in the open doorway, a sullen look on his face. After a moment of silence, he spoke up with irritation. "May I come in? Or do you expect me to stand here and shout to the admiral?"

Chastised, Ma Huan bowed slightly to the minister, but made no move to step back and allow him to enter.

"The admiral is sick, Minister Wong," he said politely as he could. "I suggest you come back at another time."

But Wong was defiant. "I will not come back another time! I demand to see Zheng He. NOW!"

Zheng He heard the commotion at the door. He strained to speak up, but all that emerged was a weak, trembling whisper. "Who is it?" he asked softly.

Minister Wong brashly pushed past Ma Huan, shoving the door open and barging into the admiral's cabin.

"It's your Deputy Envoy!" Ma Huan quickly attempted to announce. But Wong was inside before the words could leap from his mouth. "I told him you were sick," Ma Huan explained meekly to Zheng He. Wong stood at the end of the admiral's bed, clearly disinterested in Zheng He's condition.

"You know and I know that there's no guarantee we will ever arrive at our destination," Wong complained harshly. "You don't even know what our destination is!"

Zheng He motioned weakly for Ma Huan to prop a few pillows behind his head so he could sit up more easily.

"Minister Wong," he responded in a hoarse whisper, "I'm not sure I understand why you're so upset."

"I am more than upset. I am angry!" Wong declared, almost shouting. "Angry because, day after day, you continue sailing on this reckless course, putting the crew of this armada at risk!"

Zheng He was shocked at the bitter accusations spewing from Minister Wong. He fixed his eyes firmly on Wong, summoning a new strength with which to confront his disgruntled minister.

"I would be cautious with your words, Minister Wong," Zheng He told him. "Once spoken, they cannot be cast aside like dried tea leaves. They will remain with me always and will surely influence my opinion of your judgment."

Wong tightened his mouth with an unrepentant scowl. "Then mark my words well, admiral," Wong shouted back. "You are jeopardizing the lives of everyone in the fleet! The men fear for their lives."

"Frightened men are alert men, minister," Zheng He said with a great calmness. "When we are afraid, we can truly sense the precious nature of our lives. This makes us stronger and wiser and even bolder in our choices."

"How dare you twist my words to your advantage," Wong interjected sharply. "They're frightened because they see death before their very eyes. And it is at your hand they suffer! As Deputy Envoy, I demand that you stop this madness and return us to our home port at once!"

Calling upon a new strength fed by his escalating anger, Zheng He sat straight up in the bed. He summoned a strong voice from deep within his lungs, overcoming the harsh rasp in his throat to speak with a thunderously resonant tone.

"I must remind you, Minister Wong... I am here under direct orders from our emperor. And you, sir, are my subordinate. I will not turn this fleet around until such time that I feel it is absolutely necessary!"

"We could run out of food!" Wong shouted. "We could run out of water! If you'd only go out on deck and talk with the men, instead of hiding in bed pretending to be sick, you'd see for yourself!"

Ma Huan's eyes flashed between the two men, shocked by the impassioned exchange between them.

"Can't you see the admiral is sick?" Ma Huan blurted out defensively. "He needs rest..."

Zheng He raised a gentle hand to silence his servant. "No. Minister Wong may be right. As admiral of the fleet it is appropriate that I hear their concerns directly from them."

Ma Huan was startled by this reversal, concerned that Zheng He was relinquishing his position of authority. But he stifled his worries behind a troubled mask.

Zheng He considered his options in silence. Wong waited patiently now, wisely realizing that this would not be the moment to continue his challenging accusations.

Finally, Zheng He spoke. "All right, Minister Wong. I will take your recommendation. Assemble the men. I will meet with them here on the flagship at noon tomorrow."

Minister Wong nodded, secretly pleased with his power of persuasion.

Zheng He added, "And be sure to have representatives of the crews from every other ship in the fleet in attendance. I want their voices heard as well."

Knowing that it was wise to quit while ahead, Minister Wong nodded quickly and turned on his heels, heading for the door of the cabin. But in a gesture of his insolent authority, he paused at the cabin entrance, waiting for Ma Huan to open the door for him.

Ma Huan hesitated a moment, displeased with the idea of showing this rebellious minister any undue respect. But Zheng He gave a slight movement with his head, signaling the servant to follow protocol.

Ma Huan stifled his displeasure and stepped over to the door, pulling it open. He refused to look Minister Wong in the eyes, staring off blankly. Wong sniffed his disdain at Ma Huan and then vanished out the door like a foul breeze.

Ma Huan shut the door firmly and returned to Zheng He's bed. "With respect, Sir, I don't understand why you allowed Minister Wong to treat you with such insolent disregard?"

"It's a long and complicated story, Ma Huan," he said, sinking back into the pillows. "I've known Minister Wong since I was a young man. Long before Zhu Di became emperor and long before he named me to be his Chief Eunuch. Wong didn't like me then and he certainly doesn't like me now. I'm sure he finds it repulsive that I have been appointed admiral of the fleet and now outrank him."

"But that's no reason for you to let him belittle you!" Ma Huan blurted out. "I don't think you should let him do that."

Zheng He smiled philosophically. "His heart is bitter about many things, Ma Huan. While I may disagree with him, I have no desire to add to the personal misery that torments him."

As agreed, Minister Wong had arranged for appointed men and officers to be picked up from several nearby ships and brought to the flagship on launches. By noon, the main deck of the flagship was over-flowing with restless sailors, some belligerent and argumentative, as well as a handful of nervous officers.

While Zheng He remained in bed, gathering his strength, Minister Wong busied himself on the main deck stirring up emotions among the dissenters gathered there.

"I met with the admiral yesterday," he surreptitiously whispered to a group of men, "and I can honestly report that the man is confused. He has no idea what he's doing. With a common eunuch servant leading this expedition, I'm afraid all of us are in very great danger."

Wong looked into the frightened faces of the men and knew he had their attention. "Don't give in to him," he admonished strongly. "The admiral is weak at the present time. He has fallen ill. If he clearly comprehends your dissatisfaction, he will most assuredly respond properly and return us all home."

The older man that Wong had talked to the previous day stepped forward and pulled off his hat, a worried look on his face. "Begging your pardon, Honorable Sir, but I understand that if we participate in a mutiny, the punishment is death."

Wong looked at the man slyly. "Only if you fail," Wong stated with bold confidence. "Remain firm and committed to your goal. That is the key. If all of you stand as one, you will not fail!"

Still sensing some skepticism among the men gathered around him, Minister Wong pointed a finger to the sky. "Remember," he said, raising his voice so all could hear. "I, Minister Wong, am with you! I am Deputy Envoy, second-in-command of the emperor's expedition. If we act together as one and do not stumble in our effort, we can be rid of this fool servant! Are you with me?"

All the men responded, shouting their allegiance to the devious instigator.

"Are you prepared to defend your beliefs?" he asked, egging them on. Again, the men cheered, even louder now.

In Zheng He's stateroom, Ma Huan could hear the cheering from below on the main deck. He looked toward the admiral, who was now sitting in a chair beside the bed. Ma Huan winced when he heard the admiral cough. It was quite obvious that Zheng He was still very sick.

"I think you should put this meeting off for a few days," Ma Huan suggested. Zheng He waved the suggestion away, determined to get this resolved.

"No, Ma Huan, I can't. I promised I would be there, so I must. My word is important to the crew. If I can't keep my promises, how can I expect them to trust my decisions?"

Zheng He stumbled as he began to rise. Ma Huan quickly grabbed hold of him and led him toward the door with great care.

On the main deck, the crowd of men saw the admiral emerge from his third floor cabin. They looked up with nervous anticipation. A surreal hush fell over the entire ship as the officers and men watched Zheng He slowly descend two flights of stairs to the main deck below.

Wong pulled a man close to him and whispered. "See? I told you he was sick. Look how slowly he moves. He can barely stand. And his ability to think with any semblance of logic or good sense has been equally affected."

Ma Huan guided Zheng He into a wooden chair on a raised section of the deck. Lieutenant Zhang Ji had prepared the chair with a small canopy to ward off the hot noonday sun.

When the admiral took his seat and nodded that he was ready, a sailor cautiously stepped forward, respectfully removed his cap and then spoke as a representative for the rest of the men. It took him a few long awkward moments to finally get started, as he was obviously nervous.

"Admiral Zheng He, I speak for those gathered here. We have been at sea a very long time. It is no secret that we are beginning to run low on food and water. Because we have no clear idea of our destination or when we shall reach it, we believe that it may be an appropriate time for the fleet to return home."

The sailor glanced around at his companions, searching for signs that they were still in support of him. Many of them nodded their agreement and those close to the man nudged him, encouraging him to continue.

"You are ill, admiral!" the man exclaimed, startling himself with the suddenness of his own voice. "All of us can see that. We think you should return home for your own benefit and good health."

Zheng He leaned forward in his chair. He struggled to stifle a raspy cough, then took a long moment to find his voice. But when it finally came to him, it was strong and certain.

"When a soldier in battle is wounded," he said with rising volume, "he does not retreat! Just because I'm not feeling well is not a reason for me to shirk my duty. Just as your own doubts and concerns are no reason for you to avoid your great loyalty to our emperor. This expedition WILL continue!"

The spokesman for the crew nervously surveyed his comrades once more for moral support. But the look in their eyes was beginning to waver. Setting his feet wide apart and throwing himself into the breech, he made one last argument.

"But we might be killed if we keep going!" he pleaded. "What if we encounter savages or armies that are far superior to our own? There is no way of knowing what horrible terror we may find in these dark jungles."

The men behind the sailor could be heard grumbling softly, but with far less enthusiasm. They were still reeling from the strong words voiced by Zheng He.

Minister Wong watched this process with growing concern, afraid that the men were losing their taste for rebellion and descending into apathy.

Zheng He raised his hand and the waves of rumbling voices fell silent, all eyes upon him now.

"Yes... there is a risk in what we are doing," he said, allowing his voice to rise dramatically. "And it is true, as you have suggested, that we might all be killed. But what we have committed ourselves to is much larger than the salvation of our individual souls. We have pledged our loyalty and lives to the honor and glory of our country... and our honorable emperor."

There was a restless stirring among the men. Their eyes shifted away from their feet and began to rise to meet the steel-eyed gaze of Zheng He.

"Our family and friends await word of our great success. The emperor is depending on us to bravely open a door to a new world of countless unexplored wonders. If we give up now, surrendering to our personal fears... intimidated by the unknown... defeated by imagined threats and made craven cowards by our own timid reflections, then we can never rightfully call ourselves men."

At this point, Zheng He's commanding voice began to take on the fury of a typhoon, rising in force with each word spoken, each challenge hurled. "If we retreat from our duty... if we run from our obligation to country and emperor... if we deny our very destiny... none of us will ever be able to look another in the eye with pride and honor. We will carry only shame and humiliation. Is this the fate you want to bear for eternity?"

The voice of one sailor deep in the crowd suddenly arose, carried on the wind. "No!" he shouted. Others turned their eyes to him and a few even joined in with a ragged chorus of their own scattered shouts of "No!"

Encouraged, Zheng He continued. "But you men are not cowards! You men have been specifically chosen for this great honor because of your bravery. You have been selected to achieve greatness! This sets you apart from thousands of other sailors and officers. They were not chosen for this great honor. YOU were chosen! Not them. YOU!"

The men were stirred by these words. A murmur ran through the crowd. Zheng He sensed their response and he seized upon this moment of growing excitement. "To turn back now, when we are on the very brink of greatness, would be a disrespectful slap in the face of our benevolent emperor."

Another, louder, murmur rolled through the gathering of men. Zheng He pressed on. "To abandon your destiny, your country, your great emperor... would be a slap in the face of our beloved Lord Buddha!"

And now the voices in the crowd become a veritable roar of excitement, prompted by the mention of the great Lord Buddha.

"You have seen it for yourself," Zheng He shouted, summoning an energy he was unaware he possessed. "Even the Goddess of Heaven is with us."

Zheng He's eyes quickly searched the crowd for a sailor from the flagship crew. "You!" he said, pointing at one of the men nearby. "You were on deck the night of the raging storm. Tell the others what you saw."

The sailor turned to face the men, his voice rising above the restless rumble of voices. "Yes... the admiral speaks the truth. With my own eyes I saw the Goddess send us a sign... a shining light of truth upon the sails. Mark my words, if it wasn't for the Goddess of Heaven, we would not have survived that terrible tempest!"

"And she is still here with us," Zheng He added quickly, "protecting all of us! She will make certain that every man gets home safely! And with honor!"

A huge cheer went up among the men. Their hearts and souls had been stirred and strengthened. Their belief had been returned by the inspirational words conjured by their admiral.

Zheng He settled back in his chair, the very energy sapped from his body. But deep inside, his spirit felt stronger and more energized than ever before.

Minister Wong, standing at the edge of the gathering, sneered in disappointment at the unexpected shift in loyalty brought on by Zheng He. If he didn't do something quickly to turn this tide, all his efforts to sew seeds of dissension would fail.

He glimpsed a sailor nearby who seemed to be somewhat less enthused with the admiral's dramatic pronouncements. He approached the man and leaned toward him, confiding in his ear, "These men are nothing but fools. They have been greatly deceived by this conjurer of magic."

The sailor turned to him with a look of apprehension. With the hook firmly planted in this gullible fish, Wong began to reel him in. "But there is a way to stop him."

The sailor gazed at him, wide-eyed with interest. Wong smiled with conspiratorial assurance, then whispered more words of discord and unrest in the sailor's willing ear. After a moment, Wong slipped his arm around the man's shoulder and guided him away through the crowd of men.

The sun beating down on Zheng He was beginning to take its toll. He began to feel queasy. Ma Huan, sensitive to his admiral's needs, could see that something was terribly wrong. He quickly offered Zheng He a drink of cooling water. He then wiped his master's brow with a damp rag, as Zheng He leaned back with his eyes closed, struggling to regain his strength.

I saw the men watching this with concern. I stepped forward, hoping to provide some words of encouragement. I began speaking uneasily, but quickly warmed to the task. "You men shouldn't trouble yourselves with thoughts of failure and defeat," I proclaimed. "Lord Zheng He has told you to concentrate on victory! And he is right! You bring great honor to yourselves just by being a part of this historic expedition."

I quickly looked to Zheng He, hoping that perhaps he had recovered sufficiently to continue addressing the restless men. But, instead, he nodded weakly, signaling me to continue. I did so, but with great hesitancy, searching desperately for more words of inspiration.

"I'm not even Chinese!" My words burst forth louder than I had intended. I startled even myself. I brought my volume down, trying to assert a greater sense of serious intent. "But I can tell you one thing; not since the travels of Marco Polo, have men enjoyed such an opportunity for spreading trade and good will among so many people of the world. You must not stop now. All of you are on the threshold of a great achievement. All of you..."

Suddenly, a cacophony of yelling and screaming arose. It seemed to emerge from just behind the crowd of men. A guard, with blood streaming down his face, pushed through the men, threw himself down at the admiral's feet and begged for mercy. Zheng He immediately took the damp cloth from his head and told Ma Huan to use it to staunch the flow of blood gushing from the guard's head wound. While continuing to kowtow frantically, the guard pleaded for his life, begging for mercy. He made such a ruckus, crying and bowing and pleading, that Ma Huan had a difficult time holding the damp rag against the man's head.

"Get hold of yourself," Ma Huan muttered sternly at the injured man. "Just calm down and tell us what happened."

"Have mercy," he wailed, over and over. "I beg you, Lord Zheng He! Don't have me killed!"

While this commotion unfolded at Zheng He's feet, two other guards rushed forward, each holding pieces of the ship's compass. It had been badly mangled, obviously damaged to an extent that would prevent its further use.

The guards bowed with great deference, handing what was left of the delicate instrument to the admiral. Zheng He examined the piece of metal. There was a good deal of blood smeared along one side. With a glum expression, he handed the mangled instrument to me.

"Look at this," he whispered to me in confidence. "Whoever did this damage was badly injured in the process."

Zheng He took the mangled compass and handed it to Ma Huan. He turned to the fleet captain. "Captain Su... place this injured man in the ship's prison immediately."

The captain quickly motioned for two guards. They grabbed the man by his arms. A litany of praise and gratitude poured from his lips as he was escorted away.

"Thank you, merciful admiral. Thank you, thank you," he muttered over and over. "May Lord Buddha bless you for a thousand years. Thank you, Lord Zheng He. Thank you, thank you..."

He was about to be thrown into the ship's prison, yet the bloodied man heaped praise upon Zheng He. This made no sense to me. Curious, I leaned close to Zheng He's ear and asked, "Why does he praise you so? After all, you are sending him to prison."

"This man was fortunate he didn't lose his life and he knows it," Zheng He told me softly. He motioned for Ma Huan to bring him more water. "He was supposed to be guarding the ship's compass. Obviously, he failed at his job. Someone destroyed it and, unfortunately, the burden of responsibility falls upon him. Under normal circumstances, such dereliction of duty would result in his immediate beheading."

I was shocked. "You mean you would have cut the man's head off? Right here? In front of everyone?"

"Yes. But I don't have the stomach for such cruel measures," Zheng He said with calm assurance. He was truly a man who was unwaveringly certain of his beliefs. It was this that I admired so much about him.

He turned to Captain Su. "Captain! I want you to have Lieutenant Zhang Ji organize a search party. Have his men scour the ship and find out who destroyed the compass. And do it with great haste, before the offender can conceal the proof."

Captain Su immediately shouted for Lieutenant Zhang Ji, who was already in motion, having heard the original order from Zheng He's lips. The officer hurried among the men, gathering volunteers as he went.

While they searched the ship, Zheng He and I studied the broken compass. "I don't believe it can be repaired," he allowed with a heavy sigh, studying the mangled pieces.

I agreed. It was severely damaged. The criminals who did this were intent on seeing that it could never be used again. "How do you think we should proceed?" I asked, knowing full well that, given the circumstances, this was an impossible question for anyone to answer.

"We have but one choice," Zheng He said firmly, without a bit of hesitation. "We must continue on. I know it won't be easy or nearly as accurate. But we can still navigate in the traditional way... using our astrolabe. We will not let this broken compass stop us."

"Why would somebody want to do such a thing?" I mumbled, turning the twisted and bent pieces in my hand.

"I'm not certain," Zheng He replied. "But I do know that often things are not as they seem. And I believe it may be true in this case."


Below deck, a meandering trail of blood led the way to a large storage hold. Lieutenant Zhang Ji and twelve of his men followed the incriminating crimson trail to the far corner of the hold, where hundreds of wooden barrels were stacked. Some contained water and others were filled with rice.

The trail soon ended in a darkened corner, where they discovered a trembling man cowering behind several of the largest barrels, desperately trying to avoid detection. They jerked the man to his feet and unceremoniously dragged
him up several decks to the main deck above.

Topside, with a total lack of wind, it was still blazing hot and growing hotter. Zheng He's fever had become more intense, yet he refused to return to the protection of his cabin, choosing instead to stay concealed beneath the small canopy above his chair. To make matters worse, his cough began to flare up again and was making him more uncomfortable.

"How do you feel?" Ma Huan asked, already knowing what his answer was likely to be.

"I have been better," he replied, trying to wipe sweat from his face. "Do you have another damp rag?"

Ma Huan hated to see his master in so much distress.

"Maybe I should take you back to your stateroom," he suggested.

"Not yet," Zheng He replied sternly, stifling another cough. He handed the warm rag back to his servant. "I must see this through, for the sake of the men."

Suddenly, Lieutenant Zhang Ji and his men pushed their way through the crowd on the main deck, dragging the badly disheveled and distraught sailor with them. His hand bled profusely.

Lieutenant Zhang Ji forced the injured sailor to stand directly in front of Lord Zheng He. The captured suspect instinctively glanced in the direction of Minister Wong. The subtle look toward Wong did not go unnoticed by Zheng He. The minister stood at the far edge of the crowd, trying his best to disappear among the assembled men. But the admiral's sharp eye was quick to separate him from the others.

"Minister Wong?" Zheng He abruptly beckoned, motioning to him. All eyes turned to the minister, who did his best to shrink within his clothes. "As Deputy Envoy, I believe you should step forward and conduct the questioning of this suspect."

Wong was cornered. He had no choice but to wade through the men and do the bidding of his superior officer. Those few conspirators who had agreed to protect the minister from detection stepped aside, unwilling to allow themselves to somehow be implicated in this crumbling plot.

Wong stepped before Zheng He, taking an authoritarian stance, as if he were about to carry out the admiral's request. He glared at the sailor who kneeled before him ... then, without warning, he suddenly pulled a small dagger from beneath his robe, lunging at the accused man.

The sailor saw the blade flash before him and tried to wrench free of Zhang Ji's grip, leaping up and desperately dodging Wong's awkward attack. The sharp knife sliced at the side of his face, neatly cutting off one ear. He screamed in pain, dropping back to his knees, blood running down his cheek and neck. The sharp blade tore at him again. He ducked a second deadly blow from the wildly slashing minister.

Zheng He leaped to his feet and lunged at Wong, hoping to stop him from striking the defenseless sailor again. He deftly slapped the knife from the old man's hand, shoving him back.

The admiral grabbed the bloody knife from the deck and with lightning speed that I would have thought was beyond his capability, pressed it firmly against the Minister Wong's quivering neck.

Lieutenant Zhang Ji seized the injured sailor by one arm and jerked him roughly to his feet. The injured man cried out and begged Zheng He for mercy, cupping his bloody ear with his hand.

"Quiet, you fool!" Zhang Ji shouted, as he slapped the hysterical man across the face for good measure. "Stand before the admiral like a man."

"Did you destroy the compass?" Zheng He barked at the bleeding sailor, while at the same time keeping the knife firmly pressed against Wong's throat.

The accused sailor did not respond. Instead, he chose to keep his eyes focused on the deck. Zhang Ji slapped the man yet again. This time, the powerful blow caused him to fall into a crumpled heap. Feeling no remorse, Zhang Ji harshly jerked the sailor back to his feet, shouting in his face. "Answer the admiral when he speaks to you!"

Zheng He motioned for Zhang Ji to back off. Then looked deeply into the sailor's eyes. "Who ordered you to do this?" Zheng He asked, keeping his tone calm and steady.

Still the man didn't answer, his eyes filled with fear. Again he flashed his nervous gaze in the direction of Minister Wong. Seeing this, Zheng He turned to look at the minister, surreptitiously pressing the sharp blade against the bulging vein in his neck to signal his growing suspicion.

Then, turning his attention back to the sailor, Zheng He spoke with measured words. "You have brought shame to both yourself and to your family," he said. "You've jeopardized not only your life, but also the lives of all your comrades throughout the fleet. I will now give you one chance... and once chance only. Give me the name of the man who put you up to this... and I will spare your life. But if you refuse... or you lie... I will kill you where you stand."

The wounded sailor trembled, tears of shame coursing down his sweat-covered face. He raised his hand and pointed directly at Minister Wong.

"That man!" he shouted, a spray of blood and sweat erupting from his lips. "The Deputy Envoy! Minister Wong ordered me to destroy the compass."

"Put them both in chains!" the admiral ordered, taking no pity on either Wong or the injured sailor.

But before Captain Su or Lieutenant Zhang Ji could make a move, Wong broke free and furiously attacked Zheng He in a rage. But Ma Huan leaped forward and grabbed Wong by the arms, pulling him away from the admiral.

"You can't do this to me!" Wong screamed, trying to free himself from Ma Huan's grasp. "I am Minister Wong! This man lies! You can't order a minister put in chains."

Ma Huan pushed Wong through the crowd of officers and sailors as they stood quietly by, making no effort to defend the disgraced minister.

"I'll get you for this, Zheng He!" he screamed, still trying to pull free. "You will pay! I swear to you before Lord Buddha! You will pay!"

Wong's voice could be heard screaming out in protest until he was finally locked up in the ship's prison several decks below. And even after that, a faint voice still continued to echo through the vessel. In contrast, the accused sailor went quietly, escorted by silent guards.

But far below, in the deep bowels of the ship, the muffled voice of the minister still reverberated. "I am the Deputy Envoy! I was chosen by the emperor! Release me at once! Release me, damn you!"

But his words went unheeded by all.


By this time, the Forbidden City was nearly complete and Zhu Di was becoming anxious to move back to Beijing. He had never felt comfortable living in Nanking. To him, the northern capital had always been the one location that gave him greatest comfort and solace.

Even though some detailed finishing work still had to be completed, Zhu Di had firmly decided to make the final move to Beijing within the next month. But until that day came, there would still be a tremendous amount of daily business to contend with, much of it unpleasant.

The meeting that he faced on one particular day was extremely disagreeable. He had not been looking forward to it. Several weeks previous, the emperor had agreed to meet with Minister of Rites, Yang. He knew that Yang had spent considerable time with his son, Prince Han. Given Han's lack of support for Zhu Di's official policies in the past, the emperor was certain Yang was of the same mind, despite whatever he might have said to his face.


As expected, when Minister Yang arrived, he launched into a litany of obsequious compliments, groveling before Zhu Di with transparent blatancy. "I've heard your new palace is absolutely magnificent, Sire!" he trilled melodiously, an oily smile creasing his face like a tiger that had just swallowed its prey. "I can't believe that it has been finished so soon. You must be delighted."

Zhu Di accepted Yang's inflated compliments graciously, fully aware of his manipulative intentions.

"Let's just say, Minister Yang, that my new palace is 'nearly' complete. There's still much to do. But, yes, I must admit, I am quite pleased with the result."

"May I ask when you will be moving to your new residence, Your Majesty?" Yang inquired.

Zhu Di paused, taking the moment to signal a waiting servant to bring tea. He gazed up at Wang with penetrating eyes. "Soon..." he said. His word floated in the air, suspended by a curious thread of mystery. "But when I do make the move, I can assure you I will not be returning to Nanking. Beijing will be my home and Forbidden City will be my new palace. Nothing will ever cause me to leave this sanctuary again. It is where I will die."

Yang offered the emperor a coy smile that concealed many disturbing thoughts. "Not even to fight the Mongols, Sire?"

Zhu Di stared at him in silence, not appreciating the implication of his words. "I would, of course, defend the country when necessary. As emperor it is my sworn duty to protect this land and its people. But my departure from Beijing would be brief, as victory would be immediate and decisive."

Yang paced the floor, thoughts tumbling through his mind. "I have heard talk, Sire, that even now another invader may be encroaching upon our country from the north."

The servant interrupted them briefly, putting the silver tray down before the two men. He poured two cups of tea, taking his time, precise and careful in his movements. This untimely delay in the conversation created a tension to grow between Zhu Di and Wang.

As the servant departed, Zhu Di prolonged the tense moment of silence even further as he took a long sip of the steaming tea, savoring it. Finally, he spoke.

"So... you have heard about that, did you? I'm well aware of this intrusion and I don't believe it is of any consequence. General Tan informs me that it will provide nothing more than a minor inconvenience."

Abruptly, Zhu Di sat up straight with regal prominence, as if a brilliant idea had suddenly alighted upon his royal head. "Aha! Here is a thought. Why don't you join me, Minister Yang? I will be traveling with Commander Tan to encounter these petty intruders. It should not be an extremely dangerous encounter by any means. And it will afford you an opportunity to witness directly how we deal with these irritating nuisances. And best of all, it will give you a taste of real battle!"

Caught off guard, Yang was totally shocked. For a moment his mouth hung open in silence, until his voice finally forced its way up his throat and emerged with a ragged quaking.

"Uh... but, uh... me? Join you in battle? Your Majesty... I don't know if I... Well, I couldn't! It would be impossible. I have too many duties to perform here at the palace." He quickly searched for an excuse. "The, uh... Korean emperor will arrive soon. And, and..."

Zhu Di raised his hand to stop Yang's lame excuses.

"And why is it so important for you to remain here?" Zhu Di asked pointedly, leaning toward the nervous minister and feigning a stern manner. "Haven't I provided you with enough assistants?"

"Oh yes, Your Majesty," Yang whined, offering Zhu Di a humbling bow. "You've provided me with much more than I deserve. But the Korean emperor is reportedly bringing his granddaughter with him. He intends to present the young woman to you as a personal gift. I must be here to receive her properly."

Zhu Di leaned back, gazing off in thought. "How very interesting," he said softly. "A gift, you say. Do you have any idea what age his granddaughter might be?"

"She's eighteen, Your Majesty," Yang responded quickly, realizing that he had captured Zhu Di's interest. "And from what I've been told, she's been very well schooled in the art of 'personal' service." He smiled slyly at his own crudely suggestive inference.

Zhu Di continued to muse silently. "Well...I do like to be entertained by foreign women."

Finally, after a protracted period of consideration, he relented. "All right... But you must make absolutely certain that this Korean emperor receives all the honors and gifts that are appropriate for a person of his rank and stature. I want no mistakes or embarrassments, Minister Yang. Do I make myself perfectly clear?"

Pleased that his ruse has succeeded, Yang bowed deeply and backed away with great deference. "You may be assured, Sire, that your every wish will be carried out. It is my great and humble honor to do so. As always."


At sea, Zheng He's gaze was locked on the endless horizon. Two more weeks of sailing on a steady course, west by southwest, without the sighting of land, had now become a troubling concern. Supplies were running seriously low, just as Minister Wong had warned.

Before leaving on the ambitious expedition, previous eyewitness travelers had told the navigational officers to keep the fleet on an unwavering westerly course. They assured them that, with prayer and luck and good wind, the ships would eventually reach the western coast of Africa.

However, even Zheng He had now begun to secretly doubt these optimistic predictions. He feared that they might have unknowingly steered dangerously off course and were hopelessly lost in an endless sea.

It was at this nadir of hope that one of the lookouts suddenly shouted the welcome news! Land was sighted. The excited crew rushed out to the decks, squinting toward the small sliver of land that danced and flitted on the distant horizon. Before the sun had scarcely moved in the sky, gleaming white sand beaches came steadily into view, beckoning to the sailors toward the welcoming green coastline. They later learned that the land they encountered on that day was called Malindi.

After offering prayers to the Goddess of Protection for delivering them safely, Lord Zheng He sent out an advance team of soldiers to make contact with the local ruler. He was found living in a large village compound only a few miles from the beach.

The man was quite large. But he couldn't be called "fat" for his body was firm and solid as a large tree. He was addressed as "chief" and had skin so black that it appeared to be the very dark blue of a moonlit sea.

A magnificent headdress of long ostrich feathers made him appear even taller than he was. A colorful tiger skin cape wrapped his powerful shoulders. This gave him the unquestionable visage of a true leader.

We quickly learned his name was Chief D'jibuto. But to the three thousand subjects he commanded, his name might just as well have been 'god.'

When we were invited to Chief D'jibuto's compound deep in the jungle, Zheng He decided to take with him his usual entourage of Ming officials, trade envoys and an impressive unit of soldiers.

At first there was talk of taking as many as five thousand soldiers. But after talking with several local fishermen on the beach, it was decided that such a massive show of force would not be warranted and, indeed, might even be misinterpreted as a sign of aggression.

When Zheng He's entourage arrived at Chief D'jibuto's compound, it was unclear who was more astonished. The Chinese stared at the gathering of black natives with incredulous eyes. They were all nearly naked, standing amid a ramshackle village of primitive thatched huts that looked barely able to survive a rainstorm.

The African natives were equally astounded by the huge number of Chinese visitors who spoke an unintelligible gibberish and dressed in elaborately odd clothing. Tales had already begun circulating about the hundreds of wooden ships with billowing white sails that had brought them to their land.

Formal introductions took a great deal of time as the frustrated translators attempted to decipher the words of Chief D'jibuto. But finally, after much effort and a good deal of good will and patience, a pattern of communication was established between the Chinese and Africans.

Once these formalities were completed, Chief D'jibuto treated Zheng He and his men to an incredible variety of unfamiliar exotic foods, followed by much singing and dancing by the enthusiastic natives. It was like nothing these Chinese travelers had ever experienced before and they were left with deep and lasting impressions that filled their dreams for many nights to come.

As the fierce-looking dancers spun and whirled wildly, seemingly transfixed by the rhythmic sound of two-dozen jungle drums, Zheng He leaned over and shouted in my ear.

"Did you ever think we'd see such an incredible sight?" he said with a booming voice, attempting to be heard over the thundering drums. "This is all quite unbelievable!"

All I could do was shake my head in disbelief and yell back. "I prayed long and hard to get us here. Now I'm praying that these people remain friendly."

At that instant, the music and dancing abruptly stopped and Chief D'jibuto struggled to his feet. He took up a position opposite Zheng He. The natives surrounding them abruptly dropped to the ground, sitting totally still. The entire compound fell into a strange and uncomfortable silence. Zheng He remained seated, unsure how to respond in this oddly threatening situation. I discretely leaned over and whispered in Zheng He's ear. "I think he might be waiting for you to stand up."

Zheng He hesitated, uncertain. Years of observing strict palace protocol, while serving the ruler of a highly complex and advanced civilization, had not prepared him for the unfamiliar jungle diplomacy he now faced.

The nervously flickering light from dozens of burning torches did nothing to ease the tense atmosphere. Shadows shimmered eerily against a backdrop of surrounding trees and thatched huts. It was eerily unnerving to watch this powerful native chief, standing alone, glaring fiercely at a Chinese admiral... and speaking not a single word.

I gave Zheng He a hard nudge with my elbow. "Get up. Get to your feet."

Finally realizing the wisdom of my advice, Zheng He struggled to his feet, standing at polite attention before Chief D'jibuto.

Unsure of what to say, he awkwardly cleared his throat and began stumbling through a short extemporaneous speech. "I want to thank you for inviting us to your village. And I would also like to remind you that we come in peace."

The translator attempted to provide Chief D'jibuto a halting, and only partially accurate, interpretation of Zheng He's words. Sensing the admiral's nervous hesitation, I nodded encouragement for him to continue.

"Our great Chief, Zhu Di, Emperor of China, has sent us on a benevolent mission. A mission to establish friendship and trade with many foreign countries such as yours."

Again the translator tried to tell the Chief what Zheng He had said. Unfortunately, there were numerous African dialects, so it was difficult for the translator to be completely accurate. Yet, somehow, the chief managed to grasp the basic intent and meaning of what this visitor was trying to say. He bowed slightly, indicating that he was pleased with what Zheng He had expressed.

Zheng He signaled Ma Huan to have servants bring forward the gifts he had brought for the African ruler. Ten servants quickly stepped forward with costly jade and gold objects of rare beauty, distributing them to the chief and his attendants. Chief D'jibuto accepted the gifts without exhibiting any expression of interest or appreciation. His face was a blank slate.

Within a few minutes, however, hundreds of the local villagers began crowding around their tribal leader, trying to see and touch the curious objects for themselves.

We all waited nervously for any sign of the chief's reaction to Zheng He's gifts. Then, after several tension-filled moments, Chief D'jibuto turned and nodded to his people, held up a piece of jade sculpture and smiled broadly, beaming like a child with his first toy. Needless to say, Zheng He felt a great wave of relief wash over him upon finally seeing this reaction.

Chief D'jibuto then handed the sculpture to one of his attendants and clapped his hands together loudly. At once a strange sound we'd never heard before began to assault our senses. It was a bizarre chorus of loud grunts. It was low and angry sounding in the beginning, and then began echoing amidst spinning refrains of other weird noises. Before long, the odd grunts seemed to emanate from outside the eight-foot walls of palm leaves and elephant husks that completely surrounded the compound where we were seated.

The sounds were especially frightening because none of us could tell who, or what, was causing them. It turned out to be fifty or so slaves, definitely not members of Chief D'jibuto's tribe, who were forced to participate in this unusual ceremony. As the long line of slaves snaked into the compound, we could see the men grunting loudly, while each carried an unusual-looking African gift.

At least two-dozen drums began to pick up a rhythmic primitive cadence as the grunting men moved around the compound in a wavering line that undulated like a huge snake. They paused near Chief D'jibuto, staring with menacing intensity at the awe-struck Chinese.

Some of the slaves carried exquisitely carved objects of wood, ivory or stone, while others had entered the chief's compound leading one form or another of exotic wild animal.

The Chinese visitors suddenly drew back in startled surprise when an extremely tall long-necked beast with a small head was brought in. It walked stiffly on long, thin legs, yet seemed to possess an unexpected grace.

"I've never seen an animal like that," Zheng He gasped, as the strange looking beast slowly ambled past.

I sucked in my breath, wanting to speak, but my voice seemed trapped inside my lungs. Finally, I managed to whisper, "Neither have I. Not even in my own Italy."

The huge creature had a mottled orange coat. It towered over all of us. "Well, there is no animal like it in all of China," Zheng He whispered back, with reverence. "Of that, I am most certain."

Zheng He continued to stare at the odd animal. "I would like to take one of these beasts home with us, so I can show it to Emperor Zhu Di."

Once the long-necked leaf-eater had been led from the compound, two large male lions were then brought forward. They were kept at bay by just two small rope leashes and a circle of natives with sharp spears. The lions made a terrifying sound, roaring ferociously. Zheng He and Ma Huan tensed as the lions were led past them. The other Chinese guests leaned back, straining to move away from the huge animals, reacting to their large, sharp teeth and hot breath. Chief D'jibuto laughed, greatly amused by the frightened reaction of his Chinese guests to jungle wild beasts.

Chief D'jibuto muttered a comment to one of his attendants, who laughed heartily and nodded. Zheng He asked the translator what was said. Interpreting as best as he could, the translator told the admiral that the Chief felt that his guests were not very brave. They would not make good warriors."

By the time the eventful and raucous evening was over, everyone present had consumed more than their share of Chief D'jibuto's unique fermented beverage. And even though tea was the preferred drink of most Chinese, not one of the guests complained about the spirits they were so enthusiastically imbibing.

In Nanking, a different type of alcoholic beverage was being consumed; a delicate, yet powerful, rice wine. The occasion was to honor the arrival of the Emperor of Korea. After the normal thirty-course meal had been completed, Korean Emperor Dong made a short speech, during which he offered his granddaughter, Quan, to the Ming officials. Just as Yang had reported, she was a lovely young woman of eighteen, with long black hair that pulled back from her face and fastened with several distinctive jeweled combs. With large dark eyes, high cheekbones and full red lips, this ravishing woman had the look and demeanor of a true princess. And she conducted herself in a fashion that was perfectly in keeping with her lofty regal station.

Xi Chen was present at the impressive ceremonial banquet and assisted serving great portions of food and wine to the more than four hundred Chinese and Korean guests. She was not prepared, however, for what she observed near the end of the festivities. Minister of Rites Yang got to his feet and, with subtle rudeness, offered the Korean emperor a discourteous and clearly inferior bow. When she glanced in Prince Han's direction to see if he had noticed this undiplomatic slight, she was disturbed to see Han smiling discretely at Yang and giving him a surreptitious nod, as if signaling his approval of the minister's inappropriate social behavior.

Minister Yang nodded back at Han in response to the sign of affirmation, then offered Emperor Dong a barely tolerant smile and began a short speech.

"I must apologize that Emperor Zhu Di is not here in person to receive your generous gift," he stated flatly, in a tone devoid of any emotion. "I'm afraid, as usual, he's off somewhere fighting foreign infidels."

Xi Chen could sense a tension in the room. Something was not right. There was obviously a deceptive collusion transpiring between the Minister Yang and Prince Han. But the nature of it wasn't yet clear to her. As a servant, there wasn't anything she could do but observe and see what would happen next.

Because of the language barrier, the distraction of specific cultural differences and other random diversions, the Korean emperor had not yet become aware that something might be amiss.

"I trust my granddaughter will be well received by Emperor Zhu Di," Dong commented with diplomatic dryness. "She is one of my most prized possessions."

Minister Yang again offered the Korean emperor another insufficient bow.

"I'll see to it that Emperor Zhu Di is made aware of the young maiden's presence," he said, quickly dispatching the subject with casual regard. Then, with no other words, he abruptly took his seat. This left Emperor Dong and his granddaughter, Quan, standing awkwardly before everyone,
uncertain as to how they should proceed. An atmosphere of extreme embarrassment and unease filled the room. Murmurs of discontent floated nervously amid the guests.

But Emperor Dong was no fool. He knew full well that if he offered the Chinese emperor a worthy gift, protocol dictated that he should receive an equally worthy gift in return. When no gift was presented, he lost face in the eyes of all those present.

To make matters even worse, Minister Yang rudely waved his hand at the Korean emperor, indicating that he should simply sit down; no reciprocal gift would be forthcoming.

"That's it," Yang said dismissively, as if Dong was a mere schoolboy being scolded. "Your gift has been duly received. You may now take your seat."

Emperor Dong glared coldly at Yang, then very slowly slid back into his seat. Quan wavered nervously, unsure what she should do. Since she was the gift, she didn't know if she should remain with her grandfather or somehow join the Chinese dignitaries.

Dong looked up at his granddaughter with stern eyes, still fuming from the insult. He nodded sharply, signaling her to sit down beside him. She sank slowly into her seat, head bowed in embarrassment.

Xi Chen couldn't believe her eyes. She knew that observing strict protocol, especially when dealing with foreign dignitaries, was a mainstay of Zhu Di's foreign policy. To insult a representative of a foreign land, especially one as important as the Emperor of Korea, was completely unheard of and totally unacceptable. To her growing horror, the next thing Xi Chen observed was Prince Han leaning down to whisper into Minister Yang's ear. He appeared to be complimenting him on the wonderful thing he had just done. What Xi Chen had suspected all along was happening right before her eyes.

"You did absolutely right," Han whispered to Yang with a snide grin. "There's no need in wasting expensive Chinese gifts on the likes of this Korean. The girl may be lovely to look at, but she is not so pretty that we need sacrifice our honor."

Yang felt a sudden pang of guilt for what he had just done, but it was too late. He turned to Han and whispered with concern, "Are you sure that your father won't be deeply offended? I wouldn't want him to..."

Han interrupted him curtly, spitting his words out through tight lips. "Don't worry about my father, Minister Yang. What he does or doesn't know will not make any difference. Besides, it's insane for us to keep offering gifts to these useless foreigners. We must put a stop to it sometime. And that time is now."

Sufficiently chastised, Yang backed down, sinking low in his chair, still troubled by his dishonorable breech of political etiquette.


Five days later, a messenger was escorted to the Ming front lines so he could personally deliver a communication to Zhu Di. As usual, the emperor's command post had been set up near the line of battle. This proximity to danger caused the palace messenger to become extremely nervous as he approached.

He bowed to Zhu Di and handed him the message, his hand trembling. He kept a wary eye on the nearby battlefield as Zhu Di read the communiqué.

"Your Majesty," he offered with quaking voice, "I have also brought a message from the Honorable Lady, Xi Chen. She asked that I personally deliver it only to you."

He quickly handed the note to Zhu Di and, having completed his instructed mission, bowed to the emperor and swiftly backed away. He possessed little motivation to stay amidst this danger any longer than necessary.

General Tan waited patiently at Zhu Di's side while he read the private message from Xi Chen. After a few seconds, Tan was surprised to see Zhu Di crumple the note in his fist and angrily throw it to the ground.

"He has some nerve!" Zhu Di shouted. "The man is a traitor."

The general looked on with a startled expression. "What is it, Your Majesty?"

Zhu Di paced with angry strides in front of Tan, clutching the troubling note tightly in his hand. "Minister Yang has deliberately insulted the Emperor of Korea," he growled with a pained grimace.

"Could it be a mistake?" Tan offered, hoping to calm his emperor."

"It is no mistake!" Zhu Di bellowed. The officers nearby turned to look, disturbed by their leader's anger. "This word comes to me from a trusted source."

Unable to contain his anger, Zhu Di drew his sword and slammed it into the ground with all the force he could muster. The metal clanged loudly as it penetrated the rocky soil.

"I warned the bastard not to test my patience," he muttered through clenched teeth. He pulled the blade from the cut in the earth, then slammed the point down a second time, driving the wound in the rough ground even deeper.

Unexpectedly, a Mongol soldier chose that particular moment to break through the Chinese battle lines and rush forward through the cluster of distracted Chinese officers. Raising his sword, the wild-eyed attacker lunged directly at Emperor Zhu Di.

As the Mongol was about to strike, General Tan caught sight of the approaching assailant and screamed a warning. Instinctively, Zhu Di spun around and neatly decapitated the assassin's head with a powerful swing of the heavy steel weapon in his hand.

The lifeless body of the Mongol soldier, with nothing more than a stump of neck remaining, collapsed in a heap at Zhu Di's feet. Blood flowed from his lifeless body like a dark crimson river.

Livid with rage, the furious emperor raised his sword up with a bellowing howl, stabbing and hacking at the blood-soaked body on the ground, shouting Yang's name out, over and over.

"Die, you bastard! DIE!" Seeing the head of the assailant nearby in the mud, Zhu Di gave it a mighty kick, sending it tumbling grotesquely across the dirt.

General Tan finally grabbed Zhu Di's arms, forcing them to his side, pulling him away from the bloody corpse at his feet.

"He's dead, Your Majesty!" Tan yelled, struggling to hold him back. "You've killed him as dead as he will be." Tan's eyes flashed to the other officers, who watched all this with greatly disturbed expressions.

"You must show your officers the same restraint that you demand of them," General Tan said, speaking close to his ear with a powerful voice that echoed like low thunder. Tan knew he was risking his very rank as General by being so recklessly brazen with his emperor. But he also knew that if Zhu Di was to maintain the respect of his troops, he must first and foremost lead by example.

Hearing Tan's words, Zhu Di became still, his body continuing to quake from his intense rage, his own hot blood coursing wildly through his veins. After a moment, he sank to his knees, leaned heavily on his sword and began gasping for air. His lungs heaved like a searing wind that roared through trees.

Finally, as the cycle of his gasping gradually returned to normal, he turned to look into General Tan's eyes. His voice came slowly, but with great certainty. "End this battle, General," he said grimly. "Get it over with and do it swiftly. We will return to the palace immediately."

During their trek back to Nanking, General Tan finally mustered enough courage to ask Zhu Di what had sparked his great anger. Without speaking, Zhu Di pushed the crumpled note into the general's hand.

As Tan read the message, Zhu Di echoed the contents with harsh resentment. "Minister Yang has deeply insulted the Emperor of Korea," he paused, his voice lowering to a murmur of disappointment and regret. "No doubt with the help of my very own son."

Tan knew that he referred to Prince Han. "Sire, do you really think your son could..."

Zhu Di cut him off. "Yes! I do," he said firmly. "I know it for certain. Yang has been clinging to Prince Han like a sick dog for months now. I'm sure he expects that someday my son will become emperor. And when he does... he'll throw him a bone."

The more he pondered this thought, the angrier he became. "But it is I who will throw that bastard a bone. He has insulted me. Conspired against me. I'll throw him a bone, alright. And he shall choke on it!"


Upon his return to Nanking, Zhu Di immediately requested the presence of his Minister Yang. Empress Xu tried vainly to calm her still irate husband before the meeting.

"I'm sure it may just have been some sort of oversight," she suggested. "I don't think it serves any good purpose for you to get yourself so upset."

"Upset?" he growled, glaring at her. "You tell me that I shouldn't get upset? I do everything possible to achieve an honorable goal. I build a huge fleet, larger than any other that has gone before, so that we can attract foreign leaders. And what does this imbecilic minister do? He takes it upon himself to insult an important foreign leader the moment he arrives!"

"You are becoming erratic, my dear," she cautioned. "Please calm yourself. I'm sure Minister Yang has his reasons."

Zhu Di paced restlessly in front of his wife, still obviously upset. "Oh, I'm sure he had his reasons," he said with mocking sarcasm. "And I can imagine they are of a dissembling nature." He waved his arm at her. "Now tell the servant to bring him in. I want to see him now."

"Promise me you won't become upset," she said with a steady voice.

Zhu Di paused, turning to look at his wife with suspicion. "And why are you so suddenly concerned about how I behave with Minister Yang?"

She stared at him for a long moment, unmoving and grim. Then she abruptly turned away. "I will bring him to you. Just as you wish."

"Wait!" he commanded. She stopped in her tracks, slowly turning back to face him. "Your sudden interest in the welfare of the Minister is strangely curious," he said, stepping toward her. "Should I be concerned?"

Her expression betrayed no deceit, but he knew that the empress was very adept at concealing her true feelings.

Zhu Di fixed his gaze upon her, waiting for the moment when she might crack and suddenly confess her betrayal. But her inner strength was equally as strong as his own. If she were of a traitorous nature, she would surely not reveal it.

Finally, he waved her away, tired of this stalemate. As she vanished out the door, Zhu Di went to his throne and made a sincere effort to compose himself for the arrival of Minister Yang. But an angry tension hung over him like a dark curtain.

When he heard the large doors opening at the end of the hall, he quickly sat up rigidly on his throne, striking an imperious pose. Yang scurried into the room, bowing over and over with exaggerated humility, praising Zhu Di with every step.

Zhu Di motioned at the trailing servant to leave. He turned and hurriedly retreated, more than happy to be set free.

Knowing that the emperor must surely be aware of the recent controversy, Yang decided to go on the offensive and bring the subject up himself. "Your Majesty," he sang out with an uncustomary glee, "I'm certain that you would like to hear all about that ridiculously trivial incident that occurred during our recent visit by the Emperor of Korea."

Zhu Di remained stoic, measuring his words carefully to have the greatest impact. "Yes. That would be very... enlightening... indeed."

Yang's wide smile widened and he stepped closer with enthusiasm. "I'm sure that whatever nonsense you have heard has been exaggerated far beyond the actual truth, Sire. We must remember, it was Confucius who said..."

"SILENCE!" Zhu Di screamed, startling the minister with his thunderous interruption. Zhu Di leaped to his feet and shoved an accusing finger directly at Yang's eyes.

"You spineless dog!" the emperor roared. "Do you have any idea the incredible harm you have done to the honor and reputation of our country? The terrible shame you have brought to the good people of China?"

Beginning to tremble and quake, Yang sobbed a frightened reply. "But Your Majesty, you don't understand..."

Zhu Di interrupted, rising to his feet, towering over the groveling minister. "I understand perfectly!" he bellowed. "I understand that death is too painless a punishment for someone as disreputable as you. But despite this, death is exactly what I shall give you."

He turned to the sentinels at the door. "Guards!" he shouted. Two guards rushed forward and seized Minister Yang by the arms, holding him tightly.

"Listen carefully. I want a hundred gnawed bones forced down the throat of this worthless scum until his belly explodes. Then I want you to set fire to his bloated carcass. And once it has been consumed by the flames and rendered to ash, I want you to set loose a pack of the meanest and hungriest wild dogs you can find to devour whatever remains of this pathetic traitor."

Minister Yang jerked himself free from the guards and prostrated himself on the floor at Zhu Di's feet. "Have mercy on me, Sire," he wailed tearfully. "Have mercy, I beg you!"

But Zhu Di was in no mood for mercy. "Take him away!" he thundered. "I can no longer stomach the sight of this vile maggot."

As the two guards dragged the pleading minister from the room, Zhu Di called out for a servant. The young man rushed toward the throne, bowing respectfully.

"Bring me Minister Wa," Zhu Di screamed. "I want to see him immediately!"

The servant bowed again and dashed away quickly, pausing only to close the two large wooden doors to the emperor's private chamber.

Zhu Di paced back and forth, still agitated. He slumped onto his throne, trying to calm himself and gather his wits for the coming encounter with his Finance Minister.

Within a few short minutes, the doors abruptly swung open with an echoing thud as Minister Wa was escorted into the room by the dutiful servant.

He was a short, stocky man with a high-pitched voice that became an annoying screech whenever he grew nervous or agitated. "You wished to see me, Sire?" he squeaked as he approached the emperor.

"How much wealth is in the royal treasury?" Zhu Di demanded, his words awash with constricted anger.

Minister Wa hated being the bearer of bad news. He began to shake nervously and sweat profusely. "Well, the policies of the crown, Sire, are absolutely correct, of course. However, as you yourself have stated on more than one occasion, they tend to require the expenditure of a somewhat greater, uh..."

Zhu Di cut him off impatiently. "Enough of this! I asked you... How much do we have in the royal treasury?"

Wa trembled even more. "Oh, benevolent emperor," he muttered, casting his gaze downward at the floor. "I must regrettably inform you that the greatest portion of the imperial treasury has already been spent." Then, he quickly added, "But I'm quite confident that if Your Majesty were to curtail just a few of the expenditures for the fleet..."

"GUARDS!" Zhu Di bellowed. "Take this filthy lump of pig intestines and throw him into prison. NOW!"

Two guards instantly responded, rushing toward the throne. Minister Wa dropped to his knees, clutching at the hem of Zhu Di's robe, pleading and whining.

But Zhu Di was unmoved by the groveling man's desperate pleas. "And if I find anyone else among my ministers who refuses to abide by my policies, they will suffer the very same fate. Now take him away!"

The guards seized the blubbering minister and dragged him off, ignoring his desperate cries for mercy.

As the huge wooden doors slammed shut, Zhu Di leaned back on his throne and closed his eyes, sighing with a great relief at the blessed silence.

After a moment, a faint smile appeared on his lips as he pondered the enormous, thick doors of his chambers and the great service they provided. He could always count on them to drown out the pitiful begging and pathetic pleas for mercy emitted by treasonous court officials as they were taken away. "Praise Buddha for small favors," he muttered.

Exhausted by the contentious confrontations with his ministers, Zhu Di soon drifted into a peaceful slumber upon his throne, unaware that far away, deep in the jungles of Africa, Zheng He was experiencing something that was most exceptional.


After all the trade negotiations had been successfully completed with Chief D'jibuto, the African ruler invited Zheng He and several others to join him on a safari into the country's interior.

Ma Huan and I rode together on the back of a large elephant that had been outfitted with a crude type of woven basket seat. It was surprisingly comfortable and was equipped with two large banana leaves attached to a bamboo pole, providing both of us some welcomed shade from the hot African sun.

Since Zheng He was Admiral of the Ming Fleet, he was not required to share a seat with anyone else, riding proudly on his very own elephant, outfitted with an elaborately soft seat and shaded by a colorful banana leaf parasol.

Chief D'jibuto and his two wives rode together on another large pachyderm, directly behind the Ming admiral. It, too, was a magnificent beast, colorfully decorated with leopard skins and ostrich feathers, which clearly befitted the stature of its royal passengers.

Walking in two long lines in front of the lumbering jungle beasts were nearly two hundred African porters and warriors carrying spears. At the rear, behind the chief's elephant, were two-dozen Ming servants, our translator and more than a hundred Ming soldiers. Zheng He had decided it was a good idea to bring the soldiers with them as a bold demonstration of his military strength... and as a wise cautionary gesture.

As we moved slowly along the edge of a vast grassy expanse, great herds of zebra and antelope could be seen grazing peacefully all the way to the horizon. Overhead, great black vultures made lazy circles in the cloudless sky.

The sight of the huge Ming fleet may have been quite overwhelming to the Africans, but this pristine landscape, raw and untamed, with thousands of animals roaming freely, was equally overwhelming for the Chinese visitors.

I could tell Zheng He was having a marvelous time. He behaved like a schoolboy, shouting out to me and Ma Huan and pointing excitedly at every bird, animal, or unusual-looking tree that we passed.

"Have you ever seen anything like this in your whole life?" he shouted gleefully to us, as we craned our necks to see wherever he pointed next. "I think it's wonderful!"

"It certainly is very different," I shouted back to him, equally amazed at all the unbelievable sights and sounds we were encountering. "There's nothing like this in all of Italy. I can guarantee you that."

Zheng He also waved enthusiastically to Chief D'jibuto and his two wives, who acknowledged his gesture with a small smile and wave of their own. Chief D'jibuto was delighted his Chinese guests were having such a good time.

In Nanking, the world was silent. Emperor Zhu Di spent a subdued evening with Empress Xu. Ever since his son had told him that Zheng He and Xi Chen were lovers, his desire to spend time with the Honorable Lady had diminished. On earlier occasions, he had invited her to his chambers, hoping to summon enough nerve to ask her if what he had heard was true. But each time he was with Xi Chen, he found himself mired in hesitation and doubt, unable to broach the delicate subject. These unpleasant evenings passed slowly for Zhu Di and always ended with nothing of substance being spoken. Xi Chen knew their relationship had become strained but was puzzled as to the cause.

As days passed, the young woman, Quan, who had been given to Zhu Di as a gift by Korean Emperor Dong, began to look more and more appealing. She was only eighteen years old, which did cause a few pangs of conscience to stir in Zhu Di's breast. He worried that since he was now in his forties, a girl of eighteen may be too young for him. But Zhu Di always did prefer younger members of the fair sex.

He had more than fifty concubines and Honorable Ladies at his personal disposal, but many were also getting older and didn't always provide him with the sexual adventure he so often craved.

As he pondered this further, he realized that he too was growing older and his sexual drive wasn't as adventurous and insistent as it was in his youth. It pained him to admit such a thing, viewing it as an unacceptable weakness of spirit. But there was no way he could escape from the reality that, from time-to-time, he found little pleasure in having to sexually perform with enthusiasm for younger women.

Consequently, the comfortable familiarity of spending a quiet night in bed with his wife didn't seem to be quite so distasteful as it once did. Empress Xu, of course, didn't care what motivated her husband to begin spending more time with her. She was simply pleased that he had chosen her over the temptations of the many younger, more attractive concubines who were at his easy disposal.

During one such evening, just prior to the imminent return of the fleet, Zhu Di requested a glass of wine, then settled into his favorite chair. While her husband quietly sipped on his wine, Empress Xu sat across from him in her own chair, idly twirling strands of hair around her finger.

It usually only took one or two glasses of wine to put Zhu Di in a reflective mood, allowing his feelings to easily flow. "What I find so hard to accept is that our own son, Han, is so totally against what I'm trying to accomplish."

Zhu Di took another sip of wine, contemplating what he had just said. Empress Xu gazed at him, curious. Yet she said nothing, but instead began to casually comb her hair, pretending that his words were of little consequence.

"Why does he do that?" Zhu Di asked rhetorically, not really expecting her to respond. "Why in the world would he be so against the policies of his very own father?"

Empress Xu looked away, offering the defense she usually did whenever she needed to speak out in support of her son.

"I'm sure he means well."

"If he does," Zhu Di grumbled, suddenly growing testy, "he has an odd way of showing it." Zhu Di finished his wine, then restlessly changed the subject.

"You should have seen the two Korean envoys I escorted around the palace today," he said, attempting to brighten the conversation with a more positive thought. "They really tried to outdo each other in offering me compliments."

"Did you apologize to them for the reckless imprudence of Minister Yang?" she asked abruptly. The words had escaped her lips before she considered their possible effect. She silently regretted her lack of discretion.

"I apologized to them profusely," Zhu Di groused while pouring more wine. "I had to give them gifts that were three times the value of what would have been necessary had that minister not behaved in such a traitorous fashion."

Relieved that he hadn't been offended by her inquiry, Empress Xu sneaked a cautious glance at her husband... and then grinned to herself.

"I think your plan for reaching out to other nations is working quite well. Don't you?"

He thought for a moment. " Yes. It is working, isn't it?" he responded, a slight smile tickling his lips. "Praise Buddha!"

He got to his feet, excited by this thought. "You are quite right. Lord Zheng He has invited many foreign leaders to come visit our country. Several have already accepted his invitation and come to pay their regards. And all this before Zheng He has even returned from his first voyage. It is even better than I had hoped."

Xu suddenly stopped combing her hair and looked at him with pride. "It is really quite extraordinary that we have already received visitors from Champa and Korea. And more are coming. You should be very proud."

Zhu Di's broad smile slackened as another thought took hold. "Then why can't Prince Han see the truth of this? Is he blind to the obvious? Or just being an obstinate child?"

"He's a good boy, Zhu Di," the empress said soothingly, once again coming to the defense of her son. "You just need to give him some time."

"He doesn't need time," Zhu Di snapped with anger. "He needs common sense. He needs to recognize the value of loyalty to his father!"

Zhu Di sat absolutely still for a few moments, scowling and sipping on the last of his wine. "Worst of all," he sneered, "Han poisons all the people around him with his traitorous ideas."

Empress Xu resented her husband's accusations but held her tongue, not wanting to aggravate him further. Zhu Di did not like to be criticized by anyone. And when the empress disagreed with him, he interpreted this as a personal attack. "You don't see it, do you?" he countered, becoming defensive. "The boy goes out of his way to cause problems for me. Yet, YOU defend him! Why? Don't you realize the

256

harm he can cause for me? And for our people? You can mark my words, dear wife... our own son, Prince Han will cause us great harm and heartache before this is over."

Empress Xu fell into a deep silence, refusing to take the bait. She would not continue arguing with Zhu Di. It would only expose them both to more disagreement and strife.

The emperor's chamber was soon filled with a hollow emptiness. And, as with so many other evenings that had preceded it, no other words were spoken until a new day had dawned and the discord of the night before had been long forgotten.

Six months later, the fleet reassembled off the coast of Fukien Province in preparation for its grand return to the mouth of the Yangtze. Messengers on horseback carried the joyous news overland to the emperor. Zhu Di had only recently completed his move to the new palace in Beijing and was delighted the arrival of the first expedition would now be celebrated at his new Forbidden City, rather than Nanking.

While Zheng He and the fleet sailed up the coast to the place where the Yangtze River emptied into the South China Sea outside of Shanghai, Emperor Zhu Di and the rest of his royal entourage traveled overland from Beijing to Shanghai. Zheng He delayed the fleet's movement northward for several days to be certain the emperor and his guests had plenty of time to prepare for the fleet's glorious arrival.

With flags flying high, cannons booming and hundreds of thousands of cheering people lining the shore, the return of Zhu Di's impressive Ming fleet was an historic and colorful spectacle. The emperor led a grand celebration from his gaily decorated Imperial Reviewing Stand, which was crowded with family members, special guests and a host of important dignitaries. All anxiously awaited the arrival of the huge nine-masted Treasure Ships, which they could see in the distance, entering the broad bay of the Yangtze.

Zheng He and I stood at the rail of the Baochuan's open 'penthouse' and were amazed when we saw all the people lining the shore on both sides, waving at us and cheering loudly. I stared in wonder at the masses of people. Where had they all come from? It seemed to me that everyone in China was there that day.

While we happily waved back to those along the shore, rockets began to burst overhead in a brilliant display of red, white and yellow colors.

Then, as our great armada edged closer to shore, I glance in Zheng He's direction. I was surprised to see that he was no longer smiling. Indeed, his expression was glum and troubled.

"What's the matter?" I asked, hoping to brighten him up. "Today's going to be the greatest day of your life."

"I'm scared," he responded, shaking his head slightly, the words catching in his throat.

"Scared?" I said, puzzled by his response. "Of what?"

He didn't answer for a long moment. Then, he turned to me with frightened eyes and spoke the words I never expected. "Seeing Xi Chen again."

I couldn't believe it. The woman he longed for and dreamed of every night of this long voyage, and now he was frightened by the prospect of finally seeing her.

"You should be delighted you're going to see her," I scolded him. "Not scared!" I gripped his arm, squeezing it tight so he would focus on my words. "She's the woman of your dreams, isn't she?" I asked, staring him in the eyes.

But the melancholy expression on his face remained. He stared blankly across the vast expanse of water toward the cheering people on the shore.

I carefully weighed my options and finally decided to bring up a most delicate subject. I knew that once I had broached it, there would be no taking it back.

"Are you worried that she still loves you?" My words hung there for a long time as he let them penetrate his mind, not blinking an eye or moving a finger.

Finally, he spoke. "It's been two years, friar," he said solemnly. "Two long years of Xi Chen sleeping with Emperor Zhu Di."

I was shocked at this. "You don't know that!" I exclaimed, trying to inject as much certainty as possible into my protest. But, in truth, I wasn't sure at all.

He finally turned and looked me in the eye.

"There was no way she could have stopped him. Even if she had wanted to."

I walked in tight, frustrated circles beside him, trying to muster some logic that I could throw back at him. But what he had said left me flustered. Perhaps he was right. But I knew that I needed to keep a door open to hope.

"I don't think you're right," I protested, fearing that my weak voice and unsure inflection did not carry the weight of a convincing argument. How could I convince him of this if I didn't believe it myself?

I stopped moving about and stepped to his side, turning my gaze back to the shore. "I think you're just worried about nothing," I offered weakly.

We stood in silence then, as the shore and the teeming masses of people drew closer.

Immediately after Zheng He's private launch deposited the admiral and his officers at the Imperial Docks, the admiral and a large number of Ming dignitaries followed Emperor Zhu Di to the small temple by the bay, where they offered prayers to the benevolent Goddess for protecting them during the long voyage.

Afterward, Zhu Di greeted Zheng He with great affection, excitedly telling him about the new palace that he had constructed in his home of Beijing. He said it was there that he planned to honor Zheng He and the brave men of his fleet, conducting an official welcoming ceremony.

When Zhu Di asked about Minister Wong, Admiral Zheng He awkwardly deflected the question, telling him the Deputy Envoy had been temporarily detained. Zhu Di accepted this explanation without question, but his instincts told him that something was clearly not right. He could see a glint of trouble and uncertainty in Zheng He's eyes.

Before the subject could be addressed further, several trade envoys from Champa stepped forward to greet the admiral and congratulate him on the fleet's safe return.

Amidst this flurry of greetings and hospitality, Zheng He could barely focus on the news of a palace in Beijing or of an elaborate Forbidden City. His mind was elsewhere.

He searched the crowd of dignitaries and servants, hoping to catch sight of Xi Chen. But she was not among the lady servants gathered that Zhu Di had brought to Shanghai for the fleet's return.

Zheng He felt suddenly exhilarated, pleased to know that the emperor had not chosen to bring her. Perhaps Xi Chen and Zhu Di were no longer on friendly terms. She may have rejected the emperor's advances and thereby fallen out of his favor.

As these possibilities raced through his mind, Zheng He became more hopeful. But then, a dark shadow of concern descended on Zheng He as he considered other alternatives. Perhaps something terrible had happened to Xi Chen. She may have been hurt or... He stopped suddenly, trying to force these dark possibilities from his mind.

He looked out among the joyous masses and tried to think about the great honors that he would receive in Beijing. But in a flash, the negative thoughts returned. What if Xi Chen was now in love with Zhu Di? What if he has taken her as his wife? What if...?

A loud explosion shook the crowd. All eyes turned to the sky as a grand exhibition of celebratory fireworks filled the air. For a few moments, the tumultuous display of light and noise and cheering crowds pushed the doubts from Zheng He's mind. But they would return to haunt him many times during the long journey back to Beijing.

When they arrived in Beijing three weeks later, Zheng He was taken aback by the sheer size and beauty of Zhu Di's new palace, which he quickly learned was called "Forbidden City."

But the admiral was not the only one who was shocked by what he encountered. Chief D'jibuto, who Zheng He had brought back with him to China, was utterly speechless. He and the rest of his African party spent their entire first day at the palace walking through the immense courtyards and gardens, staring in awe at the incredible beauty, which surrounded them.

On the second day, true to his word, Zhu Di presided over a colossal celebration at his new palace. It was an event that exceeded everyone's wildest imagination and expectations. It truly was a celebration like nothing anyone in China had ever experienced before.

Zhu Di had an impressive Reviewing Stand constructed in front of a magnificent building called Hall of the Golden Throne. It was here that the emperor and his family, plus honored guests and imperial dignitaries, would watch the proceedings in exquisite style and comfort.

The richly decorated viewing area overlooked a huge open courtyard where the celebration festivities were to take place. Once everyone on the official Reviewing Stand was seated, Zhu Di signaled for the historic event to begin.

Thousands upon thousands lining the courtyard began to cheer, as a great procession of civil servants, selected dignitaries, musicians, dancers, exotic animals and African tribesmen began to march in a grand procession before the emperor and his distinguished guests.

And just as Zheng He had predicted, Emperor Zhu Di was totally mesmerized and speechless when three tall, gangly giraffes ambled past the Reviewing Stand on their long skinny legs. He quickly looked to his Admiral Zheng He for an explanation.

"What kind of an animal is that?" he stammered, unable to take his eyes off these strange new beasts. "I don't think I've ever seen anything like that before. Not in my entire life!"

To Zheng He's great delight, he had shocked and surprised the emperor as much as he hoped he would.

"In the African language, Your Majesty," Zheng He replied, "it is called a 'girin.' To me, it sounds very close to what we would call a 'ki-lin'."

"So that animal is a unicorn?" he blurted out in loud amazement. "Can this actually be the fabled unicorn I have always heard of?"

Zheng He knew the animal was a giraffe, but he played along with Zhu Di's imaginative fantasy, for he too had heard the legend of the ki-lin when he was a child.

"According to legend, the appearance of the ki-lin is always regarded as a sign of good fortune. Maybe this is confirmation, Sire, that heaven approves of your policies."

Zhu Di glimpsed the hint of an impish smile on his admiral's lips and a twinkle in his eye. Finally catching on, he playfully shook a finger at him.

"Zheng He, you devil," he said with a big grin. "You are playing with me. I see what you are doing." He laughed heartily, enjoying being teased by Zheng He. Then leaned close, with an earnest look. "But I do agree, it looks a lot like a ki-lin."

Laughing together, Zheng He and his emperor turned to watch the last giraffe amble by slowly, it's long neck swaying from side to side.

Zhu Di excitedly turned to the assembled guests and shouted out, "Look, everyone! It has the body of a deer and the tail of an ox, just like a 'ki-lin'!"

Emperor Zhu Di laughed cheerfully, slapping his knee. Encouraged by this, Zheng He continued his colorful commentary. "And like a 'ki-lin' it eats only herbs and is said to harm no living being."

Zhu Di joined in the jovial charade, turning to his guests. "See that, everyone. They're 'ki-lin'! Can you believe it? We have the fabled unicorn, right here at Forbidden City! It is a fortuitous sign!"

As everyone began chattering enthusiastically about the giraffes, Zheng He caught a brief glimpse of Xi Chen. She was in a nearby gathering of other women, standing at the side of a young Korean woman. He quickly glanced away, so filled with excitement that he gasped for air, his head spinning.

He returned his gaze to her, fully expecting that she would have disappeared, merely a taunting figment of his imagination. But she was still there. And now she was looking directly at him. She gave him a wry smile, shook her head slightly and rolled her eyes, as if to show that she knew these animals were not the fabled unicorns called ki-lin. Unable to restrain himself, he grinned broadly at her, his heart pounding.

At the front of the reviewing stand, Zhu Bao Zhi was having a delightful time, laughing and carousing. He was dressed in his finest clothes and made every effort to call attention to himself. Nearby, his younger brother, Prince Han, was not feeling so celebratory. He spotted Assistant Finance Minister, Jing, sitting close behind him and motioned for him to meet him behind the reviewing stand.

Jing squeezed through the tightly assembled dignitaries and found his way to the rear of seating area. The prince suddenly appeared at his side. Han grabbed Jing's arm in his tight grip. "Where is Minister Wong? He snapped. "Have you seen him?"

Jing was taken aback by the young prince's unexpectedly cruel behavior. He could barely stammer a reply.

"No, no... I, uh, I haven't seen him."

"He vowed to cause the expedition to fail," he whispered harshly. "But look at this." He motioned to the grand procession passing by in all its splendor. "This is not failure."

Han made a broad gesture towards the celebration parade. Jing nodded his agreement, hanging his head in shame. "I can't imagine where he might be. It's been more than three weeks since the fleet arrived at Shanghai. I thought that he would contact you immediately."

"When I find that old fool," Han threatened, "I'm going to teach him a lesson he'll never forget."

Han jabbed a finger into Jing's chest. "And if you see him, you tell me first. Do you understand? Give him no warning. He is mine to deal with."

Jing bowed nervously to the impetuous prince and quickly skulked away. Prince Han slipped back to the Imperial viewing area and took his seat, nodding politely to the others. But the snide, smug look on this face betrayed his true feelings.

Han continued to scan the huge delegation of dignitaries in hopes of spotting Wong. But then his gaze fell upon his father. He was surprised to see that Zhu Di was coughing badly, clutching his chest. The empress held him closely, trying to comfort him, a deeply worried look on her face.

Han was abruptly distracted by the thundering sound of over two dozen African drums. They made a terrible racket and heralded the appearance of a large undulating crowd of
African tribesmen bearing gifts for the Chinese emperor.

Tall, black-skinned natives carried large jars filled with ambergris, which they called Dragon Saliva, as well as incense and golden-colored amber. Other natives paraded past carrying rolls of decorative silks, bales of ivory, large containers of a spice called pepper and dozens of beautifully carved objects made of a hard dark wood called ebony. Much of the ebony was decorated with generous amounts of silver and gold.

Fascinated by the incredible display, Zhu Di had ceased his coughing and was staring with wide eyes at the African procession. He began to clap enthusiastically as the chief and his warriors and animals passed. But, then, he bent forward, unexpectedly struck by another fit of wrenching coughs.

"Maybe we should leave," Empress Xu suggested, holding him as he struggled to catch his breath. "The parade is nearly over."

"No," Zhu Di protested, while turning to stifle yet another cough. "I'm fine. This is our first celebration at Forbidden City. I have no intention of missing a single moment of it."

"But you're not well," she persisted, hoping to change his mind.

Zhu Di stifled another cough. "I'm not leaving until the parade is OVER!" he snapped, a little more sharply than he had intended. "Please..." he added, quickly softening his tone. "I'll be fine," he said, patting her hand gently, forcing a weak smile. "I promise. The parade will end soon."

As the long procession came to an end, Zhu Di was shocked to see Minister Wong shuffling past the Reviewing Stand, his feet and hands bound in heavy chains.

He immediately turned to Zheng He with glaring eyes, his coughing suddenly forgotten. "What is the meaning of this outrage? Why is he in chains?"

Zheng He began to explain what had occurred aboard the admiral's flagship and Zhu Di could scarcely believe what he was hearing.

But then, Wong cast his gaze up toward the emperor and Zheng He. When he saw the admiral talking frantically to Zhu Di, gesturing emphatically, he stopped in his tracks and shouted at them.

"I was under direct orders from Prince Han! He's the one who ordered me to sabotage the expedition. If my head must fall, then the head of your own son must fall as well!"

All eyes immediately turned to Prince Han, who leaped up from his seat and screamed back at his shackled accuser.

"You're a damn liar, Wong! I didn't order you to sabotage anything!"

Han glanced into the glowering face of his father, then pushed past the honored guests, jumped down the steps to the ground and quickly disappeared in the crowd.

Zhu Di was furious! He stood up and shouted at the old minister wrapped in chains.

"I want this man executed at once! Take him away!"

As the guards grabbed him by both arms and started dragging him away, Minister Wong screamed at Zheng He. "It's Prince Han's fault! You will die for this, Zheng He! I promise you, a vile and painful death will be your fate!"

Zhu Di sunk down into his chair, shocked and sickened by this unexpected turn of events. He turned pale and slumped forward. Xi Chen and Lady Servant Quan rushed forward to aid the stricken emperor.

When Zheng He saw Xi Chen's frightened face and her eyes filled with tears, it was like a dagger being thrust into his heart. Her instinctive reaction proved to him what he had feared all along.

"She loves him," he muttered to himself, hopelessly despondent. His eyes filled with tears.

When Empress Xu looked up and saw Zheng He's tears, she mistook their meaning. She reached up and gently touched his tear-streaked face. "Zhu Di's so fortunate to have you, Lord Zheng He," she whispered, tears now filling her own eyes as well. "You are a good and faithful servant. He is blessed to have you. He knows well that your loyalty and love for him is eternal."

Chapter Eight

---

## PAINFUL DECISIONS

After the debacle with Minister Wong and Prince Han, Zhu Di retreated to his private quarters and refused to see anyone. For weeks on end, he was consumed by a terrible depression, unable to stir even the smallest measure of interest in the daily events and activities around him. As emperor, he felt he had no choice but to send his son to prison and he agonized daily over whether he should have him executed as well.

For many days he shut himself off from everyone, unable to face the reality of his situation. If he started making imperial decisions once again, he would be forced to deal with the fate of his own son.

But Empress Xu could no longer bear her husband's forced isolation. She decided to take matters into her own hands, pushing her way past the servants standing guard at the door to Zhu Di's private chamber, bringing three steaming bowls of rice and fish; two for him and one for her.

Zhu Di heard a muted commotion on the other side of the door, but took little notice of what was happening. A moment later the stern voices fell silent and the empress entered the room carrying the food on two black lacquered trays, stacked one upon the other. She took a seat beside her husband holding the trays on her lap. Zhu Di did not acknowledge her presence, staring numbly without response.

"I've brought your favorite meal," Empress Xu cooed, trying to sound as pleasant and soothing as possible. "I think you should eat. It will make you feel better."

As Zhu Di became more fully aware of the savory aroma of cooked rice and fish, he slowly turned to look at her. "How did you get in?" he asked sternly, not even pretending to be civil. "I left strict instructions not to be disturbed... by anyone!"

The empress opened her mouth to respond, but he gave her no opportunity. "Where are my servants?" he snapped.

But Empress Xu was not going to let her husband intimidate her. "I've sent them away," she responded firmly, still maintaining a soft air of civility and warmth. "This evening, Zhu Di, you and I are having dinner together. Alone."

Without asking permission, she set one of the trays of food before him. He made no move to stop her. Instead, he avoided confrontation by pausing to stifle a pesky cough.

When he recovered, he picked up the chopsticks beside the bowl and sampled a bite of the flaky, white fish.

"It is very good," he confessed, savoring the delicate flavor on his tongue. "It is prepared precisely how I like it."

Empress Xu smiled to herself, pleased. She took a small bite of the fish from her own bowl. "I can remember a time," she offered softly, "when we had all our meals together. I think we should reinstate this practice. Don't you agree?"

Zhu Di gave his wife a scowling glance, stuffing more rice and fish into his mouth. But he made no attempt to contradict her suggestion.

He turned away abruptly, seized by another irritating urge to cough.

"I'm worried about your cough," she confided anxiously. "Why don't you let the physicians tend to you?"

Zhu Di picked up his bowl with both hands, letting the warm soup wash into his mouth, soothing his ragged throat. He sat silently as the moist warmth filled his chest, finally turning to his wife.

"Lord Buddha and green tea are all I need, empress," he said with polite assurance. "Physicians cannot bring me the same comfort. I will be well soon."

Accepting this, Empress Xu replaced his empty bowl with a full one. After several more minutes of quietly eating their meal together, Empress Xu decided to bring up a dangerously personal subject.

"Have you gone to visit our son?" His head turned sharply, eyes glaring at her from beneath dark, furrowed brows.

"Never!" he replied without a tinge of remorse. "He's a disgrace to our family."

"Prison is such a dreadful place for a boy," she protested, trying to appeal to his sympathy.

Zhu Di remained unmoved. "It's my solemn duty, empress..." he began with great formality.

However, she was not interested in hearing any of his speeches. "It's your solemn duty to protect the people!" she cut in abruptly, startling him. "Not to order the execution of your own son!"

Zhu Di always resented it when the empress spoke to him with such firmness and clarity, especially when she left him no room to disagree. Her words cut right to his heart like a knife and he knew she was right. He lowered his bowl with a pained expression, letting it fall to the floor with a clatter.

"What can I do?" he moaned sadly. "Prince Han has committed a terrible crime. I have no choice."

"He is our son, Zhu Di. And he swears he is not guilty," she stated flatly, making her case without emotion. "Minister Wong could have made this all up. There is much doubt, Zhu Di. You know that."

Zhu Di turned away, consumed by a nagging fit of hacking coughs. No matter how hard he tried, there seemed to be little he could do to stop his persistent affliction. And recently, during some excruciating spells of coughing, the great exertion left him struggling for breath.

After a long struggle to regain control of his wheezing breath, he found the strength to mutter, "I wish there was a shred of truth to your words. But in my heart, I do know... our son is guilty."

"How can you say that," she protested. "You haven't even talked to him!"

"And I will not talk with him!" Zhu Di barked, becoming more annoyed. "I will not subject myself to anymore of his brazen lies! He is guilty. There is no way for us to avoid this terrible truth."

After a long moment of heavy silence, he turned to look at his wife. Her face was drawn into a pitiful look of dreadful sorrow. This mask of sadness took him aback. A pang of guilt suddenly shook him and he found himself wishing that he had not been so harshly obstinate. He took a long, slow breath, attempting to draw in enough strength to continue.

His words came slowly and with a solemn softness. "I don't want to order the execution of our son any more than you do. But I am the emperor," he stated with firm conviction. "I have solemn duties and responsibilities that I must uphold."

He handed his empty bowl to his wife, making a weak attempt at conciliation. "I will let some time pass before I make my final decision. Perhaps something will change. Perhaps new information will come to light that will give me cause for reconsideration."

His words surprised her. She looked at him intently, searching his eyes for a sign of sincerity. He looked away briefly, made uneasy by her gaze.

After a moment, he stated with a cold clear flatness, "But if the facts remain as we know them, I will have no choice but to do what must be done."

He turned back to her. Tears filled her eyes and washed down her smooth cheeks. Choking back his own feelings, he remained stoically unresponsive. Then, with uncharacteristic gentleness, his fingers settled softly on her hand and rested there.

The following day, Zhu Di's perspective began to change. As the morning sun filled the sky, the world around him appeared to be a more welcoming place, brimming with renewed hope. Stirred by this unexpected optimism, the emperor now felt capable of confronting his problems with greater confidence.

Inspired by this, the emperor invited Zheng He to his private residence to talk, hoping that this might shed light on another elusive truth that he had long been avoiding. When the Ming admiral arrived, Zhu Di exerted great resolve to present an image of strength and good health, straining to stifle the coughing fits that had plagued him for many days.

Zhu Di motioned for Zheng He to take a seat beside him.
"I appreciate you coming to my residence," Zhu Di wheezed softly, trying to catch his breath. "I am finally defeating this miserable illness. Feeling better now. Much better."

Zheng He could still hear the congestion in Zhu Di's lungs and sensed that the weakened emperor could launch into a barrage of coughing at any moment. He watched him with worried eyes, but concealed his concerns behind casual words.

"Have you been drinking plenty of green tea, Your Majesty?" he asked, trying to sound positive. "I've heard it will cure almost anything."

"That's what I told my wife," he responded, grinning. He paused, gazing inward, hunched over, breathing steadily as he held back yet another irritating urge to cough. "I'm sure I'll be just fine in a few days. It's nothing to worry about."

Zhu Di took another sip of tea and waited for his breathing to come a little easier. He looked directly at Zheng He, his eyes riveted in such a way that truth could not escape his gaze.

"I want to ask you something, Zheng He. It concerns, Honorable Lady, Xi Chen."

Zheng He stiffened at the sound of Xi Chen's name. He worried what might come next, anticipating any number of uncomfortable questions from his emperor. The sound of Zhu Di's ragged breathing abruptly became more prominent, as Zheng He's breathing had stopped altogether. The room was filled with a heightened tension. Finally, after what seemed like an eternity, Zheng He's voice sprang forth, filling the wispy void.

"Xi Chen, Your Majesty?" The words seemed to escape his throat, unwarranted and unwanted.

When Zhu Di saw Zheng He's nervous reaction, he already sensed the answer to his question. But the door had been opened and he knew that he must step through it.

"It's been reported to me that there is a relationship... or shall I say, a 'special relationship,' between you and Xi Chen."

Zheng He attempted to remain expressionless, hoping that the only emotion detected by the emperor would be confusion. His effort, however, was in vain. His feelings were clearly painted upon his face like a grand panoramic mural, exposing every nuance of his intense obsession.

A sharp chill shot down Zheng He's back. He struggled to maintain his composure. His mouth began to open, but only air escaped. Before a word could follow, Zhu Di raised his hand up, erasing Zheng He's nervous tension.

"I haven't said anything to the Honorable Lady, Zheng He. You've been my servant and close friend for many years. I wanted to hear the truth from you, before I said anything to her."

Zheng He was stunned. He hung his head for a moment, staring at the floor while trying to determine what he should say now. Truth was the only door to choose. He looked Zhu Di squarely in the eye.

"It is true, Your Majesty," he began, striving to remain calm and centered despite the panic coursing through him. "Xi Chen and I have known and loved each other ever since we were children."

Now it was Zhu Di who was stunned. He slumped back in his chair, the air sucked from his already ailing lungs. His eyes searched the air, as if an answer was floating somewhere, waiting to be grasped.

Zheng He leaned forward, anxious to tell his story now, hoping that his emperor would somehow understand. "Do you recall... when I was a boy and you rescued me from General Ho?"

Zhu Di nodded slightly, thinking back to a time that was mired in a thousand other memories, trying to pull this one moment out so that he might relive it.

"The young girl who was with me at the time was Xi Chen."

Zheng He stopped, letting this piece of information find a firm place in Zhu Di's mind, then continued. "Xi Chen and I were separated on that day."

Zhu Di looked up and it was clear to Zheng He that the emperor now recalled the day, the moment, when lives were irrevocably changed. After a moment, Zhu Di motioned weakly for his admiral to continue.

"Much later... when Chief Chi Li Bu Hua surrendered to your forces at the Great Wall, you requested that he present you a number of his personal servants and Ladies-in-Waiting. I was surprised, and overjoyed, when I discovered that Xi Chen was in the group of servants and ladies that Chi Li Bu Hua offered you."

Zheng He hesitated for a moment, curiously watching Zhu Di's face, wondering what was going through his mind. But the emperor didn't look up. He was obviously lost in the past, staring trance-like as events unfolded on the canvas of his mind.

Feeling a heavy weight lifted from his soul, Zheng He continued. "My heart longed to be with her," Zheng He boldly admitted, "and yet, my service and my loyalty remained pledged to you."

Even without words begin spoken, Zheng He sensed a profound skepticism emanating from Zhu Di. "I swear to you, Sire, under oath to Almighty Allah, that I have at no time taken any personal liberties with your Honorable Lady."

Zhu Di stood up slowly and walked over to a nearby candle. The flame flickered nervously. The emperor placed his finger in the flame, holding it there for a long moment, unmoving and expressionless. Finally, he withdrew his finger, looking at the black soot that coated his skin. He smiled wistfully. The pain of the flame hurt no more than the ache in his heart.

Zheng He's revelation was devastating to Zhu Di, but it no more demanded retribution than the innocent flame. Both hurt him, but neither deserved punishment for existing.

The revelation that Zheng He and Xi Chen knew each other and had loved each other ever since childhood was more hurtful than he had expected. Yet Zheng He had stayed true to his feelings, faithful to Xi Chen and loyal to his own emperor. "I've trusted and supported you, more than I've trusted and supported my own two sons," Zhu Di said, still facing away from Zheng He.

The admiral opened his mouth to speak. But, without even turning, Zhu Di raised his hand to stop him. "What you tell me now grieves me deeply. I do care for Xi Chen... but I also care for you."

Zhu Di finally turned to look at Zheng He. He remained stoic and composed, effectively concealing any torment that he was feeling within.

"You have told me the truth, Zheng He, and that is what is most important to me. But I must give this much thought. It would not be fair for me to respond without seeking the most wise and reasonable course of action."

Zheng He bowed politely and stepped back, feeling a sense of great relief. But at the same time he had the distinct impression of a foreboding dark cloud looming ahead.

Emperor Zhu Di watched his admiral walk toward the door. Zheng He seemed somehow smaller to him now, yet also larger than ever.


Later that same evening, Zhu Di invited Xi Chen to his private residence, anxious to question her about the personal relationship she had with Zheng He.

He solemnly motioned for her to sit down in the same chair he had offered Zheng He earlier in the day. Without a trace of provocation or formality, Zhu Di bluntly announced to Xi Chen that he had spoken with Zheng He and he knew of their relationship. She fell silent, lowering her eyes in shame, shocked to hear this unexpected disclosure.

"Why didn't you tell me?" Zhu Di implored sternly, trying to maintain a façade of civility and calm. "The truth would have been most graciously appreciated.

Xi Chen glanced up, then quickly diverted her eyes, not wishing to face the emperor's penetrating gaze.

"As a Lady-in-Waiting, Sire," she began, her words falling cautiously from her delicate lips, "I serve at your pleasure. I felt that I should not do anything that would compromise my loyalty and service."

Her stiffly formal answer made Zhu Di angry. "And so you hid your feelings and bit your tongue, accepting my advances without so much as a flicker of emotion or love?"

She met his gaze now, fixing her eyes on him with a cold, resentful glare. She was no longer willing to play the weak submissive role required of lady servants.

"Your words bring shame upon me, Your Majesty," she said forcefully. "And, in turn, you bring shame upon yourself." Her voice quivered now, softened by pain and heartbreak. "You speak as if I took pleasure in deceiving you. But I did not!"

Xi Chen turned away, concealing tears. Zhu Di slid forward on his seat. He extended his hand toward her... then slowly withdrew it when she made no attempt to acknowledge his discreet gesture of concern. A long, sad silence wrapped around them.

Eventually, Xi Chen pierced the silence with her soft voice while looking off into a distant memory.

"When Zheng He and I grew to know each other many years ago, I was filled with happiness. But when we were separated, I felt I would never see him again and my heart was broken. When we were reunited, my life was shaken once more. Despite many years and great distance, Zheng He had been brought back to me. I knew then that I could never allow myself to be without him."

Xi Chen wiped away her tears with the delicate tips of her tiny fingers. Zhu Di shifted uneasily, but did not interrupt.

"But then, I soon began to realize that things were now different between us. Zheng He had changed, and I had changed as well. We were no longer young children with unrealistic dreams."

Xi Chen turned slowly so she could look directly into Zhu Di's eyes. "We were both loyal servants to you, Your Majesty. But with each day I began to notice that Zheng He was behaving differently than before. Something had changed."

Zhu Di raised a curious eyebrow at this comment. He wanted to interrupt her and ask many questions. But he knew that it would only distract her and pull them away from the subject at hand. If he really wanted the truth, he must be patient and give Xi Chen the opportunity to speak her heart.

She sensed his great willingness to listen and continued. "He acted like he still loved me. I could tell that he did. But he would hold himself back. For some reason, he could never allow himself to be intimate with me."

Zhu Di attempted to hide his elation at hearing this, but his excited movements and the hopeful sparkle in his eyes surely betrayed him. To counter his excitement, he forced himself to speak in a calm and composed tone. "Zheng He is a very trusted and loyal servant," he said evenly.

Xi Chen spread a moist tear across her cheek. Its wetness glistened, making her appear even more lovely to Zhu Di.

"But there was something more," she said. The emperor opened his mouth to speak, but Xi Chen placed her finger softly to his lips, gently stopping his words.

"Your love for me was strong, Your Majesty... and very reassuring. It gave me a feeling that I'd never known before. A feeling I'd only dreamed of ever experiencing with Zheng He. In my mind, he would always be that reckless young boy that I had loved so long ago. I tried to erase him from my mind and my heart. I knew he wasn't real. But I could never dismiss him. Not entirely. And when the long expedition was over and he returned..."

"Do you still love him?" Zhu Di asked with apprehension.

Xi Chen searched the emperor's eyes for compassion. "I will always love him, Your Majesty," she stammered, helpless to hide the truth any longer. "In some ways..."

Zhu Di's eyes narrowed. He felt a sharp pain course through his head, and then a more excruciating pain deep inside his chest. "What you must understand, Xi Chen, is that, as emperor, I cannot come second to a servant. Not any servant. Not even Zheng He."

Xi Chen felt her legs go weak. Her hands began to tremble. Suddenly she felt that she had been too forthright with the emperor. She never should have exposed the true nature of her heart to him.

"Your Majesty, please don't misunderstand what I am trying to say..."

"I've had enough talk for today," he said abruptly, cutting her off. "The servant will show you out."

Zhu Di brusquely motioned for a servant. Xi Chen stood up and bowed to the emperor. Deeply shaken by Zhu Di's harsh statement, she quaked unsteadily on her feet. As she turned to leave with the servant, Xi Chen felt tears begin flowing like wild rivers down her cheeks. The air was wrenched from her lungs as deep sobs shook her body. And yet, she somehow maintained an illusion of composure until the large door closed with a loud echoing thud behind her. And at that very instant, she collapsed on the stone floor, helplessly sobbing and convulsing until the servants finally took pity and helped her back to the her quarters.

Inside his chambers, Zhu Di seethed with confusion and anger. He abruptly snatched a prized porcelain vase from the table and hurled it at door, smashing it. "Damn them!" he shouted in a rage, "Damn them both to the fires of eternity!"

Zhu Di's resentment was easy to understand. His first expedition had ended badly, forcing him to send his own son to prison. And now, he had learned that his two most trusted and loved servants had deceived him. Life, for him, had grown darker and disappointing. His faith in people was crumbling. Once again, he retreated into his shell of stoic defiance and refused to see anyone.

Empress Xu, however, was in no frame of mind to just sit back and do nothing. The life of her beloved second son was at stake. She invited Zheng He, General Tan and Dao Yan to her private quarters. I was asked to accompany them as well.

The empress confided her grave concerns to us and then asked if we would be willing to visit Prince Han in prison. She hoped that if we could convince the young man to change his views, and perhaps even apologize to his father, Zhu Di would have a change of heart and not have him executed. We all knew that deep within his heart Zhu Di did not want to kill his own son, but he needed some way to save face.

The following day, the four of us left for the prison to meet with Han. Each in his own way was hoping and praying for the best.

We passed through an ornately decorated Stone Gate that reflected the grandeur and opulence of Zhu Di's incredible new palace. Then we followed, single file, down a long narrow stone pathway, which eventually led us to a low one-story building. Its simple, crude appearance caused it to stand out from the other palace buildings.

Four prison guards snapped to attention as soon as they saw the three Imperial Representatives approach, followed closely behind by me, a simply garbed, unpretentious monk.

"We're here to see Prince Han," Zheng He said with firm authority, the forceful tone of his voice surprising even me.
Without saying a word, one guard bowed to the Ming admiral, then quickly turned and unlocked the heavy wooden door to the building's entrance. After we entered, the guard stepped inside, locked the door behind us and then motioned for us to follow. We trailed behind him down a long, narrow corridor. Thick stone walls and rough stone floor echoed our footsteps as we moved deeper into the dank building.

I noticed that heavy wooden doors were located about every ten feet along the gloomy hallway. As we neared the heart of the prison itself, there was an eerie stillness and a gloomy darkness. Small window slits near the wooden ceiling allowed very little light to filter into the narrow stone corridor. I could tell that the others didn't like being in the prison any more than I did. Besides being horribly dark and dank, it also didn't smell very good. After a few moments, Dao Yan acknowledged, under his breath, what all of us had been thinking. "It stinks in here."

"All prison's stink," General Tan agreed, having heard Dao Yan's comment. But he offered no excuse for the obviously vile conditions. "It is a prison, not a palace. It is meant to be uncomfortable and disgusting."

A few moments later, Dao Yan leaned closer to Zheng He, speaking in a lower tone this time so that General Tan would not hear him. "Are you sure we should be doing this?" he whispered.

"It won't take long," Zheng He said softly, trying to reassure the nervous High Consul. "Let's just hope we can talk some sense into him quickly and then be on our way."

The guard stopped to open a second wooden door, allowed the four of us to enter, then stepped inside himself. Once again, he locked the door behind us with aloud thud and clank of wood and iron. After politely bowing once more to the Imperial Representatives, he led us down yet another long corridor. It was even darker and smellier than the first passageway.

Halfway down this corridor, the guard stopped at a door. He opened a tiny peephole at the center of the door and peered inside.

"Prince Han is in here, Lord Zheng He," he declared in a dull monotone that blended boredom with official decorum. He stood silently for a long moment, apparently waiting for further instructions.

"Well... open the door," Admiral Zheng He ordered sharply. As the guard responded, Zheng He rolled his eyes at us, signaling both a distinct impatience with the guard and a clear feeling that they were now entering new territory. They had all sailed unexplored seas and distant lands, but this challenge presented by the emperor made them all nervous and uncertain.

The guard twisted the heavy iron key in the door's lock and pushed the heavy portal open. Cautiously, Zheng He stepped into the gloomy cell, followed closely by General Tan and then me. I stayed further back, cautiously watching from just behind Zheng He and the general. Not surprisingly, the reluctant Dao Yan chose to remain outside in the corridor with the guard.

The prince was lying on the floor with his head on a thin filthy woolen pad. He made no attempt to acknowledge our presence.

The cell had a rough stone floor and dank stone walls covered with black-green moss that smelled of moldy dirt and fetid water. A foul-smelling gutter ran along the back wall from one cell to the next, used by the prisoners as a toilet. This open trench was a literal cesspool, stinking and fetid. It made the primitive conditions even more reprehensible.

I looked up and noticed that two small stones had been carefully removed from the back wall near the ceiling. The opening was extremely small, allowing only a very small amount of light to enter the cramped stone enclosure.

A large rat skittered along the base of one wall and then dropped down into the filthy gutter that ran under the wall into the cell next door. Prince Han took no notice of the filthy rodent's furtive visit. It was, no doubt, a common daily occurrence for him.

Zheng He stepped over to the prisoner, bending slightly to address him in a courteous tone. "Prince Han... your mother, the empress, has become very concerned for your well being. She requested that we pay you a visit to assess your health and personal condition."

Silence. No response at all. Han behaved as if no one had even entered his cell. But Zheng He wisely ignored this unresponsiveness and continued, never allowing his steady voice to betray a growing impatience.

"If you wish to ignore us, Prince Han, that is, of course, your choice. However, your mother will be extremely troubled when she learns that you have fallen into dark despair and have refused to acknowledge her genuine concern. Your mother begged us to come and..."

Suddenly, Prince Han sat bolt upright, his eyes flashing with rage and madness, shouting with an aggressive roar, spittle flying from the corners of his mouth. "Don't lie to me, admiral! It was my FATHER who told you to come! He wants to torture me! To break my spirit and my soul! Well, you can tell him for me, that I will NOT succumb. He can rot in hell!"

When General Tan heard such brash insolence from the prince, he grabbed the young rebel's dirty collar and wrenched him to his feet.

"Listen to me, you filthy little bastard!" he growled. "If you ever speak of the emperor that way again, I will..."

Zheng He placed a firm hand on General Tan's arm, stopping him from taking his angry threat further. But Prince Han was not at all intimidated by the general's violent response. He smirked with cocky smugness. "Has this pitiful trio come to inflict my round of torture? A eunuch coward to conceive my course of pain... a corrupt soldier to administer it... and a heathen friar to pray for my pathetic soul?"

He stepped toward Tan, pulling himself up taller, arrogantly puffing out his chest. "What are you going to do, General? Beat me? Torture me? KILL me?"

This bold rejoinder stopped General Tan cold. The young prince roared with a loud, mocking laugh, brazenly shoving a finger at the general's face.

"My father is a fool, General Tan, and all of you are nothing but his helpless slaves. When he says to bow, you bow. When he tells you to crawl, you crawl. You are his dogs!"

Furious, General Tan shoved the young prince to the floor and snarled, "Your words will soon cut your own throat!" He whirled around to face the admiral. "You talk to him, Zheng He. I can't bear to gaze upon his disgusting face!"

Zheng He calmly stepped toward Han, keeping his voice firm and steady, attempting to disarm the bitter prince with an amiable diplomacy.

"I told you the truth, when I said it was your mother who sent us to see you. Your father doesn't even know we are here and he would, no doubt, not be pleased if he did know. Your mother is deeply saddened and concerned..."

Han leaped to his feet. "She should be concerned! Her son is rotting in this pit of pestilence, surrounded by murderous traitors. My father wants to execute me for acts I never committed. I am innocent! Yet he wants to kill his own son!"

Han was shouting loudly now, determined that his every curse and threat would be clearly witnessed by Minister Wa, who, unbeknownst to us at the time, had concealed himself in the adjoining cell. The prince dropped to the floor, his face nearly in the fetid trench of waste, repeating his raging accusations and curses, forcing his voice to echo beneath the wall along the filthy gutter. "My father is nothing but a STUPID FOOL!"

Zheng He stepped toward Han, looking down at the young man as he squirmed on the floor, his face close to the disgusting trench. The admiral resisted the urge to push this insolent traitor's face into the gutter with his foot, choosing instead to meet him with an expression of reason and wisdom.

"Dear prince," he said with great patience, "perhaps a wiser course of action would be to offer your father an opportunity to understand your..."

Han leaped to his feet, pushing his scowling face into Zheng He's face, exploding with a hot wind of rebellion.

"NO! I will NOT discuss anything with anyone! Not my father, nor any of his great generals, and definitely not with you, Zheng He!" A strange moment of unexpected silence descended upon them. Han's thunderous voice lowered to a steady and ominous snarl. His intense eyes glowed with a disquieting certainty. "Not until my father, the great and glorious Ming Emperor, comes to me groveling on his knees, and apologizes for throwing me into this stinking cesspool."

General Tan could take no more of this insolence. "There will be no apologies to you!" he roared. "Your father has every right to punish you for the disreputable deeds you have perpetrated."

"I have done nothing!" Han shouted back. "I have been falsely accused. Minister Wong bears the guilt. Not me! If the emperor must have blood on his hands to claim justice, let him take his revenge on Wong."

Zheng He stepped between General Tan and Prince Han. "Wong is dead. And you shall soon meet the same fate unless you confess to your father and beg his forgiveness."

This startling news silenced the prince. He staggered back against the wall and then slumped slowly to the floor as he began to grasp a profound reality. His co-conspirator and only supporter was no longer there for him.

After a moment, he turned a suspicious eye toward Zheng He. "How do I know you aren't lying?"

Zheng He relished this moment, taking a long pause to savor it before speaking. "You don't."

The admiral went to the door of the cell and pounded upon it to signal the guard they were ready to depart. He looked down at Prince Han. "Although, I'm certain this nagging seed of doubt will torment your dreams and leave little comfort for sleep."

Once outside in the corridor, the four of us stood in silence as the guard locked the prince's cell. We maintained our oddly awkward silence as we marched the long passageways, from building to building. The only sound was of our feet echoing rhythmically as they slapped the stone floors.

As we emerged from the final door and stepped outside, we all took great gulps of fresh air, vainly trying to remove the terrible stale stench from our lungs.

"Praise Lord Buddha!" Dao Yan gasped. "That terrible place is even more dreadful than I had imagined."

"And the prince is more foolish and ignorant than I could have ever imagined," General Tan grumbled, still angered by the prince's insolent behavior.

Zheng He was the only one of us who seemed quite calm and collected, totally undisturbed by the confrontation with the emperor's son. "Well we certainly gave him something to think about," he observed casually.

"But what shall we tell the empress?" I inquired. "She will want to know."

"That is simple," Zheng He replied with a confident smirk. "The truth. Her son is healthy, filled with energy... and having great difficulty sleeping through the night."

Now that the bloom was off the rose with Xi Chen, Zhu Di wasted no time in getting to know his lovely new Korean servant, Quan, on a much more intimate basis. He requested that she be brought to his private bedchamber. It was here that he intended to initiate her into an experience that the servants mockingly called the "emperor's ritual lovemaking."

A great number of lighted candles had been strategically placed throughout the room and beside the bed, bathing the entire room in a soft, seductive glow.

The beautiful young Korean woman sat with Zhu Di on the soft bed covers, just as Xi Chen and many other concubines had done many times before. Zhu Di talked quietly, carefully navigating the subtle misinterpretations that might occur because of the differences between their languages. As they took frequent sips of sweet wine, they gradually began to depend less on spoken words and more on the silent language of familiar gestures, warm gazes and gentle touches.

"I want to congratulate you," Zhu Di began softly, "on your exceptional social graces. I'm deeply indebted to your grandfather for offering you to me."

The young woman lowered her eyes as she had been taught and responded graciously, even though all his words were not precisely understood.

"You are too generous, Your Majesty," she replied. "I'm afraid I don't deserve such praise."

Zhu Di eagerly took another sip of wine, feeling the relationship turning in his favor. "Tell me about your grandfather. He must be a very noble gentleman."

Quan looked up and smiled, pleased that Zhu Di referred to her grandfather as noble. "My grandfather is very dear to me, Your Majesty. I was quite young when my father was killed in battle. It was my grandfather, the emperor, who raised me since childhood and taught me the subtleties of offering proper service."

Zhu Di smiled. "I must say, he has taught you well. I am certain he would be proud."

Zhu Di noticed that Quan's goblet was empty. With a nearly imperceptible movement of his hand, he signaled to a servant who watched from behind a screen across the room.

The servant emerged immediately, silently approaching like an invisible breeze, discretely refilling Quan's goblet. Then, without making the slightest sound, he disappeared like a wisp of wind behind the screen.

Zhu Di took Quan's hands in his and kissed them tenderly, gazing into her eyes.

"Do you feel that I'm too old for you?" he asked with great sincerity. "And I would be most appreciative if you would tell me the absolute truth."

The young lady looked quizzically at Zhu Di. He sensed her hesitation and quickly interjected, "What I mean is... you are so young and so very beautiful. On the other hand, I no longer enjoy the radiance or glory of my youth. So I must ask... do you find my maturity offensive?"

Quan leaned close to Zhu Di and brushed his face with her soft lips. "On the contrary, Your Majesty. I find you..."

Much to Zhu Di's surprise, Quan suddenly pulled back and giggled. She hid her face in her hands like an embarrassed schoolgirl, peeking through her fingers.

He slowly took her wrists and gently pulled her hands aside. She blushed, looking down humbly. "Please forgive me, Your Majesty. But I find your maturity very appealing indeed. Younger men do not possess your great patience and strength. It is your experience that I find so desirable."

Zhu Di raised his chin, pleased to hear these words. He took a prolonged sip of his wine and gave a quick glance toward the screen. This time, two servants responded, suddenly flashing toward them like swooping birds. The wine glasses were filled in an instant and the servants vanished like phantoms.

Another servant appeared from the shadows and began to extinguish all the candles in the room. Only the two candles beside the bed remained lit, flickering softly.

Zhu Di guided Quan back against the soft pillows of the bed and began kissing her tenderly on the lips. As if by magic, and right on cue, soft music began to emanate from behind another decorative screen. Zhu Di's fingers began to tenderly caress the young woman's firm, up-turned breasts. His words came in a soft, whispered breath.

"I desire to show you, Lady Quan, what years of experience have taught me." Quan responded by brushing her moist lips against his cheek, her delicate tongue dancing seductively around his ear.

"Your Majesty," she whispered to him, "I await with great anticipation whatever you wish to teach me. I am your most willing student."

Quan and Zhu Di began to kiss and fondle each other with growing urgency, removing each other's clothing in a frantic rush. In short order, all their garments were recklessly discarded across the bed and onto the floor.

Forgetting imperial decorum, Zhu Di hurriedly mounted the young Korean woman and thrust himself inside her. She gasped and moaned loudly, causing him to be startled at his own animal-like aggression. He pushed himself deeper inside the exotic young maiden, overcome by lust for her tempting nubile charms.

As their lovemaking became more and more frantic, Quan suddenly pushed Zhu Di onto his back and mounted him. He looked up at her with wide eyes, shocked at her unexpected enthusiasm and passion, but overcome with immense pleasure.

Her sensual movements continued to intensify for more than an hour, taking Zhu Di on an erotic excursion of lovemaking unlike anything he'd ever experienced or imagined.

As the candles beside their bed finally began to flicker and wane, the two lovers reached a fevered climax of intense ecstasy. The culmination of their frantic passion left them bathed in sweat, wrapped in a tangle of limbs, lungs heaving, helplessly moaning and gasping for air. Zhu Di and Quan were deliciously exhausted, their heads reeling and swimming dizzily.

For a long while, they lay silently, listening to each other breathing, feeling a simultaneous throbbing pulse run through their veins and into their hearts. They hadn't even noticed that the music behind the screen had faded away long ago. Then, the last candle flickered out, leaving them enfolded together in a warm shroud of darkness.


Two days later, in the small living quarters attached to the back of my humble mission, Zheng He and I had just finished our first cup of tea. Suddenly, he rose to his feet, pacing restlessly.

"What is the trouble?" I asked. I had noticed earlier that Zheng He seemed curiously unsettled, but gave it little mind. However, his anxiety now appeared to be growing rapidly more acute. "Why don't you sit... enjoy your tea."

"I have little patience for tea today, friar" he responded with frustration. "I have been requested to meet with Zhu Di this afternoon."

"So? You meet with him often. This is not so unusual and certainly no cause for concern." I motioned for him to sit, but he turned away and resumed his nervous pacing.

"Last week I confessed to Zhu Di that I am in love with Xi Chen."

Though surprised by this revelation, I maintained a calm demeanor, so as not to incite his anxiety further. "Well... it is true. And perhaps it's better that he learned the truth directly from you now, before hearing it from another source."

"It made no difference. He was not pleased," Zheng He explained flatly. "It is clear that Zhu Di is in love with her as well."

"What? The emperor? In love with Xi Chen?" I found this surprisingly unlikely. "You must be mistaken."

Zheng He leaned toward me, revealing an intensity in his dark eyes. "If you could hear him speak of her, friar, you would have no doubt."

"But she is in love with you," I told him, hoping to strengthen his resolve. "That is what matters most."

"I don't believe she does," he said sullenly. "Not now. Not like before

"Why do you say that?"

He looked at me with a saddened expression. "After I met with Zhu Di, I went to see Xi Chen. But she would not see me. I returned several times, but on every occasion one of the other servants would tell me that she was not available."

I stood up, intercepting Zheng He's path, hoping to capture his distracted attention. "And so... now what? You are going to confront the emperor? That may not be the best approach, Zheng He."

"It is the emperor who has requested this audience. I'm certain he intends to announce how he shall deal with this unfortunate situation. And I fear the outcome will not be a good one."

I rested my hand on his shoulder to comfort him. "Fear is a friend to no man. You should remain confident. The love between you and Xi Chen is pure and strong. It has survived many tribulations over the years."

"But the persuasive authority of an emperor may be much stronger," Zheng He said, slumping back into his chair. "I feel the love that once existed between us has been breached by a power far beyond my influence. You may see an admiral before you, friar, but I am now and always will be just a Muslim boy with great hopes in his heart. I am a loyal and grateful servant of an emperor who now stands between me and the eternal love of my life."

I touched the cross hanging from my neck, wondering if I possessed the wisdom required to solve this horrible dilemma.

"You can pray for guidance, my friend. But do not expect the solution to come from God on a bolt of lightning. He will only show you the many possibilities. The true answer lies within you. It is yours to discover."

Zheng He considered this for a moment and then looked up at me with a smile. "I can always trust you to grace me with the truth, friar... no matter how heavy a burden it might place upon my shoulders."

"The weight of your burden will only serve to make you stronger," I told him with a confident nod. "Carry it well."

When Zheng He arrived at Zhu Di's private quarters, the emperor was sipping a steaming cup of green tea. Zheng He took a seat across from him, observing the elder leader as he meticulously poured more tea into his cup, savored the warm aroma and then carefully let the soothing liquid flow between his lips.

"Has your cough improved, Majesty?" Zheng He inquired.

"I believe it has," Zhu Di allowed, giving his admiral an unmistakable grin. "The green tea is helping, but so are other remedies."

"Other remedies?" Zheng He ventured, unsure exactly what Zhu Di meant.

But the emperor simply smiled with a mischievous twinkle in his eye. He waved his hand merrily, chasing the reference away, yet deeply pleased by his memory of the recent evening of lovemaking with Quan.

Quickly changing the subject, Zhu Di stated firmly, "I think I've made a decision."

Zheng He stirred restlessly in his seat, filled with a nervous apprehension. He had a distinct feeling that the emperor was referring to their mutual relationship with Xi Chen. "You've served me well for many years," Zhu Di acknowledged, his voice remaining earnest. "Your valuable assistance was very instrumental in helping me become emperor. Your service continues to be very much appreciated and never forgotten. Your leadership of the fleet on the first great Ming expedition was a remarkable achievement. It deserves great admiration."

Zhu Di abruptly stood up and walked to the window, gazing for a long moment at the trees outside.

"As far as Honorable Lady Xi Chen is concerned..." he said, suddenly turning to face Zheng He. "My heart was deeply touched when you told me of your love for her. That you did not make any intimate advances or demands upon her while she has been a servant to me is noble. Noble indeed."

Zheng He nodded with humility. He felt his chest tighten with a combination of trepidation and great relief.

"Your honorable sacrifice, Lord Zheng He, will not go without reward. I pledge to you, that from this day forward, though Xi Chen will remain my Honorable Lady, and will continue to serve me in my imperial chambers, I will no longer make any personal demands upon her."

Zheng He couldn't believe what the emperor was saying.

"But Your Majesty," he burst forth, "there's no need for you to make such a benevolent sacrifice."

Zhu Di raised a firm hand to halt his servant's sincere protestations.

Zheng He stopped speaking, bowing humbly once more. "Then I thank you from the bottom of my heart, Sire. I will never be able to repay such kindness and unselfish generosity."

Zheng He bowed deeply to Zhu Di and held himself in this humbled position until Zhu Di took him gently by the arm and raised him back up to face him.

"Now!..." Zhu Di sang out, greatly relieved that this awkwardly uncomfortable bit of business had been completed, "I want to show you something."

He leaped to his feet and guided Zheng He to a broad table where several maps were spread out and stacked loosely in disorderly piles. "Before you returned the fleet from the first expedition, I began making plans for a second."

Zheng He was surprised by this revelation. "You are already planning another expedition, Majesty? But the men have barely had an opportunity to recover from our first voyage. It was a difficult experience."

Zhu Di excitedly tapped the side of his head with his finger. "And it is fresh in their minds, my friend. The challenge stirs their souls. Their hearts desire the discovery of new horizons." He quickly traced a route across one of the larger maps, spanning a vast sea until he touched the ragged outline of a distant land mass."

"There! The land called Arabia!" he exclaimed proudly. "That is where I want you to go. How long do you think it will take to ready the fleet?"

But everything was happening so fast. Zheng He's head was spinning with a million thoughts. Only moments before Zhu Di had promised not to make any personal demands upon the woman Zheng He loved. Yet, almost in the same breath, he was telling the admiral to leave again. And to stir even greater conflict in his soul, Zhu Di wanted him to take the fleet to Arabia, the precious land he had always dreamed of visiting. Tears began to well up in Zheng He's eyes. He quickly wiped them away, hoping that his emperor had not seen the sudden burst of emotion.

Finally, he managed to squeeze words from his tightened throat. "Six months, Your Majesty," he replied, struggling to keep his quavering voice steady.

Zhu Di gave him a hard look, considering this response. "Six months?" He spun around and paced the floor, disturbed by the length of time.

"Many of the ships need to be repaired, Majesty," he replied, trying to explain. "We have to chart new routes and assess the navigational difficulties. Much work needs to be done."

284

Zhu Di turned to him with a stern expression. "Six months then. And not a day longer."

After a stunned hesitation, Zheng He bowed sharply. The emperor smiled. "Good! Then it is done," Zhu Di exclaimed happily. "And I want you to keep me posted on your progress just as you did before."

As the emperor's door closed with a loud thud behind him, Zheng He's first thoughts were of Xi Chen. His world had once again been turned upside down, leaving him in search of solid ground on which to stand. There was now a chance that the woman he loved might once again be his... and his alone. But if he must now leave her behind and sail away, what new competition for her affection might he face? And even though the emperor was willing to relinquish any personal claim on Xi Chen, would she be so easily willing to be released from the honor of his devotion and admiration? Zheng He's future now seemed as agonizingly obscure as it had before.


Determined to resolve his troublesome situation, Zheng He sent Xi Chen a request that she meet with him later that evening in the palace garden.

But her reaction was not at all what he expected. "I thought you'd be happy," he said, deeply disappointed at her solemn response.

"Why should I be happy?" she said pointedly. "Can you give me one good reason? You refuse to make love to me. And now you tell me that Emperor Zhu Di has promised not to pursue my affections as well. Where does that leave me? Am I merely a thing that the two of you barter and negotiate for?"

Her rash statement prompted anger in Zheng He. "Is that the only thing you care about, Xi Chen? The pursuit of our affections? Making love?"

She looked Zheng He directly in the eyes. "It's not the only thing. But I have begged you to love me. I begged for you to touch me and hold me. But you refuse. When we were young, all you could talk about was how much you wanted to make love to me. But now..." Her words fell away into a hollow silence.

He reached out to touch her arm, but she pulled away, averting her gaze and looking into the trees. Finally, her voice returned, soft and sad. "We're not children anymore, Zheng He. I'm not a girl. I've known disappointment and loneliness. I've felt pain. I'm a woman. And you... you are a man. I need more than just talk and promises now. We can no longer hide from the truth."

She paused, mustering the courage to go on. Suddenly, her words burst forth, as if no longer controlled or carefully measured. "If you are a eunuch, Zheng He... then just tell me!  And if you are not, then make love to me!  Right here.  Right now."

Like a flash of lighting, Zheng He suddenly slapped Xi Chen across the face with the back of his hand.  Her soft pale cheek turned crimson, darkening like a cloud.  A small cut on her lip brought forth a moist teardrop of crimson blood.

Both Zheng He and Xi Chen were shocked at his unexpected burst of violence.  Reacting with instinctive fury, Xi Chen slapped Zheng He's face with her open palm.  It cracked like bamboo snapping, sharp and loud.

Zheng He shuddered with shock and anger, the sharp sting of her rebuke cutting him like a sword.

"Never touch me again!" she screamed.  "Do you hear me?  I don't want you to touch me again... EVER!"

She spun around and raced from the garden, blinded by tears.  Zheng He stood like a rock, unmoving, cold and hard.  But in his legs he felt a trembling and weakness seize him, threatening to bring him to his knees.


For the next several days, Xi Chen went into seclusion, telling anyone who bid her presence that she had fallen ill and was desperately trying to recover.  She sat for hours in the darkness, her thoughts swirling around the details of her long relationship with Zheng He.

She couldn't make sense of Zheng He's erratic behavior.  Many had told her that he was a eunuch, but she was under the impression this only meant he had been rendered unable to impregnate a woman.  Zhu Di considered Zheng He a great friend, confidant and trusted servant.  He would never be so cruel as to have Zheng He's sexual organ removed.  Such a thing was simply unthinkable.

She was relieved to have learned that Zhu Di had solemnly vowed not to request that Xi Chen make love to him.  This would remove much of the pressure she felt and the guilt that plagued her.  But if Zheng He refused to make love to her as well, she would now be left feeling abandoned and totally alone.


On the other hand, the mood of Emperor Zhu Di had now brightened considerably.  His health was improving every day and his nights were filled with long hours of making love to Quan, his exotic Korean beauty.

Feeling invigorated and much more socially inclined, Zhu Di decided to invite his close friends to join him at the residence.  The next day,

Zheng He, General Tan, Dao Yan and I walked together across the broad expanse of the open courtyard leading to the residence entrance.

"I hope the emperor doesn't ask us anything about his son," Tan muttered dourly. He turned to Zheng He with a worried expression. "What did you report to the empress of our visit to the prison?"

"I told her the truth," Zheng He stated with confidence, offering the general a casual shrug. "I said the visit with her son did not meet our expectations."

The general looked surprised. "You...? But, but that..."

"Is accurate," Zheng He stated firmly, cutting off the general's flustered interjections. "We were disappointed by his lack of cooperation and could do little else than state our case and hope he would eventually see our point of view."

I chuckled and the others looked at me curiously. "You are quite the diplomat, Zheng He," I explained with a big grin. "You expressed the obvious truth in a manner that is easy to swallow and thoroughly digestible."

We all walked on, basking in the cleverness of Zheng He's words. But just as this explanation was about to settle on us like a gentle summer rain and render us comfortable, Zheng He spoke again. "And... I told the empress that her son had received us well."

We all stopped short, unable to believe our ears. "You said what?" Dao Yan gasped. "Received us 'well'?"

Zheng He turned back to face the High Consul with a wry smile. "As *well* as could be expected... given that he is an ignorant and deplorable tyrant."

"What else did you say?" Dao Yan burst out, excitedly realizing that there was surely more to tell.

"I also explained that Prince Han was giving very serious thought as to what he would tell his father when the two of them met in the near future."

"He certainly was giving it thought," Dao Yan mused. "And voice."

"I hope you didn't tell her what he planned to say," I ventured, my eyes bulging with the very thought of this.

Zheng He flashed me a reassuring gaze. "Give me some credit, Friar. I do have a reasonable sense of decorum."

Once inside the ruler's impressive residence, a servant led us into Zhu Di's private study, bowed politely and left. We settled ourselves into four chairs that had been placed side-by-side, facing the emperor. Several servants silently circulated among us, pouring cups of tea.

After we received our tea, Zhu Di softly cleared his throat and turned to face Zheng He. "I have a favor to ask you, my friend."

"A favor, Majesty?" Zheng asked, a bit surprised by the abruptness of the request. "What is your wish?"

"As all you gentlemen know quite well, I had to send my son to prison. Under Chinese law, I should have ordered his execution at once."

We all exchanged nervous glances. All except Zheng He, whose gaze remained steadily focused on Zhu Di.

Unable to abhor the awkward silence that followed, General Tan anxiously began to speak. "Sire, the prince is still an impressionable young man. Surely, you must take that into consideration. As he gets older, I'm quite certain he'll realize he's made a few mistakes and will decide to change his views..."

"I'd like to believe what you say, general," Zhu Di said with a deep frown, "but I'm not really confident in this assessment. My son is overly ambitious. And he is very stubborn. I've tried to talk good sense into him many times before, but all I ever accomplish is to make myself angry. And then I say many horrible things that I wish I hadn't."

Zheng He shot a brief glance at General Tan and Dao Yan, then offered a surprising suggestion. "Perhaps we could talk to Prince Han, Your Majesty. If all of us were to visit him in prison, we might be able to convince your son to repent and see the great error of his ways."

We all remained completely motionless, the expressions on our faces frozen. We did not want to betray any sign of surprise at Zheng He's unexpectedly brash suggestion.

The emperor leaned forward, resting his elbows on his knees, looking directly into Zheng He's eyes with an intense squint. "If you did... I would be..." His words hung in the air, heavy with portent. None of us could imagine what might come next. The thick tension grew even heavier. Finally, he continued, "...forever grateful to you."

There was a simultaneous expulsion of breath as a great relief swept over all of us. The Emperor beamed with warm gratitude. "I had hoped beyond hope that I might be able to convince you to take on this difficult task. I can't express how incredibly pleased I am that you have offered it to me on your own."

"It would be our honor, Your Majesty," Zheng He stated, allowing his eyes to close slowly, followed by a gracious bow of sincere assurance.

Zhu Di rose to his feet and began to pace with great energy. "If my son would simply apologize, I could save face and there would be no need to have him executed."

He turned to us and explained with great sincerity, "The empress is very worried about the prince. As you can well imagine, neither of us wants to order our son's death."

Zheng He stood up suddenly, intent upon concluding this conversation with Zhu Di before it led to further discussion of the empress and her concerns. "We will report to you the moment we have good news, I assure you, Majesty."

Zheng He bowed with abrupt politeness and swept out of the room with the three of us at his heels.


As we once again crossed the stone courtyard, General Tan finally voiced the thought that was troubling all of us. "How are we going to manage this, Zheng He? The prince has already spit in our faces and cursed his father. It seems highly unlikely that an apology will be forthcoming."

Dao Yan echoed the general's trepidation. "Yes... how can we possibly bend him to the emperor's wishes when he is rigid as iron?"

Zheng He stopped abruptly in his tracks and turned to face us, smiling with surprising confidence. "With great finesse, my friends."


The following day we entered the prison compound once again. As before, we were enveloped by the dank, shadowy enclosure, as if being swallowed by a horrible sea monster. The light within was heavy and somber. The air was laden with a musty weight that made us feel ponderous and slow, burdened by our difficult mission.

The guards led us down the long stone corridor. Zheng He, General Tan and I paused outside Prince Han's cell as the guard unlocked the cell and pulled the heavy wooden door open. Dao Yan waited in the corridor with the guards as the three of us entered.

Prince Han slumped against the dank stone wall, barely illuminated in the faint shafts of daylight that crept into the gloom through the small slits in stones close to the ceiling.

The prince glared at us with an angry insolence. His penetrating eyes were livid with cold rage, but his voice emerged with an unexpected steadiness, as if his words had been rehearsed and refined during his long hours in the gloomy darkness.

"Has this pitiful trio returned to inflict my round of torture?" he asked with spite. "A eunuch coward to inflict my course of pain... a corrupt soldier to administer it... and a heathen friar to pray for my pathetic soul?"

I let the insult pass and, in a gesture of kindness, I stepped toward him, raising a sympathetic hand that offered peace and condolences. But Prince Han spat upon my hand, and then, moving more rapidly than any of us expected, scooped up a handful of fecal matter from the vile-smelling gutter, leaped forward and shoved it into my face.

I gasped and sputtered, shocked by the disgusting attack, stumbling backward to the stone floor. General Tan grasped his sword and quickly pulled if from its scabbard. He was instantly upon Han, shoving him to the floor, the blade pressing against the soft skin of his neck. "You dare to defile a man of God!" he shouted at the squirming prince.

Zheng He helped me to my feet as I wiped the vile slime from my face, coughing and wheezing at the terrible odor.

Prince Han's face grew red with anger and spittle flew from the corners of his mouth. The sharp blade drew a small trickle of blood.

General Tan shouted angrily, "I should kill you as you grovel at my feet."

Zheng He reached out and touched the General's arm firmly. "Release him. This is not the way."

The General hesitated, then slowly withdrew his sword, stepping back reluctantly, still quaking with tension.

Prince Han sneered at Zheng He. "Don't think your mercy buys my trust, Zheng He. I know you hate me more than any other."

"I don't want your trust," Zheng He told him sternly. "I want you to heed my warning. When your father visits you... and he will visit you soon... I want you to fall to your knees and beg his forgiveness."

Prince Han met Zheng He's cold stare with his own defiant and unwavering gaze. His words came forth with a steely arrogance. "I am a prince. I do not beg."

Angered by this insolence, General Tan raised his powerful arm and slapped Prince Han hard across the face, knocking him to the floor with the crushing blow.

"If you want to live, you'd best learn to grovel like the disgusting pig you are!" the General raged.

He slammed his foot against the back of the prince's neck, shoving his face forcefully into the gutter, mashing it in the stinking muck of urine and feces. "If you're a prince, then you're nothing but a prince of swill and excrement. Fill your belly with it you miserable bastard!"

Han tried to shake and kick himself free, but General Tan wouldn't let him up, pushing harder with his foot.

"Listen to me, Han... and listen good! You will do as Zheng He commands. We will pay you another visit in three weeks and your father will be with us. When you see him... you will fall down on your miserable knees and beg his forgiveness."

Prince Han's eyes bulged with both resentment and fright. General Tan pushed harder with his foot, leaning down close with his snarling face to emphasize the harshness of his words.

"If you don't do as I say," General Tan threatened, "I will personally return to this cell and feed you nothing but shit and piss from the gutter until you are DEAD!"


As the four of us left the prison, we paused in the courtyard, while Zheng He attempted to clean the filth from my face with his dampened sleeve.

"I knew you would be a great help to us, friar. And you were," Zheng He said.

"Me?" I gasped, completely astounded by his words. "What did I do? Besides irritate the prince and cause a brawl?"

"Oh, no, my friend," General Tan said, gently laying an encouraging hand upon my shoulder. "Lord Zheng He is quite correct."

I looked at them both with puzzlement, thinking they were greatly confused. But General Tan went on to explain to me, "Your offer of kindness to that young fool prince enabled us to see his true nature."

Zheng He nodded and smiled. "Confucius said 'some men respond to the honey of a bee, others to its sting.' You helped us discover that Han is the kind of man who responds best to the sting."

"So what do we do now?" I asked, still not sure getting my face covered with feces was any help at all.

"That's easy!" Zheng He responded quickly. "All we have to do is tell Zhu Di that his son is earnestly searching for the truth. And in three weeks, he'll be ready to repent!"

"And if he doesn't?" I asked sarcastically. "Then what?"

General Tan grinned broadly.

"Then I'll start feeding the little sonofabitch something he isn't going to like!"

Chapter Nine

_____

## UNFORTUNATE CIRCUMSTANCES

Several days later, Zhu Di was delighted to play host to two newly arrived trade envoys from Korea. He had built Forbidden City to impress foreign visitors and now they were beginning to come. Outwardly, he tried to remain calm and not show how delighted he was for the opportunity he had to fulfill his dream. But now, for the first time, two trade envoys were visiting and he was actually getting a chance to put his plan into action.

The first area he showed them was an area known as Imperial City. This impressive collection of buildings was located just outside the walls of his newly constructed Forbidden City palace.

Quan, Zhu Di's newest love interest, who had recently been elevated to the official status of concubine, was invited by Zhu Di to accompany him as he gave a guided tour to the two visiting Koreans. Also nearby were the ever present eunuch servants who trailed Zhu Di's party a short distance away, but close enough at hand should they be called upon to serve.

Zhu Di stopped at a white marble bridge and began pointing out the nearby architecture to the two visiting envoys.

"Those buildings over there," he exclaimed proudly, are apartments and palaces where various ministers and government officials live who serve in my imperial court."

Next, Zhu Di pointed to a high wall in the distance.

"Do you see that high wall over there? It completely encircles this entire area, effectively separating Imperial City from the local citizens of Beijing proper."

The two envoys were delighted that Emperor Zhu Di had agreed to conduct their tour himself. The senior Korean envoy bowed graciously to Zhu Di before asking a question.

"Could I assume, Your Majesty," he intoned solemnly, "that the peasants who live in the outer city of Beijing would find it very difficult, if not impossible, to gain access to the entire area of Imperial City. Is that true?"

Zhu Di smiled at the envoy's question happy the visiting dignitary had grasped the importance of the restricted area.

"It is quite true, Honorable Envoy! Anyone wishing to visit Imperial City on official business would have to pass between one of the large wooden gates in the wall. And, as you can readily see, the gates are heavily defended. No one can just walk into Imperial City unannounced! You have to have a very good reason to get inside."

The senior envoy nodded his understanding, dutifully impressed.

"I must say, Your Majesty," he added solemnly, "your whole palace complex is quite extraordinary. I don't think I've ever seen anything like it before anywhere."

"I can assure you, gentlemen," Zhu Di replied smugly, "my tour is just beginning. Please allow me to show you the humble quarters where I live."

Zhu Di started walking across a low marble bridge which crossed a deep moat filled with water. In the middle of the bridge he stopped again so he could point out the huge stone walls and massive gate which stood before them more than twenty feet tall. It was even more massive than the previous gate Zhu Di had pointed out which separated Imperial City from Beijing City proper.

"As I told you before," Zhu Di continued. "On this side of the wall where we're standing is the area known as Imperial City. On the other side, just beyond the huge gate you see before us, is where my new palace is located. It's an area I call, Forbidden City."

"And that's where you live, Your Majesty?" the junior envoy asked, obviously shockied by what he was hearing and seeing.

"Yes, that's where I live!" Zhu Di sang out happily. "And although you can't see the whole expanse of wall from here, it does extend completely around the inner core of buildings. Inside, I think you'll be even more impressed at the incredible collection of imperial palaces and gardens that I've had constructed."

"Is this the only entrance, Sire?" the senior envoy asked, since it was the only entrance he could see.

"Oh, no!" Zhu Di declared, haughtily, but not wanting to appear too boastful. "There's a huge gate just like this one on each side of my Forbidden City complex. The gate on the side which faces the rising sun is called Eastern Glory. The gate which faces the setting sun is called Western Glory. There's a gate on the northern side which is called Spiritual Valor and here, on this southern side, the gate you see before you now is called Meridian Gate."

The two envoys looked at each other in utter amazement which pleased Zhu Di tremendously.

"Would you like to see inside?" he asked, already knowing what their answer would be.

The two Koreans offered Zhu Di a gracious bow in unison, then the senior envoy gave the emperor his predicted reply.

"We would consider it a very great honor, Your Majesty. Please show us whatever you can!"

"Good!" Zhu Di gushed enthusiastically and immediately started walking towards the huge Meridian Gate just before them, followed closely behind by the two Korean envoys, Concubine Quan and Zhu Di's two ever-present servants.

As they walked across the bridge, as if by magic, the massive wooden doors began to swing open and they were able to see a huge imposing courtyard which spread before them. In the middle of this spacious open area, on a slight rise, the envoys could see a magnificent structure that was like no other building they'd ever seen before in it's sheer size and beauty.

"The building I'm going to show you first," Zhu Di exclaimed proudly, is what I like to call my architectural masterpiece. Its official name, however, is the Hall of Supreme Harmony. If you'll just follow me for a few moments I think you're going to like what I show you."

As the two visitors approached the spectacular edifice and walked inside they were immediately struck by two images; one, the immense size of the building's interior and two, by its exquisite grandeur. Thirty huge columns, each an imposing sixteen feet high, were magnificently decorated from top to bottom with carvings of silver and gold. The columns held a massive roof which featured thousands upon thousands of intricately carved wooden beams. The two Koreans, predeictably, couldn't believe what they were seeing. Both were immediately struck speechless upon entering.

Zhu Di turned and smiled at Concubine Quan upon seeing that his two newest visitors were so impressed!

"It's, it's," the junior envoy, stammered, trying to find proper words...

"A masterpiece?" Zhu Di replied happily, finishing the man's sentence for him. "I quite agree! It is a masterpiece! There's no other way to describe it. Now, if you don't mind, I'd like to show you my throne."

In the middle of the immense structure sat Zhu Di's simple, yet exquisitely elligant, Dragon Throne. The proud ruler led them over to the seat of his imperial power so the Koreans could inspect it more closely.

"This, gentlemen," Zhu Di beamed, "is my Dragon Throne! I only use it on solemn state occasions, such as very important birthdays, new year celebrations, the nomination of generals before a special campaign, that sort of thing."

The Korean envoys were again struck with awe.

"Just like this entire edifice, Your Majesty," the senior envoy gushed, "it is magnificent!"

Pretending to be unfazed by the compliment, Zhu Di continued with his description.

"As you can see, the throne itself is six feet high. Upon my command fragrant incense is allowed to filter into the hall from those large urns you can see located on either side of the throne and also in some of the nearby galleries."

"That's very nice," the junior envoy whispered softly to himself, not wanting to interrupt the emperor, but instinctively commenting on what the Chinese emperor had just described.

Zhu Di took no notice of the interruption and continued with his description.

"As an added touch I've instructed that as I assume my place of honor upon the throne, servants softly ring small bells of gold and jade."

Both envoys looked at each other and nodded. Once again they were obviously amazed that what they were beinig shown was unlike any other palace or structure they'd ever seen before! The senior envoy then turned his attention to Zhu Di's two large cranes, which silently stood guard on either side of his throne.

"Would you please tell me about your magnificent bird statues, Your Majesty? They are quite extraordinary."

"Ahhh, they are special," Zhu Di agreed, proudly. "They're cloisonne cranes! Each is five feet tall and decorated with seven coats of fine enamel. The crane, as you probably know, is the Chinese symbol for long life."

"They are beautiful," the envoy gushed again almost reverently. "They are simply beautiful!"

"Now!" Zhu Di announced, enthusiastically, quickly breaking the spell, "I wish to show you my Temple of Heaven. Many people have said that it's the most beautiful building in all of China."

The two envoys could hardly believe what Zhu Di was now telling them!

"I can't imagine how it could be more beautiful than this magnificent structure," the junior envoy stammered, "but, if people say that it is more beautiful, I'm quite sure that it must be!"

Just as Zhu Di turned to lead the envoys out of the Hall of Supreme Harmony, General Tan approached and offered the emperor a quick bow.

"I'm sorry to disturb you, Sire, but something has come up which I think you should know."

Zhu Di hated to be interrupted by his trusted General. He knew from experienced that whenever General Tan asked for an urgent meeting it was never to give him good news.

Turning to his two Korean guests, Zhu Di begged their forgiveness.

"Will you gentlemen please excuse me? I'll just be a minute."

The two foreign guests offered Zhu Di a gracious bow as he retreated a short distance away to confer with General Tan in private.

"What's so important General Tan that you had to interrupt my tour?"

"I've just received word of another excursion against our northern frontier, Your Majesty. I don't believe the threat is serious but the invader has slipped past our defenses and is approaching Beijing. If we're going to respond, I suggest that we do so immediately."

"How did they get past the Wall?"

"I'm not sure, Sire. They might have overpowered an area that was lightly defended, or possibly a portion that was under repair. In any case, I suggest we deal with them quickly before they have time to grow stronger or resupply."

"Are you sure the invading force is small?"

"My scouts have reported the enemy has no more than three thousand men."

"What about horses and armaments?"

"Maybe five hundred horses," Tan responded, always amazed at how quickly Zhu Di's mind could turn from domestic to military matters. "As far as we can tell, Sire, they have no cannons, only bows and arrows and spears! They're definitely a small group. A little crazy if you ask me!"

"Why do they keep coming?" Zhu Di asked mostly to himself. "Don't they know they can never win?"

He then turned and waved to Concubine Quan who was talking casually with the two Korean envoys. When she saw the emperor motioning in her direction, she wasn't sure if he was motioning to her, or to his guests. When he waved again and pointed vigorously at her, she hurried over to the emperor and bowed sheepishly.

"You wished to see me, Your Majesty?" still not sure the emperor really wanted to talk to her.

"Yes!" Zhu Di responded happily. "How would you like to join me on a little excursion?"

The young woman couldn't believe what Zhu Di was asking.

"You mean, join you in battle, Sire?"

Zhu Di laughed.

"I guess you could call it a battle, but General Tan has assured me it will be a very small battle! It's what I usually refer to as a pesky excursion. Isn't that right, General Tan?"

"There should be very little danger, Honorable Concubine," General Tan confirmed, trying to help Zhu Di convince the young woman there was little to fear.

"Well," Quan responded, not wanting to disappoint Zhu Di, "if you really want me to go, I, ahhh, would be delighted!"

"Good!" Zhu Di responded happily. "It's settled! General Tan, assemble the troops. As soon as they're ready Concubine Quan and I shall make ourselves available."

When General Tan bowed and turned to go, Zhu Di unexpectedly stopped him and told him to wait. He then asked his young concubine to rejoin the two waiting envoys.

"Tell them I'll be along shortly. I'd like to ask the general about another matter. I won't be long."

When Concubine Quan bowed and took her leave, Zhu Di again turned his attention back to Tan.

"Were you able to meet with my son in prison?" he asked, obviously worried. "I'm anxious to learn if, ahhh, the encounter was satisfactory."

General Tan had been afraid Zhu Di would ask him something about his son and wasn't sure what he should say if he did ask. But, deciding to take the easy way out he stole a chapter from Zheng He's book and slightly fabricated the truth.

"I'm happy to report, Your Majesty," he began as he forced a very big smile, "that Prince Han is seriously reassessing his views. I'm quite certain that he'll be ready to express them to you in three or four weeks."

Zhu Di could hardly believe what General Tan was telling him! His answer was much more positive than he had expected.

"Why, that's wonderful news General Tan!" he gasped. "Just wonderful! Just as soon as we get rid of this pesky invader, you and I and Lord Zheng He will visit my son in prison. Hopefully everything will be resolved satisfactorily. And thank you again for bringing me such optimistic news!"

"Think nothing of it, Sire," Tan replied generously, suddenly feeling more confident. "The meeting we had with your son was…how can I say this…extremely persuasive."

At that point, Zhu Di grabbed the general's hand and started shaking it enthusiastically.

"I'll never be able to thank you and Lord Zheng He enough!" he allowed, as he continued to shake the general's hand vigorously.

"Actually," Tan added sheepishly, "Friar Odoric also went with us and turned out to be extremely helpful!"

"He was?" Zhu Di boomed. "That's wonderful! I've always said that for a foreigner, Friar Odoric is a very clever fellow!"


Less than one week later Zhu Di and Concubine Quan were sixty li north of Beijing, in the emperor's command tent listening to General Tan conduct a military briefing. A large map had been set up on an easel in front of the imperial officers and Tan busily pointed out areas to them that he knew would be important. Also in attendance were six of Zhu Di's most trusted field commanders. Zheng He had not been asked to participate in the small skirmish, because Zhu Di wanted him to concentrate on getting the second Ming expedition ready on time. The officers who were present stood behind Zhu Di and his concubine as General Tan spoke.

"We have five thousand men placed in positions at our front and on both flanks," General Tan stated firmly, "plus two thousand men here, guarding our position to the rear."

"General Tan! Would you please show me where the enemy positions are located," Zhu Di asked, mainly for the benefit of his Korean concubine.

"They're located here, Sire, in this wooded area."

"And their numbers?" Zhu Di demanded, before having to turn away and cough.

General Tan waited for the emperor to finish coughing and turn back to him before responding. "Two thousand, Your Magesty! Most, I can assure you, are lightly armed."

Zhu Di beamed.

"Did you hear that, Concubine Quan? General Tan said that the enemy is lightly armed. Didn't I tell you they would be no match for our imperial forces?"

The imperial officers in attendance hoped General Tan's assessment was correct. They looked at each other, but said nothing.

Zhu Di was embarrassed when he had to again turn away and cough. But none of the officers present acted as if they noticed. Just as the emperor turned back to the map, the sound of thunder rolled ominously in the distance.

"Sounds like we might be in for some bad weather," Zhu Di suggested to everyone present. "General Tan! Make sure the men have their tents tied down safely. We don't want to have anyone injured before the battle even begins!"

"I'll see to it right away, Sire," Tan replied quickly, then he and several of the officers left to make certain the emperor's request was acted on immediately.


That night the area was hit by a violent storm. A cold rain pelted the imperial encampment mercilessly which put a nasty chill in the air. Unfortunately the weather caused the emperor's cough to grow worse. Zhu Di was awake almost the entire night coughing, as he drank large quantities of hot green tea and hoped it would free the congestion in his chest. Unfortunately, whatever he did, nothing seemed to help!

Concubine Quan lay quietly beside the emperor in his bed and listened to struggle to breathe.

"Can I get you something?" she whispered, after a particularly violent fit of coughing wracked him from head to toe. "Maybe some more hot tea?"

Zhu Di waved her offer away as he tried to catch his breath. "I've been drinking tea all night," he gasped. "It doesn't seem to do any good!"

"Maybe I should summon a physician, Sire. He might be able to help."

After yet another retched spell of hacking and gasping for breath, Zhu Di relented. "You might be right," he gasped. "My chest hurts and my throat feels like it's on fire!"

Zhu Di tried to fluff the pillow under his head for the thousandth time, but it did little good.

"I hate to get anyone up on a night like this," he allowed hoarsely, "but I've got to try and get some relief. Do you think you could fetch the doctor for me?"

Concubine Quan immediately got up, pulled on a robe, then sat down on the edge of the bed next to Zhu Di. She leaned over and gave him a kiss on his forehead.

"I'll be right back, Your Majesty. There's more tea beside the bed if you need it."

Zhu Di reached up and touched the young Concubine on the cheek.

"I shouldn't ask you to go out on a night like this," he whispered.

Concubine Quan leaned down and kissed Zhu Di on the forehead again.

"I won't be long! Try and get some rest."

The young woman silently moved to the flap of the tent, slipped the robe's hood over her head and stepped outside.

Two soldiers standing guard just outside the imperial tent were partially protected from the wind and rain by a large cloth overhang which extended forward some ten feet. This waterproof covering was held up by four sturdy poles and held tight by strands of thick rope. A glass lantern hung on one of the poles and provided light for the two guards.

An incense stick burned off to one side and let the soldiers know when their watch would be completed. On this particular foul night both guards knew the two relief guards couldn't come soon enough.

Quan asked the guard closest to her which way she should go to reach the physician's tent? When he pointed out the way, she pulled the hood tightly about her head and instinctively ducked before stepping out into the nasty storm.

Quan moved as quickly as she could down the long row of tents which were continuly being buffeted violently by the blowing wind and rain. The guard had told her to go down fifteen lanterns before turning into the physicians tent. As Concubine Quen hurried on her way, she concentrated on counting the lanterns which hung on each tent post, but in the darkness and blowing rain it wasn't easy.

At first she tried to dodge the giant puddles that covered the ground, but soon found there were just too many to keep her feet from getting wet. After her feet did get wet she gave up on the impossible task and decided that she had better concentrate on locating the tent where she would find the physician.

When lightening struck exceptionally close, which was followed almost instantly by a horrendous crash of thunder, Quan instinctively froze, offered a short prayer that she was still alive, then ducked under the overhang of the closest tent.

"I'm trying to find the tent of Zhu Di's physician," she told the soldier who was standing guard. "Can you please tell me where it's located?"

The guard was most happy to assist.

"It's not far, Madam Concubine. Just follow that line of tents over there to those two lanterns in the distance. That's where you'll find him."

Concubine Quan bowed to the friendly soldier before tugging the hood tightly over her head once again then, after looking both ways, ducked and hurried off in the direction of the two lanterns in the distance.

She did her best to follow the row of tents the guard had suggested, but in the increasing wind and rain, Quan lost sight of the two lanterns she was supposed to find. When she paused for a moment to get her bearings, an enemy soldier appeared from out of nowhere, grabbed her from behind, jerked her head back and violently drew a dagger across her throat. The mortally wounded concubine silently dropped to the ground as the lone assassin disappeared into the night without making a sound.

When Zhu Di learned of Concubine Quan's death he ordered General Tan to take him back to Forbidden City at once! He was physically sick with a bad cold and cough but he was also terribly despondent over the loss of the young concubine with whom he had become quite attached.

As soon as he arrived back in Beijing he called for his wife, Empress Xu, and asked her to please join him in his private quarters. She was shocked that her husband was back in the city so soon, but delighted that he had asked her to join him for the evening.

When she arrived at his private quarters, she found him terribly morose and staring blankly off into space. Without even looking at his wife or saying hello, he started telling her about the death of his Korean concubine.

Empress Xu gasped when she heard the news. She wasn't particularly fond of Zhu Di's female companions, but certainly didn't wish for anything so tragic to happen to any of them, especially a woman so young as Concubine Quan. She was very glad to have her husband back, even though with his sickness he was beginning to look almost frail.

"Do you think I'm a bad person?" Zhu Di asked his wife softly, surprising her that he sounded so dispondent.

She thought it was an odd question, but what worried her most was the sound of his voice which sounded to her very hoarse and weak.

"Why would you say such a thing?" she responded evenly, not wanting Zhu Di to know that she might be worried about his health. "Of course you're not a bad person!"

Silently she took a seat next to her husband and held his hand. He still didn't look at her, choosing instead to continue his blank stare at nothing.

"I must be doing something wrong!" he lamented to her glumly, as he slowly shook his head from side to side. "Whatever I try to do, Empress, it always seems to fail."

"Quit tormenting yourself!" she scolded gently. "It wasn't your fault the young girl was killed."

"It WAS' my fault, empress!" he lamented sternly, while finally turning to face his wife. "If I hadn't invited her to go with me to the battle she never would have been killed! It was wrong for me to invite her. It was clearly wrong. Now Lord Buddha is punishing me."

Zhu Di began to cough again, harshly this time, over and over, as it tormented his body with a physical malady from which there seemed to be no escape. When Empress Xu heard the ominous-sounding rattle in his chest, she began to worry even more about his deteriorating health.

"You're not being punished, Zhu Di," she argued softly, trying to think of something positive to say. "You're just upset and you're sick! In a few weeks you'll feel much better."

Her unrealistic-sounding explanation caused him to quickly become angry.

"In a few weeks, my dear empress," he growled hoarsly, "Concubine Quan won't return to me from the dead! In a few weeks, my ministers and civil servants won't suddenly decide to support my policies!"

"Stop it!" she demanded, knowing full-well that if he continued his outburst it would only spiral downward into more recriminations of self pity. "I will not allow you to blame yourself for unfortunate circumstances."

"Unfortunate circumstances?" he shouted, even louder this time, his voice becoming stronger the madder he got. "You believe the things that are happening to me are just unfortunate circumstances? What about our son, empress? The boy's life hangs by a thread! Is that just an unfortunate circumstance?"

Things were quickly getting out of hand. She knew she had to try and calm her husband down and fast.

"Zhu Di, please, I didn't mean to imply..."

He cut her off.

"I invited you to my private quarters, empress, hoping, that of all people, you, my wife, would provide me with a little kindness and understanding."

"Zhu Di," she begged, "I don't want..."

He waved his hand, again cutting her off.

"But what do I get? As usual, I get arguments and excuses! I don't need to have you around, empress!" he hissed strongly, "and I don't want to have you around! Do you understand me, empress? I want you to get out, NOW!"

When his wife did not move, Zhu Di jumped up and yelled in her face.

"Do you hear me, empress? I want you to get out of my sight, NOW! Leave me to my own devices. I shall find a way, as I always have, alone!"

Because of the excitement and exertion, Zhu Di started coughing again but this time he couldn't stop. All he could do was stagger over to a nearby chair and collapse into it. He then turned away from his wife and waited for her to obey his command.

But Zhu Di's unreasonable outburst had made Empress Xu furious as well. She stood her ground and shouted back at her debilitated husband!

"I will NOT allow you to talk to me that way! Do you understand me? You will..."

She suddenly stopped when she saw her husband turn towards her, livid with rage. Zhu Di screamed at his wife and shook his fist in her direction!

"Get out of my sight, woman! NOW! I want you to LEAVE ME ALONE!"

His body was again racked by another series of violent coughs which, as before, he could not control.  Barely able to catch his breath, all he could do was feebly wave her away.

"Get out!" he gasped again, weakly this time, hardly able to breath. "Please...get out!"

Empress Xu burst into tears and ran from the room, upset over the way her husband continued to treat her, but also distraught over the fact that his health was obviously bad and getting worse!


Empress Xu then did something she had never done before.  She went to visit Honorable Lady Xi Chen.  In more normal times she would never have humbled herself by going to the apartment of a servant.  But these were not normal times!

When Xi Chen answered the knock at her door she was equally shocked to see Empress Xu standing there in front of her.  She looked despondent and obviously upset.  Two lady attendants waited at a discrete distance.

"Madam Empress?" Xi Chen gasped, "Is that you?"  When she realized it was the empress who stood before her she quickly bowed respectfully. Empress Xu was in no mood to worry about protocol.

"May I come in?" she asked.

"Yes, of course!" the Honorable Lady replied, quickly stepped aside and offered the woman a seat in her best chair. She knew the servants attending the empress would remain outside, so she softly closed the door, then, embarrassed, began to apologize for her meager apartment.

Empress Xu abruptly interrupted.

"Xi Chen, I'm sorry that I've bargd in on you like this, but I must ask a favor."

Now Xi Chen was more shocked than ever!  No member of the imperial family had ever come to her apartment before and asked for a favor.

"No apology is needed, Madam Empress," she responded, humbly. "You know that I'll do anything I can to be of service."

The empress slipped a silken handlerchief from the fold of one sleeve, dabbed at her eyes for a moment, then continued.

"I've just come...from a visit with my husband." she confided haltingly.

"The emperor has returned?" Xi Chen interrupted, surprised to hear that he was already back from the battle.  "Is anything wrong, Your Magesty?  I mean...I didn't think the emperor was supposed to return for another two or three weeks?"

"Listen, please!" Empress Xu interrupted again, not wanting to waste time talking about the battle. "Zhu Di is not injured, Xi Chen, but he is sick. He is very sick and he is very despondent. I've never worried about him dying before, but now…"

Empress Xu started crying again.

Xi Chen didn't know what she should do. She wanted to do something, so, instinctively, she reached out and touched the older woman on the arm and tried to offer her comfort.

"Is there something you'd like for me to do, Madam Empress?" she asked. "You know I'd do anything I could to be of service."

When Empress Xu finally got hold of herself, she looked sadly into Xi Chen's eyes and for the first time, Xi Chen could see how really worried she was.

"I'm afraid for Zhu Di's life, Xi Chen," she sobbed, starting to cry again. "He won't talk to me, but he might talk to you. Will you go to him? He's so very despondent over the loss of that Korean girl."

Again Xi Chen was shocked!

"Concubine Quan?" she gasped. "Has something happened to Concubine Quan?"

"Didn't I tell you?" Xu countered she dabbed at her eyes. "She was killed in Zhu Di's camp before the battle started! That's why Zhu Di came back so soon!"

"I had no idea, Madam Empress," Xi Chen whispered, almost to herself, stunned when she heard the unexpected news. "Concubine Quan was such a..."

She stopped in mid-sentence and decided that under the circumstances it was probably best if she said nothing.

"Surely the emperor will talk to you, Madam Empress?" Xi Chen suggested instead. "Surely..."

Empress Xu cut her off.

"I tried to talk to him, Xi Chen, but all we do is fight! You're the only person I can think of beside Lord Zheng He whom he might listen to. Go to him. Please! He needs someone,now that he's sick, to help nurse him back to health."


When Xi Chen arrived at Zhu Di's quarters she found him lying on his bed. His eyes were closed and his breathing was hard and uneven. He seemed to be sleeping, or at least he was trying to sleep. When she looked closely at his features, his Honorable Lady was surprised to find that he did look older and much more tired, just as the empress had suggested. She wasn't sure if she should quietly leave the room, or let him know that she had stopped by as the empress had wanted. Deciding that she should try to do something, she cautiously whispered softly.

"May I be of service, Your Majesty?"

There was no answer from the prostrate ruler. Not knowing what to do, she found a pot of tea on a table close by, felt to see that it was still warm, then placed it quietly on a table beside his bed and turned to go. But then, just as she was about to leave, Zhu Di whispered to her in a weak voice.

"Don't go!"

Xi Chen turned back to the emperor's bed and saw that his eyes were still closed. She then pulled a chair over by his bedside and took a seat.

"Is there, anything I can get for you, Your Majesty?" she asked softly.

Zhu Di opened his eyes and looked fondly at his Honorable Lady.

"Not really," he told her, weakly, while having to stifle another cough. "I'd just like for you to sit beside me for awhile and keep me company."

Xi Chen picked up one of Zhu Di's hands and kissed it tenderly.

"As you wish, Your Majesty."

When Zhu Di spoke she was surprised at how feeble his voice sounded.

"You and I were once very close," he whispered, barely loud enough for her to hear. Then he had to cough again.

She quickly filled a cup with the warm tea and offered it to the wheezing emperor. In between coughs, he managed to take a few quick sips, then fell back onto his pillow, and gasped for breath. His face looked almost grey.

Xi Chen had never seen Zhy Di when he looked as bad before, so she clearly understood why Empress Xu was so worried.

"Do you remember the first time we made love?" Zhu Di gasped, surprising Xi Chen with his unexpected question.

"I remember, Your Majesty," she countered with a smile. "I also remember that I was very frightened."

"Yes, I suppose you were. I was a little apprehensive myself."

When Xi Chen glanced back at Zhu Di, she could now see that his eyes were closed again, but this time there was a slight smile on his lips. He lay still for a moment and thought about their sweet encounter that happened long ago. Then, after he had to caugh a few more times, he reopened his eyes and once again looked at his Honorable Lady.

"I wish life were as simple as making love," he confessed, as a thin smile creased the corner of his lips. "...especially making love when you're young! Do you remember..."

Zhu Di was suddenly racked by several more violent coughs and was forced to cut short his sentence. When he was finally able to catch his breath, he tried to continued.

"Do you remember," he wheezed, "the first time...you started to experiment with love?"

Xi Chen was embarrassed at the emperor's personal question. She hesitated, then responded tentatively.

"I guess I do, Your Majesty. I know I shouldn't tell you this, but it was with your servant, Lord Zheng He."

Zhu Di smiled.

"I always knew Zheng He was a very lucky fellow!"

The emperor forced back another cough while he thought of what Xi Chen had just told him.

Xi Chen didn't want to talk about Zheng He, so changed the subject and asked Zhu Di about he and his wife.

"And what about you, Your Majesty? Surely you must have fond memories with the empress."

Zhu Di smiled again.

"I do, Xi Chen, especially when we were young. But that was a long time ago. Unfortunately, a lot has changed between us since then!"

"Then tell me about the happy times!" she urged. "Tell me about the two of you, when you were both young and in love. That's what I want to hear about!"

Zhu Di knew he shouldn't be talking about such things, especially to a servant, but after he stifled another cough he lay still for a moment and then tried to remember the time when he courted his wife before they were married. Xi Chen watched Zhu Di's face closely and noticed that it visably softened as he began to think about those more pleasant memories of so long ago.

"She was beautiful back then," he confided. "Actually, she was very beautiful. And I remember that I did love her. A lot of times we would sneak off together and do some things that we shouldn't have been doing."

Xi Chen pretended to be shocked.

"You and the empress, Your Majesty? That's shameful! I can't believe that you ever did such a thing."

"Didn't you?" he countered, smiling. "You can't tell me that you and Zheng He didn't sneak around once in a while!"

Xi Chen blushed.

"Well, maybe we wanted to a few times, Your Majesty, but we were talking about you and the empress. I want to hear what the two of <u>you</u> did!"

Zhu Di once again lay back on his pillow and smiled.

"Well, one thing we used to do," he admitted, the smile still dancing on his lips, "was go off and hide."

"Hide, Your Majesty?" Xi Chen interrupted, again surprised at what Zhu Di had just told her.

"Yes, hide! What's wrong with that? We used to sneak off so we could be alone and, you know, fool around. It used to drive the servants and court officials crazy."

Zhu Di was suddenly stuck by another series of violent coughs and had to stop reminiscing about courting his wife. Xi Chen quickly grabbed the pot of tea and filled his cup, but he waved her away and waited for the excruciating episode to subside. Then, when he was finally able to regain his composure, he tried to continue.

"I hate it," he gasped, "when I can't stop coughing. It hurts my chest terribly and it's embarrassing! Now, where was I?"

"You were telling me about when you and the empress used to go off and hide and the court officials couldn't find you."

"Oh, yes, that's right. They'd look all over the palace, trying to find out where we were hiding and what we were doing!"

"I thought Zheng He and I were bad," Xi Chen joked, while grinning at Zhu Di, "but it sounds to me like you and the empress were worse!"

"I guess we were!" Zhu Di laughed, which caused his lungs to hurt. "Poor Minister Wong was in charge of my upbringing. Whenever the empress and I disappeared, he had to come up with an excuse so my father wouldn't find out what was going on!"

"But what happened, Your Majesty?" Xi Chen asked, honestly wanting to know why things between them seemed to now be different. "I mean, it sounds to me that you and the empress used to have a wonderful time together. I mean no disrespect, Sire, but what caused things to, ahhh, change?"

Zhu Di lay still for a few moments and thought about what he should tell Xi Chen.

"We grew up and got married, Xi Chen! That's the sad truth. I'm sure there was much more to it than that, but as far as I'm concerned, that's what happened plain and simple."

"You got married?" Xi Chen blurted out, astonished at what Zhu Di had just tole her. "Getting married should make things better between two people, not worse!"

"It was for a while," he allowed, letting out a loud sigh, "until my father shipped me off to Beijing and made me king of the Northern Province!"

"I don't understand. You were a young king with a beautiful new wife and things were bad for you? I'm sorry, Your Majesty, I just don't understand. That doesn't sound like a bad combination to me!"

"It wasn't at first," Zhu Di agreed, as he reflected back on those earlier years. "The empress and I did have many happy times together. But then, when my father made me king he thought that I should have more servants. As you might imagine many of these servants were beautiful young ladies whose sole function was to cater to my every whim."

Xi Chen began to frown.

"I think I'm beginning to get the picture."

"As a young king," Zhu Di continued, "it was easy for me to succumb to a wide variety of selfish pleasures. Little by little my wife, who by now had grown into an older woman, became less and less attractive and unfortunately, less important to me."

Without warning Zhu Di was suddenly struck by another fit of non-stop coughing. The terrible rattle in his chest was unmistakable. When Xi Chen was finally able to put a cup of tea to his lips, he took a few sips, handed the cup back to her, then, completely out of breath, fell back onto his pillows exhausted.

"We...no longer did things together," he gasped, "like we did...when we were young."

Zhu Di had to stop to catch his breath.

"She became jealous...of the time I was spending...with my younger ladies," he wheezed. "More and more...things got worse...between us."

Xi Chen poured more tea into the emperor's cup, while he continued to explain about his early relationship with the empress.

"The more time I spent...with my lady servants and concubines," he gasped, "the less time I spent...with my wife. It was a...vicious circle, which...I now realize...caused my wife a lot of pain and heartache."

"But the two of you had children together!" Xi Chen suggested, trying to add something positive. "You must have had some sort of relationship?"

"We had...two children," Zhu Di allowed, beginning to breathe a little better, "the prince and the crown prince. But...other than that, there was little for us to talk about, or...that we had in common."

Zhu Di coughed again. Xi Chen tried to hand him a freshly poured cup of tea, but again he waved it away. There was no mistaking the fact that his mood was again beginning to turn morose.

"I was very selfish in...my youth," he mumbled hoarsly, so low that Xi Chen could hardly hear what he was saying, "and now...I'm beginning to realize that I'm just as selfish...in my old age."

"You're not selfish," Xi Chen tried to argue. "I wish you wouldn't say that! And you're not old!"

Zhu Di wouldn't listen.

"I am selfish!" he disagreed, forcefully, "and I'm a selfish...old man. I'm overbearing...and I know it!"

Xi Chen took his cup and put it down on the table beside his bed.

"I think you're being much too hard on yourself," she told him firmly.

"Too hard?" he countered, even more firmly. "Just this afternoon...I had another fight with my wife...and threw her out of my apartment. I don't even remember…what it was about. But I know one thing…I'm an overbearing fool, and a selfish old man!"

Xi Chen tried to calm Zhu Di down so he wouldn't start coughing again.

"You were just upset, Your Majesty, because of losing Concubine Quan! Anyone would be! It's a very normal reaction."

Zhu Di visibly softened for a moment, then stifled another cough.

"Maybe you're right," he relented, laying still for a few moments, his chest heaving up and down while he tried to catch his breath. Xi Chen sat quietly and waited for Zhu Di to tell her what else was on his mind.

"Now that I'm coming…to the end of my life," he stated firmly, as he struggled to catch his breath, "I'm going to change…the way I do things."

Xi Chen was again shocked by Zhu Di's unexpected comment.

"What are you talking about, Your Majesty?" she scolded. "You're not coming to the end of your life! Please don't talk like that! You're still a young man! You still have many years of great things to accomplish!"

Zhu Di looked into his Honorable Lady's eyes and offered her a tolerant smile, but his mood remained serious.

"I may have a few…years left," he wheezed, "but…I definitely do not have…many! And…if I don't find a way…to get rid of this damnable cough," he tried to joke, "I may not have…much time left…at all!"

Now it was Xi Chen who became serious.

"Please don't talk to me about dying, Your Majesty. I can't bear to even think about such a thing. All you need is green tea and it will make you as good as new!"

Zhu Di knew better.

"If I have any more green tea… my dear, I'll…float out of the palace! Ggreen tea…is not the answer…but doing something…about changing my life…is!"

"What do you mean by that?"

"From this day forward…Xi Chen…I'm going to…make a concerted effort…to have more compassion for people. I'm…also going to try…to make peace with my wife and my…number two son!"

Xi Chen watched as Zhu Di pushed himself up onto one elbow so he could more easily talk to her, but had to stifle yet another pesky cough before he could begin.

"Look!" he wheezed, while reaching out and taking hold of one of her hands. "I've made…a lot of mistakes…in my life, and now…I see you and Zheng He…beginning to make…some of the same mistakes…my wife and I made. Don't allow yourselves…to grow apart, Xi Chen. Will you…listen to me? You'll regret it…"

Zhu Di had to stop.

Xi Chen didn't want to hear what he had jut told her!

"But, Your Majesty," she argued, "I've told you how I feel about Zheng He. He has changed. He has changed a lot!  It's not the same between us..."

Zhu Di cut her off.

"Nothing in life is easy... my dear, and...I'm sorry...that I contributed to your problem.  But that was...when I was foolish...and selfish. From now on... I'm going to change...and I want you to change...as well!  I want you...to look after Zheng He. Will you...do that for me, Xi Chen? Promise me...you will."

Xi Chen turned away from Zhu Di and started to cry. She didn't want to cry, not now in front of the emperor, but she couldn't help it. Zhu Di tried to take a cup of tea from off the table and give it to her, but another series of violent coughs hit him and he had to set the cup back down before it spilled.  When his coughing finally passed, he dropped back onto his pillows and in a hoarse voice admonished his lady servant again.

"Remember what I said, Xi Chen," he gasped.  "I want you...to promise me...that you'll always look after Zheng He!"

Unable to control herself any longer, Xi Chen sobbed loudly and ran from the emperor's bed chamber in tears.  In Zhu Di's incapacitated state, all he could do was watch her go.  Sadly, he shook his head and whispered one word. "Women!"


The next day Xi Chen sent word to Zheng He that she wanted to meet with him in the garden.  When he eagerly arrived at the appointed place, he found her sitting on a marble bench that was located under a large weeping willow.  The Ming admiral was surprised to find she was already there and he was also surprised that she didn't look particularly cheerful.

Xi Chen motioned for Zheng He to take a seat beside her on the bench.

"I had a long talk with the emperor last night," she started, as she got right to the point and didn't want to waste time with pleasantries. "He doesn't look well, Zheng He. He doesn't look well at all. I'm terribly worried about him."

"Does he still have that cough?" the admiral asked, as he tried to keep their conversation light, but he already knew what her answer was probably going to be.

"It's worse than ever!" she confessed. "I hate to say this, but I'm afraid he won't ever get well."

"You can't mean that," Zheng He scolded. "Isn't he drinking his green tea?  I've heard the physicians say that green tea can cure anything."

"The green tea isn't doing any good and it won't do any good," Xi Chen responded testily. "You know that! Zhu Di's sick, Zheng He! I'm afraid he's really sick!"

Zheng He got up to stretch his legs, as he tried to think of something positive that he could suggest.

"What he probably needs more than anything else," he offered as he turned to face Xi Chen, "is some good news! I heard he was pretty smitten with that young Korean girl."

Xi Chen didn't want to discuss the Korean girl, but did agree that good news might very well be a big help.

"What about his son?" she asked tentatively. "When you talked to him in prison, was he cooperative?"

Zheng He wasn't sure how he should answer.

"Let's just say, he might be cooperative in the near future. The young prince is not an easy person to deal with."

"But something has got to be done," she pleaded. "When is Zhu Di supposed to visit his son?"

"About now," the admiral acknowledged, unhappy about the prospects of having to make another visit to the prison and clearly unhappy that Xi Chen seemed to be so extraordinarily worried about Zhu Di.

"Then set it up!" she demanded. "If the prince will apologize to his father, I think it will bouy his spirits. We've got to do something!"

Zheng He again sat down next to Xi Chen and looked her in the eyes. He didn't want to be pushed into going back to the prison, mainly because he wasn't optimistic about Prince Han being cooperative.

"What else did you and the emperor talk about, Xi Chen? Did he say anything about the new expedition to Arabia?"

Xi Chen didn't want to talk about expeditions. She shook her head "no", but then, surprisingly, added, "he mainly talked about his wife."

"The empress?" Zheng He asked, shocked at Xi Chen's unexpected revelation.

Xi Chen didn't want to waste time talking about the empress, either.

"Zheng He!" she pleaded, again becoming exasperated. "I want you to get the emperor to visit his son. It's the only thing I can think of that might help him improve his spirits! Will you do that for me? Please?"

The admiral wanted to help the emperor, but he was definitely worried about Xi Chen's motivation. Her concern, he was afraid, went much deeper than just platonic friendship between an emperor and his servant.

"I'll see if I can get General Tan to go with us," he allowed grudgingly as he got to his feet. "If I take the general along he might find a way to be persuasive!"

"What's that supposed to mean?" Xi Chen asked, curious as to why Zheng He had emphasized the word persuasive.

"Nothing!" he hedged, offering a slight grin. "But you'll do well to pray Xi Chen. Getting Prince Han to apologize for anything isn't going to be easy!"


Two days later I found myself following Zheng He, General Tan and Emperor Zhu Di into the imperial prison. None of us spoke as we dutifully followed the jail guard down the long stone corridor towards Prince Han's cell. As usual, the stench was almost unberable, but Emperor Zhu Di kept quiet and pretended not to notice.

Just as we arrived at the young man's cell I noticed that Zhu Di had to stiffle several coughs, while waiting for the guard to unlock the heavy wooden door. When the hinged structure was pulled back, Zhu Di cleared his throat and stepped inside.

Surprisingly, the prince got to his feet as soon as he saw his father enter. Apprehensively, Zheng He, General Tan and I followed the emperor inside. When Zhu Di saw his son for the first time and the condition of the cell in which he had been living, he was clearly shocked. Han had lost a lot of weight and was filthy from head to toe. The smell in the small enclosure had not improved, but if Zhu Di noticed he didn't let us know.

A large rat suddenly scampered across the floor almost at Zhu Di's feet. While the emperor's attention was momentarily diverted by the rodent, General Tan motioned sharply for Han to get on his knees. Immediately, the young prince dropped to the floor and kowtowed to his father in a dramatic expression of capitulated deference.

Zhu Di was not only surprised, he was shocked by his rebellious son's unexpected demonstration. He turned and gave Zheng He and General Tan a small nod, obviously quite pleased with his son's new show of respect. Without saying a word, he reached down and lifted the young man to his feet.

Han kept his eyes on the stone floor, in a submissive gesture, as he spoke to his imperial progenitor.


"I have shamed you, father," he began, trying his best to sound sincere. "Will you ever find it in your heart to forgive me?"

Zhu Di's face revealed nothing. He motioned for his son to step aside, so he could make a short inspection of the filthy enclosure.

Zheng He, General Tan, nor I, didn't move. We kept our eyes glued on Han, as the emperor casually inspected his son's filthy mattress with one foot and then uneasily looked into the cell's cesspool gutter at the rear.

I noticed that Han continued to watch his father closely, as he searched for any sign of weakness. When he noticed his father had to cough, hoarsely, several times during his brief inspection, the young prince cut his eyes towards us hoping Zheng He or General Tan would offer some explanation. But each maintained a stoic silence and offered the prince nothing.

When Zhu Di finished inspecting Han's small hellhole he repositioned himself back in front of his, seemingly, repentant son.

"Lord Buddha teaches," he began slowly, "that one must have compassion for others. But what you have done, my son, makes it very difficult for me to have compassion for you."

Prince Han again hung his head and pretended to be completely remorsefull, then, he slowly lifted his head and looked into his father's eyes, almost as if he'd practiced the maneuver several times, which I'm quite sure he had. Han then spoke to his father in an even, sincere, tone, as his voice dripped with emotion.

"While I've been in prison, father," he began, almost in a whisper, "I've had a chance to think about all the terrible things that I've said and done, which I'm sure have caused you great harm. I now see clearly just how foolish and selfish I have been."

I watched Zheng He and General Tan as Prince Han was making his speech. They couldn't believe what they were hearing. Each looked at the other in amazement, but pleased at the seeming transformation of Zhu Di's number two son. They remained silent.

"I wish to follow in your footsteps, father" Han continued, somberly. "I wish to do whatever I can to continue all of your grand policies..."

While Han was speaking, he glanced over his father's shoulder to see if General Tan approved of what he was saying. Almost imperceptibly Tan nodded his endorsement. Without skipping a beat, Han continued.

"...so that our country will remain strong and the accomplishments of its benevolent emperor will be known and respected throughout the world."

Zhu Di turned to his two friends and smiled, obviously pleased at what his son was saying. But then, without warning, Zhu Di was once again gripped by a series of violent, uncontrollable, coughs. When he was finally able to catch his breath, he laid his hand on his son's meatless shoulder and spoke to him from his heart.

"I pray, Prince Han," he began, willing himself not to cough, "that what you've told me...is true. If I grant you your release...I will expect you to work in support...of all my policies. Do you understand me?"

Another cough caught in Zhu Di's throat, ever so slightly. He hoped that his son wouldn't notice. He then continued.

"I will expect you...to demonstrate to all the people...that as a member of the imperial family...we stand together! Do you swear, before Allah, that you will do this my son?"

"Oh, yes, father!" Prince Han sobbed, with tears streaming down his face, "I swear to you with all my heart, before our most revered, Lord Buddha!"

Now satisfied, Zhu Di stepped forward and gingerly placed his arms around his son, clearly wanting to demonstrate some token of affection, but also evidencing that because of Han's offensive odor he didn't wish to get too close! After an appropriate amount of time, the imperial ruler stepped back and turned to his senior officer.

"General Tan! I want you to arrange…for Prince Han's immediate release."

Again Prince Han kowtowed himself on the floor in a final humbling attempt to demonstrate his utmost respect.

With their mission successfully completed, Zhu Di, Zheng He, General Tan and I took our leave and gingerly closed the door.

Unfortunately, I found out later, that as soon as we left the cell, Han raised up onto both knees and spit boldly towards the now closed door.

"Bastard!" he hissed at his departing father, "Before I do anything for you, I'll see you rot in hell!"


One month later all the preparations had been completed for the second expedition and Zheng He was ready to make his official report to Zhu Di. The Ming admiral, his servant Ma Huan and I arrived at the emperor's quarters and waited to be announced.

"Are you sure we've got everything?" Zheng He asked Ma Huan for the tenth time.

His servant held up the large stack of books and documents that he held in his arms to prove that it was all there.

"I think we've got everything, Sir!" he responded wryly, knowing they'd been over this many times before.

"What about the maps?" the admiral asked as he quickly turned to me. "Friar, we didn't forget the maps, did we?"

"No, Zheng He!" I told him with a sigh. "I've brought along all our maps, plus Ma Huan has a complete list of the new routes we'll need, all the known information we could find on Arabia, plus more lists of ship cargoes, personnel and supplies. I think you'll find that we've got everything you'll need!"

"Zhu Di is such a stickler for details," Zheng He worried out loud, as he hoped to diffuse our obvious reluctance to ease his unnecessary nervousness. "I know from past experience that he doesn't miss a thing."

Ma Huan changed the subject and hoped that his master would calm down and quit worrying so much!

"How's the emperor's health?" he asked. "I've heard a lot of talk that he's been pretty sick."

"He has been sick," Zheng He acknowledged, "but I think he's doing a little better. I wouldn't say he's well yet, but I heard that getting his son back did him a lot of good."

Just then the door opened to Zhu Di's private quarters and a servant appeared.

"Please follow me, Lord Zheng He," he intoned. "Emperor Zhu Di is waiting to see you."

Zheng He, Ma Huan and I followed the middle-aged servant into a large reception area where Zhu Di often conducted informal meetings. When we arrived, Zheng He fully expected to greet the emperor, but he was completely shocked when he also saw Empress Xu and Xi Chen also standing there to greet him as well.

Empress Xu stood beside her husband with a big smile on her face. Xi Chen had taken a position a little off to one side, as if she was waiting to serve.

Admiral Zheng He walked up to the imperial couple and bowed graciously. Ma Huan and I also bowed, but remained a discrete distance behind.

"I'm prepared to make my report, Your Majesty," he stated formally, "on your proposed expedition to the country of Arabia. I'm sure you will find that everything is in order."

"There's no need for you to make your report," Zhu Di answered while offering his servant a big smile. "I'm quite certain that, as you say, everything is in order!" Zheng He was completely taken aback by the emperor's unexpected comment. He was certain that Zhu Di would want to go over every aspect of the proposed Ming voyage, as he had in the past. Hearing that he didn't want to review any of the details was, to say the least, a very curious turn of events.

Zheng He was further surprised when Zhu Di suddenly turned and motioned towards his Honorable Lady.

"Xi Chen?" he sang out happily, "would you please come forward and stand over here next to the empress and me? I wish to make an announcement."

Now it was Xi Chen who was caught off guard. She immediately looked at Zheng He, as if to say, "what's going on?" She was obviously just as surprised as he.

Honorable Lady Xi Chen then gave Zheng He a slight shrug of her shoulders and took her place beside the imperial couple as requested. After Xi Chen was at Zhu Di's side, the emperor cleared his throat, as he so often did before making an important speech, and began.

"Lord Zheng He!" he intoned solemnly, doing his best not to cough and his very best to make his speech sound official, "You have provided me with many years of loyal and faithful service…in the palace…on the battlefield…and recently…on the high seas as Admiral of my Ming fleet. As a gesture of my great appreciation, I wish to reward you with a gift."

Again Zheng He was shocked.

"A gift, Your Majesty?" he stammered. "It's my distinct pleassure to serve the crown. I assure you, Sire, a gift is not necessary."

"Nonsense!" Zhu Di gushed happily. "If I wish to reward you with a gift, then I shall!"

At this point, Zhu Di turned and gave his wife a sly grin. Surprisingly, she returned Zhu Di's expression with a satisfying grin of her own. Zhu Di continued.

"In a gesture of my great appreciation, I wish to offer you the services of…"

Zhu Di paused for effect, as he always loved to do. He looked first at Zheng He and then at his Honorable Lady before continuing.

"…my Honorable Lady, Xi Chen!"

"Your Majesty!" Zheng He gasped, as he started to disagree strongly. But Zhu Di quickly held up his hand to stop his expected protestations.

"It is my heartfelt desire," Zhu Di continued, "that my Honorable Lady accompany you on your expedition to Arabia and offer you personal services as your own Lady-in-Waiting."

Zheng He couldn't believe what he was hearing! He was stunned! He quickly glanced at Xi Chen to see her reaction, but to his great dismay and horror he found that she offered none.

"Your Majesty," he begged again, "I humbly appreciate your most generous offer, but there is simply no way I can accept! I mean no disrespect, Sire, but you're not in the best of health. What I mean to say is that, most assuredly, you will need the services of your Honorable Lady."

"I have more servants than I need," Zhu Di told him merrily. "Although I do appreciate your concern for my health, there's no need for you to worry. Empress Xu, I'm happy to report, will be taking care of me from now on."

When the empress heard what her husband said, she looked up at him and beamed proudly.

Xi Chen then bowed formally to Zheng He, as she was expected to do. Her words were correct, but they were in no way sincere.

"I shall serve you, Lord Zheng He, as I have always served my emperor." Once again, she gave the admiral a slight bow.

Zheng He was still in a state of shock! He looked at Zhu Di, then at the empress and then back to his new Lady-in-Waiting. The emperor and empress were smiling broadly, but still, Xi Chen was not!

Zheng He bowed again to Zhu Di.

"Your Majesty!" he gushed. "Words alone can never express how I feel at this moment. I'll never be able to repay the kindness that you've shown to me, your humble servant. As always, I will do my very best to bring honor and glory to your most revered name."

Both Zhu Di and Empress Xu offered a discrete bow to their much-loved and much-appreciated servant.

Zheng He was immediately torn between two very strong emotions. One was of unbridled joy that Xi Chen had been given to him as a gift by the emperor, and the other, a terrible sadness, from the realization and fear that the only woman he had ever loved didn't want to leave the services of the emperor.

While Zhu Di and Empress Xu were in the midst of their humbling bow, Xi Chen glanced at Zheng He and mouthed the word "bastard!" She then buried her face in her hands and ran from the room crying.

Chapter Ten

---

TWO SURPRISES

A physician finally came in to check on me. He changed my bandage and told me not to move around so much. I asked him about the bleeding? He said it had stopped. I guess that's good, but my chest still hurts. It wasn't a terrible sharp pain. It was more like a continuing ever-present throb.

While the physician was trying to patch me up, servants brought me another pot of hot tea which I greatly appreciated, since what I had left had gotten cold. It's funny how life seemed to revolve around tea. Especially hot tea. If you have plenty of the refreshing liquid the rest of life's problems don't seem so onerous.

I remember that it wasn't like that in Italy when I grew up and then first joined the church. But here in China hot tea seems to be almost akin to life itself.

How many hours had it been since I started writing? Eight hours? Ten? Maybe it had been ten days? It was hard for me to tell. What happened to the cannons? I couldn't hear them firing any more. I hope Zheng He made it out of the gorge. Do I have enough paper to finish? Ahh, yes, there it is. The servants must have brought me more because now I seem to have plenty. If I could just pour myself another cup of hot tea, I might begin to feel as good as new.

Where was I? Oh, yes, Zheng He was getting ready to leave on his second expedition, this time to Arabia and Zhu Di had given Xi Chen to him as his own Lady-in-Waiting. That was the most incredible thing for the emperor to do. Thinking about it now, I can still hardly believe that he did such a thing. But he did give Xi Chen to Zheng He and I must continue to write down just how it happened.

With another huge crowd cheering wildly, the Ming fleet sailed to the mouth of the mighty Yangtze and, as before, passed in review for the emperor and his distinguished guests. On the Imperial Reviewing Stand, once again, Zhu Di and Empress Xu smiled and waved happily as Zheng He's huge flagship majestically sailed past.

This time, however, there was less celebration on the flagship.

Zheng He and his new Lady-in-Waiting had hardly spoken to each other since the emperor made his unexpected announcement. They now stood together on the open deck of the Ceremonial Building penthouse and waved casually in the direction of the Imperial Reviewing Stand. It was plain to me that neither of them had much enthusiasm for the voyage upon which they were just starting out.

Along the shore, however, it was quite a different matter. As before, almost two hundred thousand people cheered wildly and happily threw firecrackers to help celebrate the fleet's grand departure.

This time, Prince Han and Zhu Bao Zhi stood together on the Reviewing Stand and each seemed that they wanted to outdo the other as they cheered and shouted enthusiastically. Both clapped and waved merrily to everyone they saw as the emperor's huge fleet of ships rode a soft breeze towards the mouth of the Yangtze.

Unfortunately, another bad coughing spell hit the emperor before half of the huge Ming vessels had made their grand departure past the Reviewing Stand. Zhu Di bravely waved away those offering to help, but then, when a second spate of coughing struck him violently he had no choice but to retreat from his place of honor and acquiesce to their wishes.

Empress Xu wasted no time in taking charge!

"Bring the carriage!" she demanded. "I want to take him back to Forbidden City at once!"

Dao Yan and General Tan were standing on the Reviewing Stand close by and clearly saw what was happening. They wished they could do something to help their friend, but under the circumstances, the empress was clearly in control so there was little they could do. Four servants grabbed Zhu Di by both arms and half-carried him into his waiting carriage.

When the Crown Prince, Zhu Bao Zhi, saw his father in such distress, he too wanted to help. But as he tried to go to his father, Han grabbed him by the sleeve and stopped him.

"Let him go, Han," he scolded, registering no emotion or concern whatsoever. "There's nothing you can do to help!"

By the evening of the first day the ships in the fleet had settled into a comfortable sailing formation about thirty li from the coast. As before, Zheng He's huge flagship was majestically leading the huge Ming armada towards its first destination; the country of Java.

Outwardly, everything seemed to be going smoothly on that first night at sea. All the soldiers and sailors who had participated in the first expedition were having a grand time teaching the new recruits what they should be doing to keep everything operating as it should.

In the admiral's third floor bedroom suite, however, things were not nearly so friendly, nor so harmonious. Zheng He stood alone at one of the large windows of his suite and silently watched as the last rays of the sun disappeared from view. When the sun sunk below the horizon he turned to face his new Lady-in-Waiting, who was standing silently in the middle of the room waiting for him to make the first move.

"Now what do we do?" he asked facetiously, knowing full well that the lady Zhu Di had provided to be of service, didn't want to be with him at all.

Xi Chen bowed correctly to the Ming admiral before speaking.

"Emperor Zhu Di has given me to you, Lord Zheng He. As your personal Lady-in-Waiting, I'm here to serve at your pleasure."

Xi Chen's proper, but cold, response made him angry.

"Stop it, Xi Chen!" he growled. "You're here because Zhu Di ordered you to be here and for no other reason!"

Xi Chen snapped back at her new master with fire in her eyes.

"And why should I want to be here? All I get from YOU is someone who treats me with disdain, or even worse, indifference!"

"And why shouldn't I treat you that way?" Zheng He countered, his voice rising. "Ever since you arrived at the palace you practically threw yourself at Zhu Di!"

Xi Chen couldn't believe what Zheng He has just said.

"You couldn't wait until I left on the first expedition," Zheng He continued loudly, "so you could jump into bed with him!"

When Xi Chen heard what Zheng He had said she slapped him across the face as hard as she could.

"How dare you speak to me that way?" she screamed. "I was a servant and had to do what Zhu Di wanted!"

Zheng He grabbed Xi Chen by both shoulders and started shaking her vigorously.

"Bitch!" he shouted. "You didn't do what Zhu Di wanted, you did what YOU wanted!"

Xi Chen broke free and started striking Zheng He in the chest with both of her fists.

"Yes, I did what I wanted," she creamed back, "and it was wonderful! Do you like to hear that, Zheng He? It was WONDERFUL!"

Again Xi Chen struck Zheng He in the chest with both fists as hard as she could.

"Zhu Di was a MAN," she taunted, "a man who could give me what I wanted! Not a half-man! Not a EUNUCH bastard like you!"

Her words hit Zheng He like a hot poker. He slapped Xi Chen across the face and knocked her backwards onto the floor.

"Bitch!" he screamed again, shaking his fist in her face and hating her more than he had ever hated anyone in his whole life. "You think I'm half a man? I'll show you half a man!"

Zheng He tried to grab Xi Chen on the floor, but she rolled away, jumped up, grabbed a porcelain vase from off a table and threw it at him as hard as she could. He ducked and the vase crashed against a wall and broke into a thousand pieces. "Don't come near me!" she screamed, while trying to fend him off.

Zheng He lunged at her a second time, but once again she slipped away, picked up another vase and hurled it at him at almost point blank range. Again, she missed the dodging admiral, which caused this vase to smash against a large decorative screen.

Since I was sitting just outside Zheng He's bedroom suite, I could hear the muffled voices of two people screaming at each other and the sound of objects breaking. As you might imagine, I started praying for all I was worth and almost rubbed a hole in my little wooden cross.

A few minutes later, when Ma Huan came up the outside stairs, he also heard all the noise that was eminating from inside the admiral's stateroom.

"What's going on in there?" he asked, obviously worried that Zheng He and Xi Chen were having some kind of a fight.

"They're getting to know each other," I responded, calmly, trying to make it seem that such outragious behavior was completely normal between two grown adults.

Just then, we both heard another loud crash which was followed by another sharp yell.

"Getting to know each other?" Ma Huan gasped, not believing what I had just told him. "It sounds to me like they're trying to kill each other!"

"Sometimes when two lovers have a quarrel," I countered, as I forced a smile, "it's hard to tell the difference!"

Ma Huan put his ear to the door to try and hear what was happening, but now, strangely, all was quiet.

"What's happening now?" he whispered, giving me a curious look. "I don't hear anything!"

"Maybe they're getting to the kiss and make up phase," I suggested, as I held up my little cross and gave it a kiss. "At least that's what I pray is happening!"

Inside the bedroom all was quiet. Zheng He and Xi Chen were now lying on the bed, he partly on top of her, as he tried to hold her down. It looked as if both were ready for a truce.

"What are we fighting for?" he asked Xi Chen softly, his voice now much more conciliatory.

"You started it!" she shot back, continuing to pout.

Blood trickled down Zheng He's face, where she had hit him with a plate that didn't miss. She took one finger and tenderly wiped the blood from his cut lip.

"Why did you start it?" Xi Chen also asked softly, as she also sounded like she wanted to make up.

Zheng He rolled off Xi Chen and lay back onto the bed thinking. It was plain he didn't want to fight anymore.

"Because I'm jealous, Xi Chen," he told her trughfully as he kept his eyes on the ceiling and diverted from her. "I'm jealous of you and Zhu Di."

Xi Chen rolled over and tenderly kissed his cut lip, which continued to bleed slightly.

"You don't need to be jealous of anyone, Zheng He," she cooed. "You're the only man I've ever loved!"

"You couldn't have loved me!" he argued, as he turned her face so he could look into her eyes. "You spent all those nights in bed sleeping with Zhu Di while I had to sleep in my bed alone!"

Xi Chen didn't like Zheng He's continued accusations. She sat up so she could more easily defend herself.

"You had your chance, Zheng He," she countered, her voice again tinged with anger. "I begged you to make love to me for more than a year. But you wouldn't. Why wouldn't you? Is it because you're a eunuch?"

"Yes!" Zheng He shot back, his own voice tinged with anger, but his eyes betraying the fact that he was also ashamed.

The anger and hurt in his voice startled her.

"But that only means we couldn't make babies together, doesn't it?"

"No!" Zheng He spit out, as his eyes began to fill with tears. "That's not what it means at all. It means that I can't make love you to, Xi Chen. I can't make love you to EVER!"

Xi Chen couldn't believe it!

"But there were stories, Zheng He!" she pleaded, beginning to fear the worse, "stories that said you weren't forced to become a eunuch."

Zheng He wiped the tears from his eyes and also sat up in bed so he could more easily explain the delicate subject.

"Truth is elusive, Xi Chen."

Xi Chen was now more confused than ever.

"Truth? What is the truth? Will you tell me what happened, Zheng He? I want to know. Please?"

Zheng He hesitated.

Xi Chen persisted.

"I was told that Zhu Di interrupted the ceremony, that's why many people have speculated over the years that you were never castrated and weren't actually a eunuch. Zhu Di didn't castrate you, did he?"

Zheng He struggled for words. He didn't want to tell Xi Chen the truth, but he knew that he must. After taking a deep breath, he began.

"When I was taken to the ch'ang tau for castration," he told her slowly and calmly, "I was tied down by four eunuchs."

Again Zheng He hesitated as he thought about the ceremony that happened so many years ago.

Xi Chen didn't press him to hurry.

"The tao tzu chiang brought out a sharp blade and prepared to do his duty. But then, just as he was about to begin, Zhu Di unexpectedly entered the room and ordered everyone to leave. I couldn't believe it. Here I was tied down on this table, ready to be castrated, when Zhu Di entered the room and we were suddenly alone."

Zheng He paused again, as he really didn't want to think about the terrible ordeal that he had to endure, but knew that he must.

"Zhu Di asked if I trusted him? I was terrified. Being tied down, I couldn't move. Suddenly, he brought the blade down and I started to scream, but he stopped and held it there, just above my private parts. He asked me again, do I trust him? I couldn't believe it. I didn't know what to say. I could hardly catch my breath. Finally I managed to gasp, 'yes', 'yes', I trusted him and was just starting to relax, when I saw his fingers tighten around the handle of the blade."

Zheng He shut his eyes as tight as he could and tried to blot out that terrible moment that happened to him so many years before.

Xi Chen gasped, "He didn't!"

Zheng He opened his eyes and turned to Xi Chen, then continued.

"When his hand came down I opened my mouth to scream, but all that escaped was a strange hiss from inside my throat. I stared in wide-eyed shock and agony at what Zhu Di had just done. Zhu Di didn't just castrate me my love, he removed my penis as well."

Xi Chen couldn't believe what she was hearing.

"Oh, no," she moaned, "Zhu Di didn't…"

Zhu Di then told me calmly, "Never…trust…anyone."

Xi Chen's eyes began flowing with tears as she buried herself in Zheng He's arms and began to cry.

"My darling, my darling," she sobbed, "I'm so ashamed of myself for all the things that I've said to you and the terrible way I've treated you. I didn't know, my love. I had no idea. Can you ever forgive me?"

Zheng He put his arms around Xi Chen and kissed her lips hard, then began to stroke her face.

"Of course I will forgive you, my little flower. I love you. You're the only woman I've ever loved, or ever will love!"

Both held each other while Xi Chen sobbed quietly.

"If it wasn't so tragic," Zheng He continued, as his voice cracked and became emotional "it would almost be funny. Here we are, the moment we've both waited for...and prayed for...all our lives and now..."

Zheng He couldn't continue. He broke down completely and started to sob himself.

After a few moments, when he was able to get control of himself, he removed Xi Chen's necklace from around his own neck and placed it back around her neck.

"Now that you belong to me, my love," he told her softly, "I want to give you back your necklace. I've never taken it off since that day years ago when we were separated and you gave it to me. But it's yours, Xi Chen and I want you to have it back."

Zheng He then leaned over and kissed Xi Chen lovingly on the lips.

"I may not be able to make love to you," he whispered, his voice breaking again as he spoke, "but I can remember how it was between us when we were both young, when you always wore your beautiful necklace, and..."

Xi Chen wouldn't let him finish. She wiped the tears from her own eyes and took Zheng He's face in her hands.

"This is our night, my love," she cooed, "the night that we both have waited for all our lives. Nothing is going to stop us from having this night together."

She then began covering Zheng He's face with little kisses, tenderly at first, but then with growing passion.

He initially resisted her ardent advances, afraid that she was only being kind. But as he sensed that her amorouos emotion was genuine, Zheng He began responding to her and wrapped her small body tightly in his arms.

Xi Chen lthen gently opened Zheng He's robe and let her hand slide slowly toward his groin. She paused and gasped slightly when her hand felt nothing, but quickly recovered and forced a reassuring look as she continued to touch him between his legs.

"Can you feel anything there?" she asked, cautiously.

Zheng He hesitated, then took her hand and placed it on his heart.

"I feel everything here."

The two lovers kissed again fervently, as their passion grew with each moment.

Zheng He removed Xi Chen's robe, which fully revealed her soft, porcelain skin.

Both again began kissing and touching each other, all over, slowly at first, but then, more and more frantically.

"Wait, wait!" Xi Chen gasped, while she pushed Zheng He away. "I want us to do this right!"

He started to say something but she placed a finger on his cut lip and stopped him. She then got up, went over to the side of the room and picked up a small candle which flickered softly on a table off to one side. She also retrieved a small bottle of fragrant oil from the table's only drawer.

Zheng He wasn't sure what she was up to. He watched silently as Xi Chen returned to the bed and placed the candle and oil on a table beside the bed. Then, by the dancing candlelight, she slowly and seductively began to rub the oil all over her body which was completely naked except for the necklace of love around her neck.

Zheng He could hardly stand it. He had dreamed of this moment for his whole life and now, here she was, in his bed next to him, naked, motioning for him to come to her. When he did she lovingly kissed him and slowly began to rub the fragrant lubricant, slowly and sensually, all over his body as well.

For several long delicious minutes they touched and kissed and felt each other's oily, naked body, without either speaking a word.

"Are you sure you want to do this?" he finally whispered, still self-conscious about the way he had been disfigured. "We don't have to..."

Xi Chen stopped him with a kiss.

"It doesn't matter, my love," she cooed softly. "The only thing that does matter is that we have each other."

She then gently pulled Zheng He to her breast.

"Now, my love, we have each other, forever!"

As Zheng He's tongue began to explore the loveliness of Xi Chen's breasts and stomach, the beautiful lady spread her legs wide and begged to receive the man she loved. In one glorious rush of unbridled passion, he thrust his tongue, his face, his fingers, everything he could think of, deep inside the pulsating body of the woman he loved. There was no holding back for either of them. All the terrible doubt and guilt that both had harbored for years vanished between them forever.

For the next three hours the two lovers tasted the fruits of sexual pleasure that neither of them could have even imagined in their wildest teenage dreams.

They clutched at each other, desperately, forcefully and probed, over and over, every orifice of each other's body. Shamelessly, they experimented with their tongues, their fingers and toes. Deeper and deeper, again and again, joyously holding nothing back, each relived every sexual fantasy they had ever imagined.

Their lovemaking continued and became more and more frantic until, finally, shockingly, an explosion of sensual bliss erupted from deep within both of their bodies. As one, they were both engulfed in a climax of such intense sexual pleasure that they could not tell if the unexpected release was physical or emotional.

It didn't matter. As the moment of heavenly ecstasy slowly released its hold, they rolled off each other and gasped for breath, both deliciously spent, both unsure of what had just happened, or how it had happened. Then, as if on cue, the small candle beside the bed danced haltingly for a few seconds and flickered out. Now lying together in the darkness, Zheng He grinned to himself and whispered softly to the woman he loved.

"Are you ready for seconds?"

She quickly whispered back.

"...and thirds...and fourths!"

"Oh, no," he moaned happily, then silently thanked Benevolent Allah for giving him the most incredible miracle for which he had always prayed.


Zheng He's relationship with Xi Chen was now back on track and they were both enjoying the sexual life together that they had only dreamed of sharing for years.

Back at Forbidden City in Beijing, Empress Xu was getting to spend time with Zhu Di, just as she had always wanted, but it was not the happy love nest that Zheng He and Xi Chen now shared. Zhu Di was sick and seemed to be getting sicker. A gray, unhealthy-looking, parlor had settled ominously onto his face and for the first time the empress began to actually fear that her husband may not live much longer.

Whenever Zhu Di and his wife spent time together in his private quarters, more often than not, their conversation revolved around their number two son. On this particular evening there was no exception.

"I had a talk with Prince Han today," he told her soberly, between coughs, "about my plans for a third expedition."

Zhu Di's unexpected comment caught his wife completely by surprise.

"You discussed a third expedition with our son?" she asked, still not believing what she had just heard. "Lord Zheng He has just started his second expedition Zhu Di! Why in the world are you already thinking about a third?"

He couldn't answer her right away because his coughing had caught up with him and he had to endure several long minutes of debilitating torture before he could speak. Listening to the unmistakable rattle in her husband's chest caused her to noticibly wince. Finally, when the emperor was able to breathe again and speak, haltingly, he answered his wife's question.

"I was thinking about…a third expedition, empress," he wheezed, "because, I don't know…how much time I have left. When the fleet returns…I want everything organized and ready to go…so it can turn around quickly…without wasting time."

"Don't you think you're pushing yourself too hard?" she asked, continuing her knitting and trying not to appear overly upset about his precarious health. "I think you should relax, Zhu Di, until you're feeling better."

"I may not <u>ever</u> feel better!" he countered, dourly, forcing himself to speak without caughing. "I don't want to just sit around all day, empress…and do nothing!"

"But there is still a lot of opposition from officials and civil servants," she complained. "You know how excited they get whenever you announce you're going to spend more money on an expedition."

"I'm not spending the people's money," he told her testily. "You know that…To hell with them, empress!...To hell with ALL of them!"

Empress Xu put down her knitting.

"Zhu Di, please!" she admonished. "You promised me you wouldn't allow yourself to get so upset."

"I know…I know," he agreed and took a deep breath, as he tried to acquiesce to his wife's wishes. "I just can't help it! There are so many things…that I still want to accomplish!"

"Like what?"

"Well, like sending the Ming fleet to the east…instead of to the west." Zhu Di threw the statement out just to see if his wife was listening. "There are probably a lot of new…undiscovered lands out there," he continued, "large, rich lands…that we don't know anything about!"

His wife listened but she didn't like what Zhu Di was suggesting.

"That a ridiculous idea!" she crowed and reacted even more negatively then he had expected. "Please tell me you're not going to indulge yourself in something so foolish!"

"What's foolish about it?" he responded quickly as he began to enjoy the slight confrontation. "I think sending an expedition towards the east...would be a wonderful idea!"

The exasperation in his wife's voice was now unmistakable.

"You want to risk hundreds of ships and the lives of thousands of men by sending them across an uncharted ocean that may stretch on forever? And you ask me what's foolish about it? It's a crazy idea, Zhu Di! It's crazy and it's terribly risky! I want you to forget all about it!"

Zhu Di smiled inwardly to himself and was pleased that he was still able to get his wife a little stirred up. But then, before he could enjoy his little victory, he was hit by another series of violent coughs which consumed his energy and prevented him from speaking any more about it.

Empress Xu forced herself to take no notice of her husband's most recent debilitating condition and went back to her knitting. After a few quiet moments Empress Xu ventured a final comment.

"If you said anything to our son about a third expedition, Zhu Di, I wish you would tell him that you've changed your mind. Will you do that for me?" she asked, as Zhu Di struggled to get air back into his lungs.

Zhu Di wheezed a weak reply.

"It doesn't make any difference...empress...what I say to him...one way...or the other."

Empress Xu was surprised by what her husband had just said and looked up.

"Why do you say that?"

"I've had...some of my servants...watching him," he gasped, still having to struggle to catch his breath, "ever since...I let him...out of prison."

"And?"

"And...what I secretly feared...has been happening!"

"What's that supposed to mean?" she asked, part of her wanting to know the answer, but another part of her afraid to hear what he might tell her.

"Han has continued to meet...with his same lackey friends, empress... just like he did...before stirring up trouble behind my back."

"Oh, I wish you hadn't told me that." she worried out loud, continuing to concentrate on the thick threads in her hands. "Have you said anything to him?"

"No! Not yet!" Zhu Di confessed, as he shook his head up and down and tried to get more air into his lungs. "I'm just having…the servants, keep track of…what he says…and who he meets. But what they report back to me…isn't good."

Without warning, Zhu Di was struck by another spate of violent coughs. This time it was so bad the empress had to put down her knitting as she expected she would have to go to his aid. But when he was finally able to regain a little control, she forced herself to ignore his obvious distress, which, unfortunately, had become a familiar occurrence.

"I know…that if I die," Zhu Di wheezed again, barely able to speak, "Han will try to…take the throne…from Zhu Bao Zhi!"

Shocked, Empress Xu put down her knitting again and complained bitterly.

"He can't do that, Zhu Di! The crown is the birthright of our number one son!" Then, after realizing what she had just said, she instinctively yelped, "Oh!"

Now it was Zhu Di who looked up."

"Are you…all right?"

She didn't answer right away, as she was still mesmerized by the comment that she had just made. For the first time in her life Empress Xu realized that she had allowed herself to acquiesce to the actual inevitability of her husband's death.

"Yes, I'm all right," she answered haltingly. "I just don't like for you to speak of such unpleasant things."

Empress Xu reached out and tenderly touched her husband's arm.

"You're not going to die, Zhu Di. Please tell me you're not!"

"Everyone…has to die my dear," he allowed, giving his wife a condescending smile. "It's time we both…faced up…to this basic fact of life!"

"Zhu Di, please, I don't like…"

He cut her off.

"I don't like…to say this, empress," he gasped, "but should I die… I'm quite sure…that Prince Han…will try to take over the throne…and do… whatever he can…to stop the expeditions!"

"Please don't speak to me about dying," she begged, again. "It makes me frightened. I don't ever want to think of living without you!"

Zhu Di wasn't worried about dying. In his mind, he had already acquiested to that foregone conclusion. But what he did worry about was that his number two son would stop the expeditions and ruin the most important thing he'd ever accomplished in his life!

Just now, Zhu Di's huge Ming fleet was stopped in a large bay off the coast of Java. Zheng He stopped the fleet here on its first expedition and was warmly received by King Jawralla Banga-ta and his people. The admiral chose to return for a second visit, primarily because he wanted to personally thank King Banga-ta for sending trade envoys to China even before he completed his first expedition and he also stopped the fleet to satisfy a more practical matter. Zheng He knew the fleet would have to be resupplied somewhere along the way and Java was a convenient place to satisfy that basic requirement.

When Captain Su informed the Ming admiral that King Banga-ta and his official party were waiting for him on the beach, Zheng He gathered together his own party of friends and officials and proceeded to exit the huge flagship.

He led then down a large wooden stairway which had been specifically placed over the Baochuan's port side, so the admiral and his guests could safely gain access to his private launch below.

After Lord Zheng He was on board the gaily decorated vessel, two dozen Ming officers and officials joined him on the craft along with Xi Chen, Ma Huan and me.

When everyone was seated, Captain Su issued an order for the admiral's private launch to be pushed away from the huge Baochaun and the long slender oars manned. As soon as we were clear of the flagship, thirty sailors, fifteen on each side, dipped their oars into the water and gracefully began rowing us towards the shore.

The launch was fairly good-sized, a little over sixty paces in length, if you didn't count the gilded dragon's head that was carved at the bow and its tail at the stern. Along with the thirty oars, Zheng He's personal craft also featured two good-sized sails. One large mast and sail was located in front of his personal cupula in the center of the ship and another just behind. Together, with the oars, the graceful Ming vessel was able to move steadily towards the beach at a fairly good pace.

Admiral Zheng He's private launch was not alone as it approached the beach. Eighty smaller vesssels of various lengths followed a short distance which were also propelled by oarsmen and sails. Each of these wooden craft was also decked out in colorful flags and pennants and each was filled with a variety of Ming soldiers, sailors, officials and dignitaries.

As this colorful flotilla of Ming vessels moved steadily towards the white sand beach before them, a soft onshore breeze made the short trip a little more bearable. In the tropical noonday sun, even out on the water, the air was terribly humid and oppressively hot.

Thankfully Lord Zheng He's beautifully decorated cupula was open on all sides which allowed the cooling zephyrs to freely circulate. The area reserved for the admiral's guests, however, was not covered but it was equipped with comfortable chairs and plush divans. The comfortable furniture made traveling from the flagship to the shore a somewhat relaxing and enjoyable experience.

"It's beautiful," Xi Chen gushed to Zheng He when she saw the tropical scenery that spread out all around them. "I don't think I've ever seen such a lovely beach before, anywhere! Did you stop here on your first expedition?"

Before Zheng He could respond, we began to hear a hauntingly beautiful sound eminating from the direction of the shore. When we all turned to see who, or what, was making such unusual music, all of us were completely surprised to see that almost a thousand people had congragated on the beach and were now singing softly as they welcomed us back to their tropical isle.

I didn't know about Zheng He, but I, personally, had never seen such an outpouring of friendship for foreigners before, anywhere!

As we got closer to the beach we could begin to make out the Java king and queen sitting under a dozen or more large coconum palms waiting for us to arrive. Each sat on a large chair that was exquisitely decorated and made of solid teak. Several brown-skinned servants continuously fanned the royal couple with palm fronds as they waited for the Ming admiral and his Chinese visitors to arrive.

King Jawralla Banga-ta and his wife were also joined on the beach by a large number of Java government officials and dignitaries. They must have been uncomfortable in the tropical heat, as all were required to remain standing and none were allowed to sit.

Just as Zheng He's launch reached shallow water close to the beach a number of Ming soldiers quickly jumped over the side with small chairs and rushed forward so the admiral, his guests and senior officers could sit in the chairs and ride safely to the beach without getting wet!

As we were being deposited safely onto the beach the other Ming vessels arrived and quickly deposited their cargos of Chinese soldiers, sailors, officials and dignitaries as well.

While Ming officers scurred around and arranged themselves into a large, but simple formation, led of course by the Admiral Zheng He, the remaining soldiers, officials and dignitaries formed up into positions just behind. As soon as everyone was in place, Lord Zheng He nodded and the whole formation began marching up the beach to where the Java king and queen waited.

Xi Chen, Ma Huan and I scurried around the impressive-looking formation until we were able to find ourselves a place to stand that was a little off to one side, but still within the shade of one of the tall coconut palms. This wasn't difficult to do, since the palms grew in great profusion all along the edge of the white sand beach.

I knew what was coming next, as I had witnessed Zheng He's rehearsed opening ceremony a number of times on our previous expedition.

The admiral stopped a short distance from the Java royal couple and gave them a gracious bow, which officially opened the small beach ceremony.

"King Jawralla Banga-ta," Zheng He intoned seriously, "I again bring you personal greetings from his Imperial Majesty, Zhu Di, Third Ming Emperor of China!"

Lord Zheng He offered the king and queen another gracious bow which was joined this time by the senior members of his Ming entourage and staff. After King Banga-ta acknowledged the admiral's greeting with a nod, Zheng He and his entourage retreated from their bow and stood at attention as the Ming admiral continued.

"Once again I wish to present gifts to you, Your Majesty, of five hundred Ming vase and five hundred rolls of variegated silk."

As on the first expedition, two Chinese servants immediately stepped forward and held up samples of the gifts for the Java king and queen to see. While the servants went through the ritual of allowing the royal couple to inspect the vase and silk, Zheng He continued with his pronouncements.

"I'm sure you're aware, Your Majesty, that the silk you are now inspecting is of a superior quality, as are the Ming vase, which have been made of a special porcelain and exquisitely decorated by Chinese craftsmen. I present these gifts to you on behalf of Zhu Di, the Most Holy, Benevolent, Cultivated, Righteous, Martial, Refined, Virtuous and Successful, Exalted Emperor of China."

The two servants then handed the sample gifts to a Java minister, who stepped forward and accepted them on behalf of the royal couple.

After Zheng He's presentation was complete, the Java ruler began reading from a small scroll that had been handed to him by a servant.

"Lord Zheng He, Admiral of the Ming Fleet," King Jawralla Banga-ta began solemnly, "the people of Java wish to welcome you again to our humble shore. In order to demonstrate how much we appreciate and respect your benevolent emperor, we would like to offer him a few gifts. Please accept our meager offering of fifty tons of fragrant wood, one thousand pieces of decorative silver ornaments, five hundred catties of perfumed oil, one hundred pieces of precious gold and twenty-six rolls of variegated silk."

King Jawralla Banga-ta paused for a moment, looked up and offered Zheng He a smile, then continued.

"I wish to offer these small gifts to your emperor," he intoned, "and pray that, although they are insignificant, they will, nevertheless, demonstrate our willingness to recognize His Imperial Majesty as a true and lasting friend of the Java people."

Immediately, twenty-five Java servants began filing past Zheng He on the beach. Each carried a sample of the just mentioned gifts. When the servants retook their positions at the back of the Java formation, Zheng He again bowed to the Java king and replied graciously.

"Your gifts are most generous, Oh king, and will be carefully noted. I assure you, that I, Lord Zheng He, Admiral of the Ming Fleet, will personally make certain that each of your gifts is made known to the emperor."

King Jawralla Banga-ta then clapped his hands and immediately the scene erupted into a joyful celebration of singing and dancing, not only by the Java entertainers present, but by all of the Java residents as well.

I found out later that while Admiral Zheng He was busy currying favor with King Jawralla Banga-ta in Java, Prince Han was equally busy doing whatever he could to curry favor among dissident ministers in Beijing. The young prince was convinced that his father was seriously ill and had little time to live. Consequently, when he did die, he wanted to make certain that he had an abundance of ministers who would give him their full support so he could take over the crown.

Prince Han was smart enough to realize, however, that his acceptance by many of the imperial ministers, depended largely upon his friendship with Minister Wa. Unfortunately for him the popular minister was still kept under lock and key in the prison. With this in mind he decided to make a visit to the incarcerated official and knew full well that his cooperation would most assuredly be needed, hopefully, in the very near future.

As Han followed the guard down the dimly lit hallway he became irritated when he thought the man was walking too slow.

"Can't you move any faster," he growled and gave the poor man a shove that almost knocked him down. "I haven't got all day."

Without stopping, the guard turned and tried to offer the young man a bow which got him nothing but a slap on the side of his head for his trouble.

When they finally got to Wa's cell, much to Han's further consternation, the guard wasted additional time as he funbled with the keys.

"Come on, hurry up!" he grumbled at the guard again, which caused the man to fumble even more.

When he was finally able to push open the door and step back, Han bounded into the room without acknowledging the servant's service.

It had been more than a month since Prince Han last saw his, formerly, heavy-set friend. Today when Minister Wa offered him an unsteady bow, he was taken aback by his terrible appearance. The minister seemed to have deteriorated greatly since the two of them were in prison together. The young prince offered Wa a smile and helped straighten him up from his bent over position.

"I'm going to get you out of this cesspool, Minister Wa," he told him firmly, doing his best to be friendly. "I don't want you to lose your will."

Wa returned Han's greeting with a wan smile and offered a weak reply.

"My will remains strong, Honorable Prince, but my body is not faring so well. The conditions at the prison remain, I'm afraid, less than satisfactory!"

Han pulled out a bag of food that he had hidden in his clothing and handed it over to his obviously weak friend.

"Here, hide this!" he suggested quickly, after making sure the door was closed and the guard wasn't looking. "It may help to fill you out a little."

Wa took the bag, went over to his one chair, tore it open and immediately started devouring the food right in front of the startled prince.

"I will, not, forget, your kindness," he mumbled, as he stuffed handfuls of rice and chicken into his mouth. When Han saw the minister gorging himself like an animal, he was disturbed by his crude behavior.

"Can't you control yourself?" he complained.

"If the, guard, comes," Wa mumbled, while continuing to stuff food into his mouth, "they will take it from me! I can not, take the chance, Honorable Prince!"

Not wanting to watch the minister's crude display of gorging, Prince Han began inspecting the stinking gutter at the rear of the cell. The smell was no different from what he remembered and thought that it had gotten worse!

Minister Wa watched the prince closely as he slowly moved about the nasty cell, but he never stopped swallowing or stuffing morsels of food into his mouth. When Han repositioned himself back in front of the minister, Wa offered him another wan smile, but didn't stop his forced feeding.

"My father remains engaged in his stupid practice of trading with foreign countries," Prince Han stated firmly as he hoped to open a meaningful conversation with the minister. "As we both know, it's nothing but a crude deception! All he really wants to do is frighten the leaders of the countries into paying him tribute!"

This brash statement by Prince Han caused Minister Wa to momentarily stop his gorging.

"I've, ahhh, never heard anyone say that before," he stammered, obviously astonished at Han's words. "Even though I'm against your father wasting money on the expeditions, I always thought the foreign leaders wanted to trade with us! After all, we do give them expensive gifts…"

"They're not fools!" Han interrupted, as he quickly became irritated that Wa didn't immediately agree with his assessment. "Why do you think my father built such a huge fleet?"

Minister Wa started to take another bite of chicken, but Han knocked it from his open mouth and onto the filthy floor.

"If he was only interested in trade, Minister Wa," Han growled, "all he'd have to do is send out a few ships and a few envoys! He wouldn't have to send out hundreds of ships and thirty thousand men!"

WA retrieved the small morsel of chicken from the filthy floor and popped it into his mouth. He didn't even think about brushing it off. While chewing on the obviously dirty food, Wa reflected for a moment on what the young prince had just told him.

"You may be right about countries paying us tribute!' he mused, as he continued to chew and swallow steadily. "I guess I never looked at it like that before!"

While Minister Wa pondered what the prince had said, Han began to pace nervously within the small inclosure as he tried to decide what he should say to the man to insure his unqualified support. But then, to Han's surprise, Wa stopped chewing and offered an unexpecdted comment of his own.

"I don't wish to disagree, Honorable Prince," he began cautiously, "and, as you know, I'm a very strong supporter of all your policies, but it is true that your father offers foreign leaders valuable Chinese gifts that far exceed the cost of what he receives in tribute. I really don't understand how you can say the foreign leaders are only trading with us because they're afraid not to."

Prince Han was like his father in one respect, in that he immediately became angry whenever anyone disagreed with something he had said. When the young man heard Minister Wa's unsupportive comment he flew into a rage!

"That's not true!" he shouted and shook his fist in the face of the wayward official.

Without thinking, Wa shouted back.

"It is true! I don't know why the emperor wanted to build such a large fleet, but if its purpose was to extract favorable tribute from foreign leaders I don't think its working!"

With a little food in his belly, Wa's confidence began to grow. He waved a chicken leg in the young man's face as he was determined to make his point.

"The only people who have received benefit from this trading relationship, Prince Han, are the foreign leaders! That's why my government friends are so adamant about stopping Zhu Di! His expeditions do nothing but waste the good money and resources of the Chinese people!"

Han was now furious.

"My father is seriously ill," he screamed, "and there's a very good possibility he will die soon! When he does, Minister Wa, I plan to block my stupid brother and take over the crown for myself. Now! If you have any notion, of EVER getting out of this stinking hellhole, I suggest you reassess YOUR THINKING!"

With that, Han turned and headed for the door.

When Wa suddenly realized how foolish he had been, he dropped to his knees and immediately bgegan pleading for the young prince to reconsider.

"Honorable Sir, I beg you!" he wailed. "You've mistaken my words! Please don't be angry with me. If you become emperor and don't want any more expeditions, there won't BE any more expeditions! I'll make certain that laws are passed that will stop the expeditions forever!"

Han stopped at the door and turned to face the groveling minister.

"I was worried, Minister Wa, that maybe your long hours of isolation had damaged your brain. Perhaps I judged you prematurely. If I choose to visit you in the future, I will expect your full cooperation. Is that clear?"

Wa now prostrated his whole body onto the filthy, foul-smelling floor. In a quivering voice he replied shakily to the prince.

"I'll count the hours, Honorable Sir, until your next visit."

Han scowled at Wa and hissed a final warning.

"See that you do!"

He then slammed the wooden door shut with a loud bang and left the pathetic minister lying on the floor sobbing like a baby.

One month later, almost twelve thousand li away, Zheng He and Xi Chen were alone in the admiral's private bedroom suite as they prepared for another welcoming ceremony with a foreign ruler.

"You're getting fat!" she teased, as she tried to help him adjust his thick belt and sword.

"I know!" he acknowledged, pretending to be upset. "And if you don't stop making me eat so much, I'm probably going to weigh three hundred pounds!"

The beautiful lady slipped her arms around Zheng He's neck and gave him a playful kiss.

"Good," she purred softly. "Then there'll be more of you to love."

The two lovers kissed again, but stopped when they heard a knock on the stateroom door. Reluctantly, Xi Chen pulled away and went to answer it. When she pulled the door open, Lt. Zhang Ji and Ma Huan stepped inside and bowed smartly to Zheng He.

"Sir!" Zhang Ji reported. "Your private launch is ready. We've received word that the Ceylon king is on the beach waiting for your arrival."

"Good!" Zheng He responded cheerily as he gave the lieutenant a big smile. He then asked if the ruler was friendly.

Zhang Ji returned the admiral's smile with one of his own.

"Yes, Sir! He seems to be very friendly! In fact, he has already let it be known that he is anxious to meet with you and sign an agreement for trade."

"Seems to me, lieutenant," Zheng He joked, "that you and the trade minister's have already handled the hard part!"

"Yes, Sir," Zhang Ji replied, without thinking, then quickly added, "I mean, No Sir!"

"Do either of you know if Friar Odoric is ready?" Zheng He asked, as he turned to his servant.

Ma Huan responded quickly.

"Yes, Sir! He's waiting down on the main deck. Everyone has assembled and are waiting for your arrival."

"Well then, let's go meet the king!"


Within thirty minutes Zheng He's private launch was again leading a flotilla of small vessels towards a foreign tropical shore. This time it was the beautiful isle of Ceylon which was located less than a hundred li off the southern tip of India.

Once again Xi Chen gazed longingly at the lush landscape as the launch, propelled by the oars and sails, rode a steady breeze towards the distant shore. Sitting under the decorative cupula in the shade she looked longingly at the tropical beauty which she could see all around them.

"I don't think I've ever seen a place quite so beautiful in my whole life," she whispered to her love. "It's like a fairyland."

"It is beautiful," Zheng He agreed, then pointed out the different shades of blue that could be seen in the clear ocean water. "Even in this deep water away from the shore you can almost see the bottom."

On the beach, the Ceylonese king looked out onto the large bay and could hardly believe the large numbers of Ming ships which now floated on the calm waters before him.

"Have you ever seen anything like this before?" he gasped to his senior officer, General Bura, who was standing by his side. "There are almost too many ships to count!"

The general agreed and pointed out Zheng He's private launch which he could see in the distance as it led the flotilla of small ships towards the beach.

"The admiral must be in that large vessel, Sire," he told the king cautiously, "the one you can see with all the flags. He's the senior official you're supposed to meet. The young Chinese lieutenant said his name was Lord Zheng He."

Unable to keep his eyes off the huge array of spectacular-looking ships, the king could only stammer, absentmindedly, "I'll try not to forget."

When Zheng He's launch stopped in shallow water just off shore, once again a number of Ming servants jumped over the side and rushed forward to carry the important Chinese visitors to the beach. Seeing the unusual spectical, the Ceylon king was duly impressed and commented wryly to his senior officer, "Do you see that, General Bura? That's how an arrival is done!"

The senior officer laughed.

"The Chinese are very clever, Sire. Some of them don't even have to get their feet wet!"

Once on dry land, Zheng He again took his position at the head of his official contingent and when everyone was assembled, as before, started leading them up the beach to where the Ceylon king and his advisors waited. Using the same protocol that he used on Java, Zheng He bowed graciously to the local ruler then began to speak.

"King Yala Ku-mi-orh" he intoned, solemnly, "I bring you personal greetings from his Imperial Majesty, Zhu Di, Exalted Third Ming Emperor of China."

Again, just as on Java, Lord Zheng He and his senior entourage bowed respectfully in unison.

Also, just as on Java, Xi Chen, Ma Huan and I scrambled for a position under some nearby palm trees, so that we could watch the colorful ceremony in the shade. All around us was a growing crowd of curious Ceylonese villagers who were anxious to watch the historic ceremony that was taking place before their very eyes.

"I wish to present a gift to you," Zheng He continued, "of five hundred Ming vase and five hundred rolls of variegated silk. The silk is a superior Chinese quality and the vase are made of a special porcelain, which, as you can see, has been delicately decorated by Chinese craftsmen."

Keeping right on schedule, two servants stepped forward, bowed respectfully to the king, then presented the vase and rolls of silk for his inspection. While King Yala Ku-mi-orh was inspecting the gifts, Zheng He continued with his memorized statement.

"I present these gifts to you, Your Majesty, on behalf of Zhu Di, the most Holy, Benevolent, Cultivated, Righteous, Martial, Refined, Virtuous and Successful, Exalted Emperor of China."

When Zheng He's presentation was completed, King Yala Ku-mi-orh smiled approvingly and motioned for the servants to hand the gifts to his senior assistant, General Bura. When the gifts had been inspected by the general and several of the king's advisors, Yala Ku-mi-orh nodded in Zheng He's direction, then began his own short, impromptu speech.

"I wish to thank you for these generous gifts..."

King Yala Ku-mi-orh had to stop for a moment because he had already forgotten the admiral's name. When General Bura realized what was happening, he quickly whispered Zheng He's name in the embarrassed ruler's ear. Yala Ku-mi-orh offered the Chinese admiral another broad smile, then continued.

"I wish to thank you, Lord Zheng He, for these generous gifts and would like to invite you and your men to a banquet tonight which I will hold especially in your honor."

The admiral graciously bowed to the Ceylonese king once again and responded happily.

"Thank you, Your Majesty, that's very kind. We would be most honored to accept your generous invitation."

But then, instead of bringing the short beach ceremony to a close, King Yala Ku-mi-orh made an unexpected request.

"Ahhh, Lord Zheng He!" he begged, while he continued to smile broadly, "since we're all here at the beach together, I wonder if you would allow me a slight indulgence!"

I noticed that Zheng He was talen aback by the king's unexpected change of protocol, but didn't want to disappoint the foreign ruler.

"Of course, Your Majesty, what is it?"

"I've never seen such magnificent ships before," he stated enthusiastically. "Would it be possible for you to give me a short tour? I'd be forever in your debt!"

I could tell Zheng He was relieved the king's request was so simple and could easily be honored.

"I'd be delighted!" he responded quickly, then asked Yala Ku-mi-orh, "When would you like to start?"

King Yala offered the admiral another forced smile and replied calmly, "I must confer with my advisors."

Zheng He was left cooling his heels in the tropical sun for a few moments while Yala Ku-mi-orh, General Bura and several other senior advisors whispered quietly together. Then, after a short interlude, King Yala Ku-mi-orh turned back to Zheng He and again flashed his famous smile.

"It's still early in the day, Lord Zheng He. If its not too much trouble, I'd like to take the tour, now!"

"Now, Your Majesty?" Zheng He stammered, as he was unprepared for the king's unusual request.

"Yes, now!" King Yala reiterated firmly, his fake smile frozen on his face. "If you don't mind, please!"

The admiral turned to his own military advisors to see what they thought of the king's unusual request. It's plain that they too, were caught off guard and felt uncomfortable in the change of plans. No ruler had ever made such a request before.

Yala Ku-mi-orh pushed for a decision.

"My palace is some distance inland, admiral. Since I'm at the beach and my advisors are at the beach, it would be much more convenient for us to inspect your ships now, rather than later!"

Again the king offered Zheng He his wide fake smile and hoped that it would help solicit a favorable reply.

"Well," the admiral stammered, not wanting to begin their relationship on a sour note, "I, ahhh, guess it can be arranged. How many people do you plan to take with you on the tour?"

Again Yala Ku-mi-orh conferred briefly with General Bura and his advisors before answering. Then, as before, he turned and smiled broadly at the Ming leader.

"Thirty, Lord Zheng He," he replied, "that is, if it's not too much trouble!"

Zheng He took a decision and acquiesced to the king's request.

"It will be no problem, Your Majesty. If I transfer a few of my people to other boats, I should be able to accommodate you and thirty of your advisors on my private launch."

"Splendid!" King Yala gushed, while clapping his hands gleefully. "It's settled! I can hardly wait to see your magnificent ships up close!"

Later that same evening, after a full day of escorting the Ceylon king and his advisors around to the different-sized ships in the fleet, Zheng He retreated to his private living room on the Baochuan and was glad he could finally sit down for a few minutes and rest. Ma Huan, Xi Chen and I joined him after his long and tiring day, as he had to follow the king around on his unscheduled tour.

King Yala Ku-mi-orh was quite an inquisitive fellow!" Zheng He suggested to no one in particular. "I think he asked me questions about almost everything."

"And if 'he' wasn't asking questions," Ma Huan added sourly, "General Bura was! What do you suppose they want to do? Learn how to build their own ships?"

I started instinctively to rub my little cross then blurted out, "I don't trust him!" which shocked everyone present including myself.

"What's the matter with you?" Zheng He asked, as if my negative comment had somehow hurt him personally.

"I don't know," I sighed, not wanting to back off of what I had originally said. "It's just that, King Yala, something-or-other, bothers me!"

"He bothers you?" Zheng He asked, again surprised at what I'd just said. "What do you mean that he bothers you?"

"He asked too many questions!" I told him firmly, feeling more uncomfortable the more I thought about it. "Why would he want to know how much treasure we were carrying, or how many soldiers were on the ships? He even asked questions about our armament! I don't know, Zheng He, it just didn't feel right for him to be asking so many questions. And now he wants to come back and make another inspection tomorrow!"

"You're just being, Italian!" Zheng He joked, trying to ease my fear. "As far as I'm concerned, King Yala Ku-mi-orh just likes ships. That's all! It's the first time he's ever had the chance to see such a flotilla of huge ships up close. I think it's perfectly normal that he would want to find out whatever he could about them while we're here. I think you should quit worrying!"

"Maybe you're right!" I allowed with a shrug, but knew that I wasn't completely sold that Zheng He's assessment was right. "Maybe since I'm a friar," I added, "I shouldn't be so suspicious."

Zheng He wanted to drop the subject so he turned his attention to Ma Huan and Xi Chen.

"I say we should get ourselves ready to go to the king's banquet. I'm starved!"

Xi Chen couldn't resist getting in a friendly dig.

"You're always starved!" she told him happily. "I thought you weren't going to eat so much."

"When the friar starts cutting down," Zheng He declared, "then I'll start cutting down, but not before!"

I raised my eyes to heaven pretending to pray.

"Mama Mia!" I whistled as I rubbed my ample stomach with both hands. "You're going to end up looking bigger than me!"


Later that same night we all sat down at the king's grand banquet table and, I must say, all of us enjoyed ourselves immensely. Dozens of Ceylonese dancers and musicians performed while we happily feasted on large quantities of roast pig and a large selection of tropical fruits.

Xi Chen and Ma Huan sat just to the right of Zheng He while the Ceylonese king and queen sat to his left. In the middle of the festive occasion, I saw Zheng He as he leaned over Xi Chen and tried to get the attention of his male servant.

"Ma Huan!" he shouted, trying to be heard over the jumbled noise of loud music and people talking, "I just had a great idea! While the ships are being resupplied over the next few weeks, why don't we build a stone monument here on Ceylon to commemorate our visit. Do you think you can figure out something to say that we could cut into stone?"

Ma Huan was surprised by the admiral's request but wasn't the least bit intimidated.

"I think it's a good idea, Sir," he shouted back. "Do you want the inscription to be in Chinese, Persian, or Tamil?"

Now it was Zheng He who was surprised. He looked inquisitively at Xi Chen, then back at his waiting servant.

"What is Tamil?" he asked sheepishly.

"That's one of the local dialects, Sir, that is spoken here on Ceylon, Persian is the other! May I suggest, Sir, that if you're going to transcribe something onto stone, you use both of the local languages."

"Very good thinking!" Zheng He shouted back, as he tried to be heard over the noise and wished that he had thought of what his servant had just suggested. "Will it be too much trouble for you to come up with something we can say?" he shouted to his servant again.

"No, Sir!" Ma Huan replied confidently. "I'm sure I can come up with something appropriate!"

When Zheng He straightened up in his seat, he was still uneasy about the important task that he had just assigned to his servant. Once again he leaned over in front of Xi Chen yelled in Ma Huan's direction.

"Maybe you can get some of our Buddhist priests to help you with the message, Ma Huan."

Ma Huan shook his head.

"That won't be necessary, Sir! I'm quite certain I can handle it!"

"Are you sure it won't be too much trouble?"

Xi Chen was getting exasperated at all the shouting back and forth in front of her and Zheng He's refusal to accept what his servant had just told him.

"He said he could do it, Zheng He!" she now whispered in his ear. "Why don't you quit shouting at the boy and just let him do it!"

Finally Zheng He straightened up and looked over at King Yala Ku-mi-orh who was now also looking curiously at the admiral as he tried to figure out what all the shouting was about.

"Are you all right, Lord Zheng He?" he asked, seemiingly concerned, but not sure about what?

"I'm fine, Your Majesty," Zheng He yelled back happily. "Just fine!"


The next day, Zheng He, Xi Chen, Ma Huan and I were back on board the Baochuan trying to recover from the previous night's festivities. Unfortunately, I can't say that my friend was looking his best.

"What's the matter with you?" I asked him grinning. "Did you eat too much fancy food last night?"

"I guess I did," he moaned, not bothering to look up. "That sure was some banquet!"

"I told you not to eat so much," Xi Chen calmly admonished. "You know what it always does to you."

"Don't remind me!"

Zheng He's response made me curious.

"What does it do to you?" I asked, without thinking.

Zheng He frowned again.

"Don't ask!"

I shrugged my shoulders at his non-answer and started pouring myself a cup of hot tea.

"When is the king supposed to start his second tour?" I asked, as I didn't bother to hide the irritation in my voice. "He inspected our ships yesterday. Why does he have to come back today?"

"I don't know," Zheng He replied testily, not missing the fact that I was questioning the king's motive. "He probably just likes ships."

Then, after a moment he added, "Do you still feel nervous about the king? I think he went out of his way to entertain us last night, don't you?"

"I know!" I allowed as I threw my arms up into the air in mock surrender. "I just wish he wasn't so adamant about inspecting all the ships. It doesn't seem normal. That's what makes me so nervous!"

Zheng He changed the subject and asked Ma Huan if he had thought about what he might want to write on the monument last night before he went to bed?

"Do you mean, Sir, about what inscription you think we should have inscribed on the stone?"

"That's right! I'd like for you to make up something, that's sort of formal sounding, but not, too formal sounding!"

Xi Chen was surprised at Zheng He's request.

"Formal sounding?" she asked, obviously mocking her love, "but not too formal? What's that supposed to mean?"

"You know," he quickly backtracked, trying to make sure everyone understood. "I'd like for it to sound somewhat serious, rather than too casual."

Ma Huan pulled a piece of paper out of his pocket and offered the admiral a slight bow.

"I have something prepared, Sir, that I trust will be satisfactory. Would you like to hear it?"

Zheng He, Xi Chen and I looked incredulously at each other and then back to Ma Huan. None of us could believe that he'd already written something for his master's approval.

"You have something already prepared?" Zheng He stammered. "What did you do, make it up in your sleep?"

"Yes, Sir!" Ma Huan answered without thinking, then quickly changed his mind, "I mean, 'no, sir!' Would you, ahhh, like to hear what I've written?"

Zheng He knew Ma Huan was a bright young man who was capable of knowing many things and able to speak several langauges, but to have him come up with an important declaration overnight, that would be carved permanently into stone for future generations to read, was a little more than he could comprehend. All Zheng He could do was shrug, lift an eyebrow in amazement and acquiesce to his servant's request.

"Please," he responded sheepishly, "if you've already prepared something, I'd like to hear it!"

Ma Huan nervously cleared his throat, then began reading what he had written down.

"His Imperial Majesty, Emperor of the Great Ming, has dispatched the Grand Admiral, Zheng He, and others, to set forth his utterances before Lord Buddha, the World Honored One, as herein follows."

Ma Huan paused for a moment and asked Zheng He if he thought that the beginning sounded OK?

"Sounds good to me, so far!" he replied casually with a surprised look on his face. "Friar? Xi Chen? Does it sound OK to you?"

Xi Chen and I were both just as surprised as Zheng He at what Ma Huan had written in such a short period of time. We both shrugged our shoulders and nodded our quick agreement. Zheng He then waved for his servant to continue.

"Deeply do we reverence thee," Ma Huan continued, "Merciful and Honored One, of bright perfection wide-embracing, where Way and Virtue passes all understanding, where Law pervades all human relations, and the years of whose great 'kalpe' rival the river sands in number..."

Zheng He interrupted.

"Ma Huan, where did you get all of that?"

Ma Huan maintained a serious look on his face and responded solemnly, "I have a way with words, Sir."

Zheng He could only shake his head in amazement.

"Yes, I guess you do!"

"Do you think it's satisfactory, Sir?"

"Yes, it's very satisfactory. Please continue."

Ma Huan once again looked at his notes and began reading.

"Thou, whose controlling influence ennobles and converts, inspiring acts of love and giving intelligent insight into the nature of this vale of tears, Thou whose mysterious response is limitless! The temples and monasteries of Ceylon's mountainous isle, lying in the southern ocean far, are imbued and enlightened by Thy miraculously responsive power."

Ma Huan finally stopped and confessed that was as much as he had been able to write since last night. He promised that he would have all of the message completed in time for it to be inscribed in stone. None of us could believe what we had heard from Ma Huan, but we also had no doubt that King Yala Ku-mi-orh would find the inscription more than acceptable.


Three weeks later the large stone monument was completed with Ma Huan's words inscribed in Chinese, Persian and Tamil. During the formal ceremony which was attended by more than three hundred Chinese and Ceylonese offficials and dignitaries, Zheng He read from a long scroll which contained the rest of what Ma Huan had written and was now inscribed on the stone.

"Of late, we have despatched missions to announce our Mandate to foreign nations and during their journeys over the oceans, they have been favored with the blessing of Thy beneficent protection. They have escaped disaster or misfortune, journeying in safety to and fro, ever guided by Thy great virtue."

Zheng He stopped for a moment and smiled at the king, to see if everything sounded all right. The king nodded appreciatively at the Ming admiral and offered him his large fake smile. Zheng He cleared his throat twice, glanced at Xi Chen, then continued.

"Wherefore, according to the Rites, we bestow offerings in recompense, and do reverently present before the Lord Buddha, the World-Honored One, oblations of gold and silver, gold-embroidered jewelled banners of variegated silk, incense-burners and flower-vases, silk of many colors in lining and exterior, lamps and candles with other gifts, in order to manifest the high honor of the Lord Buddha. May his Light shine upon the donors."

Zheng He again stopped, this time to catch his breath. He looked at the king, who, as before, offered him his fake generous smile and nodded approvingly. Reassured, the admiral continued.

"May it be duly recorded the gifts presented to the World Honored One, include, one thousand pieces of gold, five thousand pieces of silver, one hundred rolls of silk, two thousand five hundred catties of perfumed oil and a large variety of bronze ecclesiastical ornaments, gilded and lacquered, being presented in the 7th year of the Zhu Di reign, fourteen hundred and nine."

When Zheng He finished, the king bowed appreciatively to the Ming admiral and gave him an even bigger smile.

"Please tell your Benevolent Emperor, Lord Zheng He, that I accept his generous gifts on behalf of all the Ceylonese people. I also look forward to a long period of friendship and trade with the great people of China."

The king paused briefly which indicated that his acceptance speech was now complete, but then added one more comment.

"May you and your men have a safe journey to Arabia, Lord Zheng He, and on your return voyage home, I pray that you will again stop in Ceylon and honor us with another visit."

Zheng He was more than happy to agree.

"You've been most generous, Oh, king," he intoned. "Our fleet should be returning home in about four months. If you'd like for us to stop for another visit, I don't see why it couldn't be arranged!"

"Good!" King Yala whooped, as he clapped his hands together happily. He then turned to his chief advisor and gave him an official pronouncement.

"Did you hear that, General Bura? Lord Zheng He said he will return with the fleet in four months. I'm putting you personally in charge to see that everything will be in order. The next time Lord Zheng He and his friends honor us with a visit, I want you to have everything ready so we can receive them properly!"

The next day we were again under full sail as we followed our course to Arabia. As usual, Zheng He flagship led the huge Ming armada with the rest of the ships strung out to the far horizon and beyond.

Everyone was in an exceptionally good mood, since we had just completed a successful stopover in Ceylon and were happy to be heading for our final destination. As Zheng He's flagship plowed through moderate seas, his private living room was just the way he liked it, crowded with friends!

My admiral friend, though, had not forgotten that at the beginning of our visit to Ceylon I was suspicious of the little king. Since all of us were so well treated, he couldn't resist the temptation of asking me what I thought of the Ceylon ruler now?

All I could do was let out a big sigh as I responded with a shrug.

"What can I say, Lord Zheng He? We were all very well treated. He just made me a little nervous when he insisted on touring all the ships. I apologize to everyone for being so suspicious."

Xi Chen also had a wonderful time in Ceylon and let all of us know that she couldn't be more delighted we were going to return.

"I wonder what kind of a celebration the king will have for us when we return?" she bubbled excitedly.

"Let's hope our meetings in Arabia go as well as they did on Ceylon." Zheng He said with a smile. "On Ceylon they couldn't have gone better."

"Are you anxious to get to Arabia, Sir?" Ma Huan asked. "I've heard you say more than once that it's the one place in the world that you've always wanted to visit!"

"It's like a miracle," Zheng He told his servant happily, unable to hide the smile on his face. "I've dreamed of visiting the holy city of Mecca ever since I was a boy. And now that we're actually on our way, I can hardly believe it!"

"Do you think you'll get a chance to visit the holy city like your father and grandfather?" I asked. "That would certainly be wonderful if you did!"

348

"I don't know, friar, but being in Arabia I know I'll be close!"

"It would be a shame if you didn't get to visit," Xi Chen volunteered quickly. "I know how much it would mean to you. Surely, after making such a long journey you can find a way."

"We'll see," was all Zheng He would say, while still smiling broadly. "If it's Allah's will, I'm sure something will enable me to fulfill my lifelong dream."

Ma Huan was anxious to start planning for their arrival.

"Sir! When we get to Arabia, do you plan to send Lt. Zhang Ji ahead with a group of soldiers to seek out the local ruler? If you do, I'd like permission to go with them. Maybe I could take the place of a translator since I'm fluent in Arabic."

"That sounds like a good idea to me," Zheng He agreed. "And when you locate the ruler, or whoever's in charge of the country, I'd like for you and Lt. Zhang Ji to bring him back here to me, on the flagship. That way, we can be sure to make the proper impression."

Lt. Zhang Ji asked about security.

"How many soldiers do you think we should take, Sir, two hundred or three hundred?"

Zheng He didn't take long to decide.

"Two hundred is probably a good number. I don't think you'll need more than that."

His military assessment started me to worry.

"Why do you want to take so many soldiers?" I asked. "Do you expect trouble?"

"No! Not at all, friar!" he let me know cheerily. "Those who follow the teachings of Mohammed are normally a very friendly and peace-loving people. But there is just no need for us to take any chances!"


When we arrived off the coast of Arabia three weeks later, as agreed, Zheng He sent Lt. Zhang Ji and Ma Huan inland to search out the local ruler. They quickly discovered as they moved inland that Chinese horses aren't very good for riding in deep sand. But, unfortunately, that's the only animals that our Ming ships carried for transportation. It was tough going for the horses, no doubt about that, but it also wasn't easy for the two hundred Ming soldiers who had to ride the horses Lord Zheng He said should go along, "just in case!"

After heading inland for almost a full day the Ming representatives finally came across a small camel caravan that approached them from the south. If they didn't stop, their paths would soon cross.

Lt. Zhang Ji was the first to spot the heavily loaded animals and pointed them out to his friend.

"Ma Huan, look! Camels! That's what we need. These horses aren't worth a damn in this sand!"

Zhang Ji turned in his saddle to check on his troops, who were doing their best to keep up. He could see that all of his men were sweating profusely and they all looked dog-tired. The horses they were riding didn't seem to be faring any better. They, too, were covered with sweat and mired in deep sand over their hooves.

When Zhang Ji turned back to look again at the caravan, he was surprised to see that it also had stopped. "They probably have seen us and wonder what we're up to?" he mused to Ma Huan. "I'm sure they have never seen armed Chinese on horseback before."

After a few long moments of both groups watching each other, Lt. Zhang Ji motioned for Ma Huan to move his horse a little closer to the men on the camels, so he could speak to them in their native tongue.

Slowly Ma Huan approached the camel caravan alone, then stopped at a distance close enough that his voice could be heard.

"Can you tell me where we can find the nearest city?" he asked, not wanting to say, or do anything, that might frighten the four men leading the procession of sixteen animals that were loaded down with cloth bags, wooden boxes and earthen jars.

The dark-skinned riders were shocked when they heard the Chinese foreigner speak to them in their native tongue. The fact that he could speak to them in Arabic did make them feel somewhat better, but the sight of two hundred armed Ming soldiers sitting on horses just behind the Chinese man, didn't!

When the four Arab men didn't answer Ma Huan's simple question, he saw they looking at the Ming soldiers and figured out why they probably felt intimidated.

"We come in peace!" he told them quickly, while offering a big smile to make them feel at ease. "We bring gifts for the ruler of your country. Can you please tell me where I might find him?"

The four riders conversed privately with each other before answering Zheng He's servant, then one of the men pointed across a large span of sand dunes on the horizon.

"King Juddah lives in that direction," he stated in his native Arabic. "The king lives in a large palace in the city of Sofar."

Lt. Zhang Ji sat on his horse as he watched Ma Huan speak with the four Arab traders. Since didn't speak a word of Arabic, he had no idea what was being said. Cautiously he urged his horse forward, stopped next to Ma Huan and hoped that he could find out what was going on. Ma Huan told him about the king named Juddah, who was supposed to be living in a city called Sofar.

"Did you ask him how far it is to the city?" Zhang Ji asked, mainly worried about how much longer his men would have to ride through the damnable hot sand.

Ma Huan shook his head then turned to face the Arab riders.

"How far is the city from here?" he asked again in perfect Arabic.

"Two days by camel!" one of the men replied casually, while again gesturing in the direction of the city.

"Is that where you're headed?" Ma Huan then asked.

"God willing!"

Without saying another word, the four men urged their camels forward and continued their slow, steady, trek across the ocean of hot sand. As they moved across the path of Lt. Zhang Ji, Ma Huan and the Chinese soldiers, reluctantly, the Ming representatives urged their horses forward so they could follow.

After a few minutes the four Arab men looked back at the foreign strangers and watched them as they struggled mightily to keep up in the loose deep sand. All four men shook their heads in disgust at the pitiful sight and grumbled to themselves, "Stupid foreigners!"


When the Ming travelers finally made it safely to the city of Sofar, two days later, they were hot, they were tired and thoroughly delighted to be out of the desert. When the caravan riders showed them where their ruler's palace was located, Lt. Zhang Ji ordered his men to rest under a grove of stately date palms while he and Ma Huan set up a meeting with the local ruler.

When two Arab servants arrived they led them through several large rooms which had high ceilings that were open at the top. Ma Huan was not unfamiliar with the architecture. He knew the rooms were built that way on purpose, because it allowed heat to escape through the roof at the top, while at the same time it enabled rooms down below to remain relatively cool.

Within minutes the two Chinese emissaries were ushered into King Juddah's richly decorated throne room. They quickly noticed that the room itself wasn't as large as some of the other rooms they had just passed, but it did feature eight magnificent carved columns that were covered with gold. It also contained an unusual-looking throne which was beautifully decorated with thousands of rubies and covered, almost entirely, with intricate designs of silver.

As soon as the Chinese entered the Arabian stronghold, they saw the king sitting on his throne as he beckoned them to enter.

Ma Huan and Lt. Zhang Ji were surprised that he was a rather small man, with a closely cropped black beard and clothed simply in a looslyfitting white garment. His skin was deeply tanned, which was normal for someone who had spent his entire life in the desert. To them he looked to be no more than sixty years old.

Standing behind the king, off to one side, was a slightly younger man who they guessed was probably in his early fifties. This man was more heavyset and Ma Huan guessed that he was probably the king's advisor. The man's most distinguishing characteristic, other than his dark leathery skin, was the angry-looking scowl that he kept etched on his face which made him look like he didn't trust anyone.

Six other Arab men who were younger and less intimidating-looking also stood close by, a little off to one side who eyed the foreigners silently as they approached and made their compulsory bow.

While Lt. Zhang Ji and Ma Huan bowed to the king, the senior advisor with the perpetual scowl, whose name they later learned was Abdul bin Waddi, leaned over and whispered into King Juddah's ear.

"Do not forget, Sire, all Chinese are partial to Buddha and are against the followers of Islam. Do not believe anything they tell you!"

Since the Chinese lieutenant didn't speak a word of Arabic he had to rely on Ma Huan to handle all of the communications.

"We come in peace, Your Majesty," Ma Huan began, as he offered the monarch a big smile and spoke to him in his local tongue. "We come in peace, as representatives of his Imperial Majesty, Zhu Di, the Third Ming Emperor of China."

King Juddah did not return Ma Huan's smile. Neither did his advisor Abdul bin Waddi.

"What is it you wish from me?" he asked ominously, his voice gravelly and not particularly friendly-sounding.

Ma Huan made sure he didn't act intimidated.

"We would like for you to meet with our admiral, Lord Zheng He. He would like to discuss the possibility of establishing trade between our two great countries."

Abdul bin Waddi again leaned over and whispered in King Juddah's ear.

"Send them away, Sire! Nothing good can come from dealing with Chinese!"

But King Juddah was now curious. Actually, he was flattered that a representative of the Chinese emperor would travel such a long distance to pay him a visit. With a wave of his hand he disregarded his advisor's advice, at least for the moment.

"You say that your emperor would like to trade with me?" he responded, trying to project a more friendly attitude. "What kind of trade does he have in mind?"

"Whatever your country has of value, Your Majesty," Ma Huan replied quickly, as he continued to smile and sound as sincere as he possibly could. "In China we have a number of fine products like porcelain and silk.  I know that you have an abundance of dates.  Possibly these items could be traded.  Whatever is decided, Your Majesty, it would have to be worked out between you and our esteemed Ming admiral, Lord Zheng He"

Abdul bin Waddi didn't like the way things were going. He pulled again on King Juddah's sleeve to get his attention, but once again the Arab king waved him away.

"And who is this Ming admiral, Lord Zheng He, you talk about?" King Juddah asked.  "Why isn't he with you now?"

Ma Huan was glad to be finally getting somewhere.

"Lord Zheng He, Your Majesty, waits to rreceive you on his flagship just off the coast, not more than a two day's ride from here."

Now it was Lt. Zhang Ji, who pulled on Ma Huan's sleeve.

"What's he saying?"

"Nothing yet!" Ma Huan whispered in Chinese. "Just be quiet for a minute."

Zhang Ji again pulled on the servant's sleeve and reminded him of what they were supposed to do.

"Did you tell the king that Lord Zheng He wants to meet with the king on the flagship?"

"That's what I'm suggesting.  Let me finish."

"Your Majesty!" Ma Huan began again, "Our admiral is prepared to offer you many expensive gifts.  At his floating palace on the sea, he feels that he would be able to entertain you and your royal officials properly."

Abdul bin Waddi whispered again into King Juddah's ear.

"Do not even consider it, Sire!  It would be much too dangerous!  I strongly advise against it!"

King Juddah was getting upset with the steady stream of dire advice that he continued to receive from his Chief Advisor.  He whispered back bruskly.

"They say they come in peace, Chief Advisor!  Trading with the Chinese could be very good for our country."

Abdul was not persuaded.

"If you feel you must meet with them, Sire" he warned, "then have them come here, to the desert, where you have the advantage!"

King Juddah did have to admit that this time his advisor might be making some sense. He turned again to face the two Chinese representatives.

"I'll agree to meet with your admiral," he told them cautiously, "but not on his flagship as you have suggested. He must agree to meet with me here, at my palace in Sofar. If that is satisfactory, then I will receive him in a week, not before."

Lt. Zhang Ji looked again at Ma Huan as he still did not understand what was going on. Ma Huan didn't want to take the time to explain, so he quickly whispered and told his friend what he should do next.

"Just bow and follow me out," he hissed. "I'll tell you what has happened later!"

The two young men bowed to the king, then took their leave from the throne room. As soon as they were gone, Abdul bin Waddi wasted no time in trying to convince his king that he shouldn't deal with foreigners.

"You can't trust the Chinese, Sire!" he told King Juddah ominously. "They dangle a carrot in front of your face, just to see if you'll take it!"

"What are you talking about?" King Juddah demanded, as he was obviously irritated by his advisor's steady stream of dire predictions.

"They want to start trading with us, Abdul. Didn't you hear them? What could be wrong with that?"

"That's what they tell you to your face, Sire," he gushed forcefully. "But don't be fooled. They'll make the same offer to our enemies. By playing one side against the other we run the risk of our enemies growing strong at our expense."

Confused by his advisor's irrational reasoning, King Juddah decided that it might be wise if he didn't take any unnecessary chances.

"What do you suggest," he sighed, reluctantly.

"I suggest that you slay them, Your Majesty!"

King Juddah was taken aback by Abdul Bin Waddi's harsh solution.

"Slay them, Chief Advisor? You say I should slay the Chinese? Are you sure that's necessary? What if they have come in peace to trade with us just as they have said? We would lose a golden opportunity!"

Abdul bin Waddi would not be denied.

"Think of what you're saying, Sire!" he again complained strongly. "All Chinese are infidels and cannot be trusted! In the name of Merciful Allah, when they arrive, you must SLAY THEM!"

King Juddah waved his hand at his irritating Chief Advisor and hoped that it would stop his negative flow of advice. To the king, the two young men who met with him seemed nice enough, but still, one could never be sure. It might be a trick of some kind as Abdul bin Waddi had suggested.

"If I agree to do as you say," he asked his advisor cautiously, "what would be your plan?"

The scowling advisor smiled inwardly to hisself, happy that his monarch had finally come to his senses.

"We have many troops, Sire, but maybe not enough. It was very smart of you to tell the Chinese that you couldn't meet with them for a week. That will give us time to enlist the aid of our Muslim brothers and increase our army threefold! When the Chinese leader has arrived with his puny entourage of soldiers and trade envoys, we will be ready. At the first hint of trouble we can slay all of them!"

King Juddah was still not convinced.

"But what if the Chinese bring a large army, Abdul? What will you do them?"

"How can there be a large army, Sire? The Chinese have come in boats! Little boats, I'm sure. How many little boats can there be, three or four at the most? There can be no army, Your Majesty, and there can be no danger! At the first hint of trouble we will annihilate all of them! I promise you in the name of Allah!"

"You make it sound so simple!" King Juddah replied reluctantly, as he didn't really want to be part of such a drastic action.

"It will be simple!" Abdul shouted again, gaining more and more confidence everytime his king backed down.

"After the trade talks are over, Sire, I suggest you invite the foreigners to a meal in the desert. While they're being lulled to sleep with music and dance our men can surround the area and slay them easily."

Juddah still didn't know why such a dastardly deed might be necessary.

"Are you sure we need to do such a thing?" he begged. "The Chinese say they come in peace and..."

"They have not come in peace!" Abdul interrupted again, this time loudly. "They have come to DECEIVE YOU! If you wish to keep your kingdom intact I suggest you DO AS I SAY!"


Three days later Lt. Zhang Ji and Ma Huan were back on board the flagship and prepared to make their report to the fleet admiral. Zheng He was anxious to find out how everything went, but was surprised that it took them so long.

Since Lt. Zhang Ji was officially in charge of the military contingent it was he who bowed to the Ming admiral and reported first.

"Sir! We located the local king as you instructed but we had to ride two days through the desert to find him."

"Was he friendly?" was the first question Zheng He always asked.

"Not particularly!" Zhang Ji responded tentatively, as he hated to bring the admiral less than satisfactory news.

Zheng He couldn't believe it! All the members of the Muslim faith were supposed to be friendly to strangers. Of all the countries that the fleet had previously visited, to Zheng He, the country he would least expect to have a problem with would be Arabia.

"He wasn't friendly?" Zheng He asked, unable to believe what his lieutenant had just reported. "I find that extremely hard to believe."

"I think Ma Huan should be the one to explain, Sir!" Zhang Ji admitted. "He's the one who did the talking. All I could report is what he told me."

Zheng He looked to his trusted servant to find out what really happened.

"Well? Is it true, Ma Huan? Was the Arab king unfriendly to you?"

"Actually, Sir, I think the problem was more with the king's personal advisor. He's the one who seemed to be the troublemaker! When I suggested that the king meet with you here on the flagship, it was his advisor who talked him out of it!"

"Will the king meet with me anywhere?" Zheng He questioned, obviously perplexed by what he was being told.

"Yes, Sir! He said he would meet with you at his palace in the desert. He said he'd be ready to meet with you in about a week."

Zheng He then turned and asked for my advice.

"What do you make of it, friar? You're always pretty good at figuring out things with foreigners. Do you have any idea why the king and his advisor should be have acted the way they did?"

"You should know better than me," I told him honestly. "After all, you're the one who's a follower of Mohammed, just like the king and his advisor. I don't know that much about the Muslim religion. But one thing I do know is that the people who say they follow the religion aren't supposed to be unfriendly towards strangers."

Zheng He agreed.

"That's right, my friend! It was Mohammed himself who said that if a man should ask something of you, give it to him, willingly! People who follow Islam aren't supposed to behave toward strangers the way these two men seemed to be behaving, for any reason!"

Zheng He then turned back to Ma Huan.

"Did you mention to the king that I'm also a follower of Islam?"

"No, Sir! I guess I should have, but I never got the chance. My conversation with the king was fairly brief. Unfortunately, there wasn't a whole lot I could say with that advisor whispering in his ear all the time."

Zheng He again turned to his lieutenant.

"Can you think of anything else I should know that would help me make my decision?"

"No Sir, nothing that I can think of. But I'm sure of one thing! The Arab king doesn't say or do anything without first consulting with his advisor. And that advisor, I'm afraid, is someone you can't trust!"

Zheng He took his decision.

"Well, then, we'll meet with the king at his palace, just as he has requested, but we won't take any chances. We shall be fully prepared. How far inland did you say it was to the king's palace?"

"Normally, by horse, Sir," Zhang Ji allowed, "it would be a two day's ride. But with our wagons loaded down with weapons and supplies, I'm sure getting all that desert sand will take us a good three days and maybe even four!"

"Then four days it is, lieutenant!" Zheng He replied firmly. "Notify Captain Su that I want ten thousand armed soldiers and one thousand Ming cannons brought to bear upon the Arab city. If we can't use the fleet to impress the king here on the coast, then, in the name of our Benevolent Emperor, we shall impress him in the desert where he resides!"

Zheng He finally turned to Xi Chen who had been sitting quietly next to him on the couch throughout the entire discussion.

"How would you like to get off the flagship for a few weeks?" he suggested happily. "Does a little ride in the desert sound like fun?"

"I wouldn't mind getting off this treasure ship for awhile," she confessed, "but having to ride three or four day on a horse through a hot desert, well, I'm not so sure."

"I don't think it will be too bad," Zheng He countered, trying to be enthusiastic. "In fact, I think it will be kind of fun!"

Not wanting to spoil the party, Xi Chen then teased the fleet admiral in front of his collection of friends.

"On the flagship, or on a horse, Lord Zheng He, I will be most happy to follow you anywhere."

Jokingly I smiled and kissed my little cross when I heard Xi Chen's obvious pandering.

"Mama Mia!" I whistled happily, as I offered them both a big smile. "I wish I had someone beautiful who would follow me around like that, anywhere!"

Three days later we began to struggle through the deep sand of the desert on our way to King Juddah's palace. It was hot, it was tiring, and as Ma Huan and Lt. Zhang Ji already knew, it was not much fun.

Our eager anticipation of taking a vacation from the constant rocking of the flagship had now turned into an exercise in agony. We were all having a terrible time trying to put up with the shifting sand while we sweated profusely in the oppresive heat.

But it was worse for the Ming soldiers than it was for us! Their plight was made even more deviling because they had to march through the sand on foot while they dragged and pushed a thousand cannons.

That first night, exhausted from their first ten-hour struggle, all the men were delighted to set up tents and get a much-needed rest. If any Bedouin tribesmen happened upon the Chinese encampment in the dark, they certainly wouldn't have believed their eyes. Thousands of small lanterns and campfires now dotted the desert like sparkling jewels for several li in all directions.

As a precaution, Zheng He made sure he set out multiple guards on the far perimeters of our encampment, just to to make certain that we wouldn't be surprised at night. Danger could be lurking among any of the many sand dunes which surrounded the Chinese encampment, but for the Ming admiral and his lady servant there was no hint of any danger or discomfort.

When they retired for the evening, they did so in the admirals large tent which had been richly furnished with an oversized bed, several black lacquered tables, half a dozen ornately decorated chairs and three thickly woven carpets. When laid upon the sand, the carpets made of fine Chinese silk provided the couple with an interior that was as comfortable to walk on as it was pleasing to the eye.

To Xi Chen the desert excursion was more like a picnic than it was a military maneuver. It was hot during the day, no doubt about that, but as evening approached the heat evaporated and it actually became quite chilly. But in their spacious tent, laying on the large bed as she snuggled in her lover's arms, life could not be better. She looked lovingly at Zheng He as she casually popped a juicy grape into her mouth.

"Did you ever think, Zheng He, in your wildest dreams, that someday you and I would be together in Arabia? I can't believe that we're actually here!"

Zheng He leaned over and kissed Xi Chen on the cheek.

"I feel the same way, my love," he allowed, shaking his head at the incredible thought. "But what's even harder for me to comprehend is here we are, going to meet our Muslim brothers, armed to the teeth, and worried that we might have to engage them in battle!"

Zheng He paused for a moment to reflect on what he'd just said.

"I always saw myself traveling to Arabia one day, just like my father and grandfather, making a pilgrimage to the holy city of Mecca. But now, not only do I not know where Mecca is located, my most trusted men believe that we could be walking into a trap! The thought of it is truly unbelievable."

Xi Chen picked up another grape and put it into her mouth, then seductively rolled herself on top of Zheng He and passed the grape from her mouth into his.

Zheng He smiled.

"What did you do that for? That was sexy?"

"Because I want you to stop being so serious. All you do is worry about things that could go wrong. We're in Arabia together and we're in love! Who would have thought such a thing was possible just six months ago? It has got to be a miracle from Allah!"

Xi Chen put her lips against Zheng He's lips and gave him a long, hard, sexy kiss. When she finished she touched his lips with her finger.

"I don't think I'd be complaining about Allah's miracle if I were you!"

Zheng He pretended to bite her finger, then returned Xi Chen's kiss with one of his own.

"You're so practical!" he whispered softly, while stroking her face with his hands. "I guess that's why I love you so much!"

The admiral pushed aside the plate of fruit and lay Xi Chen over on her back. He then whispered to her again, this time, in a husky voice.

"On the flagship we practiced making love a hundred different ways. I've just thought of a hundred more!"

Xi Chen pulled Zheng He close to her breast and purred sexily.

"Oh, Zheng He...you're..."

He grinned and started nibbling her ear.

"Shameful? Yes, I know! I'm terribly shameful!"


Three days later, Zheng He made sure that flags flew and hundreds of horns, cymbals and drums heralded the arrival of ten thousand Chinese soldiers, plus five hundred officers, officials and trade envoys, as they triumphantly marched through the main entrance to King Juddah's city.

Sofar's Sharif Gate was a large wooden structure which stood at least twenty feet high and was meant to keep everyone out who wasn't invited. But when King Juddah saw the incredible Ming force that approached Sofar from across the desert, he quickly decided that discretion was the better part of valor and ordered for the gate to be opened as wide as it would go. He wanted to be sure that the visiting Chinese could enter his city unimpeded.

King Juddah stood on the front balcony of his palace a short distance away and watched, dumbfounded, as the unbelievable display of Chinese Ming might slowly made its way through the wide open portal towards the palace.

King Juddah's Chief Advisor stood by his side.

"I trust you've arranged to protect us from the small group of Chinese visitors," King Juddah stated sarcastically.

"Your, Majesty," Abdul stammered, "I can't believe what I'm seeing! Where could they have come from?"

The king didn't bother to answer and started to leave, but then turned back and offered a piece of advice to his advisor.

"When you meet the Chinese admiral, Abdul, I suggest that you concentrate on making a favorable impression instead of trying to think up ways to have him killed! You may live longer!"


Later that same evening after an initial round of trade talks had been completed, King Juddah entertained his Chinese guests at a grand banquet. I remembered the grand banquet that the Ceylon king hosted in Zheng He's honor just a month before and thought there was no way an Arab king could top such a festive occasion. But I'm happy to say that I was wrong!

Before the food was served, each of us were given large cushions to sit on and were told that we should place them on the floor. Not being able to sit on a chair was somewhat surprising, but the cushions were comfortable and it didn't take long before the unusual custom was enjoyed by all.

King Juddah had all of us sit around large round tables that had been piled high with mounds of delicious food. Curiously, no eating utinsils were provided for our meal. But then, when the Arab ruler saw that we weren't sure how we should proceed, he smiled, scopped up a portion of rice and meat with his right hand and plopped it into his mouth.

Such an unusual display of eating was quite unconventional to all the Chinese present, but when Admiral Zheng He followed King Juddah's lead and ate with his right hand as well, all of the Chinese guests began to experiment with the Arab eating custom. Sitting on the floor while eating with my hand, I have to admit, was different, but the food was delicious, the cushions were comfortable and Zheng He and Xi Chen seemed to enjoy the experience immensely.

Zheng He was also relieved that none of Ma Huan or Lt. Zhang Ji's dire predictions had come true.

I didn't realize it at the time, but Xi Chen did become a little uncomfortable when she noticed that there were no other women sitting around the table with the Arab king. She whispered to Zheng He and asked him to ask the king why there was only a small table of women sitting together on the other side of the room?

King Juddah told Zheng He that his wife had invited a few of her lady friends to the banquet and it was she and her friends who were seated on the other side of the room. He then told Zheng He that in his country, normally, women were not allowed to sit with men during meal time. Zheng He was obviously puzzled. He asked the king why women weren't allowed to sit with men to take their meal? King Juddah thought for a moment then told him soberly, "In our country we believe that it is easier for men to talk about men things when women are not around and it is easier for womem to talk about women things when men were not around." King Juddah then smiled at the Ming admiral and concluded his explanation by saying, "It's better that way!"

I'm not sure if what the king told us was true, but that is what he told us. King Juddah then went on to explain that because of the special nature of the evening's event, he had given his wife permission to attend.

From where we were sitting some distance away, it was easy to tell which of the women was the king's wife. She was the only lady in the small group of women who wore a full-length dress that was white, complete with a matching veil that completely covered her from head to toe. All the other ladies at the table wore long dresses and head coverings as well, but their clothing was dark in color and not white.

When the music and dancing paused briefly, I thought it might be a good time to pass on a little information that I thought the king needed to know. So I leaned over and asked Zheng He if I could please say something to the king?

"If Ma Huan will translate for you," he suggested with a shrug, "I'm sure you can ask him anything you want!"

Now the problem was catching Ma Huan's attention. He was sitting on the other side of the Ming admiral busily flirting with one of the female Arab dancers who was resting nearby.

"Ma Huan!" I whispered, as loudly as I dared, "Would you please tell the king that I'd like to ask him a question. I need you to translate something for me. It won't take long!"

Ma Huan was a little embarrassed that I had caught him flirting with the young dancer, but recovered quickly, got to his feet and offered the king a slight bow. When I saw Ma Huan scramble to his feet, I tried to do the same thing, which wasn't easy because my legs were stiff from sitting on the floor.

"King Juddah?" Ma Huan announced in Arabic, "Our Italian friend, Friar Odoric, would like to ask you a question."

"Yes, of course!" Juddah responded happily, while turning and offering me a friendly smile. "Please tell the friar that I would be delighted to respond to anything he might ask."

When I saw Ma Huan nod, to let me know that it was OK to ask my question, I offered King Juddah a polite bow and began.

"Thank you, Your Majesty," I started cautiously and offered him a nervous smile.

"Did you know that Lord Zheng He is not a disciple of Lord Buddha, as are most Chinese?"

When King Juddah heard Ma Huan's translation, he gave the Ming admiral a surprised look. I quickly continued.

"He is, in fact, a disciple of Mohammed! You and Lord Zheng He are Muslim brothers!"

This time, when King Juddah heard Ma Huan's translation, he reacted with even greater surprise.

"Is that true?" he gushed, as he spoke directly to the admiral in his native tongue. "I thought that all Chinese were followers of Buddha!"

Out of respect for the king, Zheng He struggled to his feet and bowed to the king.

"I understand, your question, King Juddah," Zheng He replied in broken Arabic, "as I speak a little of your language myself, but I'm much more comfortable speaking in my native Chinese if you don't mind. My able servant, Ma Huan, can translate for us."

"As you wish," Juddah responded, still not over the revelation by the Ming admiral. "But, please tell me, Sir! How is it that you're a Muslim and not a Buddhist?"

"It's really quite simple, Your Majesty," Zheng He told him easily, once again speaking Chinese. "My family was originally from Persia. When they moved to China about a hundred years ago they did not forsake their Muslim beliefs. Consequently, I was raised from childhood following the teachings of Mohammed!"

When Ma Huan translated what Zheng He had said, King Juddah leaned over and whispered to his now sullen Chief Advisor.

"I told you your concerns were unwarranted! Lord Zheng He is a Muslim brother like you and me!"

Abdul didn't want to give up so easily.

"You can't be sure, Your Majesty," he whispered ominously. "The admiral could be lying!"

Completely disgruntled with his advisor's continued stream of bad advice, King Juddah scowled at Abdul and waved his hand, as if he were trying to dismiss him entirely.

"Do not subject me to any more of your poisonous thinking," Juddah growled angrily. "Keep quiet, so I can enjoy myself with a fellow Muslim!"

The king then turned his back on his Chief Advisor, gave Zheng He another big smile and waved broadly to his musicians.

"Play! Play!" he shouted, merrily. "I want to hear music! There's a celebration going on!"

Immediately the musicians started to play another lively tune and all the young female dancers jumped up and took to the floor. Ma Huan hated for his newly found love interest to leave his side, but he had a marvelous time watching her float effortlessly across the floor.

The way that each of the young women danced was really quite interesting. Each had a small cymbal attached to their thumb and middle finger. When they clicked the cymbals together, it enabled the dancers to keep time with the high-pitched drums and flutes as they whirled merrily about the floor.

The girls spun around and around as they danced to the lively music and put on quite a demonstration for the king and his Chinese guests. I can say for certain that the unusual dance routine was appreciated by all the Chinese, but none, I'm also certain, was watched with as much interest as Zheng He's talented servant Ma Huan.

When the banquet finally wound to a close that evening, I imagine Ma Huan prayed earnestly to All Mighty Allah that Zheng He would go straight to bed and not request his services. Just what he wanted to do with the young Arab dancer, I don't think that I would want to speculate?

Chapter Eleven

---

DEADLY BETRAYAL

Back in Beijing, Zhu Di was growing weaker every day and was now confined to bed. The energy that it took to communicate with his wife was almost too much for him. But the time they had begun to spend together each evening had now become a favorite ritual and he hated to give it up. More and more though, much to Empress Xu's chagrin, their conversations together focused on Zhu Di's mortality. He was sure that he didn't have much more time to live, so was concerned, almost obsessed, with the fact that succession to his throne was assured. The empress didn't want to even think about such a thing, much less discuss it.

"We've been together since we were children," she complained and always became terribly upset every time he broached the subject. "Please don't talk to me about dying, Zhu Di, I won't have it!"

Zhu Di had to surpress a smile when he answered her weakly.

"You won't have it my dear? But if Lord Buddha calls, there's not much you or I can do about it!"

Empress Xu refused to talk anymore about Zhu Di dying so changed the subject.

"Have you had any news from Lord Zheng He? He's been gone for more than a year. Shouldn't we be hearing something from the fleet soon?"

Zhu Di was seized by another fit of terrible coughing and wasn't able to answer. After a few tense moments, he finally was able to catch his breath and gasp a short reply.

"We'll hear something…soon enough…empress!" he wheezed. " I'm not worried…Zheng He is a very capable admiral."

Xu refilled Zhu Di's cup and tried to get him to drink a little more green tea.

"Why don't you drink a little of it," she coaxed. "It will make you feel better."

Zhu Di shook his head and waved her away.

"Please!" he gasped, as he fought to catch his breath. "I don't need… more tea!"

After a few minutes he changed the subject.

"Have you seen…our son lately?"

"You mean Zhu Bao Zhi?" Empress Xu replied, while she tried to play dumb and hoped that was the son he was referring to.

Zhu Di had to cough again, harder this time, which caused a sharp pain that felt like a dagger in his chest. With a tangle of fingers he clutched at his robe and tried to pull the sickness from his body. He hated the pain, but he also hated his wife's stupid response.

"Not Zhu Bao Zhi!" he gasped, still clutching at his chest. "He's not the one…I worry about! I want to know…about Han! Have you seen…Prince Han?"

Empress Xu sat by her husband's bed and wished he wouldn't bring up the subject of their number two son. It was always so upsetting for him.

"No!" she replied, as she sighed heavily. "I haven't seen him. He's probably away from the city."

"He isn't away, empress," Zhu Di whispered. "He's here…close by, waiting for me…to die!"

Zhu Di's ugly comment caught his wife off guard. She knew that he was now overly preoccupied with death, but she had no idea that he brooded about it so intently. Empreee Xu reached out and tried to hold her husband's hand.

"Zhu Di, please! Don't talk to me about dying. I told you, I don't like to hear it!"

Zhu Di pulled his hand away.

"I'm not talking…about dying, empress," he scolded, struggling to catch his breath, "I'm talking about…our number two son…who want's to stop the expeditions."

"You don't know that," Empress Xu complained. "Surely he would want to support your expeditions, Zhu Di. He said that he would!"

"He only said that…so I'd let him out of prison!"

"He may have wanted to get out of prison," she had to agree, "but he has changed! You said so yourself!"

"I was wrong, empress!" Zhu Di shot back. "I was stupid…to think otherwise. Prince Han hasn't changed…and now I'm…too old and sick…to do anything about it!"

"You're getting better," she pleaded and once again reached out to hold his hand. "I'm sure, Zhu Di, that in no time you'll be as good as new!"

"I'm not going to get better," he told her firmly. "I know it…and you know it! And the only one now…who might be able to talk some… sense into our son…is you!"

"Me?" she gushed, obviously surprised.

"Yes, you! You're strong!" Zhu Di pleaded, as he tried mightily not to cough. "You can do it, empress! Han will listen to you…you're his mother. I want you…to talk to him." he gasped as he began to run out of strength. "I want you…to convince him…that he must not stop…the expeditions!"

Seeing her husband sick and desperate was bad enough, but now he wanted her to get their son to do something that she knew he didn't want to do. All of it was just too much for her. Suddenly she was overcome with emotions she couldn't control and began to cry.

"Now what's the matter?" Zhu Di gasped, as he fought to catch his breath.

"Please don't ask me to talk to our son," his wife pleaded with tears streaming down her face. "You know I can't make him do anything!"

Zhu Di struggled up onto one elbow so he could address his wife more directly.

"Stop crying…and listen to me," he wheezed and hoped that she would look at him while he spoke.

"The world is full of men, empress," he gasped, as he fought to catch his breath, "men with vision…and fresh ideas." Just then another fit of violent coughs made him stop from what he was saying. This time it was so bad that it caused him to spit up blood. His wife recoiled in horror when blood splattered the sheets of his bed and drooled down a corner of his mouth. She tried to get him to take another sip of tea. But Zhu Di pushed the cup away and forced himself to continue.

"This…exchange…of ideas," he gasped again, as he tried to spit blood out of his mouth and suck air into his lungs, "is vital to China's future."

Zhu Di coughed again, but this time it wasn't as bad and he didn't spit up any more blood.

"Lie back down," she pleaded. "You must save your strength."

Again he pushed her away.

"No...let me finish." His words were weak now, barely above a whisper. "You've got to...tell our son...how I feel. You've got to...make him understand!"

"But how?" she again pleaded. "What can I do? He won't listen to me Zhu Di. He NEVER listens to me!"

"If you can't change his mind," he hissed, his eyes narrow slits, "then you...must...stop him! I don't care...how you do it, empress...just stop him! Somehow...you must...find a way."

Zhu Di could no longer continue. He fell back onto his pillows and gasped for air, with his eyes closed, completely exhausted.

Empress Xu continued to dab at her eyes with a silk hankerchief, while she looked at her prostrate husband on the bed. What she saw was just the shell of a once powerful man, who ruled China like a dragon and dominated the lives of millions of people. It tore at her heart to see him now, old and sick, reduced to begging favors from his wife.

She took her hankerchief and cleaned the spittal and blood from his mouth, leaned over and gave him a loving kiss, then picked up her things and silently left the room.

While Zheng He was in Arabia, King Juddah asked the Ming admiral if he had ever made a holy pilgrimage to Mecca? He told the king that he had not, but did tell him that his father and grandfather had made the journey to Mohammed's birthplace on two occasions. When King Juddah asked Zheng He if he would like to go, my friend immediately accepted and began telling him about the stories his father and grandfather had told him when he was a boy.

Zheng He said that his relatives had regaled him many times with stories about Mecca and the magnificent quadrangle that contained a Great Mosque right in the middle. As a young lad, he used to marvel at their description of the huge open area that was completely surrounded by thick walls more than twenty-five feet high. They also told Zheng He about the beautiful minarets they had seen at Mecca that were built of white stone which gleamed like beacons in the early morning sun.

All of these marvelous stories burned in Zheng He's heart as a boy, which made him want to make the pilgrimage to the holy city himself one day when he was grown..

Zheng He told King Juddah that what he most wanted to see and what he most wanted to do when he made his own holy pilgrimage, was go to the Kaaba, the rectangular building that was located in the middle of the inner sanctuary and follow other good Muslims around the structure seven times. His father and grandfather had circled the

Kaaba seven times, fifty years before. Zheng He knew that Muslim's must do this before they are allowed to go inside and touch the sacred Black Stone and drink from the holy well of Zemzem.

I'm happy to report that my friend was able to do all of these things and thanks to the Arab king, was able to satisfy his lifelong dream.


By the middle of March Lord Zheng He had returned from his pilgrimage to Mecca and was anxious to start his return voyage home. Surprisingly, at least to me, the Arab king and queen accepted the fleet admiral's invitation to travel with him back to China. The admiral told me that King Juddah wanted to travel to China so he could personally meet with Emperor Zhu Di and work out a mutually beneficial trade agreement between the two countries.

King Juddah selected several envoys to travel with him to China on the admiral's flagship, but someone who was not selected to travel was his devious advisor, Abdul bin Waddi. For providing the monarch with a continuous stream of very bad advice, he was unceremoniously demoted from his position of Chief Advisor to that of Transportation Coordinator for the kingdom.

As Zheng He and King Juddah were having lunch together on the back deck of the Baochuan Treasure Ship the Arab king told the admiral about the title he had recently bestowed upon his Chief Advisor. When he heard the king's description he responded politely, "That sounds like he still has a pretty impressive position."

"It may sound like an impressive position to you," the ruler laughed, "but it's really nothing more than a fancy title for someone who looks after camels!"


On the first voyage, when Lord Zheng He was on his return voyage home, he followed the African coast northward to D'jubo, Somali, then took the fleet across the Western Sea to Calicut, India. After they resupplied their ships, he then took them on a southerly heading down the Indian coast where he stopped first at Cochin and then at Atchen, before rounding the southern tip of India north of Ceylon.

On that first voyage Zheng He did not stop at Ceylon, as he decided he would save more time if he headed straight for Lambri on the northern tip of Sumatra. But on this second voyage, the fleet admiral promised King Yala Ku-mi-orh that he would stop the fleet on his return trip home.

During lunch on the outside deck with his distinguished royal guests, Lord Zheng He told the Arab couple about his plans to stop at the beautiful tropical isle.

"On the way to your country, Your Majesty, we stopped for several weeks in Ceylon, so we could resupply the fleet. The king, who has the unusual name of Yala Ku-mi-orh, was generous enough to suggest that we pay him another visit on our return voyage home. If you and your wife have no objections, I would like to stop at Ceylon so I can honor my committment to the king!"

King Juddah looked at his wife to see her reaction. As usual she just smiled and shrugged, as she was more than happy to leave any major decisions up to her husband.

"It's fine with us, Lord Zheng He," King Juddah responded happily. It will probably do us good to stretch our legs on dry land for awhile. Is this island nation very far out of the way?"

"Actually, Sire, it isn't out of the way at all! We've got to stop somewhere to take on water and fresh supplies. If we didn't plan to stop in Ceylon, then we would have to stop at Calicut on the Indian coast, just like we did on our first expedition."

"Makes perfect sense to me," King Juddah replied happily. "I've never traveled beyond my desert kingdom before. Ceylon sounds like a wonderful place to make my first visit!"

"It is very beautiful, Your Majesty!" Xi Chen added enthusiastically. "I had never seen such clear blue water before in my whole life. And the lush tropical trees just seem to grow everywhere. I loved it when we stopped there on our way to your country."

"It all sounds absolutely wonderful!" King Juddah's wife agreed. "I can hardly wait!"


Several weeks later Zheng He's huge flagship sailed majestically through the mouth of the large bay which was situated on the western coast of Ceylon. The rest of the huge flotilla had not yet arrived as it was still strung out almost as far as the eye could see.

Unfortunately, everything was not as it seemed. Unknown to the Ming admiral, several weeks before, King Yala Ku-mi-orh had stationed a number of Ceylonese troops all along the coast with orders to notify him the moment they saw the Chinese fleet approach. Two hours earlier one of the lookouts had seen Zheng He's huge Flagship on the horizon and immediately sent word to notify the king.

Consequently, King Yala Ku-mi-orh now stood on a high hill close to the bay's intrance and watched as Lord Zheng He's mighty Treasure

Ship slowly approached. Also on the hilltop lookout was the king's senior military advisor, General Bura, plus six officers of lessor rank.

"Is everyone ready, General Bura?" Yala Ku-mi-orh asked. His fake smile was no longer evident. "We'll only have one chance at success!"

General Bura gave the king a big smile to let him know that he was supremely confident.

"There's no need to worry, Sire," he sang out happily. "Success will be ours. I personally guarantee it!"

King Yala Ku-mi-orh then turned and walked over to his carriage that was waiting close by. A servant helped him into his seat. The king then turned back to his confident general and addressed him through an open window.

"Both our lives will be riding on your personal guarantee, general", he warned solemly. "Make certain you do not fail."

"I will not fail, Your Majesty," Bura again boasted bravely. "In fact, with the military preparations I have put into place, there is absolutely no way we can lose. The Chinese won't know what hit them! Are you going back to the palace?"

"Yes!" King Yala replied cautiously, not nearly as confident as his senior advisor. "I must prepare to receive the Ming admiral. Mostly, though, I will be on my knees praying for our success. May Allah be with you!"

General Bura bowed deeply as the king's ornately decorated carriage pulled away. When General Bura was sure he had gone, he scoffed hauttily, "I won't need Allah's help for anything!"


An hour later the massive anchor on Zheng He's Baochuan Treasure Ship splashed into the water and sent a mountainous geyser of water into the air. Thick iron links of chain rattled noisily into the water then were quickly wrapped around a large wooden anchor post and snubbed tight.

Lord Zheng He, of course, had no idea that anything could be wrong on the peaceful tropical isle. He happily escorted his Arab guests to the open deck of the Ming Pagoda penthouse so they could have an unobstructed view of the water and lush tropical hillsides that he had described to them during lunch a few days earlier. The magnificent scene which spread around them on three sides was so beautiful it almost took their breath away.

But what was unfolding on the clear blue water right before their eyes, was as equally breathtaking! Hundreds of small boats that were decorated with flags and flowers could be seen coming out into the middle of the bay to greet them. I remember I was standing on one side of the Ming admiral watching the little boats, while Xi Chen and the Arab king and queen stood on the other. All of us were completely mesmerized by the unexpected sight of these little boats, each beautifully decorated, filled with smiling Ceylonese who were waving and singing to us on the bay.

Down on the main deck a large number of Ming soldiers and sailors pressed up against the railings of the huge ship, so they could also cheer and wave back at the friendly people in the small boats that were coming out to greet us.

King Juddah could hardly believe his eyes!

"You told me the Ceylon king would go out of his way to be hospitable, Lord Zheng He, but I never expected anything like this!"

"To be honest, Your Majesty," Zhend He had to laugh, "neither did I!"

"Allah has blessed us with the right decision in coming here," King Juddah's wife added happily. "I know we're going to have a wonderful time!"

"Let's hope so!" Zheng He quickly agreed, then turned to kid me about my earlier reservations.

"Well, friar! What do you think now? Are you still apprehensive about the king's good intentions?"

I, too, was completely flabbergasted at the incredible reception we were receiving on the bay.

"It is an amazing sight!" I allowed sheepishly. "I don't think I've ever seen a more friendly people anywhere."

Out of habit, I rubbed the little cross that hung about my neck and gave it a quick kiss, then started waving and shouting with everyone else to the friendly people approaching in the little boats.

While all of us were waving and shouting, Ma Huan came up the steps to the penthouse deck and bowed to Zheng He.

"Sir! Captain Su wants you to know that your launch is now ready for departure."

"Excellent!" Zheng He sang out, as he was anxious to get started. "If everyone is ready, I think it's time for us to go meet the king!"

As before, we all rode to the shore while seated comfortably in the shade of the beautifully decorated cupula. But now we were right in the middle of all the gayly colored boats with the friendly Ceylonese. The Arab queen couldn't take her eyes off their beautiful smiling faces. But she was equally mesmerized by the tropical greenery that surrounded us on three sides.

"It's just as beautiful as you said it would be, Xi Chen." she told Lord Zheng He's lady servant reverently. "We certainly don't have anything like this in Arabia!"

"Nor have I seen such a tropical-looking place in all of China," Xi Chen replied happily to the queen. "It is really quite lovely."

When four small boats drifted close to the admiral's launch, young Ceylonese girls began throwing flowers at the Chinese visitors, much to the joy of Xi Chen and the Arab queen. Both women reached out and begged for the girls to throw them even more of the beautiful tropical flowers.

General Bura now stood at the back of the wide beach with the six officers who were with him a few hours earlier on the hilltop, as they watched the small flotilla of Ming landing vessels approach. As soon as Lord Zheng He's launch came to a stop in the shallow water just off shore, the officers stepped out from under the shade of several tall coconut palms and began walking down the beach to greet the returning admiral.

When the Ming soldiers and sailors deposited Zheng He and his guests high and dry on the beach, again in comfortable chairs without getting wet, General Bura walked up to the Chinese explorer and bowed graciously.

"Lord Zheng He!" he gushed, both bowing and smiling at the same time. "On behalf of King Yala Ku-mi-orh I want to welcome you back to our humble isle!"

Zheng He returned the general's welcome with a broad smile of his own.

"Thank you, General Bura, and let me say, I'm more than delighted to be back!"

The fleet admiral then turned so he could introduce his two royal guests.

"Please allow me to introduce to you His Royal Highness, King Juddah bin Juddah from the country of Arabia and his lovely wife the Queen."

General Bura made another gracious bow.

"Your Majesties!"

"The royal couple are traveling with me back to China," Zheng He added quickly. "When I told them about King Yala Ku-mi-orh's wonderful hospitality on our previous visit, they were quite anxious for me to stop."

"It is indeed a pleasure, Your Majesties," General Bura responded again and offered another courteous bow. "I'm certain that my king will make every effort to see that you are not disappointed."

General Bura then turned and pointed to a dozen horse drawn carriages which could be seen sitting nearby under a row of tall coconut palms at the edge of the beach.

"And now, Lord Zheng He, if you will please follow me, King Yala Ku-mi-orh has provided carriages for you and your guests, so you can travel in comfort to his palace. As you may remember the king's palace lies some distance inland just beyond the mountains. His Majesty waits for you there in his palace."

With the initial formalities concluded, General Bura led the Ming admiral and his guests, plus a small number of Ming officials, towards the waiting transportation under the trees. Xi Chen, Ma Huan, Lt. Zhang Ji and I, as usual, trailed along behind.


Back in the huge tropical bay, two sailors, Du Wei and Xiao Jiangong, leaned casually on the railing of an eight-masted horse transport and watched as the Ming admiral and his distinguished entourage entered the waiting carriages.

"Are they lucky, or what?" Du Wei groused to his friend.

"Why do you say that?"

"What do you mean, why do I say that?" Du responded as he pretended to be mad. "Look at them, all dressed up, going to a fancy banquet, while we got to stay here on this stinking ship! I say it ain't fair!"

Xiao Jiangong wasn't impressed. "You're just worrying about a lot of nothing!" he scowled, while continuing to watch the dignitaries enter the fancy carriages. "If you ask me, Nothin' in life is fair!"

Du Wei turned toward his friend and moaned unhappily, "You can say that again!"

When Du turned his gaze back towards shore, the old sailor continued to banter at the rail with his friend. "When we get home," he said sadly, mostly to himself, "I'm going to quit this life at sea and settle down."

"If your old lady will have you back!" Xiao teased, unable to hide a smile. "I thought that's why you left in the first place, cause she threw you out!"

Du Wei took off his hat and playfully started hitting his friend over the head.

"Who asked you?" he hollered as he pretended to be mad. "You ain't even got an old lady!"

Under the tall coconut palms the waiting carriages were now filled and General Bura was getting ready to move out. He mounted his sturdy black horse and checked one last time to make sure everyone was ready. When he saw that all the coaches were filled, he hollered to one of his officers close by.

"Everyone is ready, Commander. You can move them out!"

The Ceylon officer saluted General Bura smartly, then kicked his horse in the ribs and began trotting forward towards the head of the column.

At the head of the column, fifty Ceylonese soldiers and a dozen officials waited patiently on horseback as they waited for the command to move out. Just behind this Ceylonese contingent were the twelve horse drawn carriages that were filled with the Chinese guests and dignitaries. Located just behind the carriages were three hundred Ming soldiers who, unfortunately, were going to have to walk to the king's palace on foot.

"Prepare to move out!" was shouted forcefully by Ceylonese officers up and down the line.

While all this activity was taking place at the head of the column a group of Ming soldiers had just arrived in small boats at the water's edge. Afraid they were going to be left behind, the men had to jump into the shallow surf and run across the beach in a desperate attempt to take their proper positions in the Chinese formation.

Near the head of the column, the Arab king and queen were seated comfortably in the admiral's carriage as they waited patiently for the command that would actually get them going. Zheng He was happy that both of his guests seemed to be so excited about the trip they were about to undertake.

"The last time I visited the king's palace," Zheng He told them happily, "I had to ride through the mountains on a horse. This fancy carriage is going to be a lot more comfortable!"

"The Ceylon king is making me look bad," King Juddah joked with a twinkle in his eye.

"If I remember right, I made you struggle through deep sand to have a visit with me!"

Zheng He laughed goodnaturedly, but before he could reply, the senior Ceylonese officer shouted the command they were all waiting to hear.

"Move out!"

Slowly, all the carriages began to roll.

"Here we go!" Zheng He sang out cheerfully. "I think you're going to like this ride, Your Majesty. Once we get inland a short way and start up into the mountains, the countryside becomes even more lush and tropical-looking!"

The Arab queen laughed.

"I think it's lush and tropical-looking here at the beach!"

As the Ming troops started to march away from the beach, Ma Huan and Lt. Zhang Ji sat on horses near the rear of the formation and watched the men pass.

"Which carriage is Lord Zheng He in?" Ma Huan asked his friend, as he looked around for stragglers.

"I think he's in the first carriage, riding with the Arab king and queen." Lt. Zhang Ji replied, while he took off his cloth hat and started fanning himself briskly. "Personally, I'm just as happy we're outside riding on these horses."

Ma Huan was surprised.

"Why do you say that?"

"Those carriages look nice, Ma Huan, but I'm sure they're going to be hot! Mark my words, ridings these horses will be a whole lot cooler!"

Ma Huan noticed two more Ming soldiers who were running up the beach to catch up with their formation which had already pulled out. Each man was fully dressed from head to toe and loaded down with weapons and armament.

"We'll sure be a lot more comfortable than the soldiers!" Ma Huan agreed, as he smiled at his lieutenant friend. "They've got to hike through the mountains for more than an hour while they carry all that heavy equipment!"

"We better keep them moving," Zhang Ji added, "or the formation will get too strung out."

The lieutenant and Ma Huan heeled their horses in the side and rode up behind the soldiers who were just getting into formation.

"All you men stay in formation!" the lieutenant shouted, doing his best to sound authoritative. "Don't drop back! Keep moving!"


Within fifteen minutes the formation of wagons and men had already moved into the mountains. After thirty minutes of continuous marching, a lot of it uphill on a rough dirt road, the Ming troops were already hot, they were getting tired and their formation had already begun to string out in more than a few places. It was slow going for the men and animals as they slogged wearily forward towards the Ceylon king's palace.

In the carriages, just as Lt. Zhang Ji had predicted, it was also hot and muggy, but it was not nearly so uncomfortable and tiring as what the troops had to experience on the ground.

As they passed crept over a high ridge, thankfully, the men were able to get a little rest as the road began to dip down into a rather steep ravine. Not far away the men could see a waterfall that cascaded down from some higher elevation above. It looked beautiful to the men as it crashed dramatically over a number of large boulders before it rushed under a small wooden bridge on the valley floor and spilled over onto the dirt road. The water was cool and nice to look at, but it did cause a fairly wide area of mud through which the animals and marching soldiers had to pass.

This inconvenience, however, was not noticed in the carriages. Zheng He and his guests were too busy watching a bevy of beautiful white birds which they could see flying nearby. When the admiral saw the birds he hung out the window of his carriage like an excited schoolboy and shouted the news to his lady servant, who was riding in the carriage just behind.

"Xi Chen!" he whooped loudly. "Did you see those white birds? They were beautiful!"

I was riding in the carriage with Xi Chen and we were both shocked when we heard Zheng He hollering out the window. I rolled my eyes to let the lady servant know that I certainly didn't approve of his childish behavior.

"Will you please tell him to keep quiet, Xi Chen?" I complained softly. "I don't think it's dignified!"

Before she could reply Zheng He leaned out of his carriage window and hollered again.

"Xi Chen? Did you see them?"

Now it was Xi Chen who had to lean out the window so she could communicate with her love who was embarrassing her. She answered as quietly and as dignified as she could, while at the same time waving for him to please quit shouting.

But Zheng He was having too much fun to worry about protocol. He ignored her admonition and continued to hang out of the window and point out every bird he could see.

"They're all over the place, Xi Chen!" he whooped, again. "Have you ever seen so many beautiful birds in your whole life?"

Sheepishly, Xi Chen waved at Zheng He again.

"I see them, Zheng He! They're beautiful! Now will you please be quiet?"

Inside the carriage I was becoming more and more exasperated.

"He's going to embarrass us all!" I complained again. But then I had an idea. "Don't say anything to him at all, Xi Chen. Maybe if you don't respond he'll quit yelling!"

And sure enough, that's what happened. When the admiral couldn't get Xi Chen to respond to him anymore he kept his head in the carriage. I can only imagine that he had to apologize to his two Arab guests when they observed his boorish behavior.

The king said nothing but did change the subject.

"I've never seen such a beautiful variety of plants and flowers in all my life," King Juddah stated to the Ming admiral as he tried to make a serious observation. "They must get an awful lot of rain here!"

"They do get a lot of rain, Your Majesty," Zheng He agreed, delighted that his Arab friends were enjoying the scenery.. "That's what makes everything so green and beautiful!"

The soldiers marching in formation behind the carriages didn't care a thing about the beautiful scenery. All they wanted to do was stop someplace soon so they could get some rest. The trail had once again begun to head upward which reminded every one of them that they were hot, they were tired and they wanted to stop!

But then, almost before they knew it, the dirt road once again began heading down hill! This time the troops could see high rock walls on either side of them which let them kknow they were going to pass through another ravine. This one looked even higher and steeper than the previous one they had passed through.

Once within the high rock walls the sun was blocked out, which made it slightly cooler and the soldiers thought was a pretty good thing. But then after marching in the shadows for several minutes they also found out that the high rock walls blocked out any semblance of a breeze, which caused them to sweat and become even more uncomfortable.

"How much further do you think we've got to go?" one soldier asked his buddy as they trudged together through the hot, sticky ravine.

"I don't know," his buddy replied grimly. "But I know one thing. If we don't stop pretty soon, I'm gonna have to drop out! I son't think I can go on much further."

Before long they came to a place where water from another stream drained over the road and the soldiers had no choice but to slosh through the messy quagmire. They were so exhausted at this point that none of them even noticed. Then when they got to the end of the ravine, they had to once again start following the road up another steep hill.

"Did you see those birds back there," one soldier gasped to his friend as he tried to keep his mind off how tired he was.

His friend, close to exhaustion himself, continued to plod along without taking his eyes off the road.

"To hell with birds!" he growled. "All I want to do is get our of this damn hellhole so we can stop!"

Fifteen minutes later, inside Lord Zheng He's carriage, the Arab queen was becoming extremely uncomfortable. She used a small paper fan to try and cool herself.

"It's a very warm day!" she complained slightly, not wanting to say anything that was rude. "I think it's more humid here than what we experience in Arabia."

Zheng He could only agree.

"It is humid, Your Majesty, and awfully hot! I'll see if I can find out how much further it is to the king's palace."

When Zheng He leaned out the window, this time for a good reason, he saw Ma Huan and Lt. Zhang Ji on their horses close by following the carriages.

"Ma Huan! Can you find out how much further it is to the palace? If it's much further, we'll have to stop and rest the troops."

"Yes, Sir," Ma Huan responded quickly as he began to coax his horse forward. "I'll ask one of the Ceylonese officers."

Zheng He retook his seat inside the stuffy carriage.

"I don't think it's much further," he suggested to the royal couple, trying to sound optimistic. "If it is, I've got to stop for a few minutes so the soldiers can rest!"

Back in the marching column the Ming soldiers would have been delighted to know that their admiral was at least thinking about them. But the soldier who didn't care a thing about looking at birds earlier was now exhausted and ready to stop.

"That's it!" he muttered to himself. "I'm falling out! I can't go any further!"

But just then his friend caught a quick glimpse of some small buildings just ahead that appeared through the trees.

"Wait a minute!" he gasped as he grabbed his buddy by the arm. "I think we're finally getting somewhere!"

The exhausted soldier looked up and much to his relief, also saw several wooden structures that were partially hidden behind a stand of banana trees.

"Merciful Buddha!" he gasped, barely able to speak. "You might be right!"

Within minutes the banana trees gave way to long rows of wooden houses, many of them ramshackled-looking in appearance and almost all of them covered by thatch roofs.

As they got closer to the center of the city where King Yala Ku-mi-orh's palace was located, the men found themselves marching down dusty streets that were filled with a variety of townsfolk, farmers and merchants, all of whom seemed to be shouting at once as they tried to sell their chickens, ducks, copper utensils, or beautifully woven baskets. The entire middle area of the city was busy, noisy and dusty, not at all unlike the cluttered shopping bazaars of Arabia with which King Juddah and his wife were familiar.

As the long Chinese procession passed through the din of confusion, friendly Ceylonese merchants stood on both sides of the street and waved happily to the visitors as they passed.

The Ming soldiers who were ready to drop just a few minutes earlier now began to march straighter and with more precision.

"You gonna make it?" the first soldier shouted to his friend as he tried to be heard over the jumbled din of the cities noise.

"I'll make it," his friend grimly shouted back as he tried to keep his mind off how bad he hurt. "But I still want to get somewhere where I can get off my feet!"


Yala Ku-mi-orh's magnificent palace did sit almost in the center of the noisy, busy city. But once the Chinese got within the high rock walls which completely surrounded the palace and its gardens, they found a calm sea of welcomed tranquility. Surprisingly the high walls almost blocked completely the noise and dust from the city streets. The palace itself was situated in the middle of a large, grassy, landscaped area that was clean, relatively quiet and extraordinarily beautiful.

As the carriages rolled slowly through the gardens just before dark, the Arab guests were amazed to discover that the walls of the King Yala Ku-mi-orh's palace were covered with thousands of highly polished glazed tiles, not unlike the decorative tiles which adorned King Juddah's palace in Sofar. The tiles on the Ceylonese palace were mostly a beautiful shade of green, while King Juddah's palace tiles tended to radiate colors that were mostly blue.

High ceilings covered a wide area at the front of the palace which featured thick teak beams. Each teak beam had been decorated with carvings which depicted scenes of Ceylonese life. Large round columns, also made of teak and similarly carved, held up the huge ceiling which graced the entrance to the king's wide palace porch.

When General Bura stopped the Chinese procession he made certain that Lord Zheng He's carriage was positioned right in front of the grand palace steps. As soon as the Ming admiral and his Arab guests were helped from their carriage, the first thing they saw was the face of King Yala Ku-mi-orh who was smiling and waving at them from the top of the steps.

"Welcome to Ceylon, Lord Zheng He," he crooned happily. "I'm delighted that you've honored me with another visit."

The king then walked down the wide steps so that he could personally greet his returning friend.

Zheng He bowed graciously to Yala Ku-mi-orh as he approached.

"Your palace is just as magnificent as I remembered it, Your Majesty," he sang out happily. "I'm delighted to return."

Yala Ku-mi-orh then noticed the Arab couple who had also stepped from the carriage and were now standing behind the admiral waiting so they could be introduced.

"And who are these distinguished looking people?" Yala Ku-mi-orh gushed, doing his best to sound sincere.

Zheng He turned to his two royal friends so he could introduce them properly.

"It's my very great pleasure to introduce you to His Royal Highness, King Juddah, from the country of Arabia and his lovely wife the Queen. The king and queen are traveling back to China with me so they can personally pay their respects to Emperor Zhu Di."

King Yala Ku-mi-orh then offered the royal couple a slight bow, while he gave them them his most appealing smile.

"What a wonderful surprise, Your Majesties! I'll do everything I can to see that your short visit here in Ceylon is memorable!"

King Yala then noticed Xi Chen and me standing quietly together behind the king and queen. We had just exited our carriage and came over so we could also pay our respects to the Ceylon monarch, should we get the chance. Even though Zheng He's lady servant and I were nobodies, the king surprised us both by acknowledging our presence.

"I think I remember your other two friends, Lord Zheng He," he sang out generously. "Weren't they with you when you stopped a few months ago?"

I could tell that Zheng He was surprised that the ruler went out of his way to speak to us, but I could also tell that he was pleased.

"This is my lady-in-waiting, Xi Chen," my friend responded happily, "and my very dear friend, Friar Odoric, from Italy. He was, how shall I say this, quite impressed with your magnanimous hospitality the last time we visited!"

Xi Chen and I both bowed generously to the king as we were being introduced, but I did raise my eyebrow a little to let him know that what he had said, in my estimation, used somewhat questionable judgement. The admiral paid no attention to my curious look and quickly turned his attention back to King Yala and his two Arab guests.

"I've told King Juddah and his wife how well we were treated by you on our last visit, Your Majesty. They are quite anxious to experience for themselves your generous hospitality."

King Yala again smiled broadly at his two Arab visitors and cheerfully responded, "I shall not disappoint them!" He then turned and started marching up the palace steps.

"Enough of all this stuffy formality," he sang out happily. "Let's all go inside so I can treat you, as promised, to a magnificent Ceylonese banquet. I think you are going to like what I have had prepared for you!"

Yala Ku-mi-orh waved merrily for everyone to follow him up the broad steps of his palace. We did, as each of us began to eagerly anticipate the delicacies the king had in store.


Ten minutes later the last of the Ming soldiers had filed inside the palace grounds and were finally allowed to halt. One of the officers stopped them on a portion of the wide lawn at the side of the palace where huge tree ferns, coconut palms and a wide variety of tropical flowers grew in perfusion. To the exhausted soldiers the well-manicured lawns offered a much deserved and welcomed respite.

The two soldiers who had encouraged each other to keep moving back in the mountains looked around at their impressive surroundings as if in a daze.

"This isn't bad!" the optimistic soldier told his grumpy friend. "This isn't bad at all!"

"It still ain't good!" his weary friend groused, standing on one foot and then the other. "And it ain't gonna be good 'til I can get off my feet!"

Just then the Ming officer started barking instructions.

"All right, men! Listen up! We're going to stay in formation for a few more miknutes so we can move over to that stone building you can see just in front of us. The king has arranged for us to spend the evening in the building that's within the palace walls. There will be plenty of food and drink for everyone and maybe even a little wine!"

This last comment drew a loud cheer from the disgruntled troops. The officer had to wave his hand to quiet them down.

"I want all of you to behave yourselves and act like Ming soldiers. Remember! We're guests of the Ceylon king and we're the personal representatives of His Imperial Majesty, Zhu Di. I want you to conduct yourselves accordingly!"

The officer then rode off while other Ming officers, who were also on foot with the troops, started shouting orders of their own as they moved the men across the open palace grounds towards the stone building close by.

As the sun dropped behind the walls of King Yala Ku-mi-orh's palace the Ming soldiers were thankful that their tiring day of marching was coming to an end. Finally, they hoped, they would get a much deserved rest and maybe start working on getting very, very drunk!

Unknown to Zheng He or the Ming soldiers at the time, General Bura had assembled a formidable army of fifteen thousand Ceylonese soldiers whose sole mission was to attack and destroy the Chinese fleet. After the general delivered the Ming contingent to his king, he immediately slipped away and rejoined his military commanders at the coast.

General Bura had located his command post close to the top of one of the high hills which ringed the bay. From his lofty position he and his officers could easily look down upon the entire Ming armada which now rested peacefully at anchor on the bay below.

As darkness approached, oblivious to the danger that surrounded them on three sides, the Chinese sailors began setting out lanterns for the night. The small boxes of light which hung at different locations on each ship looked like hundreds of twinkling stars to the Ceylonese officers and men when they viewed from their vantage point high on the surrounding hillsides. Seen from above the whole bay began to sparkle like a fairyland.

While General Bura fiddled with a strap on his silver helmet he shook his head in amazement at the unbelievable sight that was being played out below.

"Can you believe it?" he stated to a junior commander. "The stupid Chinese are lighting all their ships to make sure we won't miss!"

The officer holding the general's sword was equally amazed!

"Did you ever think, general, in your wildest dreams, that the Chinese would anchor all their ships so closely together?"

"Never!" Bura chuckled to himself smugly. "This is going to be almost too easy!"

A second officer dared asked General Bura the question they had all been thinking.

"Sir? How much treasure do you think the Chinese are carrying? That's an awful lot of ships down there on the bay!"

Bura completed tightening the strap on his helmet then accepted his ornately carved sword from the junior officer.

"Not all the ships carry treasure," he told them firmly as he felt the sharpness of his sword's blade, "but the big nine-masted vessels that you see lined up down there, gunnel to gunnel, aren't called treasure ships for nothing!"

Bura slammed the sword into its metal sheath.

"I say we start putting our plan into action gentlemen, so we can find out how much treasure they have! Is everyone ready?"

On board the Ming ships a lot of sailors started drifting topside so they could engage in talk and kill a little time now that the sun had gone down and it was getting a little cooler. The mood definitely was relaxed and everyone was happy they were on their way home.

Below decks on one of the large horse transports Chow Ze watered the last animal he was assigned to take care of and prepared to join his friend, Shu Wa Ji, on the main deck above. Chow Ze grabbed a lantern that was hanging on a nearby post and carried it up the steps to where he knew his friend would be waiting. When he got to the top of the passageway, he set his lantern down on a nearby hatch and joined Shu Wa Ji at the rail.

As the two friends looked out across the open water together they were amazed to see, what looked to them, like hundreds of small campfires being lit on the hillsides all around. The small flickering fires gave an almost surreal look to the entire scene.

"That sure is a beautiful sight," Shu Wa Ji whispered to Chow Ze wistfully. "What do you suppose all them Ceylonese are doing? Cooking supper? I wish my wife could be here with me to enjoy this sight instead of you!"

Chow Ze, who was overweight and couldn't be described as particularly handsome, pretended he was shocked at his friend's uncomplimentary remark.

"What's wrong with me?" he howled, pretending to be mad. "Ain't I pretty enough for you?"

Shu Wa Ji growled back, smiling.

"You're pretty enough, Chow Ze, you just smell too much like those damn horses we're carrying."

Unaffected by his friend's friendly barb, Chow Ze turned away from the beautiful lights on the beach and casually leaned back against the rail.

"Look who's talking! You don't smell like a rose yourself!"

As General Bura had observed from his hillside Command Post earlier, most of the Ming ships were tied together, gunnel to gunnel, in long rows, all across the bay. This made it easier to keep the ships anchored in one location and it also made it easier for the men to move from one ship to the next so they could fraternize with each other.

Not far away from Chow Ze and Shu Wa Ji's horse transport, four other sailors conversed with each other on one of the large nine-masted treasure ships. There was no hiding the fact that the youngest sailor in the group was tired of having to live on the ship and was anxious to get home.

"How long do you think we'll be tied up here in Ceylon?" he asked one of the older hands, trying to make a little conversation.

The older hand was in no mood to coddle the homesick youngster.

"When Lord Zheng He says it's time to go," he sneered, "we'll up anchor! Not a day before!"

"What kind of an answer is that?" the youngster complained. "I know we'll leave when the admiral's ready to go. I just wanted to know how longer you thought that would be?"

"If you plan to spend the rest of your life working on ships," the old hand growled again, as he made no attempt to be friendly, "you better start thinking of this ship as your home and not some other far off place that you're always trying to get to! This ship is your home, my young friend and the sooner you get used to it, the better!"

Another sailor who was also leaning on the rail close by came to the young seaman's aid.

"Don't be so hard on the lad." he pleaded. "He's new to the sea. It takes a little time to get used to. It took a little time for all of us!"

"Well he better start getting used to it soon," the old salt grumbled, "or he'll make himself and everyone else he's working with miserable!"

Tired of the abuse the young man turned away from the older sailor and started looking out over the water towards shore. Much to his surprise he saw what looked like a large number of small boats which were silently approaching the Ming ships.

"Hey, look!" he yelled to the others. "Aren't those the same little boats that came out to greet us earlier today?"

All the men turned at the rail and peered out into the darkness as they tried to see what the lad was talking about.

"What are they coming back tonight for?" another sailor asked no one in particular. "Lord Zheng He's not with the fleet."

The old salt wanted to make amends for being so hard on the boy did what he could to lighten the mood.

"Maybe its them native women," he whooped loudly as he grinned from ear to ear, "coming out for a moonlight visit!"

All the men began to laugh and wished that his joke was true. A third sailor didn't want to be left out.

"Yeah!" he sang out, trying to be louder than all the others. "They probably heard that all us Chinese sailors are good lovers!"

All the men had a good laugh at the baudy comment, except for the young sailor who was beginning to get worried as he watched the little boats edging closer. Only now they looked like they were beginning to spread out into some kind of formation around the entire fleet.

"What are they doing?" he wondered out loud. "I think I better go warn an officer!"

As the young sailor started to leave, the old salt grabbed him by the shirt and pulled him back.

"Where do you think you're going? The first thing you gotta learn when you go to sea is that you don't go sticking your neck out for nothing! Just sit back and enjoy the fun."

While the old salt was still holding onto the young man's shirt, the other men at the rail were suddenly mesmerized by another curious sight. All around them the figures in the boats were beginning to light torches. The older sailor turned loose of the boy's shirt and hollered to his friend, Shu Wa Ji, who he saw standing at the rail of the horse transport close to the baochuan.

"Shu Wa Ji!" he shouted, "what the hell's going on out there?"

Shu Wa Ji cupped his hands to his mouth and started to shout back just as a Ming officer rushed up from below and dashed to the rail.

"What's happening out there?" he shouted to the collection of sailors gathered at the rail. "Does anyone know who's in those little boats?"

Silently a lone fire arrow arched high into the tropical night sky and actually flew over the heads of the startled men on the treasure ship. Before any of them had a chance to say or do anything, thousands of fire arrows begin arching into the night sky from the surrounding hillsides and little boats all around. Within seconds the fiery arrows started crashing down onto the mass of ships in the bay which immediately caused fires to spring up everywhere.

Shu Wa Ji and Chow Ze ran for cover below decks just as three of the deadly missiles slammed into a storage bin filled with hay. Immediately the hay started to burn furiously!

Below decks the horses panicked!

Shu Wa Ji and Chow Ze were quickly joined by other members of the crew, who had also rushed below decks. Everyone wanted to hide from the fire arrows that attacked them from the hillsides above and the boats on the water below. But they also knew they needed to control the hundreds of frightened horses on board that were now beginning to panic. Trapped in their wooden pens the animals started to stop, neigh and snort wildly as they tried to escape the noxious smoke and spreading flames.

As more shipmates rushed below decks to help, some of them started a bucket brigade, while others grabbed blankets and began beating at the ever-growing conflagration. The noise of hundreds of shouting men and three hundred panic-stricken animals was deafening!

As Shu Wa Ji tried to lead four horses out of the holocaust below, Chow Ze grabbed the bit of another terrified animal and started trying to pull it to safety as well. Unexpectedly, the plunging beast twisted violently and crushed Chow Ze against a thick stall post which killed him instantly!

On the main deck of the treasure ship, the situation was no better and getting worse. The old salt held the lifeless body of the homesick sailor in his arms and cursed the villain who had killed him. Tears streamed down his face as he tried to pull out the shaft of a smoldering fire arrow that was still deeply embedded in the boy's neck.

On the hillsides the scene was much different. Instead of crying, death and destruction, there was unbounded celebration and joy! Four Ceylonese soldiers laughed and joked happily as they each dipped an arrow into the campfire at their feet, fastened the shaft to his bow then sent the burning missil flying towards the ships below.

On all the hillsides surrounding the fleet in the bay the same scenario was being replayed over and over. Without stop a continuous rain of fiery destruction cascaded down upon the defenseless ships in the bay which remained tied together in almost one, anchored, floating mass.

On some of the vessels soldiers and sailors crazed with fear tried to escape the spreading flames by jumping overboard. But on other ships a different scenario began to play out. Officers and men who seemed oblivious to the danger started to do everything they could to mobilize a counter attack.

Lt. Dwong Su and two dozen men in his unit hacked frantically at the thick ropes which bound their treasure ship to the one riding next to it. Within seconds the ropes parted and almost immediately the huge ship begin to slowly drift free.

The lieutenant positioned himself on the main deck near the bow and started to shout orders to other sailors who now began to scramble high into the rigging high overhead. These men had to keep their balance while beating out fires with one hand and raising sails with the other.

As a slight breeze began to fill several of the sails that were now unfurled, Dwong Su shouted another order, this time to the helmsman at the stern.

"Keep her head off the wind. Try to ground her on the beach."

The lieutenant saw other men running to man the small cannons which were located both at the bow and the stern.

"You men! Aim for the hillsides and START FIRING!"

Within seconds three Ming cannons roared to life in a tremendous volley of fire and smoke. Almost immediately other Chinese sailors on other ships began firing their own cannons as well, which sent more deadly projectiles hurtling onto the hillsides. None of the Ming sailors tried to hit any particular target. They just fired blindly towards the glowing fires that dotted the hillsides around them and hoped for the best!

Slowly Zheng He's Flagship drifted towards the beach and wallowed to a stop in shallow water close to shore. Lt. Dwong Su ordered fifty Ming soldiers to follow him over the side.

"We'll form up along that tree line over there," he shouted, "just beyond the beach! Is everyone ready? MOVE!"

Quickly the officer and men started sliding down ropes into the shallow water below. As soon as their feet hit the water they realized, too late, that it was still too deep to touch bottom. All they could do was try to hold their bow and arrows above their head and start swimming towards the shore. When it got shallow enough to wade they pushed themselves frantically towards the beach as quickly as they could as they continued to dodge the flying missiles of fire that hissed into the water all around.

Not all of them made it!

Two were cut down sliding down the rope. Three others were lost as they tried to swim in the water or run across the open beach. As soon as Lt. Dwong Su made it into the trees he turned and shouted to his friend Lieutenant Zu, who was crouched on the edge of the beach as he waited for Dwong Su's signal to run.

"Are you ready?" Dwong Su screamed. "My men will cover you! RUN!"

Six of Dwong Su's men started firing their own arrows blindly into the dark hillside above their position as they hoped to discourage some of the Ceylonese soldiers from firing theirs. The small display of Chinese offense was partially successful, but two more of the Ming soldiers were wounded as they ran across the open beach, including Lieutenant Zu, who fell into Dwong Su's arms with an arrow stuck in his arm.

"Pull it out!" he screamed, gritting his teeth against the pain.

"I can't!" Dwong Su shouted back. "The barb is too big!"

"Then push it through," he pleaded. "Hurry!"

Lieutenant Zu screamed again as Dwong Su broke the shaft and jammed the ragged point through the fleshy part of his arm before he was able to pull it free. He then quickly tore off a piece of Zu's shirt and wrapped it around his arm to staunch the flow of blood.

When the wounded lieutenant struggled to his feet, Dwong Su grabbed Zu by his bloody shirt and pulled him back to the ground.

"You'll never make it!" he screamed. "You've got to go back to the ship."

Dwong Su pointed to two men.

"Take Lieutenant Zu back to the ship. The rest of us will try to reach the admiral!"

"It's too dangerous," Zu gasped, as he pressed Dwong Su's make-shift bandage to his bloody arm. "You'll never make it!"

"I've got to make it," Dwong Su countered, determined to get his men moving as quickly as possible. "We don't have any choice!"

Without another word the rest of the soldiers scrambled to their feet and followed Dwong Su across the road as he made a mad dash for the dark trees beyond. It was the same dirt road that Lord Zheng He and the Ming soldiers followed into the mountains earlier in the day.

Using the dark trees on the side of the road as cover the Ming soldiers moved silently away from the beach and up the rising hillsides beyond. Just above them they could see dozens and dozens of small campfires as they flickered through the trees. They could also see the steady stream of fire arrows that continued to arch into the air before they made their long lazy spiral onto the fleet below.

Dwong Su was thankful that more and more of the Ming ships had begun to return fire and it did seem to cause some disruption of the Ceylonese offensive. But, as far as he was concerned, there wasn't anything he could do about the firing. What he had to do was get through to Lord Zheng He and let him know what was happening.

At General Bura's command center he and two of his officers stood together and surveyed the scene below.

"I knew it would be easy," he bragged to his junior officers, "but I never thought it would be this easy!"

"I'm also shocked," one of the officers crowed. "The stupid Chinese have barely put up a fight!"

"What about the Ming admiral?" another officer asked as he smiled broadly. "When are we going to take him?"

Bura laughed cruelly.

"Whenever we want! I don't think he's going anywhere!"


Back on the ships in the bay thousands of men were now frantically trying to throw bucketfuls of water onto decks and rigging and seemed oblivious to the fire arrows which continued to pummel them from above. Not all the arrows found their mark, however. Many fell harmlessly into the sea and were immediately extinguished while still others glanced off the sides of the large ships and did no damage. But enough of the arrows did strike some of the men, sails and superstructure so there was real concern that they may lose the fleet.

Lieutenant Dwong Su couldn't waste time worrying about what was happening in the bay. He had to lead his men along the edge of the dirt road, higher and higher, and make sure they avoided any contact with the Ceylonese enemy.

More than once Dwong Su's soldiers asked for permission to slay unsuspecting Ceylonese soldiers that they encountered on the road, but each time his response was the same.

"Leave them be! It's more important that we get to Lord Zheng He. Keep moving!"

Only once during the tiring climb did Dwong Su allow his men to stop for few minute's rest. As they dropped to the ground to catch their breath, instinctively, each turned and looked back down into the bay below. The sight they saw made them wish they hadn't! Light from more than a hundred burning ships reflected off a thick blanket of smoke, which hung like a layer of doom over the entire fleet. The scene was so depressing that Dwong Su cut short the men's rest period and ordered them back to their feet.

"We're not going to accomplish anything sitting around here," he barked. "Let's keep moving!"

In an effort to make better time, he moved his men directly onto the dirt road and began to slowly jog them up and down the tortuous mountain road in the darkness. The lieutenant knew he was taking a big risk and there was danger they might be discovered, but he also knew that if they didn't get to the admiral quickly and alert him of the danger there may not be enough time for him to mount a counterattack and save the fleet!

At King Yala Ku-mi-orh's large banquet hall everyone was having a wonderful time. There was still plenty of food, lively music and an abundance of attractive young women to entertain King Yala's guests. There was no hint of danger, there was no hit of trouble, anywhere.

In the middle of all the merriment King Yala leaned over and casually informed Zheng He that he was terribly sorry, but that he had to leave the banquet hall for a few minutes.

"I won't be gone long," he assured the admiral happily. "Please continue to enjoy yourselves!"

King Yala motioned to several of his servants standing nearby.

"See to it that our guests have plenty of food and wine," he gushed, "and anything else they might desire!"

The king then got to his feet, offered the Ming admiral a slight bow and quickly left the banquet hall, followed closely by four senior envoys who trailed behind.

At the time none of us suspected a thing. But while the musicians played and the beautiful Ceylonese women continued to entertain us with their graceful dance, other Ceylonese officials slowly begin to get up, one by one, and casually take their leave from the noisy merriment.

I was the only person in Lord Zheng He's contingent who seemed to notice. As more of the officials got up and left the hall I began to get increasingly uneasy. I didn't want to make too big a fuss, but I did lean over and whispered to Xi Chen.

"Would you please tell Zheng He that I'd like to talk to him for a minute. It's urgent!"

When Xi Chen did as she was asked, Zheng He leaned over his lady servant to find out what I wanted.

"What is it, friar?" he asked happily, "Aren't you having a good time?"

"I was," I told him nervously, "but now I'm beginning to get worried! Something's not right! Take a look around. The king is gone and almost all of his advisors have left with him!"

When Zheng He looked around he did seem mildly surprised that what I had told him was true, but he didn't seem overly worried since the king had told him a few minutes earlier that he was going to leave for a short while but would return soon. If Zheng He had thought about it he might have realized the king didn't say anything about all of his advisors leaving with him.

"It is strange, friar, I have to agree with you on that, but I'm sure they will all return soon!"

Zheng He's words sounded nice but I wasn't convinced. I grabbed him by the sleeve before he could turn away and asked if he would grant me a favor.

"Would you please have Ma Huan look around," I pleaded. "Maybe he can find out what's going on. There's something about that Ceylonese king that I still don't trust!"

Before Zheng He could even look for Ma Huan the huge doors at the end of the banquet hall burst open and Lt. Dwong Su stumbled inside with a handful of dirty and exhausted men.

"Admiral!" he shouted from across the room. "We're being attacked! The fleet is being destroyed!"

Immediately the music and dancing and talking in the room stopped! Zheng He took another quick look around for the Ceylon king and saw that he was still gone! Without hesitation he grabbed Xi Chen by the arm and started moving her towards the door, while at the same time issuing orders.

"Friar! Help me get everyone out of here! Ma Huan? Look after the king and queen! Lt. Zhang Ji? Get the troops! They should be in the building next door. Have them form up on the grounds just outside the front entrance. We've got to get back to the ships FAST!"

A very frightened Captain Su rushed up to the Ming admiral unsure of what he should do.

"What's happening, Lord Zheng He? Why are we being attacked?" Forty years of guarding coastal waters hadn't prepared the old man for what he was about to face.

"Captain!" Zheng He urged calmly. "Please follow the lieutenant. You can help him get the men formed up on the grassy area just outside the front entrance. We've got to get back to the fleet as quickly as possible!"

Pandemonium began to break out all over the hall! Several Ming servants and envoys started to strike out at anyone who was Ceylonese. A few of the dancers and musicians tried to defend themselves, but most just stopped what they had been doing and started running for their lives. When Zheng He saw the confrontations that started to take place in the banquet hall he shouted again.

"Leave them alone! I want everyone outside. NOW!"

Outside, there was even more confusion! Lt. Zhang Ji went to the stone building and brought the soldiers back to the palace on a run. He then tried to get them to form up into a marching formation as quickly as possible.

King Juddah tried to remain calm and also tried to stay as close as he could to the Ming admiral. But his wife was clearly terrified and barely able to function. All she could do was cling desperately to her husband's arm too afraid to speak.

Zheng He grabbed Ma Huan and Zhang Ji.

"Get the horses and carriages and bring them around to the front steps quickly!"

The two young men sprinted to the stable and threw upon the large wooden doors. Inside, they found nothing but empty stalls.

Zhang Ji cursed under his breath. "They took the carriages too!"

By the time Zhang Ji and Ma Huan sprinted back to the front of the palace most of the soldiers were in the semblance of a formation. When the lieutenant and servant rushed up to Zheng He they didn't bother to bow.

"They're gone!" Ma Huan shouted out of breath. "The horses, the carriages, they're all gone!"

Zheng He was surprised but didn't want to waste time worrying about it.

"All right," he ordered, "we'll walk! Lt. Zhang Ji! Put half the soldiers in front of the Ming officials and guests, the other half behind. As soon as everyone is in place start moving out! HURRY!"

In less than two minutes, amid a flurry of shouted commands, Lt. Zhang Ji was able to get the soldier's moving away from the palace at a fast walking pace, with Lord Zheng He's small group of Ming officials, friends and guests in the middle.

As they moved quickly through the darkened streets of the now deserted city, my friend shouted encouragement to everyone who could hear.

"Stay together now," he urged, "we'll be all right! I want everyone keep moving! Don't anybody fall behind!"

As the Chinese entourage hurried through the city streets some lanterns still burned within several of the houses along the way. But just as soon as the occupants inside heard the Chinese coming they quickly closed their shutters and extinguished any light.

Being overweight made it difficult for me to maintain the strenuous pace. Each time I started to fall back Zheng He always noticed and urged me to keep up.

"Come on, friar!" he shouted, probably for the third time, "I don't want you to get so far behind. You've got to keep moving!"

"I'm trying," I gasped, as I became more and more tired which each step. "I'm trying!"

Like the Arab queen, Xi Chen held tightly to her man's arm and refused to turn loose. The pace, however, was also too much for her. Zheng He had to continuously coax her as well not to fall back.

Luckily there was a full moon that night which made it easier for us to follow the dirt road through the mountains. If it had been pitch black I don't know what we would have done.

One thing that wasn't easier was the fact that we now had to walk on foot and not ride in one of King Yala's fancy carriages. Plus we all knew in the back of our mind that somewhere along the road we could be attacked at any time!

The poor soldiers weren't able to recover from their march to Yala Ku-mi-orh's palace earlier in the day. Now they had to turn around and endure a second march without being able to recover from the first.

There was no way I could have walked all the way to the palace on the first trip and now I had no idea how I was going to survive the march we were now on. Having to plunge uphill and down, again and again, brought me to the end of my endurance.

I knew we had to get to the ships as quickly as possible. But if we were attacked along the way, well, there just wasn't anything we could do about it. All I could do was pray for all I was worth and rub my little cross. The rest I left to the Father.

"Is everything going to be all right?" Xi Chen gasped as she struggled to keep up. "I'm terribly frightened!"

"We're going to be all right, Xi Chen," he told her as he continued to pull her along with one hand.. "Just make sure you stay close to me!"

"I remember…the last time…you told me…everything was going to be all right," she reminded him, as she did her best to hang on to his hand and not let go, "it didn't work out…that way!"

"This time will be different," he assured her as confidently as he could, "I promise!" But the look on his face didn't give her the confidence she was looking for. .

About then, Zheng He must have looked around for me and saw that I had again lagged behind. He turned loose of Xi Chen's hand and told her to keep walking, then dropped back to see if he could give me a little more encouragement.

"I know it's difficult, friar," he coaxed gently as he started to pull me along by the sleeve, "but you've got to keep up!"

At that point I was too exhausted to speak. All I could do was give him a desperate look as I tried to keep moving. When Zheng He saw there wasn't much he could do for me he rejoined Xi Chen and tried to encourage those around him.

"Keep up everyone! We're almost there! It's just a little further!"

As we reached the crest of a fairly high hill, Ma Huan was the first to see the eerie glow of light in the sky. He mentioned the ominous vision to the admiral.

"Look!"

When Zheng He saw the unnatural-looking light that reflfected off the low lying clouds he knew immediately what it meant.

"I don't want to look, Ma Huan," he told him despondently "Just keep moving!"

As the column of Ming soldiers continued to plod stoically down the dirt road the soldier who had complained on the way to the palace was still at it.

"When I get back on that ship," he groused to his equally tired friend, "I ain't never getting off again!"

"IF we get back!" his usually more positive friend replied.

The complainer couldn't believe it!

"What's the matter with you? You're always the optimistic one."

"I got a bad feeling," he responded ominously. "A real bad feeling!"

Fifteen minutes later as the soldiers sloshed wearily through the shallow stream at the bottom of the ravine a single fire arrow streaked downward from somewhere above and slammed without warning into the soldier who had the "bad feeling!" He took the burning missile in the back of his neck and was dead before he hit the ground.

Immediately all hell broke loose!

Thousands of fire arrows and spears began raining down upon Zheng He and his defenseless troops all at once. Some men screamed and tried to duck while others threw themselves against the nearby rock walls in a desperate attempt to find cover. But there was no cover to be found anywhere!

Zheng He also pulled Xi Chen next to the canyon wall and tried to protect her with his body, but all this did was subject both of them to an open barrage of fire arrows and spears fired from the opposite rim.

Small fires began to spring up wherever the arrows struck the ground and took away whatever was left of the moonlit darkness. Any hope of finding a place to hide was out of the question.

Through the thickening smoke Zheng He saw the Arab king and queen out in the open with no idea of how they could save themselves. But then almost immediately a dozen Arab servants ran forward and threw themselves on top of the royal couple in an unselfish disregard for their own lives.

While desperately searching for a way to escape the Ming admiral saw me unprotected also out in the open. I didn't have any servants who would lay on top of me, but I did have God. So I dropped to my knees, lifted my eyes towards heaven and rubbed my little cross.

Then I heard Zheng He shout. "Odoric! Take cover!"

With all the screaming and noise from the soldiers and envoys I could barely hear him shout my name. When I did hear him an amazing thing happened. A soothing calm came over me. I don't know what happened. I don't know how it happened, but suddenly I felt as though I was at peace. I calmly got up off my knees and walked over to my friend as he had instructed.

"We must escape this hellish betrayal," I yelled as I tried to be heard over the growing din.

Zheng He yelled back.

"We're trapped friar! There is no escape!"

"Only because we can't see it," I told him feeling no fear whatsoever.

The admiral must have appreciated my wisdom because he immediately picked up Xi Chen and guided her into my arms.

"Protect her with your life," he also responded calmly, while he refused to express fear by ducking the flaming arrows and spears which continued to fall around us.

"As my loyal friend I want you to promise me that you will protect her with your life."

What could I do? I had no choice. Of course I would do whatever I could to protect Zheng He's most cherished possession.

"I will, admiral," I told him as I reached out to Xi Chen and pulled her close to my body. "You have my word. No harm will befall her. To my God I swear. To your Allah…"

Before I could finish a barrage of flaming arrows slammed into a small tree next to us and exploded in flames. I instinctively shielded Xi Chen from the eruption of heat and flying embers.

She trembled against me terrified.

Zheng He picked up the sword of a fallen Chinese soldier and turned to face a converging hoard of Ceylonese warriors who were moving toward us like phantom spirits through the eerie smoke and flames.

Two warriors burst into view and charged Zheng He as they tried to kill him. But with lightning power he swung his blade and cut both of them down as easily as he would slice through stalks of young bamboo. I saw their severed limbs fall at his feet as if in slow motion while they continued to spew blood.

Zheng He saw something move to his left down the ravine towards the stream. A line of men in silhouette masked by the smoke moved steadily toward us. He turned to face them with his sword held high ready to fight them to the death.

But then just behind him another Ceylonese warrior exploded from the cloud of ashes and attacked the admiral with a long spear.

I saw him and called out.

"Zheng He watch out!"

But my voice was lost in the harsh cacophony of battle. In an instant without thinking I pushed Xi Chen aside and leaped towards my friend to protect him. The razor-sharp spear struck me in the upper chest and knocked me backward onto the ground.

When the warrior pulled the spear from my chest he whirled around to face Zheng He. But Zheng He was already upon him. In an instant he brought his sword down with such brutal force that it decapitated the man with one mighty swipe. He then yanked Xi Chen back to the false safety of the wall and shouted at two soldiers who cowered nearby.

"Get Odoric back to my ship! NOW!"

Just as my friend stopped to help the soldiers pick me up, three more Ceylonese warriors charged us with spears and swords. King Juddah bin Juddah appeared from the dense smoke like a savage spirit and slaughtered all three of the attackers with one mighty swipe of his sword.

Zheng He's eyes searched the thick smoke for Xi Chen who was now standing alone and vulnerable. Their eyes met. She reached for him and began to move in his direction.

Suddenly scores of more Ceylonese soldiers appeared on the ridge and raised their bows. Before Zheng He could move they fired. More than a dozen lethal missils slammed into Xi Chen and punctured her frail body with crimson wounds. She froze like a statue as if the arrows had locked her in time and space but then, slowly, she crumpled to the ground.

Zheng He was horrified. He screamed.

"Xi Chen! Noooooo!"

He rushed to her and fell on his knees. Tears poured from his eyes. As gently as he could he dragged her limp body over next to the wall and screamed in anguish to Allah.

"Help meeeeeee!" he begged, as he desperately shook his fist at the unseen enemy above. "Help meeeeeeeee!"

Zheng He held Xi Chen's lifeless body in his arms as he racked his brain and tried to figure some way out of King Yala's trap.

Then out of the blue an answer came to him. It was as clear as if Allah Himself had spoken to him face-to-face. The answer didn't seem to make sense but he sure was not going to argue with what Allah had revealed!

He lay Xi Chen's body on the ground then carefully removed the necklace from around her neck. Her blood had splattered onto a few of the stones so he wiped them clean before he replaced the ornament of love back around his own neck.

Zheng He then kissed her on the lips one last time and got to his feet.

"All right!" he screamed as loudly as he could. "I want everyone UP! Lieutenant Zhang Ji? Ma Huan? Where are you?"

Amazingly as if by magic both men appeared from out of the smoke and flames. Ma Huan had taken an arrow in his leg and was limping badly but was still ready to serve his master.

"Help me get everyone moving," he told the two men as calmly as he could. "Our only chance is to get back to the palace!"

Lt. Zhang Ji couldn't believe it!

"The palace, Sir?" he questioned, thinking Zheng He had lost his mind. "We'll all be killed!"

"We'll all be killed if we stay here, Lieutenant! Get everyone up NOW and start following me!"

When the soldiers saw the Ming admiral striding bravely through the gauntlet of spears and arrow while he slashed his sword at the attacking

Ceylonese warriors along the way they began to gather their own courage and slowly started to follow.

"START FIRING!" Zheng He shouted to his men as he encouraged them to do something. When they saw the admiral cut down another warrior with his sword it jerked the men into action. Now beginning to forget their own fear they began firing their arrows blindly towards both sides of the gorge as they also began to slash at the Ceylonese ememy with reckless abandon. Miraculously this flurry of Ming offense caused the Ceylonese will to collapse.

Zheng He shouted again.

"Keep it up men!  IT'S WORKING!"

Within minutes what was left of Zheng He's battered troops escaped King Yala's trap in the gorge and began following him back up the dirt road towards his palace.

"Keep moving!" Zheng He shouted again. "Don't stop!  We've got to keep moving!"

Lt. Zhang Ji helped Ma Huan to limp down the road when he looked forward and thought he saw Zheng He beginning to struggle. He quickly handed Ma Huan over to a nearby soldier and moved forward to see if he could help.

"Can I help you admiral?  It looks like you need to rest!"

"I can manage," Zheng He replied stoically, as he didn't want to slow down. "I'll be all right.  Just stay with Ma Huan like I asked.  He needs your help more than I do!"

"But I've got a soldier watching him.  He's doing OK!"

"Then see if you can help the Arab king and queen.  I'm sure they can use a little assistance.!"

Zheng He appreciated the lieutenant's offer to help, but the pain that he felt was in his heart over the death of his beloved Xi Chen. It didn't have anything to do with any physical stamina he might need to get back to King Yala's palace and seek his revenge.

"I love you, Xi Chen," he whispered to himself, over and over, as he took each tortured step back to the palace.   "I love you, I love you, I love you!"

With each step that Zheng He took fueled his hatred for the Ceylonese king.

Lieutenant Dwong Su who had helped bring the news to Zheng He about the deadly attack took two arrows during the battle in the gorge, one in his side and one in his leg.  No matter how hard he tried to keep up his strength left him and he could go no further.  The exhausted lieutenant fell to the ground at the side of the road and forced himself to roll into the brush.

Dwong Su knew that to stop would mean almost certain death. The Celyonese would be follwing them in the darkness and would kill any wounded Chinese they found. When he saw their torches coming towards him in the darkness he did what he could to squeeze himself under the branch of a fallen tree and hoped they wouldn't see him. But before he could sufficiently hide himself the light from one of their torches illuminated his hiding place and he was discovered.

Three Ceylonese soldiers unceremoniously dragged the wounded lieutenant into the middle of the road and formed a small ring around his prostrated form. As he lay on his back and looked up at his captors they screamed at him in a language he didn't understand. When he didn't respond he watched in horror as each soldier set an arrow in his bow and deliberately pulled the string back as tightly as he could. Then before Dwong Su could cry out or beg for mercy they released their deadly projectiles into his chest and left him to die.

When the Ming entourage of soldiers and officials made it back to the outskirts of the city Lord Zheng He passed the word that he wanted everyone to make as little noise as possible. Quietly the dishevelled group of exhausted Chinese shuffled wearily through the deserted streets of the Ceylonese capital.

Wounded were helped and comforted as much as possible as each man did what he could for the next as they slowly and silently shuffled their way forward towards King Yala Ku-mi-orh's palace.

The Arab king and queen were exhausted from their bitter ordeal. Both had long ago handed their lives over to Allah but continued to follow orders from Admiral Zheng He.

The Ming admiral was exhausted but he was also determined that nothing would deter him from his holy mission.

When they got back to King Yala's palace he quickly issued an order to Lt. Zhang Ji.

"Get some of the soldiers and come with me! I think I know where we will find the king!"

Inside the palace Yala Ku-mi-orh and his ministers were already congratulating themselves on their victory over the Chinese.

"Our plan worked better than I ever could have imagined," the monarch exclaimed happily while holding up a half-full glass of wine.

"Let's all toast again our glorious army and especially General Bura who planned the campaign and executed it so brilliantly against the filthy heathens."

General Bura had recently returned from the battlefield on another road. He nodded graciously to his king as he happily accepted the plaudits of all the government ministers.

Just at that moment as everyone again triumphantly downed another glass of wine Juddah bin Juddah suddenly apeared like a ghost on the other side of the banquet room. He stood tall with his feet apart and smiled facetiously at the Ceylonese king.

"May I drink too?" he boomed in a loud voice. "I am also a filthy heathen.

All the celebrating Ceylonese stopped their toast cold as everyone stared in disbelief at the Arab apparition. In just that instant while eveeryone's attention was drawn to King Juddah, Lord Zheng He slipped behind King Yala Ku-mi-orh from the shadows of a colonnade and pressed his dagger to the king's throat.

"You have made an error in judgement, Your Highness," he growled fiercely at the now sticken monarch.

Seeing that their king was in imminent danger General Bura and all of the Ceylonese officials froze.

Juddah bin Juddah took another step forward.

"Deception is a two-headed snake," he snarled.

General Bura reached for his sword but Lt. Zhang Ji and several of his men stepped from the shadows of another large column with their own swords drawn. Swiftly the lieutenant placed the sharp tip of his sword on the back of General Bura's neck. General Bura didn't move.

"Withdraw your troops immediately," Zheng He barked as he pressed his blade forcefully into the neck of Yala Ku-mi-orh.

"Order them to lay down all of their weapons and surrender."

King Yala hesitated.

"NOW!" Zheng He screamed forcefully.

King Yala summonded his courage.

"If...I'm harmed..." he stammered, "my men...will slaughter you...and your heathens...instantly."

A Ceylonese guard who stood within striking distance of Zheng He gripped his spear tightly. He could easily lunge and kill the Ming admiral, but Zheng He did not flench.

"You have already destroyed all that I love and everything that I live for. I would welcome death."

The admiral then pressed his blade even harder against the king's throat which caused a streak of blood to drip down his neck.

Yala Ku-mi-orh screamed out in pain and motioned to General Bura.

"Order them to surrender," he shouted frantically.

Bura hesitated.

"But Your Majesty,"

Again Zheng He slid his blade across Ku-mi-orh's throat which drew even more blood. The Ceylonese king screamed even louder and instinctively tried to push the admiral's blade away. But his action only caused the blade to dig deeper. Now in full panic the monarch screamed again at his stubborn general and ordered him to obey.

"Surrender the troops damn you!" he wailed at the top of his lungs. "Surrender them NOW!"

Lt. Zhang Ji pushed his own blade hard into General Bura's neck which also drew blood and caused him to lose his will. Bura immediately grabbed his neck and screamed out in pain!

"All right, all right!" he moaned pitifully as he fell to his knees and clultched at his bleeding neck. "I'll surrender the troops! Just don't kill me! Please!"

But Lt. Zhang Ji wasn't through. He roughly jerked Bura back to his feet and applied even more pressure against the general's bloody neck.

"I didn't hear you swear?" he hissed as he made another sharp cut which drew even more blood.

"I swear! I swear!" Bura wailed loudly. "I'll issue the order!"

While Zheng He kept his own blade pressed tightly against the neck of the Ceylonese king he issued his lieutenant an order.

"Escort General Bura back to the coast. If he doesn't order his men off the fleet immediately I want you to KILL HIM!"

Zhang Ji again pressed his sword into Bura's bloody neck and turned him towards the door.

"It will be my pleasure, admiral," the Ming lieutenant growled. "I hope the bastard gives me the excuse!"

As Lieutenant Zhang Ji and his men marched General Bura towards the door Yala Ku-mi-orh started to plead for his life.

"Please don't kill me, Lord Zheng He," he cried pitifully, as he immediately dropped to the floor on his knees. "I beg you to have mercy on me. It was all General Bura's fault. He forced me to go along with him!"

General Bura heard the king's begging and screamed back at him from the door.

"LIAR! You can't blame it all on me!"

Zhang Ji jabbed the general in the neck again, harder this time, which drew even more blood and an even louder anguished scream. Roughly he pushed the bleeding antagonist out the door.

Yala Ku-mi-orh didn't let up. From his knees he again screamed out at Bura as the general was being led away.

"It's all your fault, you bastard!" he shouted. "Give the order to your men or I'll have you killed myself!"

Zheng He was not fooled by Yala's cowardly charade. He slapped him across the face as hard as he could, which dropped him into a heap at his feet.

"That was for Xi Chen," he hissed fiercely. "I would like to kill you now with my bare hands, but as admiral of the Ming fleet I must take you back to Beijing as my prisoner. Emperor Zhu Di will know what to do with you."

The once boastful Ceylonese ruler now laid on the floor at Zheng He's feet crying like a baby.

Chapter Twelve

---

TRAGIC CONCLUSIONS

When order was restored Lord Zheng He had King Yala Ku-mi-orh and General Bura thrown into prison on board his flagship. He decided that it was his duty to take both of them back to Beijing so Zhu Di could personally decide their fate.

Ma Huan made it back to the flagship alive but, as I have reported, Zheng He's much loved lady servant, Xi Chen, did not. Before leaving Ceylon I was told that he returned to the gorge where she was killed and personally carried her body to a high ridge that overlooked the bay. There, under a large breadfruit tree he buried the only woman he had ever loved and placed a small stone marker over her grave which read: Xi Chen, My Only Love Forever, Zheng He, Admiral of the Ming Fleet.

I also heard that Zheng He lingered on that wind-swept ridge for almost a full day as he cried and begged Allah to take his life. But Allah did not take his life and he had no choice but to dry his eyes, kiss Xi Chen's necklace that hung about his neck and return once more to his duty on board the flagship.

While Zheng He begged for Allah to take his life on Ceylon, back in Beijing Empress Xu begged Lord Buddha to save the life of her husband, Zhu Di. The Third Ming Emperor was now close to death and the fate of all Chinese people hung on each tortured breath!

Zhu Di was now confined to bed at Forbidden City. When he tried to speak with his wife he could only do so in a voice that was now barely above a whisper.

"Is there any news…from Lord Zheng He?" he gasped.

Empress Xu didn't know if she should answer her husband or beg for him to save his strength. She glanced uneasily towards two imperial physicians who stood quietly together on the other side of the room. She hoped they would tell her what she should do. Silently one of the men nodded with his head to let her know that it was all right to communicate with her terminally ill husband.

Several friends and family members were also in the room close by. They, too, mostly waited quietly and said nothing. All watched and waited for the inevitable they knew would happen.

"The admiral will be home soon," Empress Xu lied as she tried to make Zhu Di feel better. "Why don't you try and get some rest?"

After taking a few more deep breaths, Zhu Di opened his eyes and struggled to ask her another question.

"Where's Xi Chen?" Obviously confused he vainly searched the room for her presence. "I wish to see…my Xi Chen."

Empress Xu got up and went over to a large window on the side of the room and pulled the drapes closed. This made the dismal scene even more dreary than before but she hoped that it would also make it easier for her husband to get some rest. She then went back to Zhu Di's bedside and started stroking his forehead.

"Close your eyes, Zhu Di." she cooed softly. "Everything's going to be all right. Just try to rest."

Dao Yan and General Tan were also in the room. They stood side-by-side along with the others and quietly waited for the end. It was hard for them to stand idly by and do nothing, but they also knew there wasn't anything they or anyone else could do at this point. They listened and waited as Zhu Di's labored breathing grew weaker.

Prince Han and Crown Prince Zhu Bao Zhi were also present. They waited silently on the far side of the room behind one of the beautifully decorated screens. The Crown Prince whimpered softly to himself as he was unable to hide his grief. Prince Han on the other hand was unaffected by his father's sickness and found it difficult to mask his delight.

"Shut up and stop your sniveling," he hissed at his distraught brother. "I'm sick and tired of listening to you!"

"Our father is dying," he told Han angrily. "Don't you have any feelings?"

"I have feelings," Han responded coldly, "but not for him!"

On the other side of the room Emperor Zhu Di's breath became more and more shallow. His face was a mask of ashen-grey. Everyone expected him to take his last breath at any moment. But then, surprisingly, he opened his eyes and forced himself up onto one elbow. You could see that Empress Xu was frightened. She didn't know what was happening. Her eyes darted in the direction of the two physicians and hoped that they would tell her what was going on. One physician put a finger to his lips and indicated that she should say or do nothing. Everyone in the room held their breath, mesmerized by the unexpected scene that unfolded before them. And then, as they all held their breath, Zhu Di seemed to see someone close by and clearly spoke his name.

"Zheng He," he whispered, "is that you?"

Zhu Di hung there for a moment and reached out for the apparition that only he could see, then, as his strength evaporated he fell heavily back onto his bed. The rattle in his chest ominously silent.

Empress Xu looked into the open eyes of her husband and knew that he was gone. Those forceful eyes which once held a magnificent vision for China now stared blankly into the forever of eternity.

Unable to hold back her tears she buried her face in her hands and began to sob uncontrollably.

An imperial physician stepped forward and gently closed Zhu Di's eyes. The other physician covered the emperor's body with a long blue robe.

Dao Yan and General Tan moved forward and tenderly led the crying empress from the room.

Behind the decorative screen Crown Prince Zhu Bao Zhi was beside himself with grief. He desperately wanted to go to his father's side but was afraid. All he could do was hide his face in his hands and whimper like a baby.

Prince Han was not afraid of anything and definitely was in no mood for tears! He strode purposefully from the room and headed straight for the palace prison.

When Han arrived at the prison he gleefully ran down the long stone passageway as he shouted to the guards and anyone else who might be close enough to hear.

"The emperor is dead!" he shouted overand over as the words echoed strangely off the thick stone walls. "The emperor is dead!"

The guards were shocked at the young man's cruel indifference as they hurried after him down the prison corridor, but also knew they had better do whatever he requested. After the door to Minister Wa's cell was unlocked, they pushed it aside and bowed quickly as they didn't wish to aggrivate the impetuous prince. But Han was in no mood to aggrivate anyone today. He was so excited he almost jumped inside the minister's cell.

"I've got good news for you, Minister Wa," he shouted happily. "My father is dead and YOU are now a free man!"

Minister Wa was going to make certain that he made no mistakes the next time Prince Han visited. He stepped back and looked approvingly at the happy prince.

"Am I looking at the new Ming emperor?" he asked, as he did his very best to flatter the ecstatic young man.

Prince Han wasnow all smiles as he turned himself around in the middle of the cell and pretended that he was the emperor who everyone wanted to see.

"All I have to do is take care of my weak brother," he crowed confidently, "and with your help, Minister Wa, that should be easy! I trust that you won't forget our bargain?"

Minister Wa immediately dropped to his knees.

"I'll gather together our friends at once, Sire," he groveled. "I can assure you that every one of my friends will give you their fullest support!"

"And will the stupid wasteful adventures of my father be stopped?" Prince Han asked, as he eagerly anticipated Minister Wa's predictable reply.

Wa did not disappoint him. He prostrated himself fully at the young man's feet.

"As you have requested, Sire. They will be stopped forever!"


Less than a week after Prince Han met with Minister Wa in prison Empress Xu requested a clandestine meeting with General Tan.

The general had no idea why the empress would want to see him in her private quarters. When he arrived he was again surprised when she personally opened the door instead of relying on a servant. He bowed politely when he saw her at the door.

"Madam Empress, you wish to see me?"

Xu didn't want to waste time with formalities. She quickly motioned for him to enter and pointed towards an overstuffed chair that was located next to hers.

"Please take a seat, general," she began obviously nervous. "I, ahhh, wish to speak with you in the strictest confidence. It's about something that's, ahhh, very important."

General Tan took a seat after the empress had seated herself, but was now more perplexed than ever. Just at that moment a servant entered the room with tea. Again to General Tan's surprise when Empress Xu saw the servant she quickly waved him away.

Han could tell that something was not right, but he didn't know just what.

"I'm not sure where to start."

"Is something the matter?" General Tan asked, still perplexed as to why Zhu Di's wife seemed to be so upset.

Surprisingly she ignored his question and then started to explain why she had invited him to her quarters.

"Many years ago," she began, "when my husband was still province king, it was necessary for him to poison two imperial generals. Do you remember the incident General Tan?"

Tan was taken aback by the woman's unexpected question but tried not to let her know what he was thinking.

"I remember," he told her evenly. "At the time your husband felt that it was, ahhh, important to..."

Empress Xu waved her hand to cut him off.

"It doesn't matter," she told him curtly and quickly returned to the reason why she had invited him for the visit.

"I understood from Lord Zheng He that it was <u>you</u> who obtained the poison for my husband. Is that true?"

Tan didn't like the direction the conversation now took but could do nothing but swim along, so to speak, and see what Empress Xu was up to.

"I, ahhh, may have, Madam Empress," he replied a little nervously, "but can you please explain where all this is leading?"

Xu did not answer his question but continued with what she was trying to tell him.

"At the time, General Tan, my husband ordered you and Lord Zheng He to help him carry out what he considered a most necessary deed."

Empress Xu searched General Tan's eyes to see if she could figure out what he might be thinking. But his eyes revealed nothing so she continued.

"Before Zhu Di died he begged me to protect his life-long legacy and, if necessary, do whatever I needed to do to make certain his legacy was not destroyed. Do you understand what I am trying to tell you?"

General Tan began to figure out where all this was headed. He hoped that maybe he could change Empress Xu's mind with a few cleverly-crafted words.

"Madam Empress," he offered softly, but she waved her hand and again cut him off.

"I need you to obtain some poison for me General," she stated firmly and without emotion. "Will you do it?"

Tan tried to argue.

"Madam Empress, I assure you, there's no need for you..."

She cut him off again.

"Prince Han is <u>my</u> son, general. Zhu Di begged for me to find a way to stop him and so I shall!"

By the time the fleet arrived off the coast of China two months later I was feeling well enough to move around the ship a little, as long as I used a cane. Consequently, I was with Lord Zheng He and the Arab king and queen on the flagship's penthouse when we made our grand entrance into the mouth of the Yangtze.

We searched eagerly for the customary boats, fireworks and cheering crowds which had always been on the shore to greet us, but this time, strangely, none of the usual festivities were anywhere to be seen. A few people wondered over to the sides of the river to watch our ships as they passed by, but there were none of the large firework celebrations which we had seen in the past and expected. Zheng He and I looked at each other uneasily, as we both had a feeling that something definitely was not right. The admiral didn't want to alarm the Arab couple that something might be amiss, so he said nothing about the lack of a normal welcoming celebration as he feared it would cause them to worry.

Ma Huan was almost fully recovered from his wound as well. He came up the inside stairs and bowed respectfully to the Ming Admiral.

"Shall I prepare your launch, Lord Zheng He?" he asked, also somewhat apprehensive that something didn't seem right. "We'll be dropping anchor soon."

"Yes! Please see to it," he told him with little enthusiasm. "Let me know when you're ready."

When the launch was prepared, Zheng He asked the Arab king and queen if they would like to join him for the ride in to the imperial docks? They, of course, said they would like to go, so after the king and queen were seated, Ma Huan, Lt. Zhang Ji and I were helped into the launch but took seats off by our self at the rear of the cupula area.

As we rode together towards the docks I don't think any of us spoke. To say the least, the mood was extremely somber. If the king and queen thought anything about it they were generous enough not to say.

High Consul Dao Yan, General Tan and a small number of low level officials were at the dock to greet us when we finally tied up along side. Both the General and High Consul waved and did their best to appear friendly, but Zheng He and I both knew by this time that something was amis.

"Welcome home, Lord Zheng He," Dao Yan offered simply while giving his friend a forced smile. "It seems like you've been gone forever."

"I feel like I have been gone forever," Zheng He returned his greeting, also with little enthusiasm.

I could tell that my friend was worried about the lack of a proper welcoming ceremony and the High Consul's obviously forced demeanor.

"Has, ahhh, something happened that I should know about?" Zheng He asked tentatively. "How is Emperor Zhu Di? Is he doing well?"

Both Dao Yan and General Tan visibly blanched when the admiral asked about the emperor, as neither wanted to give him the unfortunate news. Finally General Tan decided that it was he who would relay what had happened, so he cleared his throat and offered Zheng He a slight bow before speaking.

"I regret to inform you, Lord Zheng He," General Tan began, "that Emperor Zhu Di..."

The words caught in his throat and he couldn't finish.

"What is it?" Zheng He asked, as he now feared the worst. "Has something happened to the emperor?"

Dao Yan replied simply.

"Emperor Zhu Di is dead!"

Zheng He was stunned. The news was worse than he had feared.

General Tan, now recovered, continued.

"Prince Han tried to take the throne from his brother and also tried to stop the expeditions, but..."

"But what?" Zheng He inquired cautiously.

"His mother, Empress Xu, followed Zhu Di's wishes and ended her son's life with poison."

Zheng He couldn't believe it!

"You are telling me that Zhu Di is dead and Prince Han has been poisoned by his own mother? Who's the emperor? Crown Prince Zhu Bao Zhi?"

The Crown Prince is now emperor," General Tan acknowledged gravely, "but it's uncertain just how long he'll be able to retain control."

Again Zheng He was shocked by General Tan's revelation.

"But how can that be?" .

"Prince Han had a lot of friends, Lord Zheng He," Tan continued. "Even though he's gone their influence has remained."

Zheng He did his best to compose himself then bowed formally to his two friends.

"I want to thank both of you for meeting me here today," he told Dao Yan and General Tan sadly, "and I do appreciate that it was you who informed me of the dreadful news. I know it must have been difficult for both of you. But now, if you don't mind, I'd like to be left alone."

Without saying another word, General Tan and Dao Yan bowed respectfully to Zheng He as he turned and walked away from them towards the end of the dock. Ma Huan, Lt. Zhang Ji and I remained sitting on the launch watching. We knew that something wasn't right but since we weren't able to hear the hushed tones of their conversation at the time neither of us knew just what? The royal couple could also sense that something wasn't right but were smart enough to sit quietly for a few moments and wait until someone came forward to tell them what they should do next.

Zheng He stopped at the end of the dock and stared blankly into the brackish water, completely mezmorized by the terrible news that he had just been told. As he thought about what had happened to all of his loved ones it was almost more than he could bare.

"My beloved Xi Chen is gone" he thought sadly to himself, "and now I find out that Emperor Zhu Di is gone as well. Why Allah?" he cried out within himself. "For what purpose? Why have You taken them from me? I want you to take me! Take me Allah, I don't want to live any longer. I begged you on Ceylon to take my life. Why must I live when everyone I have ever loved are gone? Have you no mercy? Why do you want to punish me? Haven't I spent my whole life trying to serve You?"

A flood of tears began to fall from Zheng He's eyes and he wished mightily that he could stop. But no matter how long or how hard he cried out to Allah, there was no answer for his aching heart.

As soon as Zheng He returned to Beijing he went to visit Zhu Di's grave which was located just north of the city among the gentle slopes of the Junda Mountains. As might be expected the tomb complex was extremely large and consisted of more than a dozen ornately decorated buildings and gardens. The admiral remembered that Zhu Di started construction on the complex while he was having Forbidden City built, but pushed it to completion when Concubine Quan was unexpectedly killed and he began to question his own mortality.

When Zheng He visited the tomb site he took with him his servant Ma Huan who had now fully recovered from his injuries. Together they approached the emperor's final resting-place with tears and unabashed wonderment. The tomb area that Zhu Di had constructed for himself was even more grand-looking than Zheng He had imagined it would be. A large impressive avenue that was decorated on either side with large stone statues of soldiers and animals led directly towards the magnificent garden area which held Zhu Di's tomb.

The two men rode down the avenue together silently. Their somber mood made even more gloomy by the presence of a soft rain which had fallen since early morning.

"Zhu Di would have loved this!" Zheng He thought to himself as he marveled at the beautiful surroundings. He also said a silent prayer of thanks for Empress Xu and Zhu Di's number one son, Zhu Bao Zhi, who had seen fit to make certain the emperor was laid to rest with a proper interment. He knew that if Prince Han had been ini charge Zhu Di probably would not have been honored at all!

When Zheng He and Ma Huan approached the actual grave site the admiral stopped his horse a short distance away, handed the reins of his horse to his servant and stepped from the saddle.

"Wait here." he told him gently. "I won't be long."

Zheng He smiled as he passed through an area of beautiful red roses which he knew were Zhu Di's favorite. He then stopped at a grassy area upon which rested Zhu Di's white marble sarcophagus.

"The roses are a nice touch," he thought to himself. "Zhu Di would have loved every one of them!"

The Ming admiral then ran his fingers across the emperor's name which had been carefully carved into the hard white stone.

ZHU DI, THIRD MING EMPEROR OF CHINA.

"And that you were, my friend," Zheng He spoke within himself. "The Third Ming Emperor of China. You had a 'Mandate', Your Majesty," he thought to himself, "a 'Mandate' which you used to benefit, not yourself, but all the people of China."

Thinking about all the marvelous things that his emperor had accomplished brought a tear to Zheng He's eye.

"People didn't know the sacrifices you made," Zheng He continued. "They didn't understand the incredible wisdom and benevolence that you graciously expressed. It's been a glorious time for China, Your Majesty, and a glorious time for all of those you touched."

Zheng He stood alone beside Zhu Di's sarcophagus and began to cry openly for his emperor, as the rain dripped silently off his uncovered head. The more he cried, the more he began to realize just how unfair it was for it all to be finished!

"In the name of Merciful Allah," he cried out loud as he thought about the terrible injustice. "I can't allow a few ignorant officials to destroy everything that you ever tried to build!"

Zheng He felt a strong resolve move within his soul and knew now what he must do. He stepped back, bowed solemnly to Zhu Di's grave, then started to purposefully stride back through the gardens to where Ma Huan waited with the horses. His face was no longer sad. It was flushed with resolve and a new determination.

"By damn," he shouted loudly, as he shook his fist at the roses and stone statues, "I'm NOT going to allow those know-nothing ministers to destroy everything that you ever tried to build! Do you hear me, Zhu Di? I will not ALLOW IT!"

Ma Huan heard his master shouting on the other side of the garden and had no idea what was going on. When he finally saw him taking great strides in his direction he was startled further to see the admiral as he shook his fist and shouted in his direction.

"We've got work to do, Ma Huan!" he bellowed loudly, his voice no longer sad and actually booming. "Do you hear me? We have lots of work to do!"

Ma Huan couldn't believe the unexpected transformation of what had just happened as he watched Zheng He step boldly into the saddle and grab the reins from his still surprised servant.

"What, ahhh, happened?" was all Ma Huan could venture tentatively.

"What happened?" Zheng He boomed again as he waved his hand in the air excitedly. "I just realized that Zhu Di's vision CAN NOT be allowed to die! He alone brought our country to the very pinnacle of power and success in the world!  I CAN NOT and I WILL NOT allow his death to have been in vain!"

The admiral then pulled the head of his horse around with a jerk and shouted firmly again to his servant.

"Come on, Ma Huan, its time to ride!  The Crown Prince needs our help NOW!"

Zheng He kicked his horse hard on both flanks and galloped as fast as he could back down the avenue that was lined with the dramatic-looking statues.

Ma Huan didn'twant to be left so he gave his own horse a kick in the side and galloped after him.

"Hold up, Zheng He, wait for me!"


After Zhu Di died and Prince Han was poisoned by his mother the Crown Prince, Zhu Bao Zhi, followed his father to the throne and did became the Fourth Ming Emperor of China.  Unfortunately, because of Prince Han's previous influence, Zhu Bao Zhi's ministers gave him little support. The new emperor did work closely with Lord Zheng He and did send out one more expedition which was led by the Ming admiral.

Tragically, when Zheng He stopped the Ming fleet for supplies at Calicut on his return voyage home, he unexpectedly died.  No official reason was given for his death, but I always believed that it could only have been from a broken heart.

True to Muslim religion, Ma Huan brought the admiral's shoes back to China, along with a lock of his hair, when the expedition returned. Today they're entombed in a shrine at Nanking which is dedicated to the Zheng He and his historic voyages.

On a personal note, when Ma Huan returned with the admiral's shoes and hair, he also brought me Xi Chen's necklace which he always wore around his neck.  I've got it around here someplace.  I like to keep it as a personal souvenir.

One other thing I should mention before I finish is what happened to King Yala Ku-mi-orh and General Bura when Zheng He brought them back to China. They were not executed as might have been expected.  The new ruler, Zhu Bao Zhi, didn't want to start his rule by causing problems with a foreign king. Consequently, Yala Ku-mi-orh was transported back to Ceylon on Zheng He's next expedition with the sole admonition that he give up his throne, which he did, to a close relative.

It was lucky for Yala Ku-mi-orh that he wasn't living in France at the time!  I heard from a Frenchman who recently passed through Beijing that a nineteen year old girl named Joan of Arc was burned alive at the stake last year, for far less reason than Yala Ku-mi-orh's grievous action.

Surprisingly, after a short rule of just over a year, Emperor Zhu Bao Zhi died. No one ever announced the reason for his untimely death, as he was still a relatively young man. But the opposition that was stirred up by Prince Han quickly gained the upper hand and did have laws passed which stopped the expeditions forever!

Me? I'm staying here in China. That's where my heart is now and where I plan to remain. I guess I've got too many memories to leave. With my little mission, I have been able to accomplish what I set out to do, so I can't say I have any regrets. Back in Italy I'm sure my bishop is long gone by now. But, if he's watching from heaven, I do hope I've made him proud!

# EPILOGUE

As was stated in the story, when Emperor Zhu Bao Zhi died civil servants and ministers in cooperation with the newly elected emperor had laws passed which effectively stopped all fleet movements forever. These laws specifically stated that, "all ships off Fukien must return immediately to Nanking" and from this day forward, "the building of sea-going ships for barbarian countries will cease forthwith."

Of the volumes of expedition maps and detailed fleet records that were recorded by the Ming Admiral, few remain! Zheng He, or San Bao, as he was also known historically, presented full records of his voyages to the government. But before the century ended, "most of these records were destroyed by administrative thugs in the service of the Confucian anti-maritime party."

During the reign of Cheng-Hua (1465 to 1487), an order was given to search the state archives for documents concerning Zheng He's expeditions to the western world. Liu Ta-Jsia, then Vice-President of the War Office, took the documents and had all of them burned, as he considered their contents to be "deceitful exaggerations of bizarre things, far removed from the testimony of people's eyes and ears."

After the expeditions ceased, China's isolationist policy caused a number of serious problems. Japan emerged as a significant naval power and dominated the seas which surrounded China to the east. Because of China's policy against "sea-going ships," Japanese pirates were able to prey on Chinese coastal ships without fear of reprisal.

In addition to the problems with Japan, control of the Indian Ocean was lost to the Arabs and commerce between China and many countries ceased. Because of this stoppage of commerce, large sums of money were lost to the imperial treasury as customs revenue and tribute became nonexistent.

During the same century that Chinese wisdom decreed "dealing with barbarians must be stopped," the Portuguese military officer Vasco de Gama and the Italian explorer Christopher Columbus discovered new worlds and opened vast areas of trade to the Europeans. In just a few centuries many western countries were able to not only catch, but surpass, the Chinese in cultural, scientific and economic advantages.

When Christopher Columbus discovered America he had with him three ships: the 'Nina', 'Pinta' and 'Santa Maria', with a total crew of about 90 men. The 'Nina' was 48 feet in length, the 'Pinta' 55 feet and the flagship of Columbus's fleet, the 'Santa Maria', only slightly larger at 60 feet.

Sixty years earlier, Zheng He left China with three hundred ships and twenty-seven thousand men on remarkable expeditions of trade and exploration. Each expedition included sixty 'Baochuan' treasure ships that were 430-feet long, 92-feet wide and featured nine masts, 12-sails and a 3-story Ming pagoda. He also had with him more than two hundred other ships which were only slightly smaller in size. The difference in cultural and scientific development which existed between China and Europe in the early 1400's is obvious, at least in the comparison of ship size and numbers.

Unfortunately, when one thinks of world exploration, inventions, political discourse among nations and cultural advancement, as it existed five hundred years ago, a vision of European achievement usually comes to mind. But in the early fifteenth century a Chinese person who traveled to Europe would have found these western countries backward and lacking the accoutrements of what they believed to be civilized culture.

Zheng He's expeditions developed navigation and extensive geographical knowledge throughout much of southeast Asia, the coast of India, all around the Arabian Sea and down the coast of Africa to Zanzibar. Throughout this huge area of the world he expanded China's trade and promoted international cultural and economic exchange at a time when such activity was almost unheard of!

One story often told by overseas Chinese is that on each trip Zheng He would carry with him a large number of big white gourds. The gourds had three important functions. One, they were used to carry fresh water on the journey, so his men would always have something cool to drink. Two, since the gourds would easily float, they could be used as life preservers in case of shipwreck. And three, they were used to carry mud from a number of wells in Beijing.

This mixture of local sand and water was carried strictly for pedestrian reasons. Whenever the Ming fleet arrived at a foreign destination Zheng He always made certain that some of the mud he carried was put into the local wells. He believed that the Beijing mud would provide his crew with a "reminder of home," and would help them "become accustomed to strange conditions more quickly."

In the countries visited by Zheng He, especially in Southeast Asia, stories of the great navigator are still told today. Since he was known to carry his pao, or sexual organs in a jeweled box, he was also known as San Bao, or the 'Three Jewel Eunuch'. Today there is a San Bao Harbor, a San Bao Pagoda and a San Bao Temple in Thailand. In a temple near Bangkok, local people built a statue of San Bao and continue to burn incense in his honor to this very day. In Malaysia there is also a San Bao town and a San Bao well. Many people believe that San Bao's heroic feats became the basis of the stories and adventures of 'Sindbad the Sailor.'

Whether he's remembered as Zheng He, or San Bao, this Chinese eunuch admiral was a humane emissary who clearly deserves greater recognition in world history! Under his able direction, China developed unsurpassed navigation and geographical knowledge during the early Ming period. Thanks to the admiral's dynamic leadership, China was able to greatly expand its trade with foreign countries more than fifty-fold, while at the same time it promoted international cultural and economic exchanges which were precedent setting.

It's interesting to reflect on how much one decision can affect the overall growth, or stagnation, of an entire nation for generations. If China had continued its marvelous maritime expeditions instead of stopping them, or if China had pursued its explorations eastward instead of towards the west, one can only wonder if its economic, political and cultural position in the world would be different than it is today. It's probably safe to assume that it would be!

# ACKNOWLEDGEMENTS

It's not possible to list all the people who helped me with the research, writing and editing of this story.  But here are a few names of individuals and corporations I would like to acknowledge for their very valuable contribution:  Dr. Daniel Lee, Bradley Hahn, Evelyn Harris, David O'Malley, James Broughton, Robert Frankiewicz, George Grosz, Paul Yin, The Explorers Club, The Royal Geographical Society, China Film Co-Production Corporation, China International Culture Art Center, Vice-Chairman Wang Guangying, Zhang Mingzhi, Fujian Marine Design and Research Institute, Lin Da Hua, Zhou Younglian, Du Wei, Xiao Jiangong, Wang Limei and Mary L. Pei.

## ZHENG HE'S BAOCHUAN TREASURE SHIP

**Length**: 125.65m, **Width**: 50:09m, **Depth**: 10:00m, **Draft**: 6:00m, **Masts**: 9, **Sails**: 12,  **Pagoda**: 3-Tower Ming,  **Mast Heigth**: 60m, **Rudder**: Ferreus Mesua, 2,000 to 3,000 kg., **Anchor**: Iron with with Four Flukes, **Ship Weight**: 14 gross tones,   **Armament**: 16 medium bored guns, 1 royal gun, 6 france guns, 3 gun barrels, 60 jet cylinders,  30 bird-beak guns, 100 dust bottles, 500 strong bows with arrows, plus 11 strong-bows with poisonous arrows.

## TYPICAL ZHENG HE EXPEDITION

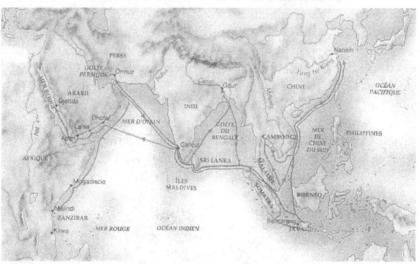

Admiral Zheng He and his huge armada of Ming Treasure Ships left in late Spring near Shanghai. They conducted a 4 to 6 week shakedown cruise, then anchored for 1-month off Min River in Fujian Province. After holding training exercises until eary fall, Zheng He sailed his fleet in January during favorable monsoon. He first sailed through the Taiwan Strait into the South China Sea and then stopped at Hainan Island to re-supply. Next he sailed southward to Qui Nhon, Champa which is modern-day Vietnam. Normal transit time from Hainan to Champa was 10-days. The fleet then sailed to the West coast of Borneo and into the Java Sea, whre they stopped at Surabaja, Java, again for supplies and waited for good winds in July. Then Zheng He took the fleet through the Malacca Strait via Palembang and on to Ceylon which is modern-day Sri Lanka. The Ming fleet then sailed to Calicut on the West coast of India, where the fleet was divided into several 'task forces'. Some ships sailed to Chittagong, while others traveled to Hormuz, Aden, Jidda and Africa and usually reached Hormuz by Jan. 1st. The fleet then returned to Malacca by March to again re-supply the ships. After waiting for favorable weather, they sailed north to Yangtze River and usually arrived by middle or late July.

CPSIA information can be obtained
at www.ICGtesting.com
Printed in the USA
LVHW062151060322
712779LV00010B/390